# The Annual

## of the
## Society of Christian Ethics

1998

Volume 18

**Editorial Offices**

Department of Religious Studies
Brown University
Providence, RI 02912

Department of Religion
Florida State University
Tallahassee, FL 32306-1520

**Publisher**

The Society of Christian Ethics
c/o Dennis P. McCann, Religious Studies
DePaul University
2320 North Kenmore
Chicago, Illinois 60614-3298

**Distributor**

Georgetown University Press
3619 0 Street, N.W.
Georgetown University
Washington D.C. 20007



*The Annual of the Society of Christian Ethics* (ISSN: 0732-4928) is published once a year in November and is the official publication of the Society of Christian Ethics. Only manuscripts presented at a meeting of the Society of Christian Ethics or invited by editors of the professional resources section of *The Annual* are eligible for publication. Members of the Society may propose topics for the professional resources section to the editor or to members of the editorial board. Institutional and nonmember subscriptions are $18 a year. Members of the Society should direct address changes and claims for missing issues to the executive director of the Society of Christian Ethics. Institutional subscribers and individual subscribers who are not members of the SCE should direct inquiries about subscriptions (or standing orders), claims for missing issues, and notifications of address changes to Georgetown University Press, P.O. Box 4886, Hampden Station, Baltimore, MD 21211; remittances should be made payable to Georgetown University Press. Orders for back issues may be placed with Georgetown University Press. Inquiries about reproducing or reprinting material originally published in *The Annual* should be directed to the editors. Single articles may be ordered from UMI Company, 300 North Zeeb Road, Ann Arbor Michigan 48103.

# Contents

## Conversations with Related Societies



## Historical—Constructive Studies



## Social Ethics

## Just War Tradition



## Applied Ethics



## Professional Resources

# PREFACE

The current volume of *The Annual of the Society of Christian Ethics* reflects the diverse interests of the Society's membership, and thus of scholars working in Christian ethics. Lisa Cahill's Presidential Address, for example, takes first position in the volume, addressing the often heated argument between advocates of liberalism and of communitarianism. Cahill argues that much of the heat generated by these positions is "misplaced," resulting from the mistaken perception that the labels represent mutually exclusive points of view. And our volume closes with a section on professional resources related to health care; particularly with respect to the contributors' repeated calls for more theological reflection on such matters, this section also reflects concerns that are widely and deeply held among members of the Society.

Between the Presidential Address and the Professional Resources Section, readers will find materials for a rich intellectual feast. A panel of authors expresses appreciation for the contributions of Fr. Stanley Harakas, whose steady stream of writings express the conviction that the traditions of the Orthodox communities contain important resources for contemporary work in Christian ethics. And, in a new feature, which we have christened "Conversations with Related Societies," Werner Wolbert and William Schweiker exchange views about the relationships between the study of ethics in Europe, and in North America. As the SCE expands its international contacts, we hope this type of exchange may become at least a semi-regular feature of the *Annual*.

The main body of this year's issue, as in the past, is formed from essays presented during the annual meeting of the Society of Christian Ethics, and from the meeting of the Society's Pacific Coast Section. As with last year's selections, the co-editors have chosen to group these essays in ways that emphasize certain clusters of interest. Maria Antonnacio's essay on contemporary attempts to recover the historic discipline of spiritual practices, and John Crossley's exploration of Schleiermacher's thinking about the distinctiveness of Christian ethics, emphasize the links between historical study and constructive reflection. In the area of social ethics, four authors contribute to the long-standing discussion among members of the Society as to the relationships that obtain between theological ethics and philosophical or social scientific reflection. For example, Peter Browning's discussion of the import of sociological interpretations of contemporary religious life for reflections on the nature and mission of the Church continues an important and well-established line of writing associated with H. Richard Niebuhr, James Gustafson, and others. William O'Neill's essay on human rights similarly furthers reflection on the relationships between Christian ethics and philosophical writing concerning the nature of one of the most important trends in contemporary social-political life—the expansion of rights language as a political vocabulary. Cheryl Kirk-Duggan's essay on the debate surrounding the Oakland, California School Board's policies regarding ebonics draws on materials from linguistics and cultural studies in connection with a womanist construal of the relevant issues. Cristina Traina's discussion of "Passionate Mothering" brings material from women's studies and the human sciences to bear on the place of erotic love in parent-child relationships.

Two essays mine the tried and true vein of just war thinking in Christian ethics, and in so doing, push such thinking in new directions. Martin Cook, for example, attempts to further the discussion of aerial bombardment related to "in-between" targets—targets, that is, that have their primary importance in connection with civilian life, but which, in time of war, become important as military assets. The Gulf War raised important questions about such targets, which include computer communication systems, and transportation and electrical networks. Tobias Winright, by contrast, takes up the more theoretical question joined recently by James Childress and James Turner Johnson (among others): Does the just war tradition build on a presumption against harm, or not? Arguing in large part from contemporary criminological theory, Winright argues that, in so far as one takes the metaphor of "policing" as capturing important aspects of just war thinking, the answer must be positive, and Childress and others who argue in favor of such a presumption must be correct.

Finally, two essays take up issues in applied ethics. Timothy Renick's essay on cloning interprets opposition to the notion of cloning human beings in terms of notions about "the abominable," as developed by Mary Douglas and Jeffrey Stout. And George Randels argues that contemporary theological, especially feminist critiques of capitalism are misplaced. Recent work in business ethics suggests a different picture of capitalism, at once less patriarchal and more democratic, than such critiques envision.

Together, these essays provide a fair representation of the diverse interests of members of the Society of Christian Ethics, as already suggested. We are grateful to the authors for such excellent contributions. And, it ought also to be said, the number of worthy submissions turned down for reasons of space was notable. While such an abundance is an important sign of productivity among members of the Society, one could wish that more space was available!

The publication of this issue of the *Annual* would not have been possible without the contributions of many workers. The co-editors wish to thank all those serving on the Editorial Board, and to take special note of three whose term of service on the Board ends this year: Martin Cook, Emilie Townes, and Allen Verhey. Further, we are grateful to those members of the SCE who served as referees; to all the authors who submitted their papers for consideration; to Kim Barber of the Academic Publications Office of the Florida State University; to Susan Minnerly and Gail Tetreault, of the Departments of Religion at Florida State and of Religious Studies at Brown University; to the staff at Georgetown University Press. Above all, the production of this volume would not have been possible without the dedicated and skilled labors of two graduate assistants: from Brown University, Andrew Flescher; from Florida State University, Garry Crites. Both of these worked above and beyond the call of duty. They deserve special thanks.

John Kelsay
Sumner B. Twiss
Co-editors

# PRESIDENTIAL ADDRESS

**Thirty-eighth Annual Meeting**
**The Society of Christian Ethics**

**1998**

# Community Versus Universals: A Misplaced Debate in Christian Ethics

*Lisa Sowle Cahill*

As many previous presidents have noted to me in a commiserative tone, the oratorical duties of the SCE president fall into an unenviable genre. It is, after all, an after-dinner speech. Peers expect it to be amusing, though not frivolous; meaty, but not ponderous; collegial, yet challenging; of general interest, yet incisive; and most importantly, of some profoundity—without having unduly detained the audience. Add to this the fact that one's listeners have been through a long day and a large meal, and the speaker is confronted with a daunting task. In the SCE banquet format, the Protestant penchant for late-night work meets the Catholic insistence on festive libations in an unfortunate ecumenical collaboration.

Given the odd genre of the Society's banquet address, the landscape of this one will be dotted with anecdotes, not necessarily humorous ones, but helpful I hope in sustaining your interest. Three of my stories have to do with taxicabs, in which I gather a good deal of theological ethics takes place.

First, though, let me insert a brief personal recollection of John Yoder. In addition to its other identities, this year's presidential address will carry something of an elegiac tone, though not for that an entirely sombre one. John Howard Yoder was an inspiration to many of us, as well as a theological *provocateur*. A man of strong convictions, he was always willing to engage collegially with those who differed. At last year's SCE meeting, John invited me to meet at lunch to share some ideas about a future SCE session we might plan together on Christian discipleship. Although that session is not now to be, my remarks this evening do derive partly from John's pointed challenges to ethical "business as usual," and partly from his essentially ecumenical spirit.

Another source of my ideas, as well as of my ecumenical leanings, is my own doctoral mentor—and that of many of you—James Gustafson. I have expropriated the title of one of his best and most effective essays (and one of his own favorites), that did exactly the right job at the right time. The title of Jim's essay, originally published in the *Harvard Theological Review* in 1965, was "Context Versus Principles: A Misplaced Debate in Christian Ethics."[1] My title is "Community Versus Universals: A [An Equally] Misplaced Debate in Christian Ethics"—and also in religious ethics more broadly construed. In some ways, this may be the same debate. But the recent version has gone on under the strong impact of postmodern philosophy and deconstructive approaches to moral ideas and behavior. I believe I am not alone in thinking the rejection of any universals at all to be incompatible with the moral stands that religious ethicists and others should and do take toward clear injustices in the world around us. I think both John Yoder and Jim Gustafson would agree with me there, though perhaps for different reasons than those I and other Roman Catholic theologians would tend to give.

Not everyone would grant that it is still important, or even ethical, to throw around terms like "moral universal," and there are some good reasons on their side, too. The possibility of moral unanimity across communal boundaries, or even among different individuals, has become acutely contentious. Moral philosophers and theologians are exceedingly attuned to historical variation, cultural diversity, the irreducible individuality of personal experience, and the radicality and strangeness of faith-based moral claims.

Nonetheless, many Christian ethicists, as well as other social critics (including feminists), have raised red flags at the proposition that communities and conceptions of human goods are so diverse as to be incommensurable. I will cite just one recent, excellent example—from Wendy Farley's *Eros for the Other*. Granted the importance of key postmodern insights, it is not enough, says Farley, to pronounce that "Hitler has his reality, and I have mine."

> Both the absurdity and the moral odiousness of this view become only more evident when one considers the horribly distorted social worlds of torture chambers, death camps, or Gulags. These unworlds produce infinite suffering; they do not produce the reified thing ideology claims their victims to be.[2]

Many people are mistrustful of vocabulary like "universals," "common morality," "shared values," or "human rights," because these terms can be used to judge and exclude others on the basis of standards that are *not* really shared. Katie Cannon's plenary address this afternoon gave an account of the trial of a black woman accused of killing a white man in the 1950's, a trial and conviction that illustrated powerfully the unjust effects of moral and legal standards that do not represent equally all those to whom they are applied.[3]

But another important point is that this same vocabulary is also a way of creating connections with other people and acknowledging one's responsibility to them. The language of common humanity is capable of encouraging us, as Katie said, to "*Do something*, for the time we know now, we shall soon know it no more." The ecumenical task, as I see it, is to appreciate difference, while maintaining a strong, accountable, sense of connection. As Katie Cannon has written elsewhere, womanist theology makes it possible to clarify that "theo-ethical structures are not universal, color-blind, apolitical, or otherwise neutral," and at the same time to prod "society at large" into rescinding its denial of "shared humanity."[4]

Undoubtedly, the rhetorics of "difference" and "deconstruction" are effective strategies for change within an oppressively tight cultural mindset and worldset. Difference talk is not only an effective strategy, but a relatively safe one in societies (like North American liberal democracy) where certain basic goods or rights are at least guaranteed in principle, if not always in fact. Here, the rhetoric of rights provides a culturally well-rooted counterbalance to the idea that the only people with whose welfare any group needs to be concerned are its own members. In liberal societies like ours, the rhetoric of difference can function as a rhetoric of *inclusion*. Claiming or proclaiming difference is not so much a denial that one's basic requirements of food, housing, health care, employment, and physical safety are unintelligible to one's fellow citizens, but to urge wider *access* to these goods and institutions, as well as to the circles in which their local meanings are refined. But the emphasis on difference is not equally useful in every context.

Last October, a riveting and disturbing article appeared in the *New York Times Magazine*. It was entitled "God Created Me To Be a Slave."[5] It told the story of Fatma Mint Mamadou, one of 90,000 black African slaves serving Mauritania's ruling Arab tribes for over 500 years. In Mauritania, slaves are so numerous that they are frequently dismissed without support or refuge, when feeding them becomes an economic burden to masters. Fatma's daily life under her master had consisted of lugging home water, at dawn, from miles away across the desert; of cooking and sweeping up sand; of tending goats; and nursing the babies of the mistress, though her own might cry for milk. Although Fatma had run away across the desert after a particularly brutal beating, and out of fear that her master would "slaughter" her, she still thinks of herself as an Arab and as a slave. "She has no other identity in a society where individualism is anathema, a world where to belong is to be."[6] "God created me to be a slave," says Fatma quietly, "just as he created a camel to be a camel."[7] Freedom, self-determination in major decisions, planning ahead for one's future or that of one's children—all of these are foreign to Fatma. Such concepts, ideals, or realities lie beyond her worldview, experience, and capacities. When asked by the interviewer if she had ever been raped, Fatma could not make sense of the question, even though it was rephrased repeatedly. Finally, she replied, "Of course they would come in the night when they needed to breed us. Is that what you mean by rape?"[8] Fatma's story combines factors of race, class, gender, economics, and certainly cultural difference. Both Fatma and her master view slavery as a normal part of social existence; rape, for a slave, is not even an available category. Does that mean it does not exist there? Is Fatma in fact the "thing" that the master-slave ideology socially constructs her to be? Surely, here is an instance of radical worldview difference, of a case in which self-understandings and social institutions are very far removed from those of virtually all readers of the *New York Times*. But why did the *Times* print this story? Wherein lies its power, and why do I choose to tell it to you now? Something in us resists, and resists for and on behalf of Fatma, and other women like her. We feel deeply and profoundly that there is some truth they do not know, and that is violated in their unknowing. The sense of radical difference and radical connection engendered by a story like Fatma's captures the heart of the debate between today's communitarians and universalists.

In 1965, Jim Gustafson differentiated between an approach centered on "formal prescriptive principles," and one centered on the "existential response to a particular situation." He thought the controversy over the two misplaced because it focused on realistic moral judgments about practical courses of action, while obscuring the fact that sooner or later, one has to explain and defend particular action-oriented norms and responses.

Postmodern moralities that discredit continuities among contexts are the fully flowered theoretical correlate of narrowly focused contextualism. But—opposite to the situation Gustafson diagnosed in the 60's—postmodern communitarian thinkers can become so fixed on radical *theory* that they lose sight of the kind of humanistic convictions that concerted moral *action* against existential suffering demands.

My reappropriation of Gustason's title is intended to join the debate between contemporary communitarians and universalists, but also to transcend it, by *relocating* the question of what is "universal" or shared in morality. Given my present limits of time and space, I will not fill this talk with specific references to other authors. I will use the terms "communitarian" and "universalist" generally, admitting that there is great diversity within each category, and also that the labels I have chosen are not necessarily the best. Yet there is a basic distinction to be made among approaches in theological ethics. Communitarians stress the particularity of Christian moral experience and therefore its distinctive moral witness; while "universalists" want some foundations or essentials in human moral experience to provide a common ground for social justice. I am going to try to affirm these insights and bring them together.

My programme for ecumenical rapprochement has two parts. The first is to defend the proposition that there are basic human needs and goods, but to talk about moral common ground in a more cautious and historically nuanced way. The second is to take the point of those who see Christian ethics as more communal and particular, that concern for the well-being of others, as for oneself, is extremely difficult to sustain across interest groups. In other words, what is often thought of as a doctrine about particularity, and hence incommensurability, of goods is really a doctrine about sin. We do not so much disagree about goods in themselves, as we do about who is entitled to share in them.

So, first, then, on a more nuanced discourse of goods and well-being. If we are attentive to the irreducible individuality of other human beings, we realize that they have real existence apart from our "constructions" of them, and that it is precisely in their similarity to the self, and not only in their difference from it, that they evoke attraction, hatred, awe or terror. And all human beings require that basic physical and psychological needs be met to flourish, as we know full well when we perpetrate violence against others.

The question is not whether we can know generalizable human goods at all, but how we do so inductively, differentially, and with adequate attention to the particularity of sites of knowledge and the irreducibility and partiality of different vantage points. And particularity is especially important as we consider specific instances of harm or benefit. I will return to and reemphasize this point later. But there is still a recognizable similarity among communities and persons about goods, as they lay claim to things needed to survive and flourish.

Next, the *second* step in my ecumenical reconstruction is to go back to the caveats of the communitarians, as against the universalists, and to take them seriously, but to relocate their real bite *beyond* knowledge of basic goods as such. We can know basic goods, but do we will or seek them for everyone equitably? The most trenchant criticisms of universalist ethics are aimed at what Reinhold Niebuhr termed "collective egoism." The real issue of social ethics, as of Christian distinctiveness, is the circle of concern or solidarity within which human persons are willing to extend a share in basic goods; or, conversely, to identify outsiders as not equal, not deserving, or not even fully human.

Let me illustrate this point with the first of my taxicab stories. In March of last year, I was leaving the first Cardinal Bernardin Conference of the Catholic Common Ground Initiative, held at the palatial Mundelein Seminary, built by Cardinal Cody as befits a prince of the church.[9] My companions in a taxicab were Joseph Komonchak, an ecclesiologist from Catholic University; and Ernie Cortes, a Latino community action organizer from San Antonio, Texas. Joe Komonchak and I were in a heated debate about the meaning and viability of "natural law." Joe insisted that knowledge of Christian morality depends on faith. I insisted that such notions undermine the very possibility of social ethics, and that the most essential human goods (like life, family, peaceful society, and conditions of health like clean water) could be known experientially and inductively, just as Thomas Aquinas had claimed in his "Treatise on Law."[10] Ernie Cortes, who had been silent up until this time, broke in. "Yes," he said. "But goods *for whom*?"

Ernie made this taciturn yet profound remark close to a year ago. It has been echoing in my mind ever since. I am increasingly convinced that the differences social ethicists often name as being about incommensurable visions of the good are really about competing visions of who has access to or is barred from practices of the good life whose essential value is self-evident. Certainly this is true regarding issues like slavery, the subordination of women, sexual violence, racism, just and unjust wars, and the gap between rich and poor.

Let me try this hypothesis out on that norm of Christian behavior perhaps most frequently ventured as distinctive or unique: nonviolence. Now, to embrace a nonviolent way of life as demanded by the gospel and fidelity to Christ's cross is not, after all, to say that *only* Christians can perceive that life is good, or that being the object of physical attack and killing is bad. What is ultimately at stake is Ernie Cortes's "for whom?" question. Those committed to a nonviolent way of life are committing themselves to a circle of solidarity in respect of the good of life from which no one will ever be excluded, no matter what the circumstances. In every foreseeable instance, and even unforeseeable ones, every other individual will be treated as equal to the self, even if the death of the self, of loved ones, or of other innocents is the result.

This absolute solidarity, pacifists would say, is mandated by Jesus' preaching of the kingdom of God as overturning all boundaries of status and exclusion, including the most despicable with the most beloved. The parable of the Good Samaritan, the Sermon on the Mount, the parable of judgment in Matthew 25, the command to love God above all else, and one's neighbor as oneself—all these point to the same moral inclusiveness, the same attentiveness to the radical particularity and value of each person. To each person's need we can and must respond; for each, we seek life, food, drink, clothing, shelter, and safety in proportion to concrete need, not as measured against our own sacrifice, to recipients' affiliation with our group identity, or to their ability to pay us back.

Of course, "solidarity" within and across communities will exist on different levels, just as communities themselves do. Our attention, compassion, and action can be directed more intensely toward those with whom we associate most closely, or to whom we have the most urgent responsibility. But we can learn to extend compassion and action quite generally, nonetheless. Where we cannot act directly, we can reach others through social practices and institutions.

My second taxicab story also reinforces my point about Christian ethics and inclusive moral commitment. This one goes back to Gustafson. He begins the book entitled *Can Ethics Be Christian?* with a personal anecdote that actually begins in a bar, though it winds up in a taxi. In this story, two colleagues are enjoying a nightcap and conversation when they observe a young, quite inebriated soldier being overcharged by the bartender and evidently unable to manage his own affairs. In a modern version of the Good Samaritan, one of the friends takes charge in putting the young man into a cab, paying the driver, and sending him more or less safely on the way to his hotel. Since the Samaritan was not in this case a believer, Gustafson then explores the question in what way and why the action of a Christian might have differed. He concludes that a Christian might act on the basis of a distinctive narrative, virtues, and attitudes, though the action itself could be substantively the same.

First of all, this story illustrates that the distinctiveness of Christian ethics has to do with patterns of morally inclusive and self-offering behavior, rather than with the fundamental nature of the goods such behavior promotes. Both Jesus'

Samaritan and Gustafson's Samaritan are seeking unquestioned benefits for individuals whose moral relation to the agent is the questionable element. Of course, Gustafson's taxicab story shows its age. It does not shock barriers of class, race, and gender. It does not threaten institutions vital to the primary agent's group or interests. But it does present the agent as having had a history and a character formed by it, as well as acting in the midst of roles and relationships that engender indeterminate patterns of response, rather than static structures. This is precisely the postmodern insight: the interdependence, permeability, and fluidity of individual being and contextual possibilities.

The most real and authentic understanding of human goods in relation to persons will be knowledge that is intimate and particular, even though in essential aspects shareable. The circle of moral concern defines the specific locale in which different persons deliberate together about concrete configurations of goods and routes of access, and so in turn contributes to participants' nuanced appreciation of what "goods in practice" mean. It is significant that Gustafson uses a very specific incident to communicate a point that might have been ventured in more philosophical terms. The parables of Jesus do the same thing, and so compel our personal and imaginative response. Both resist transmogrification into a casuistry of detailed prescriptions.

Now let me tell my third taxicab story. It is about the difficulty of being either concrete or globally inclusive when one is a professional theological ethicist. Last November 14, Gil Meilaender and I were in a cab on a snowy night, moving from the Hastings Center in rural, woodsy, rather upscale Garrison, New York, to La Guardia. We had been at a conference on religion, public policy, and cloning. More because we both love to argue and neither easily gives up, than because we had much of a substantive disagreement, we fought back and forth for over an hour about whether New Testament ethics is more grounded in love or in faith. (I will leave you to guess who was on which side of that one, the Catholic or the Lutheran.) Meanwhile, a third party to the ride, Abdulaziz Sachedina, an Islamic ethicist from the University of Virginia, was dozing in the front seat. And over the car radio—of which I was barely aware at the time—was being broadcast coverage of a possibly impending U.S. military action in Iraq. Irate Iraqi citizens were demonstrating in favor of Saddam Hussein, whom they termed the "father and mother" of the oppressed Iraqi people. They paused to express strong anti-American sentiments. To this, the cab driver muttered an occasional, "Can you believe that?" and other unintelligible or unrepeatable political commentary.

In retrospect, I take this ride as a parable of the backseated cluelessness of *some* Christian ethicists (I won't speak for Gil), who are theoretically engaged with other North American academic theologians in defining goods and pondering solidarity in the abstract, while different religions and cultures are politely not consulted about the relevant particularities. Real life and death conflicts, based, after all, more on in-group/out-group enmity than on disagreements about what human flourishing requires for the deserving, need this kind of particular, culturally differentiated attention. As it is, the age-old problem of group against group violence threatens to overwhelm our already dim prospects for a peaceful, participatory, and just global society.

Yet we only distract ourselves from the most crucial issues for social ethics, religious ethics, and Christian ethics, when we argue as though the basic necessities of human well-being for other groups or cultures are alien to us, as are our goods to them. I find that rarely if ever do those human beings actually undergoing radical suffering maintain such a thing. Victims of crushing poverty, sexual violence, torture, and genocide call for justice, mercy, compassion—in a word, for recognition that their full humanity makes us accountable, if we are fully human, too.

Yes, certain basic goods are humanly self-evident, a point Jesus took for granted when he described the man left in a ditch by robbers (Luke 10), and approached the woman about to be stoned for adultery (John 8). The biggest moral challenge Jesus presents is not to uphold a unique vision of the good, but to reach across class, race, gender, and culture to create greater solidarity around goods. Practical solidarity, which is the same thing as action, can then yield dialectical and dialogical understandings of what will further human well-being on particular occasions, and in particular relations.

Religious language can have an important role here, even beyond Christian believers, and even in the public sphere. This is so because talking in the abstract about solidarity is not enough to motivate people to act. Christian symbols and stories can educate our sensibilities, widen our vision, overturn our expectations about those to whom we do or do not have responsibilities. Jesus' parables and symbols such as kingdom of God, Cross, resurrection, and judgment on the hardhearted stimulate the moral imagination, and awaken our *human* capacity for compassion with an unusual force. Sometimes this can even happen across traditions, as with the worldwide effect of Mother Teresa, Mahatma Gandhi, Elie Wiesel, and the Dalai Lama.

Now: back to the controversy and the ecumenical border between the communitarians and the universalists. From the universalist side, no one with a glimmer of postmodern consciousness would defend the proposition that the most detailed instantiations of goods are known universally, or that knowledge of moral goods can be deduced from rational first principles. And the truth in communitarian skepticism about universals is that disclosure and embodiment of goods are always historical and always arise in particular forms. Communalist Christians see rightly that mercy and forgiving love are distinctively Christian virtues (if not unique to Christians), and that they require communal practice for their nurture and realization. They also see that it is wise not to generalize naïvely about mutual concern and a willingness to sacrifice for others.

The real scandal of Christianity is not the particularity of its moral vision, but the vacuousness and contradictions of its moral life (to recall 1 Cor. 13). If human beings use religion to override compassion, and to evade their responsibilities for one another, then the human ability to experience God as both loving and just is compromised. If Christians, for one, take the incarnation seriously, struggle to make their churches "body of Christ," and respond with empathetic attention to the pain of others, then God will be present in the world through a faith active in love.

Whether we ultimately *do* believe that reconciliation is more powerful than evil is not dependent on an abstract Christian symbol system, and not even on the "authority" of an ancient literary collection of stories about Christ. Finally, it comes down to concrete practices that mediate in the very texture of human life the *realities* of trust, compassion, and forgiveness—or their opposites.

We gather here as scholars; as theological ethicists, we rightly analyze these matters theoretically. As religious persons and members of religious communities, and also specifically for we who are *Christian* ethicists, it is further incumbent upon us not only to recognize goods all persons *should* share, but to nurture communities in which they *are* shared, through life, exhortation, liturgy, and prayer. Only within *practices* of love and concern for one another (not, of course, limited to Christians) can human beings come to believe in a merciful and reconciling God. And, if we do know a merciful and reconciling God, we can envision a future in which selfishness, hatred, and violence are actually defeated. Our skepticism about that future is the result of our lack of faith, but our lack of faith is the result of our failures to be with one another as God in Christ has made it possible to be. "The good life with and for others, in just institutions"[11]—to borrow Paul Ricoeur's phrase—is the ideal of all ethical behavior. To understand such a life well is the ideal of all ethical theory. The ideal of all theological ethics is reflect upon that transcendent power that is the ground and promise of a transformed life, and in so doing, to nurture the actual solidarity of all persons in it.

## Notes

[1]James M. Gustafson, "Context Versus Principles: A Misplaced Debate in Christian Ethics," *Harvard Theological Review* 58/2 (1965): 171-202; reprinted in James M. Gustafson, *Christian Ethics and the Community* (Philadelphia: United Church Press/Pilgrim Press, 1971): 101-126.

[2]Wendy Farley, *Eros for the Other: Retaining Truth in a Pluralistic World* (University Park, PA: Pennsylvania State University Press, 1996), 6.

[3]Katie Geneva Cannon, "Race, Sex and Insanity: Transformative Eschatology in Hurston's Account of the Ruby McCollum Trial," Opening Plenary Address, Society of Christian Ethics, January 9, 1998, Atlanta, Georgia.

[4]Katie G. Cannon, "Hitting a Straight Lick with a Crooked Stick: The Womanist Dilemma in the Development of a Black Liberation Ethic," in Lois K. Daly, ed., *Feminist Theological Ethics: A Reader* (Louisville KY: Westminster/John Knox Press, 1994), 37.

[5]Elinor Burkett, "God Created Me To Be a Slave," *New York Times Magazine* (October 12, 1997), 56-60.

[6]Ibid., 60.

[7]Ibid., 56.

[8]Ibid., 56.

[9]The setting of this taxicab story, as of the two to follow, suggests that one could do an interesting social and class analysis of the reasons why professional ethicists spend significant time (and funds) riding to and from distant locations in cars driven by other people.

[10]*Summa Theologiae*, I-II. Q. 90-94.

[11]Paul Ricoeur, *Oneself as Another*, trans. Kathleen Blamey (Chicago and London: University of Chicago Press, 1992), 172.

# PANEL ON THE WORK OF STANLEY HARAKAS

# Fr. Stanley Harakas: Introductory Comments

*Vigen Guroian*

My role here is probably the least defined of the five persons at this table. It is not as a mere moderator that I stand before you nor exactly as a presenter either. I might have taken the opportunity to speak longer than I intend to do, but I think my three colleagues are going to raise more than enough observations regarding the work of Fr. Stanley Samuel Harakas and his contributions to Christian ethics to fill our plates. We also want to hear from Fr. Stanley himself. And so I have chosen to make my remarks brief.

At the outset, however, I ask you to forgive me if I continue to refer to my friend and counselor with what sounds like unneeded formality, as Father Stanley Harakas. We Orthodox don't much know how else to address a clergyman, even when in a familiar tone, than as Father or Bishop. And these terms in the respective vernaculars can and do take on very familiar accents among Greeks or Armenians.

First, let me thank the Program Committee of the Society of Christian Ethics for acknowledging the significance of Fr. Stanley's presence among us and on the whole scene of Christian ethics in America. We have come a long way, but not nearly far enough, I must add, in recognizing the academic importance of the great and ancient tradition of Orthodox Christianity that Fr. Stanley Harakas represents in his person and in his writing.

I take it that this session is one strong indication not only that this society recognizes the importance of Stanley Harakas's work but also that we are collectively coming to the realization that Christian ethics in America can no longer be done or taught without consciousness of and greater attention to the Orthodox tradition. The next step is to make that realization a conviction that is reflected in our academic programs at colleges, in our graduate programs, and at our seminaries. World political events of the last decade alone ought to have awakened us to this obligation. The academy and this nation will hardly be able to make right sense of the stirrings and transformation in Eastern Europe and the former Soviet Union without a proper understanding of Orthodox Christianity. Our dealing as a nation in the Middle East and our encounter with Islam is fatally flawed because this understanding of Orthodox Christianity does not exist. Our programs in Islamic studies at the major institutions must be complemented by programs in Eastern Christianity, or we are at the very least being intellectually dishonest. There is a huge lacuna in our comprehension of Christian history, as it impacts upon contemporary events, when that history is taught as if Byzantium and the Ottoman Empire never existed, or as if these histories are peripheral to Christian self-understanding or to multicultural studies.

Now how does this man whose life and work we honor today fit into this big picture? Let the answer to that question be my limited task in the remainder of my remarks.

The Rev. Stanley S. Harakas is a priest of the Greek Orthodox Archdiocese of North America. Let me pause here for a moment. This is the first sentence of his curriculum vitae. Stanley S. Harakas is a priest. It is to this vocation that he has given first attention during his adult life, short of his being a husband and father. During his thirty-year term at Holy Cross Greek Orthodox School of Theology, he also served as Dean for ten years and Dean of the associated Hellenic College for five years. But during this time, Fr. Stanley retained connections with local parishes and served as priest to a number of them. Fr. Stanley has told me that this service as a priest and pastor was grounding and always reinvigorating. It reminded him that the church is his mother and that theology is an expression of love for her and her bridegroom. I cannot speak from direct experience of Fr. Stanley's service to parishes. But I will tell you that to me he has been more than a friend, he has been a spiritual director and spiritual father. We have often been paired at sessions of annual meetings of this society with all the expected intellectual airs. But my real delight is to hold Fr. Stanley in my prayers and to thank God and to thank him for the vocation he has filled as priest, pastor, and doctor of the soul.

Until his retirement in 1995, Fr. Stanley Harakas taught and led at Holy Cross Greek Orthodox School of Theology—the principal Orthodox seminary of North and South America. The impact of his several roles there must be brought to your attention, for it is major not only with respect to the modern history of Orthodoxy in America but also to the practice and study of Orthodox theology. To begin with, under his leadership both the School of Theology and Hellenic College were brought to accreditation. This alone is a major piece of American religious history.

Over the years, Stanley Harakas has also left an indelible and nearly unparalleled mark in the Orthodox world in his dominant role as an educator of not only priests but also Orthodox theologians. His influence and impact in this regard hold few peers in America, matched only by Georges Florovsky, Alexander Schmemann, and John Meyendorff.

His scholarship and writing is prolific—eleven books and literally hundreds of articles. His books include: *Toward a Transfigured Life: The "Theoria" of Eastern Orthodox Ethics, Health and Medicine in the Eastern Orthodox Tradition, Let Mercy Abound: Social Concern in the Greek Orthodox Church*, and most recently *Of Life and Salvation: Reflections on the Fourteen Biblical Readings of the Eastern Orthodox Sacrament of Holy Unction.* Even in his retirement, in addition to his major theological projects, Stanley Harakas writes a weekly column for the weekend English section of the Greek language daily, *The National Herald.*

In conclusion, it is fair to say that Fr. Stanley Samuel Harakas has traveled roads no Greek Orthodox theologian in America has traveled before. So far as I know, he was the first Orthodox person ever elected to the Board of Directors of this society, and this year he is serving as the first Orthodox president ever of the American Theological Society. He has been the pioneer in Orthodox bio-medical ethics, and his profound concern with ecology and the creation is represented in the fact that he serves as a Commissioner of the World Council of Churches Unit III on "Justice, Peace and Creation." His many honors include an inaugural appointment as the "Archbishop Iakovos Professorship of Orthodox Theology" at Holy Cross School of Theology and a "Distinguished Alumnus" award from the Boston University School of Theology.

Today we honor Fr. Stanley S. Harakas and his contribution to Christian Ethics.

# A Short Response to Stanley Harakas

*Timothy F. Sedgwick*

Some people have written Christian ethics in order to figure out what they believe. If you will, they seek to write an apology for themselves as much as for others—I think, for example, of Reinhold Niebuhr's early work, *An Interpretation of Christian Ethics,* or Paul Ramsey's early work, *Basic Christian Ethics*. And then there are those who seek to give an account of their tradition. Their texts in Christian ethics are more the conclusion of their scholarly work than beginning explorations. Stanley Harakas's work is clearly of the second sort. The contribution of such work in general and Stan's work in particular is great both for those within his tradition and for those of us who find ourselves in different Christian traditions. How this is so is the gist of what I want to say in the limits of time that I have.

First, as a work within Orthodoxy, Stan has done for Orthodox Christian ethics something similar to what George Lindbeck sees as the task of theology: to develop the grammar of faith. What makes Stan's work a work of Christian ethics is that he has developed a grammar of the beliefs and practices of Orthodoxy. His work, though, is more than a reiteration of the faith once received. In developing the grammar of Eastern Orthodox ethics he has provided a critical and constructive account that is of the greatest importance for the Orthodox tradition and as well as a significant resource for others seeking to develop Christian ethics.

In his two major works in Eastern Orthodox ethics—*Toward Transfigured Life: The Theoria of Eastern Orthodox Ethics* (1983) and *Living the Faith: The Praxis of Eastern Orthodox Ethics* (1992)—Stanley has first of all brought together into one voice the range of sources that form Orthodoxy, primarily scripture, Patristic writers, Eastern Fathers, and the prayers of Eastern liturgies and tradition. This, though, is no simple matter of articulating a received tradition. Stan has orchestrated these voices as answering a series of questions. In this way, Stan has provided a critical perspective on the Orthodox tradition. More specifically, he has described Orthodoxy as an ethos or way of life grounded in prayer and worship in terms of the questions of ethics—understandings of God, the good, moral agency, and the criteria for Christian behavior.

Stan's Eastern Orthodox ethic is rich and detailed (some of which we have heard in this Society in papers that he has offered over the last twenty-some years). Central to this description are certain claims that once articulated seem to express the heart of Orthodoxy—for example, the claim that the Christian life is grounded in a Trinitarian understanding of God and human life. Human life mirrors the divine life as that life is best conceived as "divine *eros*" (*theios eros*) in which humans participate in a love reaching out in communion with all of creation. Particular features of this Trinitarian understanding include the claims that human life is interpersonal, corporate, and sacramental.

Together the conceptual framework and the historical presentation of the Orthodox tradition enable and require critical reflection by those who stand within Orthodoxy. Once such an account is given, it is impossible for those who have eyes to read and ears to hear to say Orthodoxy is an ethos or the divine liturgy itself in which tradition speaks sufficiently and unambiguously. Suffice it to say here, Stan's work is among the first critical and constructive attempts to offer an account of an Orthodox understanding of Christian faith and life that would enable the Orthodox tradition to engage critically Western contemporary culture and society in order to form an indigenous church and a Christian people in that society—two essentials for Orthodoxy if it is to be interpersonal, corporate, and sacramental.

Two concluding, further assessments. First, forms of contemporary Christian ethics are far more captive to their own historical traditions and social locations than they know because of their failure to read critical and constructive work of Orthodox theologians in general and Stanley Harakas in particular. For example, Stan provides a constructive account of Christian love in which *agape* is grounded in *eros*, but this is little known and less reported despite a good number of recent publications on faith and the nature of love.

Second, in articulating the grammar of Orthodox belief and practices in light of changing circumstances and understandings, Stan has remained conservative. This is to say, Stan has articulated the traditional claims of Orthodoxy. His critical approach, however, raises in principle far more radical questions that cannot be simply answered on the basis of tradition. One such question is that of what is essential regarding human persons as male and female given that such understandings are informed (though not determined) by cultural conditioning and by the biological sciences. This, I believe will require a more radical questioning of Orthodox understanding of role differentiation between men and women, woman's ordination to the priesthood, and proscriptions against homosexuality. These are but particular cases raised by the development of a critical, historical perspective. Stated in more general terms, the question Stan has raised is, "What is central to Orthodoxy as a matter of Christian faith and life and what is culturally particular?" Eventually this question must be addressed if the Orthodox Church is to become indigenous so that it may effect its mission to form the people of God in contemporary Western culture.

Explorations in areas that raise questions about the essential nature of human beings will, I would suggest, give rise to other critical and constructive frameworks for Orthodox ethics (such as Christos Yannaras's existential personalism developed in *The Freedom of Morality*). Similarly, explorations of the mission and shape of the church in contemporary Western culture will raise questions about the character of the Christian life, including understandings of vocation and responsibility towards the state. The exploration of these problems will result in the development of still other, different frameworks and different construals of Orthodox ethics (such as that developed by Vigen Guroian). In other words, once critical and constructive accounts of Orthodoxy begin, there will be a pluralism of accounts of Orthodoxy, family differences to the outsider, major challenges to the insider. Together this is the beginning of a new stage of scholarship and critical understanding. For these fruits that are of value to Orthodoxy and to others seeking to do critical and constructive work in Christian ethics, the work of Stanley Harakas has made a singular contribution.

# Cosmic Theocentrism: Remarks On Stanley Harakas's *Toward Transfigured Life*

*James Gustafson*

The title of my remarks is too simple. At least one other adjective should be there, that is, "trinitarian." But before I turn to more substantive comments, I want to express my gratitude and admiration for the work of Father Stanley in all he has taught me through his publications. I recall reading an announcement of the forthcoming publication of *Toward Transfigured Life*, and ordering it immediately. Light and Life Publishing Company at that time, at least, was not the most efficient of distributors, and I waited a long time for my copy to arrive.

Two purposes were served, two lacunae were partially filled. One was my own edification. The only exposure to anything from Eastern Christianity I had during my graduate studies was the work of Berdyaev, hardly an orthodox Eastern Orthodox theologian, though one too soon ignored in the faddishness of theologies. Our studies in the history of Christian thought centered on theological controversies; ethics is still hard for historians of theology to include. James Luther Adams, along with scores of other bibliographic suggestions, once noted Professor Benz's work, so I had read his little book on *The Orthodox Church*. Apart from references in histories, I had not read works of the mystical tradition until the *Library of Christian Classics* came out, and I became acquainted with Methodius only when a Swedish friend, Lars Thunberg, presented me with his massive study. Father Stanley's book was edifying, and valued for several personal reasons. It explicates and interprets a tradition—itself something of a novelty in a time when authors were making their marks by radical revisions and rejections of tradition. It does justice to the centrality of theology in that tradition, to the close integration of the ethical with the theological, and to the equally close integration of the sacramental life to the moral life of the believer. Yet its contemporary context of writings in moral philosophy and Christian ethics provides access via current discussions to both the distinctive features of Eastern Orthodox ethics and to comparative evaluations. Together with Vigen Guroian's work, Father Stanley's books and articles make ignorance of Eastern Orthodox ethics totally inexcusable.

The second lacuna was pedagogical. My personal conviction is that Christian ethics is a field: there is a body of literature drawn from various traditions and perspectives to which students need to be exposed—to be studied both empathetically and critically. The agenda for teaching, for me, came from the literature—the theological, philosophical, ethical, methodological, and practical issues imbedded in the materials from the Bible forward, and selectively but in a representative way, from identifiable traditions. After the publication of *Toward Transfigured Life*, each time I lectured on "Introduction to Christian Ethics" at the University of Chicago, and recently when I took Emory graduate students through contemporary literature from major Christian traditions, it has been required reading. Its footnotes have, insofar as I have had time and need to expand my background for teaching, guided me. Since presumably students continue to learn from significant books, Father Stanley's works, not only the one I am most concerned with here, will be part of the syllabi of courses in Christian ethics at various levels of instruction.

One final personal postscript. I think we shared only one student, a young woman of deep Greek Orthodox piety and loyalty whom I tutored during her College education at the University of Chicago, and who, because of her medical professional family, was very interested in medical ethics. She matriculated to the seminary in Brookline, and returned to Chicago to study theology in the Ph.D. program.

All this has been an effort to provide some specificity to my gratitude to, and admiration for Father Stanley. He has been my teacher, and helped me to teach, in distinctive ways.

For me, not steeped in literature of Eastern Orthodoxy historically, nor learned in much of the recent literature—in part due to my learning deficit in foreign languages (!)—it is difficult to line out Father Stanley's distinctiveness within Orthodox ethics. Guroian's work provides some help in this way, for those features are readily available in Vigen's work. But then, Fr. Stanley is part of a tradition in which continuity with its past, particularly its great sources, is more valued than radical deviations from that past. Surely one of the intended readerships of his work are members of Orthodox churches whose context of life is our contemporary culture and society in all their aspects, and who can benefit from books which are faithful to the tradition while addressing matters that are current. I know this from careful reading of his, Vigen's, and other recent materials from the Orthodox tradition, as well as from the historical materials, where I have my deepest disagreements and departures from it. I will, here, only iterate some of the themes Father Stanley develops which are alluring to me—maybe even spiritually and theologically tempting. The great divide for me, here as with all Christian theological orthodoxy, is the Christological assurance of the complete and final redemptive goodness of God. But this presentation is not about my work.

One alluring feature is what I call cosmic theocentrism. The Protestant theologian who came closest to this is Joseph Sittler, primarily in his famous plenary address at the Assembly of the World Council of Churches in Delhi. God depicted by Harakas is not just a God for the human, but the energizing orderer of all that was, all that is, and all that will be. To be sure, God's redemptive power and purposes are efficaciously present through faith and sacramental life in and through the lives of Christians, but the human, the historical, the social, are all part of a grander total reality, of the cosmos. Poetry, I believe, more than abstract metaphysical speculation, captures this allure. Recall with me, Gerard Manley Hopkins' "God's Grandeur."

> The world is charged with the grandeur of God.
> It will flame out, like shining from shook foil;
> It gathers to a greatness, like the ooze of oil
> Crushed. Why do men then now not reck his rod?
> Generations have trod, have trod, have trod;
> And all is seared with trade; bleared, smeared with toil;
> And wears man's smudge and shares man's smell; the soil
> Is bare now, nor can foot feel, being shod.
>
> And for all this, nature is never spent;
> There lives the dearest freshness deep down things;
> And though the last lights off the black West went
> Oh, morning, at the brown brink eastward, springs—
> Because the Holy Ghost over the bent
> World broods with warm breast and with ah! bright wings.

The smudge and smell of the human, the bareness of the soil, the fallibilities of social orders and cultures, the evil outcomes of the activities of fallen creatures do not subdue the sense of the generating and regenerating process of theosis, of divination, that pulsates through the stars we see and those beyond, the living matter we are and that is around us, through our natural desires as properly directed. This is not Western Christianity's God of history, though the *divinitas sensus* of Calvin and Edwards and others can be touched by it, and Haydn's oratorio, *The Creation*, glorifies it in its own eighteenth-century way.

This cosmic theocentrism is not the end of an inductive logical process from the consequences of living in the world to their primordial necessary condition. It is a *mysterium* in the deepest sense; a reality felt because it is known, though through a glass darkly, and a reality known because it is felt through a depth of piety—for Father Stanley's community, in the liturgy and the sacraments. It is what was caught to some extent by Anglicans who wrote about the sacramental universe, and by others.

Of course, for Father Stanley and his tradition it is a *trinitarian* cosmic theocentrism. Father, Son, and Spirit inform and form, if my understanding is correct, this cosmic energizing of all that is. The ethical import of this is pervasive; this is no Anabaptist ethic of faithfulness to Jesus; this is no Reformation ethic that sharply divides the law and the gospel; this is no ethic of pietism and evangelical conversionism, though it has confidence in the altering efficacy of baptism and the Eucharist. Nor is it, alas, for many people, an ethic of radical social prophetic history. If one chooses to use the term, this is a transformationist ethic, not a transformation of the perspective of the Christian alone, but an actual theosis, divinization of all that is, which human actions "endorse" (to use a terms of Barth's) and actualize. The reality of the Divine is The Reality, prior in every respect to the human. Father Stanley's is an ethic of trinitarian cosmic theocentrism.

A second alluring feature is the moral anthropology, which has both historic philosophical and theological elements interpenetrating. This is theosis operative in humans, the synergy of the human and the divine, the cooperation of the human with God that gives shape and direction to the dispositions of human beings. Father Stanley interprets the tradition's use of the term *autexousion*, distinguishable from the preference of many moderns both in Christian and other ethics for "autonomy." *Autexousion*, he writes, "must be understood not as some absolute power of human beings to control and determine, but as an ability to decide concerning a multiplicity of influences in our lives." (p. 105) To be sure, choice is involved, and something like Rahner's fundamental option is described: we must choose to subject ourselves either to God or to the "world." But this basic option is exercised, if I interpret correctly, in determining which of the influences on us (and, I presume, on events in society, culture and nature that are affected by us) we endorse and carry forward in a synergistic relationship to God, to grace.

While it would distort the theology of this position to drop the penetration of grace in cooperation with the human in synergy, the anthropology seems to me to recognize and account for a mediating position between the claims of radical human autonomy, on the one hand, and simple concurrence in the course of the influences upon us and upon our circumstances, on the other. It is too much to say that this is the same as participating in the patterns and processes of the interdependence of all things so as to relate them to God's ordering power. The allure of grace, in theosis, could lead one, however, to feel at one with Father Stanley's interpretation of the human and human action in relation to the Divine. Dispositions, as well as acts, are stressed, and choices are made among "influences" that are prior to our actions. "Self-determination among influences" is more congenial than radical autonomy.

A third alluring aspect of *Toward Transfigured Life* is Father Stanley's interpretation of discernment, *diakrisis* as the central feature of moral choices. He cites an ancient Christian source, "The queen of all virtues is diakrisis, discernment." Its allure may be due to its congeniality to efforts of my own in the dimensions developed. Because of the recurring theme of theosis, however, it has both theological and religious dimensions which are distinctive to the Orthodox tradition. Fr. Stanley explicates discernment by taking into account critical elements, which add up to a mixed theory of moral choice: conscience as a process, rights, laws and rules, consequences, intention, motives, means, values and dis-values, the process as an ecclesial, corporate one, and the perception of what is appropriate in the particular context. One can find formulae, which are equivalently inclusive and complex in other traditions as well. It is the inclusiveness that is commendable; no simple minded differentiation of types of ethical theories (and judgment about a religious ethics based on conformity to one or another of such theories) is adequate in this view.

I could say more about alluring and off-putting aspects of *Toward Transfigured Life*. I close, in the interests of fair time sharing with another expression of my gratitude and admiration, but mostly with an odd statement. If the theology and the spirituality of Father Stanley and his tradition were intellectually and experientially authenticated in my life and thought, my empathetic enthusiasm for his work would issue in more than what we now share—which is *Soli Deo Gloria*!

# The Work of Fr. Stanley Harakas: A Panel Discussion

*M. Therese Lysaught*

I want to start by thanking Vigen Guroian for inviting me to join this panel and share my thoughts on the work of Fr. Harakas. I will admit, I was both honored by the invitation, and humbled by the prospect of the task and the company in whose presence I'd be standing. What I would like to offer is less a 'paper' and more a set of reflections. I initially intended to shape my comments around two questions: (1) how has Fr. Harakas' work influenced me and my own work and (2) what, from my perspective, do I see as the important contributions Fr. Harakas has made to the discipline of theological ethics that remain important challenges for the work of those of us in this Society?

In writing this up, however, I realized that these two questions are not so easily separable. As is probably evident to you, I represent on this panel a slightly different demographic from that of my colleagues, namely, that of a junior scholar. Consequently, in some ways I represent, or I hope my work represents, 'future' directions or the next generation of this discipline of theological ethics. I also bring to this panel a different perspective in another way, insofar as I am liturgically or denominationally a Catholic who has been trained primarily by Protestants, who finds Orthodox theology increasingly compelling, and whose work is practiced in the context of a Catholic university. Thus, I will include in my remarks reflections on the ways the distinct discipline of Catholic moral theology might profit from conversation with Fr. Harakas and Orthodoxy.

## Preliminary Caveat

Let me begin, however, with a preliminary, autobiographical aside. My introduction to Fr. Harakas' work came rather indirectly, that is, I did not encounter it explicitly in my training in the dominant conversations and literature of academic theological ethics. I first encountered Fr. Harakas' work in my hiatus from traditional academia, when I went to work in the world of "bioethics," at the Park Ridge Center in Chicago. I had recently completed my dissertation on the Sacrament of Anointing of the Sick as a theological locus for bioethics—a completely novel and innovative idea, as far as I knew. At the Center, I happened upon a book in their series on health and medicine in the religious traditions, a book written by Fr. Harakas, and—much to my amazement—what did I find but a chapter on "Holy Unction." Here was someone else looking to the sacrament of anointing in the context of bioethics! I was intrigued, and I knew I needed to learn more about this man. At the same time, my work to that point had been influenced by Vigen Guroian's work on the relationship between liturgy and ethics. Vigen's work is deeply indebted to Fr. Harakas; once you know that it is obvious, but at the time I was unaware of this connection. Thus, Fr. Harakas' work long preceded mine and had in fact influenced mine directly and in profound ways, but I did not realize it. This, in itself, is important, for I think it points to the marginalization or underappreciation of the rich contributions of Orthodoxy as a tradition within the discipline of theological ethics. This is a problem that seriously needs to be addressed in the future by this Society.

## Fr. Harakas and Bioethics

Given this preliminary caveat, I would like to organize my remarks into three areas, namely, the significance of Fr. Harakas' work for bioethics, for the methodology of theological ethics in general, and the renewal of Catholic moral theology. In the interest of giving Fr. Harakas as much time as possible, my remarks will regretfully remain a bit general, focusing primarily on Fr. Harakas' contributions to the field of bioethics. First, I address Fr. Harakas and bioethics, or more specifically, 'Christian' bioethics. For most of the relatively brief history of the contemporary discipline of bioethics, Fr. Harakas has been either the sole or the authoritative voice bringing the resources of the Orthodox tradition to bear on issues in or the practice of bioethics. Fr. Harakas was the lone Orthodox voice present at the "birth" of bioethics in the U.S. in the late 60's. As early as 1969, we find Fr. Harakas writing on issues raised for Orthodox Christians by science and technology ("The Orthodox Theological Approach to Modern Trends"). Here, he stands clearly in the company of other significant figures who created the field of bioethics, such as Daniel Callahan, Willard Gaylin, Paul Ramsey, and Richard McCormick. An indication of Fr. Harakas' unique and respected standing in the bioethics community at this time is reflected in his authorship of the entry on "Eastern Orthodox Bioethics" in the first edition of the *Encyclopedia of Bioethics* (1978).

Fr. Harakas' work is unique in at least three ways. First, in his work in bioethics, he has consistently endeavored to present the tradition of Orthodoxy, as a wholistic reality, to a non-Orthodox audience. In this capacity, he has authored the first—and to my knowledge, only—comprehensive work on Eastern

Orthodoxy in the context of health and modern medicine, the book I referred to earlier, his *Health and Medicine in the Eastern Orthodox Tradition* (1990). He has likewise supplied the relevant chapters on Orthodoxy to Numbers' and Amundsen's *Caring and Curing* (1986) and for the 1991 and 1993 editions of the Kluwer volumes *on Theological Developments in Bioethics*. In doing so, he has not only introduced this audience to a 'new' (yet ancient and rich) tradition; as Martin Marty notes, this introduction produces "a fundamental reorientation . . . for the non-Orthodox . . . [as] the visitor to the tradition learns to look at his or her own heritage in a new way" (xi). Thus, in simply being faithful to his identity as an Orthodox theologian, ethicist, and pastor, Fr. Harakas has served as, perhaps we could say, an icon for others, fostering the now growing sub-field of 'Christian' bioethics. The field of Christian bioethics is thus indebted to the work of Fr. Harakas. But with the exception of the work of Vigen Guroian, which has been directly influenced by Fr. Harakas, and a recent issue of Christian Bioethics focusing on Orthodoxy (undoubtedly at the inspiration of editor H. Tristram Engelhardt), Fr. Harakas remains the major representative of Orthodox bioethics.

But Fr. Harakas' audience has not solely been the non-Orthodox majority. Again, uniquely (relative to his counterparts—even those in the Roman Catholic church)—one of his primary audiences has been Orthodox Christians. A significant component of his corpus seeks to "educate" the Orthodox community on its own tradition, vis-a-vis bioethics, as well as specifically providing lay Christians with pastorally-sensitive yet authoritative guidance on such topics as contraception, abortion, death and dying, euthanasia, and organ donation (*Contemporary Moral Issues*, 1982). To date, much of Christian bioethics remains highly theoretical and academic, while those who write for lay audiences often lack adequate theological training.

Thirdly, Fr. Harakas' work in bioethics is unique methodologically. Again and again, his works begin with a rehearsal of the history of Orthodoxy in the Christian tradition, identification of the Church Fathers and other influential theologians, and/or an account of the spectrum of fundamental Orthodox theological convictions, *ethoi*, and aspects of sacramental spiritual life. Thus, attention to specific issues in bioethics is always framed by a discussion which integrates the following: Patristic authorities; an account of the relationship between medicine and the Church in the Byzantine period; those fascinating saints known as the Holy Unmercenaries; the apophatic/kataphatic character of the Orthodox doctrine of God; God as Trinity; humans as embodying both the image and likeness of God, with the corollary doctrine of Theosis; the divine energies; sin; incarnation; resurrection; eschatology; as well as an account of the prayer and liturgical life of the church, with specific attention to the sacraments of marriage and unction. In employing this approach, he is simply reflecting an Orthodox approach to theology. As he notes:

> Worship and liturgy, spiritual and mystical life, monastic *askesis* and

> polity, communal focus, pastoral care, doctrinal purity, and the cultivation of an ethos of love in the Christian life interest Eastern Christian tradition much more than formulations of abstract ethical constructs. Given this viewpoint, the Orthodox Church has not developed, in the main, complex rationalistic methodologies for bioethics. Those positions that it has developed are rooted in religious perspectives and not speculative reasoning ("Eastern Orthodox Bioethics," *Theological Developments in Bioethics*, 1991, p. 85).

This approach is clearly perceived as 'unusual' among those who do bioethics, even those who have an interest in relating religious traditions to bioethics. Again, I think Martin Marty's comments are interesting in this regard:

> The first time I read this manuscript I found that, following his helpful introduction, the author took up liturgy and stayed with it. When, I asked myself, will he concentrate on the history of doctrine, since Orthodoxy cherishes true teaching? When will he come to the works of justice and love that are such a part of religion, of Christianity? . . . Then it occurred to me: Harakas is talking about the teaching of Orthodoxy, about the action within it, whenever he takes up liturgy in detail. As this realization dawns upon readers, they are likely to become more patient with the accent on liturgy and then see their patience grow to fascination (*Health and Medicine*, x).

While I think it's interesting—and revelatory—that Marty found himself "impatient" with the manuscript, I think his final comment indicates the more important issue for us. For not only is Fr. Harakas simply being faithful to Orthodox methodology, in doing so he has provided the next generation of theological bioethicists with an alternative, compelling, fruitful, and much more relevant methodological model, especially for those whose lives are affected by the issues in bioethics that we academics discuss.

## Fr. Harakas and the Methodology of Theological Ethics

Moreover, Fr. Harakas' work provides a compelling alternative not only for developments in theological bioethics but for theological ethics in general. I would like to make two comments relative to methodology. First, as I have noted, this attention to sacraments and liturgy as an intrinsic part of the Christian tradition has significantly influenced my own work. Here, again, Fr. Harakas' work either precedes or appears early on in the recent turn in theological ethics toward liturgy as a theological locus. As early as 1974, he is writing on the Sacrament of Holy Confession, the role of the priest in the Divine Liturgy (1976), icons and ethics (1987), and the teaching function of liturgy (1989). Although he argues against a contemporary reductive tendency to see the Eucharist as the one, exclusive source or resource for Christian ethics or to reconceive the entirety of the Christian life through a Eucharistic lens, he provides a model for reappropriating Eucharist and other liturgical and spiritual practices—both sacramental and non-sacramental—as central within the multiplicity of sources of Christian life and Christian ethics. While one finds almost an explosion of work on the relationship between liturgy and ethics among liturgists and liturgical theologians, the appreciation of this linkage among theological ethicists remains sporadic. Given the increasing appreciation within the academy of the epistemological and ethical importance of "practices" as an object of theoretical study, it seems logical that ethicists move in the direction of liturgy. However, factors such as the lack of "openness" of liturgical practices (that is, the lack of ecumenical inter-communion) as well as their theological particularity may inhibit this development.

This latter point raises a second methodological contribution of Fr. Harakas work. Theological ethics often look less and less "theological." Implicit in all that I have said to this point is an inalienable characteristic of Fr. Harakas' work: it is thoroughly theological. At no point is his social location as an Orthodox theologian-ethicist-pastor obscured or not abundantly obvious. Moreover, he consistently draws almost exclusively on theological resources. Here he differs significantly from most academic theological ethicists who draw equally or exclusively on non-theological sources—be they philosophical (e.g., Aristotle, MacIntyre, Stout), linguistic, critical theory (Foucault), political (Rawls, Marx), feminist, etc.—for their basic frameworks or conceptual categories. Fr. Harakas clearly participates in the contemporary conversation—arguing concepts and topics such as "tradition" (1992), ecological ethics (1988, 1990), just war and peace (1981, 1986, 1993), human rights (1982), or church-state relations (1986, 1992). But he does not become entangled in the problematic tasks of either trying to "fit" theological tradition to secular frameworks or of trying to argue for or justify the use of a theological approach. He simply does it. Although his early works do show more resonance with this contemporary pattern—see "An Orthodox Evaluation of the 'New Theology'" (1967), "An Orthodox Christian Approach to the New Morality" (1970), "The Church and the Secular World" (1972)—they are still primarily focused on the articulation of an Orthodox theological vision. While personally I find this rather refreshing, I think more importantly it ought to admonish those of us who understand ourselves as theological ethicists to self-evaluation, to examine whether the resources, concepts and agendas that control our work are truly theological.

## Fr. Harakas and Catholic Moral Theology

I would like to close my reflections with a few brief remarks on the implications of Fr. Harakas' work for the practice of Catholic moral theology. Although I am Catholic and teach at a Catholic university, my work clearly does not fall within the realm of Catholic moral theology, as traditionally defined. A main reason for this is that I don't find the methodology of Catholic moral theology particularly compelling or theological. Fr. Harakas' work, in his discussions of the historical developments and differences in Eastern and Western theology, has been helpful for me in clarifying why this is the case. But more germane for our purposes, in addition to showing how moral theology ought to be theological and take liturgy seriously, Fr. Harakas, over the course of his career, has provided Orthodox readings of concepts and topics central to Catholic moral theology—for example, natural law, just war and peace, human rights, church-state relations, conscience. While not afraid to be "distinctively" Orthodox, he still sees a role and possibility for Orthodox thought to influence public policy. It might be interesting, for example, for a Catholic moral theologian to compare Fr. Harakas' presentation of the Orthodox position on *symphonia* to the work of John Courtney Murray. Alternatively, he offers an account of natural law that minimizes both the biological and juridical components. Insofar as he offers an alternative reading of a tradition that is in large part shared between Orthodoxy and Roman Catholicism, his work provides the most accessible and persuasive Orthodox counterpart—indeed, perhaps the only Orthodox counterpart—for contemporary Catholic moral theologians. Catholic moral theologians might take note of the productive rapprochement between Orthodox and Catholic systematicians, as evidenced, for example, in the influence of the work of John Zizioulas on communion ecclesiology. And finally, Fr. Harakas and his Orthodox colleagues offer positions that are more theologically-grounded, pastorally-sensitive, and reasonable than Catholic positions on precisely those issues which are most troubling for the contemporary U.S. Catholic church—contraception and the ordination of women. Might Orthodoxy provide Catholicism with the means for breaking out of the impasse on these issues? I would suggest so.

In closing, I hope my remarks have indicated my deep appreciation for Fr. Harakas' contributions to an endeavor I deeply cherish, and I hope I have suggested constructive ways in which we, in the future, might build on his work.

# Response

*Stanley S. Harakas*

Let me begin by expressing my thanks to the Program Committee of the Society of Christian Ethics for honoring me with this panel session. My membership in the Society of Christian Ethics of almost a quarter of a century has been for me a precious and valuable learning experience. Plenaries, and a myriad of sessions with an extremely wide range of topics, presented by highly competent, thoughtful and sensitive people of many persuasions, have been for me provocative, humbling and challenging. Participation in the academic arena of the SCE has impacted on my thought and writing in many ways. Most of all, however, the Annual Meetings of the SCE have made it possible for me to meet and engage in conversation with numerous sincere, dedicated, committed and highly competent ethicists who represent a wide range of starting points and traditions. These personal encounters have been enriching and instructive.

In the light of today's panel discussion on my work, I feel it is necessary for me to also add that it has been my hope that in some small way I have been able to bring to the attention of the membership of the SCE the method, concerns, and the theoretical and practical perspectives of the Eastern Orthodox tradition in ethical reflection. It began as a lonely effort, supported primarily by my teachers and fellow students at Boston University's School of Theology and by colleagues in the Boston Theological Institute, in particular Lisa Sowle Cahill and Max Stackhouse. I owe much to my doctoral mentor, Dean Walter George Muelder—much more than I can ever repay.

Soon, however, I was joined by several Orthodox colleagues who came and went, but in particular, my special friend and colleague Professor Vigen Guroian who moderates this session. I thank him for his most generous and kind remarks about my work and me. Vigen's kindness comes out of his good heart, and out of many hours of joint reflection, and personal sharing. His chairing this session is something that is not unusual in our common pursuit of Orthodox Christian ethics in the SCE. For years, he has chaired sessions in which I presented the lone Orthodox ethical paper on the program of our Annual Meeting; and I, in return, presided at sessions over the years, in which Vigen presented the lone Orthodox ethical paper on the program. A panel or two on Orthodox ethical topics served to expand the presence of Orthodox ethicists in recent years, and I'm pleased to say that this pattern has moved into a new phase. The Breakfast with an Author at this year's meeting on Vigen's book *Life's Living Toward Dying* was convened not by an Orthodox ethicist but by a Roman Catholic scholar, Mara Kelly-Zukowski of Felician College. And, to top it off, the session was full.

When I first saw the title of this session, "The Work of Reverend Stanley Harakas," was a bit taken aback. I can't remember very often seeing the ecclesiastical title "Reverend" in the title of a panel or session at SCE. But, upon reflection, I felt that it was appropriate. In my work, I have tried to stay focused on the ethical tradition of the Orthodox Christian Church, and so the ethics that I deal with is ecclesial, with no apologies. I have tried to make that clear in many ways, including the way I dress. I wear clerical garb all the time (except when working around the house and in my garden). Some years, I have been the only person in attendance dressed this way. Yet, I have not ever considered coming any other way. Perhaps it is my conviction that Christian ethics cannot be anything, if it is not at first and at its core, ecclesial. So, in all that I have done in this society, I have tried to send the message that my work is in, for and about an ecclesial reality—Christian ethics.

As an Orthodox Christian ethicist, I have spoken first of all to my own community, raising up for them forgotten or minimized dimensions of ethical reflection in their own tradition. My work however, also seeks to provide a dimension of reflection for the larger Christian ethical sphere of discourse, and beyond that, for the public domain. For example, the theological and sacramental approach of the Eastern and Oriental Orthodox Christian traditions on the ecological question, I believe, speak in a different accent than those of the Western Christian traditions. These Eastern perspectives can serve to remind all that from the beginning of Christian history and not just recently, Christianity's faith and experience have never been limited to Europe or even just Western Europe.

So, I am deeply grateful to my friend and colleague Vigen Guroian for accepting to moderate this session.

## Timothy Sedgwick

I am grateful also to Prof. Timothy Sedgwick for his thoughtful comments and assessment of my Eastern Orthodox approach to Christian Ethics. He raises an important point in terms of the role of Christian Tradition in relationship to the study and investigation of Christian ethics. I think it is fair to say that my effort over the years has been to examine the Eastern Christian tradition and to seek to articulate it in a way that is not only historical, but also in a way that sees it as an important source for addressing new concerns and issues. Though this has taken place in this forum, most of my work has sought to develop, for the first time in any systematic fashion, Orthodox Christian ethics in the English language. My audience, deliberately chosen, has been the Orthodox Church, so that I have not sought, primarily, to engage the larger Christian ethics community directly and consciously. Since my work was ecclesial, it was of necessity, even in its most theoretical expressions, pastorally focused.

Sedgwick characterizes my work as developing "the grammar of faith." I think he is right on this, but I prefer to call what I do as exploring and seeking to understand and express "the mind of the Church" in the area of Christian ethics. On the one hand, it unashamedly seeks to understand ethics as coming out of the Eastern Christian tradition, yet my approach also experiences the tradition as illuminating the ethical task for yet unknown and still unresolved ethical issues. The tradition functions both instructively and heuristically. Thus, examining the tradition cannot be a reactionary return to the past. It is a search for methods and values that illumine the human condition and is a risky search for normative direction in the face of on-going human problems and totally new issues and developments.

In his comments, Timothy speaks of Orthodox Christian ethics as drawing on "the wide range of sources that form Orthodoxy, primarily scripture, patristic writers, Eastern Fathers, and the prayers of Eastern liturgies and tradition." That is also a fair assessment. However, in that mix "reason" should also be included. Not rationalism, but reason that seeks to root itself in human experience and knowledge, and which is most true to itself when it acknowledges the presence of what might be called "rational mystery" and transcendence, especially regarding the mystery of faith. That is why I would hold that reason is useful for much of our work, especially that of the academy and public discourse. But can it be Christian ethics if the religious presuppositions and warrants are not accented or highlighted even more than reason?

After all, we are dealing with ethical discourse. Discourse searches, discusses, reflects and enters into sustained conversation. It should not be perceived as confrontation, but an effort to clarify and illuminate problems that face us as Christians and as human beings. Discourse, by definition, must be conducted in open and ecumenical dialogue. In all this, I wonder how Christian ethics can seek to do its work without articulating and affirming its most precious religious, theological, liturgical and spiritual sources as primary data?

That's why I'm glad Timothy Sedgwick noted that commitment to the Orthodox Christian tradition "enables and requires critical reflection by those who stand within Orthodoxy." I see Christian ethics as standing at the nexus of faith and life, responding to a series of questions about the meaning of ethics itself and about "living the faith" questions. To do ethics from within this tradition requires rootedness in the tradition of faith, but engagement with it in a constructive way in many situations. This is all the more true as Orthodox ethics seeks to address even its age-old questions in the new context of the modern and post-modern mind set. Without doubt, there are ancient ethical affirmations that will never find adequate reasons for change or adaptation. But new circumstances challenge even traditional ethical reflection for fresh analyses and responses.

It is true that there is an increasing pluralism in what Sedgwick calls "family differences to the outsider, major challenges to the insider," in the practice of Orthodox Christian ethics. But I believe this is an accurate assessment because of the tendencies to reductionism in ethical reflection. Ethics, in my judgment is concurrently necessarily personal, ecclesial and outreaching. Often, perceptions of the Christian tradition reduce its meaning and content to just one of these three foci, distorting the wholeness and balance of the tradition. In my own work, I have sought to keep these three dimensions in a mutually informing and interpenetrating relationship. It may be that this wholistic perspective is one of the major contributions that Orthodox Christian thought could make to the Western Christian mind set.

## James Gustafson

I can't describe to you how deeply I appreciate Professor Gustafson's presence on this panel. There were many things he could have said that differentiate his own "cosmic theocentrism" from the views of Eastern Christianity, but he has chosen to lift up some of the convergences that he finds particularly congenial. The most important of these convergences is what I have alluded to above, what we might call the "ecumenical" nature of ethical discourse. I don't mean by this a polite conversation, but rather the mutuality of an expanding fullness of perspectives: a fullness that cannot approach its completion without a sense of the divine, if not a communion with the divine.

Professor Gustafson has caught and commented on the central affirmation of Eastern Orthodox ethics, its Trinitarian cosmic theocentrism. Focusing on my book *Toward Transfigured Life*, which seeks to articulate the "*theoria*" of Eastern Orthodox ethics, Gustafson has rightly posited the derivative character of Christian ethics, not from rationalism, nor from mysticism, nor from natural law, nor from human experience, but from the Triune God, who encompasses the world as Creator, Redeemer, and Sanctifier -Father, Son and Holy Spirit. The book, he correctly observes, seeks to present Christian ethics as derived from theology, and to relate the sacramental life with the moral life, and to bring to bear on current issues the whole vision of the theological stance, without apology or circumspection.

The idea that theology and worship are the key to understanding ultimate reality and our place in it and our responsibility for it means that the discipline of Christian ethics is of necessity pedagogical. I deeply appreciate Professor Gustafson's use of Orthodox Christian ethical material in his course offerings, because it helps me comprehend the potential of this material for stimulating thought and reflection in the thought of our day.

It is interesting to me that he has chosen three themes to lift up for comment. His own work in focusing on a theocentric perspective for Christian ethics sees God as central to ethics. God is, however, in Orthodox theology and ethics, a God who is a community of divine persons, the Holy Trinity. That God becomes not only the cause and the sustenance of all that is not God, but also in a certain way, the Triune God is the model for being genuinely human.

Gustafson is right, however, in faulting historic Eastern Orthodox Christianity for not being a model of social change in some ways. Yet, part of my life-long work has been to present to my students the social thought of the Bible and the Eastern Church Fathers. Part of this includes the Church Fathers' ethical understandings, for example, of economic justice. Surprising for many is that Patristic economic ethics is so radical that it stands as a perpetual challenge to every age and time, especially in one in which individualistic capitalist values predominate. There is a reason for that challenging stance. The majority of Church Fathers were monastics. Their monastic calling was based on a demanding and radical eschatological vision that constantly challenges the Church in the world, especially when it accommodates itself too readily to the ways of the world. The monastery is an eschatological counter-culture in the midst of the Church. Healthy monasticism keeps the tension between what is and what ought to be in the life of the Christian and the life of the Church.

Professor Gustafson's second theme is the anthropology of Eastern Orthodox theology, which is concurrently a matrix for Orthodox Christian ethics. The Orthodox understanding of the human condition sees human beings, even in our fallen condition, as reflecting the "divine image" in our constitution, as rational, self-determining, creative, and moral persons in community. But it understands the message of our being in the "likeness" of God as the potential of growing toward God-likeness. We use the term "theosis" or "divinization," to describe the fullness of human existence and life.

So, in spite of the oft repeated misrepresentation of Orthodox thought and life as stagnant and lacking in dynamism, Orthodox theology and ethics understands the norm of growth toward God-likeness as an ongoing and never-ending process toward the fulfillment of our human *telos*, both as individual persons, members of the ecclesial community, and as the community of the whole of creation. This has powerful ethical implications, some of which Gustafson mentions. In my book, *Living the Faith: The 'Praxis' of Eastern Orthodox Ethics*, I try to show how this works itself out in the personal and ecclesial dimensions of the Christian life.

Because I try throughout my work to be as comprehensive as I can, Professor Gustafson was insightful to lift up the importance that I give to the virtue of discernment (*diakrisis*) in Eastern Orthodox ethics. He describes what he calls a mixed theory of choice in ethical decision-making. There is no single and exclusive criteria for ethical decision-making that can be identified in the Eastern

Christian ethical tradition. And I would venture that no living, ecclesial Christian tradition would sustain such a view of decision-making if it were studied objectively. In my study of the concrete sources of ethical decision-making in the biblical, patristic and canonical sources in Eastern Christianity, the moral appeals are found to be extremely wide-ranging. This is another instance of the wholeness, inclusiveness and transcendence of an ethic that grounds itself in ultimate reality of the Trinitarian God, who creates, redeems and sanctifies all that is, including human moral decision-making that ought to be in conformity with the struggle for growth in God-likeness.

I'm grateful to Professor Gustafson for focusing his comments on the theological core of my understanding and presentation of Orthodox Christian ethics.

## M. Therese Lysaught

I must confess to you that I am nearly always caught by surprise when someone in the academy tells me that she or he has read one of my articles or books. Since my primary intended audience is to be found within the Orthodox tradition—my publisher Light and Life sells mostly to the Orthodox Christian reader—and the theological tradition I speak from is Eastern rather than Western, the surprise is understandable.

So when Therese Lysaught shows knowledge of more than a few of my publications, it strikes me as astonishing! I'm particularly grateful that she, as a Roman Catholic ethicist teaching in a Roman Catholic university, finds the message of my books and articles of interest and value.

Professor Lysaught raises up for attention my work in bioethics. She is correct that early in my work in Orthodox Christian ethics, I found the emerging discipline of bioethics a interesting sphere to test my working hypothesis that the resources within the tradition of Orthodox Christianity could address new and fresh situations in a creative fashion. The method that evolved over the years for doing this was to search the living and sometimes forgotten tradition in its multiple embodiments for expressions of faith and life that "speak" to the newly developing issues in the sphere of bioethics. In this, I have been told, my method has some affinity with Jewish rabbinic scholarship. Similar to it also, has been a willingness to be criticized and corrected by the circle of scholars in the Orthodox tradition. Thus, in semi-popular books such as *Contemporary Moral Issues Facing the Orthodox Christian*, positions have been ventured for the Orthodox Community on bioethical problems which are rooted in some aspects of the tradition, but applied to totally new and unanticipated bioethical situation. Sometimes, these positions have taken on a certain authoritative and normative character for both clergy and laity. Attention to bioethical questions, thus, was on the one hand, an exercise in ethical method for a tradition-based ethic, while on the other hand, a contribution to the on-going formation of the ecclesial mind-set for many.

In discussing the relationship of Orthodox ethics with Roman Catholic moral theology, Professor Lysaught touches on a long-standing interest I've had in the Eastern Christian approach to Natural Law. In my doctoral dissertation I examined the muted, yet real and functionally important place of natural law thinking in the Ante-Nicene patristic period, comparing it with modern Greek Orthodox thought on the subject. One of the first papers I read at the SCE was on Eastern Christian approaches to Natural Law. One of the distinctions between this perspective and that of the developed Roman Catholic tradition is that Eastern Christian Natural Law thought remains within a theological matrix, while not limiting itself to the Christian revelatory framework. In its early Christian expression, the Natural Law was a low-level, minimalist ethic that could be empirically determined to have much to do with the sustenance and maintenance of human communities in any kind of social context. It was "rational" in the sense of American philosophical Pragmatism. It was "natural law" precisely because it worked to hold together any social whole. Maybe Therese is right that such a perspective might contribute to some Roman Catholic re-assessment of its own tradition of Natural Law.

Professor Lysaught has been most kind in her assessment of my writings. Her familiarity with them is much appreciated. As a member of the ongoing Roman Catholic/Orthodox Dialogue, the longest lasting continuous ecumenical dialogue on the North American continent, I pray that my work contributes, even in a small way, to a deeply desired reconsideration of our divisive pasts, and the formulation of a new future.

# A Select Bibliography of Works by Stanley Samuel Harakas

## Published Books

*Living the Liturgy*. Minneapolis: Light & Life Publishing Co., 1974.

*Partakers of Divine Nature*. Trans. George Stavropoulos. Minneapolis: Light & Life Publishing Co. 1976.

Nom de plume, "Exetastes." In *Contemporary Issues: Orthodox Christian Perspectives*. New York: Greek Orthodox Archdiocese Press, 1976.

*Contemporary Moral Issues Facing the Orthodox Christian* (Expanded and revised edition of *Contemporary Issues*). Minneapolis: Light & Life Publishing Co., 1982.

*Let Mercy Abound: A Chronicle of Greek Orthodox Social Concerns*. Brookline: Holy Cross Orthodox Press, 1983.

*Toward Transfigured Life: The Theoria of Eastern Orthodox Ethics*. Minneapolis: Light & Life Publishing Co., 1983.

*The Orthodox Church: 455 Questions and Answers*. Minneapolis: Light and Life Publishing Co., 1987.

*Proclaiming God's Word Today: Preaching Concerns in the Greek Orthodox Archdiocese of North and South America*. Minneapolis: Light and Life Publishing Co., 1989.

*Living the Faith: The Praxis of Eastern Orthodox Ethics*. Minneapolis: Light and Life Publishing Co., 1992.

*Health and Medicine in the Eastern Orthodox Tradition*. New York: Crossroad, 1990. Second printing, Minneapolis: Light and Life Publishing Co., 1996

*Of Life and Salvation: Reflections on Living the Christian Life (Based on the Fourteen Scripture Readings of the Orthodox Christian Church's Sacrament of Holy Unction)*. Minneapolis: Light and Life Publishing Co., 1996.

## Other Writings

"Alexander N. Tsirindanes on the Present Age." *The Greek Orthodox Theological Review* II, no. 1 (1956): 75-82.

"The Natural Law Teaching of the Eastern Orthodox Church." *The Greek Orthodox Theological Review* IX, no. 2 (1963-1964): 215-224. Reprinted in *New Theology* no. 2, ed. Martin E. Marty and Dean G. Peerman (New York: The Macmillan Co., 1965): 122-133.

"The Orthodox Theological Approach to Modern Trends." *St. Vladimir's Theological Quarterly* 13, no. 4 (1969): 198-211.

"'Η 'Ηθική Διδασκαλία τοῦ Πεντηκοσταρίου" ("The Ethical Teaching of the Pentecostarion"). *Θεολογία* (Athens, Greece) 39 (July-September 1968): 368-385, and (October- December 1968): 586-612.

"An Orthodox Approach to the New Morality." *Greek Orthodox Theological Review* XVII, no. 1 (Spring 1970): 107- 139.

"The Church and the Secular World." *Greek Orthodox Theological Review* XVII, no. 1 (Spring 1972). Abstracted in *Journal of Ecumenical Studies* 10, p. 4.

"Greek Orthodox Ethics and Western Ethics." *Journal of Ecumenical Studies* 10, no. 4 (Fall 1973): 728-751.

"The Meaning of the Adaptation of Orthodoxy to the Contemporary World." *Theologike Epiteris tes Theologikes Scholes tou Panepistemiou Thessalonikes* 19 (1974):127-140.

"Ethics in the Greek Orthodox Tradition." *Journal of Ecumenical Studies* XIII, no. 4 (Fall 1976): 574-578. Also, *Greek Orthodox Theological Review* 22, no. 1 (1977): 58-62.

"Eastern Orthodox Perspectives on Natural Law." *Selected Papers: The American Society of Christian Ethics* (1977). Ed. Max L. Stackhouse: 41-56.

"L'etica nella tradizione Greco-ortodossa." *Unitas* 32 (1977): 95-100.

"The Centrality of Conscience in Eastern Orthodox Ethics." *Greek Orthodox Theological Review* 23 (June 1978):131-144,

"Eastern Orthodox Medical Ethics." In *Encyclopedia of Bioethics,* vol. 1. Ed. Warren T. Reich. New York: The Free Press, 1978: 347-356.

"Population: An Eastern Orthodox Perspective." In *Encyclopedia of Bioethics*, vol. 3. Ed. Warren T. Reich. New York: The Free Press, 1978: 1251-1254.

"Christian Ethics in Ecumenical Perspective: An Orthodox Christian View." *Journal of Ecumenical Studies* 15, no. 4 (Fall 1978): 631-646.

"Eastern Orthodox Perspectives on Natural Law." *American Journal of Jurisprudence* 24 (1979): 86-113.

"Reflections on the Ethical Dimensions of the Topics of the Great and Holy Synod." *Greek Orthodox Theological Review* 24 (Summer/Fall 1979): 131-157.

"Social Concern and the Greek Orthodox Archdiocese." *Greek Orthodox Theological Review* 25 (1980): 377-408.

"The Morality of War." In *Orthodox Synthesis: The Unity of Theological Thought*. Ed. Joseph Allen. Crestwood, NY: St. Vladimir's Seminary Press, 1981.

"Orthodox Social Conscience: Archbishop Iakovos, A Modern Case." In *Orthodox Theology and Diakonia: Trends and Prospects*. Brookline, MA: Hellenic College Press, 1981

"Church and State in Orthodox Thought." *Greek Orthodox Theological Review* 27, no. 1 (Spring 1982).

"Human Rights: An Eastern Orthodox Perspective." *Journal of Ecumenical Studies* 19, no. 3 (Summer, 1982): 13-24. Also, published in *Human Rights in Religious Traditions*. Ed. Arlene Swidler. New York: The Pilgrim Press, 1982.

"An Orthodox Theology of Development." In *Just Development for Fullness of Life: A Responsible Christian Participation*. WCC-CCPD Orthodox Consultation in Kiev, USSR, 22-30 June, 1982. Geneva: Commission on the Churches' Participation in Development, The World Council of Churches (1982): 49-81. Reprinted in *Θεολογία* (Athens, Greece) 54, no. 4 (1983): 817-847.

"Orthodox Method for the Ethics of Christian Praxis." in *Xenia Oecoumenica* (Helsinki, Finland), 1982.

"Foundations of Orthodox Christian Social Vision." *Diakonia* XVIII, no. 2 1983.

"A Case Study in Eastern Orthodox Ethics on Rich and Poor: Alexios Makrembolites' 'Dialogue Between the Rich and the Poor.'" *The Annual of the Society of Christian Ethics*, 1984.

"The Stand of the Orthodox Church on Controversial Issues." In *A Companion to the Greek Orthodox Church*. New York: Greek Orthodox Archdiocese, 1984.

"Christian Faith Concerning Creation and Biology." In *La Theologie Dans L' Eglise et Dans Le Monde: Les Etudes Theologiques de Chambesy*. Chambesy, Switzerland: Publications of the Orthodox Center of the Ecumenical Patriarchate, 1984.

"Educating for Moral Values in a Pluralistic Society." *Greek Orthodox Theological Review* 29, no. 4 (Winter, 1984): 393-399.

"The Greek Orthodox Church." In *Euthanasia and Religion: A Survey of the Attitudes of World Religions on the Right-to-die*. Ed. Gerald A. Larue. Los Angeles: The Hemlock Society, 1985, pp. 45-54.

"Eastern Orthodox Christianity and Ultimate Reality and Meaning: Triune God and Theosis - An Ethician's View." *Ultimate Reality* 8 (1985):209-223.

"Health and Medicine in the Orthodox Church." In *Caring and Curing: Health and Medicine in Western Religious Traditions*. Eds. Ronald L. Numbers and Darrel W. Amundsen. N.Y.: Macmillan Publishing Co., 1986.

"Eastern Orthodox Christian Ethics." in *Dictionary of Christian Ethics*, 2nd ed. Philadelphia: The Westminster Press, 1986.

"The NCCB Pastoral Letter: 'The Challenge of Peace' -An Eastern Orthodox Response." In *Peace in a Nuclear Age: The Bishop's Pastoral Letter in Perspective*. Ed. Charles J. Reid, Jr. Washington, D.C.: The Catholic University Press, 1986.

"Orthodox Christianity and Bioethics." In *Orthodox Christians and Muslims*. Ed. N. M. Vaporis Brookline, MA: Holy Cross Orthodox Press, 1986. Reprinted in *Greek Orthodox Theological Review* (1986): 181-194.

"Thalassemia: A Theological Perspective." In *Thalassemia: An Interdisciplinary Approach*. Ed. John T. Chirban. Lanham, Md: University Press of America, 1986.

"The Teaching of Peace in the Fathers." In *Un Regard Orthodoxe sur la Paix*. Chambesy - Geneva: Editions du Centre Orthodoxe du Patriarcat Oecoumenique, 1986.

"Icon and Ethics." *One World*, no. 131 (1987): 12-14.

"The Integrity of Creation." A paper for the Orthodox Consultation on the "Integrity of Creation." Sophia, Bulgaria, Sept.-Oct., 1987. *St. Vladimir's Theological Quarterly* 32 (1988): 27-42.

"Rational Medicine in the Orthodox Tradition." *Greek Orthodox Theological Review* 33 (1988): 19-43.

"The Teaching Function of the Liturgy." In *The Pastor as Teacher*. Eds. Earl E. Shelp and Ronald H. Sunderland. New York: The Pilgrim Press, 1989.

"Health and Medicine in the Eastern Orthodox Tradition: Salvation as the Context of Healing." The Annual Georges Florovsky Memorial Lecture, Orthodox Theological Society in America, 1989. *Greek Orthodox Theological Review* 34, no. 3 (1989): 219-235.

"Integrity of Creation: Ethical Issues." In *Justice, Peace, and the Integrity of Creation: Insights From Orthodoxy*. Ed. Gennadios Limouris. Geneva: WCC Publications, 1990.

"Ecological Reflections in Contemporary Orthodox Thought in Greece." *Epiphany* 10, no. 3 (1990): 46-61.

"Rational Medicine and the Eastern Orthodox Tradition" with Greek Summary. In Vol. 5: *'Αναφοράν είς τήν Μνήμην Μητροπολίτου Σάρδεων Μαξίμου*. Chambesey, Geneva: Patriarchal Center, 1989.

"Statement by Stanley S. Harakas." In "Feature: A Time to Die: The Cases of Nancy Cruzan and Janet Adkins." *Bulletin of the Park Ridge Center* (September 1990): 24.

"Giver of Life- Sustain Your Creation." In *Come, Holy Spirit: Renew the Whole Creation: An Orthodox Approach*. For the Seventh Assembly of the World Council of Churches, Canberra, Australia, 6-21 February, 1991. Ed. Gennadios Limouris. Brookline, MA: Holy Cross Orthodox Press, 1991.

"Sources in Orthodox Christianity for Bioethical Decision-Making." *Diaconia* XXIV, no. 2 (1991): 109-120

"Eastern Orthodox Bioethics." *Bioethics Yearbook*: Vol. 1: *Theological Developments, 1988-1990*. Netherlands: Kluwer Academic Publishers, 1991.

"Is There an Orthodox Just War Position?" *Orthodox America* 1, no. 2 (1992). Washington D. C.: Ethics and Public Policy Center.

"Reflecting On the Body . . . and Ethics." *Second Opinion: Health, Faith, Ethics* 17, no. 4 (April 1992): 89-92.

"Earth, Water, Light." In *The Renewal of Creation in Eastern Orthodox Epiphany Rites. The Living Pulpit* (April-June, 1993): 14-16.

"Orthodox Christianity Facing Science." From a Seminar on "Orthodox Christianity Facing Science, Education and Politics, March 16, 1987." *The Greek Orthodox Theological Review* 37, nos. 1-2 (1992): 7-15.

"Tradition" in Eastern Orthodox Thought." Presented at the 1990 Meeting of the American Theological Society. *The Christian Scholar's Review* XXII, no.2 (December, 1992): 144-165.

"Sunday Closing Laws Revisited- An Orthodox Approach." In *Sunday Closing Laws Revisited: A Biblical, Ethical, and Sociological Study of a Common Day of Rest*. Boston: Massachusetts Council of Churches, 1993.

"Eastern Orthodox Bioethics." *Bioethics Yearbook*. Vol. 3: *Theological Developments in Bioethics, 1990-1992*. Netherlands: Kluwer Academic Publishers, 1993.

"An Eastern Orthodox Approach to Bioethics." *The Journal of Medicine and Philosophy* 18 (1993): 531-548.

"Resurrection and Ethics in Chrysostom." *Ex Auditu* 9 (1993): 77-95.

"Peace in the Nuclear Context." Presented at the Third International Conference of Orthodox Theological Schools, September 1987. *The Greek Orthodox Theological Review* 38, nos. 1-4 (1993).

"Ethical Teaching in St. Gregory the Theologian's Writings" Presented at the St. Gregory the Theologian Conference, April 1991, Holy Cross Greek Orthodox School of Theology. *The Greek Orthodox Theological Review* 39, no. 2 (1994): 141-150.

"Orthodox Christianity and Bioethics." *Chelovek* (February 1994): 79-90.

"Faith and Culture in Contemporary Orthodox Theology." In *Rightly Teaching the Word of Your Truth: Festschrift in Honor of His Eminence Archbishop Iakovos*. Ed. N. M. Vaporis. Brookline: Holy Cross Orthodox Press, 1995.

"Eastern Orthodox Bioethics." In *Encyclopedia of Bioethics*. 2$^{nd}$ ed. Ed. Warren T. Reich. New York: Macmillan Publishing Co. & Simon and Schuster Publishing Co., 1995.

"Population: An Eastern Orthodox Perspective." In *Encyclopedia of Bioethics*. 2$^{nd}$ ed. Ed. Warren T. Reich. New York: Macmillan Publishing Co. & Simon and Schuster Publishing Co., 1995.

"Ethical Teachings in the Canons of the Penthekte Council." Presented at the Holy Cross Conference on "The Council 'In Trullo': Basis for Ecclesiastical Reform? Commemorating the 1300 Anniversary of the Penthekte Ecumenical Council." *The Greek Orthodox Theological Review* 40, nos. 1-2 (1995): 165-181.

"Orthodox Christian Perspectives on Issues of Population and Development." Solicited and submitted to The World Conference on Religion and Peace (WCRP) for the 1994 International Conference on Population and Development in Cairo, Egypt. In *Religion, Population and Development: Multi-Religious Contributions*. New York: The World Conference on Religion and Peace, 1994.

"Testimony of Rev. Dr. Stanley S. Harakas on Behalf of the Greek Orthodox Church, Archdiocese of America." In "Assisted Suicide: Legal, Medical, Ethical and Social Issues: Hearing Before the Sub-Committee on Health and Environment of the Committee on Commerce, House of Representatives, One Hundred Fifth Congress." First Session, March 6, 1997. Serial no. 105-7. Washington, DC: U.S. Government Printing Office, 1997, pp. 25-26 ff.

"'Ορθοδοξία και Βιοηθική" ("Orthodoxy and Bioethics")." Vol. 2 in *'Ορθοδοξία.- 'Ελληνισμός: Πορεία στήν Τρίτη Χιλιετία τῆς 'Ορθοδοξίας* (*Orthodoxy – Hellenism: Journey to the Third Millenium of Orthodoxy*). Holy Mountain Athos: Publications of the Holy Monastery of Koutloumousiou, 1997, pp. 277-289.

"To Clone or Not to Clone?" *Reflections: Newsletter of the Program for Ethics, Science, and the Environment*. Department of Philosophy, Oregon State University. (Special Editon, May 1997): 3-4.

"Orthodox Christian Ecological Reflection in North America." In *Agape and Diaconia: Essays in Memory of Bishop Gerasimos of Abydos*. Ed. Peter A. Chamberas. Brookline, MA: Holy Cross Orthodox Press.

# CONVERSATIONS WITH RELATED SOCIETIES

# Christian Ethics in Europe: A Perspective from the *Societas Ethica*

*Werner Wolbert*

When I was asked to present a paper on Christian Ethics in Europe, I accepted the invitation gladly. Afterwards I had some scruples. To begin with, I am not competent to report on ethics in all European countries. There is, for example, the problem of the Eastern (Central) European countries, among which Poland is especially important. For historical reasons, there seems to be in force a rule in Western Europe: "Slavica non leguntur." Especially among German-speaking people, there is little incentive to learn any Slavic language, because German is often a kind of *koine* between people of different Slavic countries.

The problem of language is only an indicator of a more fundamental problem. After the fall of the iron curtain, another curtain could be strengthened or built up again, namely, the demarcation between the Europe of Latin and that of Byzantine tradition. The wars in former Yugoslavia illustrate that danger.

Despite these problems, the *Societas Ethica* has had members from the countries behind the former Iron Curtain participate in conferences. Most of these colleagues have been from Poland and Hungary. But only very rarely have we had orthodox participants.

The languages in our society are English and German. This means, of course, an obstacle to people from the Romance countries, especially from France. The (linguistic) difficulty for people from Italy or Spain is decreasing because, in these countries, English has already taken the place of French as the first foreign language. Still, there is very little representation from France, Italy, Spain, or Portugal (although there are now some members from French-speaking Switzerland, and the president is from Ticino, living and working in Zürich). Most members are from Central Europe, the Netherlands, and the Nordic countries. The presidents have always been from these countries.

The society was founded by H. van Oyen, a Dutch scholar who taught in Basel from 1948 on. His original idea was to gather those European colleagues who taught ethics in Protestant theological faculties, and he sent letters to many of these in the early 1960s. In this letter, he shared his plans for the foundation of a *Societas Ethica*, which subsequently was formed in 1964. The first members were mainly from Germany, the Netherlands, and Switzerland. Later on, they came also from Eastern Europe, Austria, and Scandinavia. In the German-speaking countries, the Protestant theological chairs for ethics were (and are) mostly not dedicated to ethics exclusively; rather, ethics was taught by systematic theologians. Van Oyen himself had a chair for systematic theology (beside Karl Barth), but concentrated on ethics. Although one of the founding members was a Catholic philosopher (Hans Reiner), in the beginning the society was predominantly Protestant, and in the early years, only one fifth of the membership was allowed to be Catholic. This rule was abolished later on; there also came to be (even non-religious) philosophers among the members.

This short outline of history and present situation of the *Societas Ethica* can already give us some hints on the situation of Ethics in Europe, which I will sketch in three points: 1) the relation between philosophical and theological ethics; 2) communication and cooperation between ethicists; and 3) the debate on communitarianism in Europe.

1. My first point concerns the relation between philosophical and theological ethics. From the fact that one of the founding members was a philosopher one should not infer that German-speaking philosophers dealt much with ethics at that time. So far as I know, Hans Reiner was the only one to hold a chair for philosophical ethics in his time. In 1974, a collection of essays in two volumes was published in Germany under the title *Rehabilitierung der praktischen Philosophie*.[1] This title indicates that, among philosophers, practical philosophy had not been taken seriously for some time. So far as I know, the situation was similar in Romance countries. Ethics was studied mostly from an historical perspective. Now, of course, philosophers regularly contribute to public discussions on matters of practical ethics. Moral theologians, therefore, no longer have a monopoly in these matters, even though their voices are still important, at least in Central Europe. In France, on the other hand, only recently has a theologian become a member of the National Ethics Committee (after roughly ten years of its existence). In the meantime, philosophers as well as theologians are consulted and elected to respective commissions by the public authorities on the regional, national, or European level. But even if there is some exchange and cooperation, one can observe that theologians are familiar with the contribution of philosophers, but, in general, not vice versa. Theologians are rarely quoted in philosophical essays.

This description, so far, applies to Central Europe and (I think) also to the Nordic countries. In the Romance countries, especially in Italy, the situation is remarkably different. Here, the terminology is treacherous. Italian writers distinguish between *morale cattolica* and *morale laica.* And *laica* often means: anticlerical. There is a gap between theologians and philosophers that is caused, among other things, by the fact that there are no theological faculties within the state (and even ecclesiastical) universities. Thus our Italian colleagues lack the reputation (and independence) of university professors. The gap is also related to the proximity of the Roman magisterium, whose interventions have become more and more heavy, as an Italian colleague has complained. If a theologian is invited to a philosophical conference, he is esteemed only as an ally (for instance, if he shares a pacifist position with them), but they are not very interested in his arguments. What makes the relation still more difficult is the fact that most philosophical ethicists hold a non-cognitivist position, as the title of a book *L'etica senza verità* illustrates.[2] This does not fit very well with the "splendour of truth," which the pope conjured up in his encyclical.

The Italian situation reminds me of some remarks I read about Ireland in a short article by the Irish theologian E. Conway, entitled "Theology at the Margins." [3]

> Most theologians are free-standing, therefore dialogue between theology and other disciplines seldom occurs. These are some of the reasons why, in the popular mind, theology is seldom distinguished from religious education or from Church teaching and generally theologians lack a distinctive identity and relevance in Irish society.

About the future orientation of Irish theology he said

> It is appropriate that we would try to locate such issues in the wider European theological context. Up until now we have tended to look more to North America for enlightenment. Many of our theologians studied there, many of our own people have emigrated there, and we speak the same language—more or less. However, there is a growing awareness that the future landscape of faith in Ireland is more likely to resemble that of present day mainland Europe and that careful study of the situation in which our European neighbours now find themselves would be rewarding."

The next remark is relevant for ethicists:

> Do Irish theologians have any contribution to make to Europe today? It has been noted at meetings of the Irish section [of the European Society for Catholic Theology] that theological exploration of the Irish experience of colonialism might help develop and maintain a sensitivity in Europe to the plight of developing countries. Regrettably Ireland also

has considerable experience of sectarianism, and theology has been more part of the problem than of the solution.

Moral theology in such situations (as Italy or Ireland) is in danger of being pushed to one side, and thus limited in its ability to proclaim the ethical message of the New Covenant to all people.

The situation is remarkably different in Spain, where there is no open dissent from the magisterium, but a moderate freedom to express one's view. Such freedom may be an important reason why, in Spain, philosophers can afford to proclaim themselves as Catholics without losing their reputation. Philosophers contributed to a book, *Conceptos fundamentales de ética teológica.*[4] In Spain, it is not a *morale laica* that is considered as a basis for a democratic society, but an *etica civil* that is understood as a common undertaking, as *expresión de la convergencia de ideales de vida publica, de ideales de perfección*. To understand this relation one has to keep in mind that, in Spain, both theologians and philosophers were critical of the dictatorship, against which they fought together, and prepared the way for democracy. The theologians in Spain don't claim any monopoly. Vidal speaks of the "superamento dell 'imperialismo morale.'"[5] Even the bishops proclaim the dialogue between Christian ethics and other ethical models in a pastoral letter. Christian ethics no longer claims to be the only moral guardian. It seeks the cooperation of all people of good will. Again, perhaps such an approach helps to explain the way Spanish philosophers appear much more willing than their counterparts in other countries to regard theologians as partners in a common task.

A last remark concerns Sweden. On the one hand, theologians there have a respected position within the university like in Central Europe. On the other hand, there is still to be felt the influence of Axel Hägerström, whose philosophy was similar to logical positivism and to Cambridge Analysis. As Justus Hartnack has said, "Like logical positivism it was antimetaphysical, and also like logical positivism, it rejected the supposition that moral sentences have a truth-value."[6] It was, of course, antitheological as well. Theologians in Sweden still have to fight against the impact of Hägerström.

2. My second point concerns the means of communication and cooperation between ethicists. As the history of the *Societas Ethica* demonstrates, there is no regular congress of German-speaking Protestant theological ethicists. The *Societas* (at least at present) does not succeed in fostering communication between these people. On the other hand, they have a common periodical, the *Zeitschrift für evangelische Ethik*. The German-speaking Catholic moral theologians didn't succeed in establishing something similar, but they do have their congress every second year. Moral theologians from other countries have their regular meetings as well. The Italians and Spanish also have periodicals, the *Revista di teologia morale* and the *Moralia* respectively.

From my personal experience, regular personal contact in the setting of a congress is an important means of communication. Let me first concentrate on the communication between ethicists of the same Christian denomination. My experience is limited to the congress of the German-speaking Catholic moral theologians and social ethicists. The regular congresses have a decisive role in discussion, especially among moral theologians. They were important in developing consensus, in understanding the positions of others, for mutual acquaintance between professors and representatives of the new generation.

The impact of these meetings may be illustrated by a recent example. In Germany, there has been a lively controversy on questions of organ transplantation, especially its legal regulation. The *Zustimmungslösung*, according to which an organ may be explanted from a dead body only if relatives have consented to this during the lifetime of the person, was questioned, and the *Widerspruchslösung* was considered, according to which an explantation is allowed if neither the person nor relatives have prohibited it. This latter solution is practiced in Austria. These considerations caused an intense controversy on the criterion of brain death, which had not been questioned in earlier years. This controversy was mainly between Protestant theologians (and also among some physicians). A common declaration of the German Catholic Episcopal Conference and the Council of the Evangelische Kirche in Deutschland, published in 1990, suddenly became the object of harsh criticism because it had accepted that criterion.

Among Catholic moral theologians there was widespread consensus in favor of the brain death criterion. At least one reason for this difference from the Protestants, in my view, was the opportunity to discuss questions of common interest and to develop common convictions (or at least, more mutual understanding) that a regular congress makes possible. In the history of the congresses, we can observe the discussions on central subjects of the respective periods, for instance, the problem of the *optio fundamentalis* in the sixties, problems of natural law and normative ethics (teleology-deontology) after 1968 (*Humanae Vitae*) or the question of the *proprium* of Christian ethics. I myself observed a growing consensus in this last debate which was a bit late in Catholic moral theology. Within Protestant theology, this question was raised especially by Karl Barth and Anders Nygren. For some years, there was an intense controversy between two positions, called autonomous ethics and ethics of faith, of which the latter contended (albeit inconsistently) that some moral norms were understandable only on the basis of Christian faith (or theism). In the middle of the 1980s, there was a consensus that the *proprium* is at least not to be found in particular moral norms. The recent controversy between liberals and communitarians may confront us with this question from another point of view.

One negative side effect of these congresses is that only very few of my Catholic, German-speaking colleagues have participated in the meetings of the

*Societas Ethica* in the past. However, in the last few years we have observed an increase in the participation of younger Catholic moral theologians.

3. In the time remaining, I would like to give an example of a different approach to a particular question, different between European countries and between Europe and the United States: the debate on communitarianism. In Europe, communitarianism does not seem to be as great a challenge to liberalism or universalism as in the U.S. One reason may be the specifically American context of the debate: the appeal to more common sense, the critique of atomistic individualism, the thinking back to basic common values. On the other hand, the U.S. has not experienced religious wars like Europe. The problems resulting from religious division in Europe are impressively depicted in Stephen Toulmin's book *Cosmopolis*, which I have never found mentioned in a communitarian publication.[7] The conflicts in the former Yugoslavia (and in the former Soviet Union) were horrible examples of extreme communitarianism. Is not an uncritical loyalty to one's own community as dangerous as a limitless individualism? Bosnia may illustrate the question of which F. Rickens claims to have found no answers in the publications of prominent communitarians: how is a common conception of the good possible in a pluralistic society?[8] Perhaps it is possible in the tradition that brought forth the liberal state, but how vigorous is this tradition in pluralistic societies? The least communitarian country in Europe seems to be France. The French have suppressed all regional languages, dialects, and traditions. And the people who fought for the rights of foreigners were sometimes the ones who strongly opposed the veil of Muslim girls in public schools.

The debate on communitarianism does not seem to have had an impact on Spain. *Ètica civil* is a universalistic approach. Let me sketch the main ideas of this approach already mentioned above.[9] Civil ethics is supposed to lead people of different convictions (religious, agnostic, atheistic) to loyal cooperation for aims that go beyond purely individual interests. This kind of universalism is, therefore, not thought to be based on an individualistic or egoistic approach. Moral motivations have to be distinguished from religious convictions. Civil ethics is autonomous from the state and the church, but this autonomy does not mean indifference towards different denominations.

The Spanish seem to have a basic confidence in the convergence of different ideals. A democratic ethos, of course, is not uniform. But there are indispensable common moral values: freedom, justice, equality, political pluralism. Civil ethics is not confined to a basic minimum; it encourages civic virtues: resistance against every violation of human dignity, courage (*valentia civica*), etc. Civil ethics is supposed to foster pluralism as well as express common moral values (for instance, tolerance not as a kind of indifference, but as a joint responsibility). The difference from Italy may be illustrated by the following quotation:

> Ha llegado la hora de percartarse del patrimonio moral común acumulado y de romper . . . con toda razón perezosa (fideísta o laicista)

> que evita aportar argumentos, sino todo deseo de autocomplacencia resignada que por el miedo evita el testimonio.[10]
>
> (The hour has come to take notice of the common moral heritage and to break . . . with all idle reason, whether fideistic or laicistic, that avoids the presentation of arguments, with no desires for a resigned complacency that fearfully avoids testimony.)

The theologian regards civil ethics as a bridge or mediator between an atheistic ethics and the ethics of a believer (he may appeal for this conviction to Romans 2:11-16). Faith has to be active and to intervene in the field of civil ethics with its own intuitions and challenges. Christian ethics must incarnate itself in the respective culture so that it may foster the conversion of the hearts, social and structural transformation (cf. *Redemptor hominis* 14). The tolerance proclaimed by civil ethics is not indifference, but a *tolerancia preferential* or *intolerancia justa* fighting for emancipation, participation, equality, and real democracy. Civil ethics is not a distant observer or a negotiator only. It is the struggle to preserve personal and cultural differences as sources of originality, of creativity, of the richness of the society and the church. Summing up, it is characterized as "una mediación y un instrumento apropiado para afrontar hoy los graves problemas de la convivencia."[11]

There is more awareness of the communitarian challenge in the Nordic countries. As an example, consider the controversy between Arne Rasmusson and Göran Bexell in *Svensk Teologisk Kvartalskrift* 1997. The thesis of Rasmusson is "There is no humanity in general." Rasmusson admits that theological ethicists in Sweden know about the changes in the debates of moral philosophy that have happened roughly since 1980, but that these have had no impact on their basic consent. Ethics in Sweden is conceived as a Lutheran creation ethics. Morality is something common to all human beings. Specifically theological motives are the idea of creation and the doctrine of natural law. The universality of ethics is stressed, and one looks for an adequate ethical method. This universality is, in Rasmusson's view, the ideology of the national state and the national Lutheran church of Sweden. The reflection on the correct method mirrors the philosophical ethical reflection of this century, especially in the Anglo-Saxon world.

As an example, Rasmusson discusses the ethical approach of Bexell. Bexell's conception of ethics is grounded on the reflection of three factors: the necessities of humanity, the social situation's claim, and the ethical phenomenon. Are these factors common for all human beings? Are they the basis for a common morality? Rasmusson objects that all our experience is mediated by our language. Experience and human necessity cannot be described in neutral terms. Our moral convictions influence our language and our view, even in descriptive systems such as, for example, psychology. Modern psychology, sociology, biology, and economy often recommend egoism and aggression as basic human behaviour.

Rasmusson mentions Adam Smith, for whom following one's self-interest is a means for the achievement of the common good.[12]

It is true that, for Rasmusson, we have to work for the well-being of the individual and of the community, but the really difficult question is, what is the best in the concrete situation? If one avoids this second question, ethics becomes minimalistic and sometimes justifies all: marriage and other forms of partnership, pacifism and just war, celibacy and intercourse for homosexuals, etc. Unambiguously condemned is something outside of Sweden: apartheid. Rasmusson doubts the usefulness of the distinction between basic principles and their concrete application. Principles, for him, are not abstractions from specific cultural and social moral practice. Rasmusson does not plead for more unambiguous precepts, but for a virtue ethics. He illustrates this preference with a comparison. A good soccer player is not somebody who obeys the rules. His behaviour concerning the rules says nothing about his ability or skills. Virtue ethics looks for the good life, how it can be lived. The question of acting rightly cannot be answered independently of the actor's understanding of his life. For Bexell, first are the rules; afterwards they are practiced.

In the discussion between different traditions, one does not need arguments from an absolute point of view. One has to argue for what is convincing from our own point of view. We cannot discover unity, neither can we presuppose it.

In his reply, Bexell stresses first that creation ethics is neither *typically* Lutheran nor typically *Lutheran*. The German Lutheran theology after the last war was very critical of creation ethics. This kind of ethic had not distanced itself from the Nazi regime. It is not typically Lutheran because this approach is also typical for Catholic moral theology. This coincidence was the basis for a recent ecumenical document in Sweden on the responsibility of state and church for the society. For Bexell, it is a matter of course that nobody can have a point of view totally outside his own tradition. But he stresses the difference between genetic questions (about the origins of certain convictions) and the question of the validity of an argument. He does not understand his position as absolute or neutral, but he thinks that his conviction is right until he can be convinced of the opposite. But of course, there is no absolute point of view above all particular ones. There is something common to all moralities, but this cannot be found outside a cultural context. Bexell's difference with Rasmusson concerns the question of how much can be said about this common content. Bexell has more trust in the possibility of a neutral description of the human necessities, the social claim, and the ethical phenomenon, even if there is no absolute objectivity. Science can answer only those questions that science itself raises and which its methods permit. It is not so difficult to demonstrate the utility and significance of the commandment of love. If, from a purely neutral point of view, love were harmful, how could it be justified from a Christian perspective?

Bexell protests against the verdict of legalism (does Rasmusson mean a deontological theory in the way of *fiat iustitia-pereat mundus*?). We do not need to know if a person is good to be able to judge that person's action.

Concerning universalism, Bexell tries to clarify. There is an intercultural, interreligious, international ethic. One has to distinguish universalism in a descriptive and normative sense. Even a particularistic ethic can have a universal meaning in a normative sense. Particularism holds that there is nothing intercultural to be found in either the descriptive or normative sense. Ethics, then, is totally determined by its context.[13]

My last example is Otfried Höffe, who questions the alternative between Kant and Aristotle, the latter of whom is often regarded as the church father of the communitarians.[14] For Höffe, Aristotle is not a communitarian or anti-Kantian *avant la lettre*, because he does not defend traditions that were not judged according to common obligations. The very different language of the two authors may conceal what they have in common. Kant's aim, like that of a spiritual leader, is practical: the purification of moral theory. A false moral theory may corrupt morality itself.

Neither Kant nor Aristotle offer a theological foundation of moral theory. Reason has a central role. At least for some part of his ethic, Aristotle claims universal validity for the life of *theoria*. Kant's universalism does not intend to dissolve the national states (therefore it does not exclude some kind of patriotism), but he tries to give rules for their peaceful coexistence. Aristotle, on the other hand, regards the teachings of his ethics, politics, and rhetoric (e.g., *eudaimonia* as supreme end) as valid for any person and any polis. For communitarians, the way of life is rooted in a particular community. Of the four ways of life discussed by Aristotle, only two (political and theoretical life) are acceptable from a universal ethical point of view. The exact shape of a virtue like courage may depend on the particular community. But in any case it has something to do with the domination of an affect, namely fear. It is the appropriation of morality, not morality itself, with its rules and virtues, which is particular. The virtues are required not because of some convention, but, insofar as they conform to reason, because they are the way to *eudaimonia*. Aristotle does not present a catalogue of human rights, but he distinguishes the *physei dikaion* from *thesei dikaion* and proclaims the protection of property, life, freedom, and political participation.

I am not sure if these three examples concerning the question of communitarianism are representative, but they at least may illustrate a more cautious attitude toward the communitarian challenge. A possible impact on the Catholic church might be an attempt to have it both ways: the church could argue in a communitarian way *ad intra* to strengthen the role of the magisterium, and in a universalistic way *ad extra* to be able to speak to all people of good will. But that would not be a good solution.

## Notes

[1]Manfred Riedel, ed., *Rehabilitierung der praktischen Philosophie*, 2 v. (Frieburg i. Br., 1972).

[2]Uberto Scarpelli, *L'etica senza verita* (Bologna, 1982).

[3]Eamon Conway, "Theology at the Margins," *ET-Bulletin* 6 (1995): 90-91.

[4]Marciano Vidal, ed., *Conceptos fundamentales de ética teológica* (Madrid, 1992).

[5]Marciano Vidal, "Le teologia morale in Spagna," *Rivista di Teologia Morale* 29 (1997): 484.

[6]Justus Hartnack, "Scandinavian Philosophy," in *The Encyclopedia of Philosophy*, ed. P. Edwards (New York, 1967), 295.

[7]Stephen Toulmin, *Cosmopolis: The Hidden Agenda of Modernity* (Chicago, 1990).

[8]Friedo Ricken, "Tradition und Natur. Über Vorgaben und Grenzen praktischer Rationalität," *Theologie und Philosophie* 70 (1995): 64.

[9]Cf. Agustin Domingo Moratalla and Bartomeu Benássar, "Etica civil," in *Conceptos fundamentales de ética teológica* (Madrid, 1992), 269-291.

[10]Ibid., 277. Cf. also José-Roman Flecha Andrés, *Ética y fe cristiana*, in *La pregunta por la ética civil*, ed. Angel Galinda Garcia (Salamanca, 1993), 183-210.

[11]Ibid., 289.

[12]In my view, the allusion to Smith is not very appropriate here. Rasmusson fails to distinguish between egoism as the opposite to love as impartiality and an ethical egoism as a way to achieve the best for all people involved. Smith's own attitude is characterized by Lindren in the following way:

> "The picture of the good life that Smith entertained was devoted neither to self-indulgence nor vaulting ambition, qualities often associated with 'economic man.' Instead it was marked by 'self-command,' by moderation of one's actions in accordance with the sentiments of the supposed impartial spectator. That emphasis on self-restraint is more reminiscent of the normative theories of the Roman Stoics than of the egoism either of Thomas Hobbes . . . or Bernhard Mandeville" (J. Ralph Lindgren, "Smith, Adam (1723-1790," in *Encyclopedia of Ethics*, ed. Lawrence C. Becker and Charlotte B. Becker (New York, 1992): 1162.

I mention this one-sided characterization of Smith because it manifests a problem that I sometimes have with communitarian authors when they stress the differences between various ethical approaches, different cultures and traditions. Sometimes these assertions are too superficial. Some differences are only verbal and, at least, one has to ask which differences are real and which are only apparent (and to what amount).

[13]Rasmusson wrote a final response to Bexell in another 1997 issue of *Svensk Teologisk Kvartalskrift*, but due to space constraints, I have not considered it for this essay.

[14]Otfried Höffe, *Ausblick: Aristoteles oder Kant - wider eine plane Alternative*, in *Aristoteles, Die Nikomachische Ethik*, ed. idem., (Berlin, 1995), 277-304.

# Christian Ethics in Europe: A Response to Werner Wolbert

*William Schweiker*

## Introduction

I want to begin my response to Professor Wolbert with a word of thanks. He has provided an insightful overview of ethics in Europe—in all of its historical, social, linguistic, and religious complexity. That alone would seem a daunting task, and yet Professor Wolbert handles it with care and subtlety. I also want to thank him for presenting this to the Society of Christian Ethics, that is, for his effort and labor in coming to tell us about the European situation. In this, he has put into practice a central good presented in the paper itself, namely, the struggle to increase communication. Thank you.

In the short time allotted me to respond to this paper, I will not, by the nature of the case, be able to do it justice. What I want to do, then, is to isolate what I take to be the main point, and then press issues for further discussion. This may seem, of course, like a strange alchemy of thought, the mysterious transformation of a report of developments into basic conceptual and practical questions. But hopefully the alchemy will produce some gold and not just iron!

## The Basic Argument

Professor Wolbert's paper appears to have four interrelated movements. He begins with a complex analysis of the situation in Europe: how differences of language, culture, and religion shape the social context within which the *Societas Ethica* works. These points of difference are simply the substructure of pluralistic nations and also societies. And I should note here parenthetically that we Americans should probably stop talking about "pluralism," "diversity," and "otherness" until we take the time to learn the languages necessary to understand others in their own tongues. The paper gently—but rightly—chides the linguistic Pax Americana. In any case, Professor Wolbert's move is to offer a complex social analysis.

The second step is to argue that the *Societas Ethica* be seen as a communication process where all of these differences can meet and interact around basic moral issues. In this respect, the *Societas* functions something like civil society, but with explicitly international roles. No doubt, in an age of globalization, such mediating communicative structures—various institutions and societies that work between political and economic unities—are increasingly important and needed. I will return to this point in a moment.

The third step in the paper is to show concretely the kinds of problems than can be discussed and how this mediates linguistic, cultural, and religious differences in the interest of addressing actual moral issues. Wolbert mentions three: the relationship of philosophical and theological ethics; cooperation between ethicists; the debate about communitarianism. These are, of course, all well-known topics; it is comforting to know that our European colleagues labor in the same vineyards as we do!

The final step of the argument, as I read it, returns us to the point about the *Societas Ethica* as a mediating, communicative institution, yet mindful of the three problem areas Wolbert notes. The way I read this paper—and I hope that Professor Wolbert will either confirm or deny this reading—is that he is arguing that in order to have such mediating institutions (sorely needed in an age of pluralism and globalization), we cannot be satisfied with a simple communitarian ethic. We have to take up again the challenge of universalism in ethics while being mindful of the need to sustain active moral communities. In this respect, the very work and life of the *Societas Ethica* (and, I might mention, The Society of Christian Ethics), is just the kind of social reality we ought to be thinking about in order to develop such an ethic beyond the conflict of universalism and communitarianism. In this respect, we should note, the method of the paper is to move from social analysis to normative reflection, all within the compass of ethics. Bravo!

## Questions for Consideration

That, then, is my reading of this paper, and it is a challenging argument that works at several layers of reflection. What to make of it? I have no interest in challenging Professor Wolbert's description of the *Societas Ethica*; that would be an act of sheer stupidity. Nor do I want to contest the fact that the topic he isolates as a point of debate among ethicists is genuine. Throughout this meeting of the Society of Christian Ethics each of those topics—philosophy and theology, cooperation, communitarianism—will be debated. So how to respond to a paper I found so helpful? I can do so only by trying to provoke further reflection on the very topics he has already noted. What do I mean?

If my reading of Wolbert is right, that is, if I am correct that he is pressing for some way beyond communitarianism and universalism by looking at the actual practice of the *Societas Ethica*, then we can provoke reflection. Three questions come to mind in this regard. First, what is the distinctly theological ground and warrant for that move? It is interesting, at least for me, how little theology enters the picture. So a question for reflection: can we set out the theology informing the concerns of this paper? This is to engage the philosophy/theology relation constructively and substantively. It seems to me that there is much interest among European thinkers on this point. Pierre Hadot speaks about spiritual exercises; Jacques Derrida explores negative theology and the idea of "gift;" Emmanuel Levinas wants to make ethics first philosophy, but also show that the divine is a trace in the encounter with the face of the other. So too, there are important movements afoot in theology. Theologians like Jürgen Moltmann and Michael Welker are rejuvenating the importance of the Spirit in theology; hermeneutics continues to influence theology in the work of Dietmar Meith; even the papacy is concerned with questions about labor, persons and also moral absolutes. We are ripe for a new consideration of the relation of theology and philosophy. Can reflection on mediating institutions like the *Societas Ethica* help?

A second question arises. The interest in cooperation and communication between ethicists begs further reflection. As I understand it, there is immense interest among European intellectuals on this point. One theme is the idea of "otherness" itself and the communicative structure of human life. I have already mentioned Emmanuel Levinas in this regard, but one thinks of Paul Ricoeur and others as well. Another theme is the whole idea of "communication" that dominates much sociology, especially so-called "systems-theory" in the thought of Niklas Luhmann, but also in the work of Jürgen Habermas. Here, too, theologians are at work. Edmund Arens, in Münster, uses Habermas in his work on christopraxis; Wolfgang Huber of Heidelberg/Berlin, draws on some systems-theory in his work on responsibility. There are others, no doubt. The point is that ideas about communication must be pressed further if we are to use them to reflect on a viable normative ethic for our time. So the question becomes: are these matters informing the argument of this paper?

A third question springs from the observation that we are not simply in a situation where there is, on the one hand, linguistic, religious, and cultural diversity and, on the other hand, various mediating institutions. We are also in a time in which cultural, religious, and linguistic identities are mediated and remade via a spreading, global media-system and also the economic market. As social anthropologists like Arjun Appadurai (*Modernity at Large*[1]) have aptly shown, the media and market traffic in images that people use to form and construct their identities. There are global flows of images and economies that are shaping how persons understand their world. This is part of the breakdown of colonialism, which Wolbert mentions, that carries its own dangers and possibilities. In thinking about mediating institutions like the *Societas Ethica*, we need also to explore how identities and social worlds are formed. This would seem important if, normatively speaking, the interest—which I applaud—is in moving beyond communitarianism and old-style universalism. So the question emerges: how should we be thinking about media and market as they impinge on mediating institutions in shaping and forming selves and social worlds?

## Conclusion

I hope you see that these three questions about the implied theology, ideas of communication, and forces shaping social worlds and identities are merely provocations to continue the work already set forth in this paper. And they imply a whole host of conversation partners that I believe Christian ethicists ought to be engaging. But my conceptual alchemy, in which I have changed a report on a society into an intellectual challenge, is not simply for its own sake. I am suggesting that our self-understanding as societies of ethicists should itself be content driven. We should form our societies around questions pressing upon us and our world; we must venture into new realms. And on this point, I think Professor Wolbert agrees. He is pressing us forward in thought and in our self-understanding as ethicists, and for that, I can but again say: bravo!

## Notes

[1]Arjun Appadurai, *Modernity at Large: Cultural Dimensions of Globalization* (Minneapolis: University of Minnesota Press, 1996).

# HISTORICAL—CONSTRUCTIVE STUDIES

# Contemporary Forms of *Askesis* and the Return of Spiritual Exercises

*Maria Antonaccio*

## ABSTRACT

This paper examines recent philosophical retrievals of the ancient idea of *askesis* and argues that they face a dilemma. On the one hand, these retrievals embrace certain assumptions often associated with "antitheory" and moral particularism in ethics; yet ancient forms of *askesis* were based on assumptions that most antitheorists would reject. After presenting a threefold critical typology of approaches to *askesis*—existential (Hadot), aesthetic (Foucault), and therapeutic (Nussbaum)—the paper demonstrates the limitations of each model and presents an alternative reflexive model, drawn in part from the work of Charles Taylor and Iris Murdoch, as a more adequate approach.

## Introduction

In his groundbreaking study of the spiritual exercises of ancient philosophy, Pierre Hadot makes the following remark concerning the *Meditations* of the Stoic philosopher Marcus Aurelius: "There have been a great many preachers, theoreticians, [and] spiritual directors . . . in the history of world literature. Yet it is extremely rare to have the chance to see someone in the process of training himself to be a human being."[1] This idea of self-training is at the heart of Hadot's thesis that ancient philosophy was not primarily an abstract mode of discourse, but rather a form of *askesis*, a practice of shaping oneself according to an ideal of wisdom.

Consider, for example, the following passage that Hadot cites from the *Meditations*: "When you have trouble getting up in the morning, let this thought be in your mind: I'm waking up in order to do a man's work."[2] This and other such passages have prompted Hadot to observe that the *Meditations* fascinate contemporary readers because "we have the feeling of witnessing the practice of spiritual exercises—captured live, so to speak . . . [W]e feel a quite particular emotion as we catch a person in the process of doing what we are all trying to do: to give a meaning to our life . . . and to give each of life's instants its full value."[3]

Hadot's observations on the enduring attractiveness of the *Meditations* may help to account for the recent resurgence of interest in the idea of spiritual exercises more generally. What has captured current attention is precisely the notion of *askesis*, the Greek noun meaning "exercise," "practice," or "training," which Hadot distinguishes from the modern and Christian notion of asceticism associated with "complete abstinence or restriction in the use of food, drink, sleep, dress, and property, and especially continence in sexual matters."[4] Although ancient philosophical forms of *askesis* influenced the later development of Christian asceticism and were sometimes accompanied by renunciatory practices themselves, Hadot argues that the term *askesis* was originally used by ancient philosophers exclusively to designate philosophical thought-exercises, "inner activities of the thought and will" intended to cultivate certain habits of mind conducive to a life of wisdom. These practices included reading, meditation, memorization, therapies of the passions, remembrances of good things, accomplishment of duties, and so forth.[5]

Recently, scholars in both moral philosophy and religious ethics have sought to recover this ancient meaning of *askesis* as exercises in self-training or self-formation in relation to some ideal.[6] In doing so, they have reconfigured our familiar notions of both ethics and asceticism. In moral philosophy, for example, interest in *askesis* has coincided with a renewed attention to ancient Hellenistic ethics and to the idea of philosophy as a training in virtue. Besides Hadot's work on this subject, Martha Nussbaum's book on the theory and practice of Hellenistic ethics, *The Therapy of Desire* (1994) and Michel Foucault's second and third volumes *of The History of Sexuality* (1985, 1986) analyze the ancient philosophical practices of the Stoics, Epicureans, and others in an attempt to retrieve a conception of philosophy as a "lived ethics" or "art of life." In religious studies, a similar turn to concrete experience has sparked recent scholarly interest in the spirituality of Christianity and other traditions, in contrast to the more traditional emphasis on theological discourse and doctrine.[7] The turn to *askesis* is also strikingly evident in the current popular fascination with alternative and so-called New Age forms of spirituality, secular therapies, and self-help manuals, not to mention the proliferation of diet, exercise, and health regimens which might be seen as broadly "ascetic" in nature.

In another area of religious studies, a number of scholars have sought to recover the core meaning of *askesis* through an interdisciplinary inquiry into the theory and practice of historical asceticism. Vincent Wimbush and Richard Valantasis, for example, have been in the forefront of recent efforts to reconfigure the ancient notion of *askesis* in relation to asceticism, ethics, and contemporary cultural analysis. In the introduction to their massive volume of papers collected from the International Conference on Asceticism, they argue that "ethics [is] the modern secular term that usurped the place of historical asceticism . . . . The root of asceticism remains ethical formation . . . and ethics cannot function without addressing personal formation."[8] They further contend that, by severing ethics from its roots in *askesis*, modern moral theory has lost a crucial dimension of ethics. Since the process of personal formation "happens consistently in every society" whether we acknowledge it or not, failure to scrutinize critically the practices by which this occurs breeds a society in which persons are "assimilated into various functioning systems" of formation and yet "finds itself incapable of molding people who live ethically."[9]

These examples of recent work on *askesis* have opened a provocative new line of thought in current moral inquiry by exploring multiple dimensions of the idea of self-formation as an ethical, religious, and cultural problematic. This paper builds on this opening by interpreting some recent philosophical retrievals of *askesis* in the context of contemporary ethics and culture.[10] These retrievals, in my view, represent an effort by scholars of ethics to correct modern moral theory's perceived lack of attention to the problem of ethical formation; but they also attempt (whether implicitly or overtly) to articulate a normative view of ethical formation for contemporary culture. The purpose of this paper is to analyze recent retrievals of *askesis* at both of these levels by examining some of the general assumptions underlying the return of *askesis* in current moral inquiry and attempting to offer an interpretive framework for evaluating the normative implications of such proposals.

My argument, in brief, is that the current turn to *askesis* in moral inquiry is driven by some of the same concerns that characterize recent challenges to modern moral theory by narrative ethicists and others who defend some version of moral particularism. In this respect, it shares some features of what has been called the "antitheorist" trend in recent ethics, which has shifted the focus of ethical inquiry away from the universalist pretensions of ethical theory toward the task of forming particular selves in specific communities of ethical practice. However, I intend to show that these antitheorist assumptions render the contemporary retrieval of *askesis* problematic, since ancient forms of *askesis* were based on assumptions that most antitheorists would reject. In seeking both critically and constructively to address these tensions, my aim is to demonstrate the need for a more adequate theoretical framework in which to understand the idea of ethical formation in contemporary ethics and culture.

The argument will proceed as follows. In the first part of the paper, I situate the turn to *askesis* in relation to other challenges to "theory" in recent ethics in order to identify the tensions that arise from the attempt to retrieve these practices in the present. In the second part, I offer a typology and critique of three recent philosophical approaches to *askesis* drawn from the work of Pierre Hadot, Michel

Foucault, and Martha Nussbaum, each of whom has published important studies of ancient spiritual exercises which have gained wide attention in recent thought. My purpose is not to assess the historical adequacy of these studies as accounts of ancient ethics; rather I attempt to expose the tensions in each approach in order to clarify what is at stake in contemporary reappropriations of *askesis*. In the third part of the paper, I attempt to shed some constructive light on these issues by offering a model of *askesis*, drawn in part from the work of Charles Taylor and Iris Murdoch, which can answer the deficiencies in the other approaches.

## The Critique of Theory and the Return of Spiritual Exercises

In order to situate the turn to *askesis* in the context of contemporary ethics, I begin with the contention that there are two related concerns driving the current interest in *askesis*, both of which should be familiar to students of recent ethics: 1) the concern that modern moral theory has severed itself from the lived experience of actual moral agents; and 2) the concern that the study of ethics has too often been reduced to the analysis of general rules, principles, and codes of conduct while ignoring the formation of persons in particular moral contexts. Both of these concerns attest to the pervasive suspicion of universal principles and the increased attention to moral particularism that have characterized various forms of narrative and character ethics especially, as well as recent "postmodern" ethics.[11] In this respect, the current return to spiritual exercises may be understood against the background of the current critique of "theory" associated with a diverse range of thinkers in ethics.[12]

While it is not my intention to engage the debate over theory in detail, nor to quarrel with the rather constricted definition of theory it assumes (in which theory is identified with some version of Kantian rationalism), I contend that the current critique of theory helps to illuminate some of the assumptions underlying the return of spiritual exercises. There are two features of so-called antitheorist arguments that are relevant to my purpose: first, its critique of abstract universalism as failing to provide normative guidance to actual agents facing particular moral dilemmas; and second, its suspicion of theoretical forms of discourse as unable to capture the density and complexity of actual moral experience. Both of these have led to a third, more general claim about the priority of practice to theory in ethics. Let me summarize each of these points briefly in order to show their relevance to the current turn to *askesis*.

According to one recent account of the antitheory position, antitheorists "emphasize opposition to any assertion . . . that morality is rational only insofar as it can be formulated in, or grounded on, a system of universal principles;" rather, morality is seen as "primarily concerned with the particular virtues of particular cultures."[13] As Dwight Furrow has put this point, the antitheory position

> is motivated by the perception that when moral agents think about moral

> questions, they do so not in terms of abstract principles with an aim to systematize some large chunk of moral experience, but in terms of concrete relationships with other people . . . [and the] histories and the institutions in which they are embedded . . . . To the extent that we think about principles and rules, they are viewed as emerging from the aforementioned concrete relationships.[14]

This feature of antitheory, as Furrow notes, coincides in many instances with the rereading of Aristotle.[15] One finds it, for example, in Alasdair MacIntyre's argument for a tradition-constituted rationality and in Stanley Hauerwas's defense of a narrativist conception of ethics. These positions may be considered antitheorist insofar as they reject the theorist concern to "identify universally binding principles which govern all rational persons" as well as the proceduralist conception of moral rationality often associated with it.[16] My point is that the concern of these thinkers with the formation of persons in particular contexts and the practices by which this formation occurs suggests a point of convergence with the idea of *askesis*. In fact, MacIntyre's definition of a practice and Hauerwas's defense of the role of narratives in forming character and teaching the skills needed to pursue a particular form of life make this emphasis on practices explicit.[17]

The second feature of antitheorist arguments I want to note concerns the critique of theoretical forms of discourse. According to the account I have been citing, antitheorists deny that "the intellectual virtues of theorizing, such as universality, explicitness, consistency, and completeness, are essential to the moral life."[18] Rather, they contend that ethics is a contextual form of reflection that requires literary and other figural modes of expression as better suited to the concrete task of moral thinking.[19] Thus such thinkers as Martha Nussbaum, Stanley Hauerwas, and Richard Rorty have embraced novels and other forms of literature as indispensable to ethical inquiry. As Nussbaum argues, these literary forms "are likely to confront and explore problems about human beings . . . [that] a philosophical work . . . that does not focus intently on the stories of concrete characters, can lose from view in the pursuit of systematic considerations or to the end of greater purity."[20]

This critique of theoretical modes of discourse also emerges in contemporary accounts of *askesis*. For example, Hadot contends that ancient philosophical treatises had an explicitly practical intention and were "written not so much to inform the reader of a doctrinal content but to form him."[21] Accordingly, such treatises often subordinated the concern for systematic coherence to the goal of spiritual effectiveness by presenting short, striking formulations of maxims intended to engage the student and penetrate the memory.[22] Similarly, Nussbaum argues that Hellenistic philosophy rejected two types of argumentation still widely recognized in philosophy today: deductive arguments that derive conclusions from first principles, and dialectical arguments that proceed by calm questioning.[23] Instead, the explicitly therapeutic aim of Hellenistic philosophy required innovative techniques of narrative designed to engage the student's memory, imagination, and emotions.[24]

Taken together, the two aspects of antitheory I have been discussing (that is, its critique of abstract universalism and its suspicion of theoretical modes of discourse) have contributed to a third, more general assumption, frequently noted in current ethical inquiry, about the priority of practice to theory. This assumption is driven in part by the conviction that the abstractions of theory have effaced the concrete reality of persons and the practices that have shaped them. Thus so-called postmodern ethicists argue that the language of ethical theory cannot do justice to the radical otherness of persons,[25] while feminists and others contend that the supposed universalism of ethical theory fails to take into account certain human beings whose experience has been excluded from the mainstream traditions of ethical thought in the West.[26] In response to these perceived deficiencies, many thinkers have challenged the primacy of theory in modern ethics, arguing that the concrete stories and practices of particular persons and communities are the prior base from which general principles and theories of moral agency arise in the first place, rather than the reverse, as is often assumed.

In summarizing these features of the antitheorist trend in ethics, my point is not to argue that all thinkers who attempt to retrieve forms of *askesis* in the current context are necessarily antitheorists in the sense I have been discussing. Rather, I want to suggest that contemporary retrievals of *askesis* share certain rather widespread antitheorist concerns regarding the critique of abstract universalism, the need for alternative forms of moral discourse, and the insistence on the primacy of practice over theory. This will become evident in the three thinkers whose work I will be considering in the next section of this paper—Pierre Hadot, Michel Foucault, and Martha Nussbaum—each of whom sees ancient forms of *askesis* as productively challenging some of the key assumptions of modern moral philosophy and ethical theory.

Yet when understood against this antitheorist background, these recent retrievals of *askesis* face certain tensions which I will address in the remainder of this paper. These tensions arise from the fact that many ancient forms of spiritual exercises (such as those of the Stoics) understood *askesis* as training the self to adopt a universal or cosmic standpoint, in keeping with the claim that human beings are by nature rational and participate in the rational order of the universe. Contemporary retrievals of *askesis*, consistent with their antitheorist assumptions, tend to eschew (or at least challenge) these universalist and naturalist presuppositions in order to affirm some form of moral particularism. Such contemporary attempts at retrieval, therefore, seem to face a contradiction. For the goal of the successful *askesis* in the ancient context was not, ultimately, to constitute the self's identity as a member of a particular moral community, but rather to bring about a *universalization* of the self in relation to a norm that transcends particularity. How, then, are we to conceive the meaning of *askesis* in the absence of universalist and naturalist assumptions? And to what extent does the normative force of *askesis* depend on these assumptions?

I begin to address these questions in the next section of the paper, where I present a threefold typology and critique of recent approaches to *askesis*. My thesis is that with the loss of the conceptual background of a universal order of nature, these approaches to *askesis* tend to exhibit two tendencies that would be recognized as problematic on the ancient model: 1) an emphasis on the training or formation of the self without sufficient attention to the normative ideal which *askesis* is meant to serve (thus risking a type of subjectivism); and 2) an emphasis on the primacy of practice over theory, such that *askesis* becomes a procedure or method which is separable from a substantive body of moral truth (thus risking a type of voluntarism).

My contention is that each of these tendencies is associated with the antitheorist cast of recent ethics; and to that extent, contemporary retrievals of *askesis* may be undermined by their own antitheorist assumptions. Yet I also want to argue that, given the force and the persistence of the particularist turn in current thought, any adequate contemporary model of *askesis* will have to come to terms with these assumptions one way or another. Therefore, after presenting my analysis and critique of the available models of *askesis* in Part II, I will consider in Part III whether a more adequate model of *askesis* can be constructed which can successfully negotiate the tensions noted above.

## A Typology of Approaches to *Askesis*: Existential, Aesthetic, and Therapeutic

My typology of contemporary approaches to *askesis* is drawn from the following works: Hadot's *Philosophy as a Way of Life: Spiritual Exercises from Socrates to Foucault* (1995); Foucault's *History of Sexuality*, volumes 2 and 3, titled *The Use of Pleasure* (1985) and *The Care of the Self* (1986), respectively; and Martha Nussbaum's The *Therapy of Desire: Theory and Practice in Hellenistic Ethics* (1994). As is the case with all typologies, the one I will present necessarily abstracts from the historical depth and conceptual complexity of these studies in order to illuminate the difficulties facing contemporary retrievals of *askesis*. Any adequate discussion of these individual works would obviously require far more nuance than I can provide here.[27]

I have constructed my typology starting from the premise that a central problem for contemporary retrievals of *askesis* (as noted earlier) is the loss of the assumptions that informed ancient models of *askesis*. Those assumptions may be briefly summarized as follows. In the ancient world, as Charles Taylor has noted, "the good life for human beings is as it is because of humans' nature as rational life."[28] That is to say, a life lived according to nature was a life lived according to reason because "what we are by nature is rational life, and hence acting by reason is the key to the good for us."[29] This ontological connection between human reason and a rational order of nature provided the conceptual background to ancient forms of *askesis*. Their efficacy rested on the idea that the cultivation of a proper vision of the world would bring rational order to the soul and mastery over the chaotic life of the passions. In this respect, ancient thought was both universalist and cognitivist in its assumptions: universalist, in the sense that to be rational was to perceive the order of the cosmos and one's place in it as a rational being; and cognitivist, in the sense that this vision or apprehension of a rational cosmic order provided the motivational force for the effort to conform oneself to this order.[30] In short, to see the good was to love it (and vice versa) and to attempt to live by it.[31]

Using this ancient or "naturalistic" model of *askesis* as our point of reference, we can now outline a threefold typology of approaches to *askesis* along a continuum that progressively moves away from universalist and cognitivist assumptions. The first type, which I will call "existential," represents an approach to *askesis* that remains strongly universalist but weakens the claims of cognitivism at a crucial point; this type is exemplified by Hadot's work. The second type, which I will call "therapeutic," qualifies both universalism and cognitivism in complex ways, especially with regard to the meaning of the self-transcendence enacted in *askesis*; this is demonstrated by Nussbaum's approach. And the third type, which I will call "aesthetic," represents the furthest extreme from the ancient model in rejecting both universalism and cognitivism, as Foucault's work will show. In my exposition, I will outline the two most extreme types first, the existential and the aesthetic, and then define the second, therapeutic type as the most ambiguous of the three to characterize by the terms of this typology.

According to the existential approach, the purpose of *askesis* is to cultivate the vision of a universal or cosmic order that would provide a critical perspective on the disorder of the soul caused by the passions. This type preserves the naturalism of the ancient model in its correlation between an ideal of wisdom defined by a universal order of nature and an inner attitude of soul which attempts to conform itself to this order. Spiritual exercises are designed to help mediate this connection between the order of nature and the order of the soul. In doing so, they solve the problem of the passions (which are considered false opinions) by teaching the soul about the true nature of reality and its own nature as rational. Yet the existential approach to *askesis* departs from the ancient model in embracing a certain type of voluntarism. That is, it conceives the adoption of a cosmic perspective as a matter of personal choice, rather than a metaphysical necessity. In this respect, the existential model breaks with the ancient dictum that to see the order of the good is automatically to love it and seek to live by it; rather, on this model one *chooses* to lead a life of wisdom. This sets up an apparent tension within this position, since it is hard to see how one could affirm the universal perspective which it holds is essential to *askesis*, while weakening the cognitive and metaphysical link between the order of the soul and the order of the cosmos.

Hadot's work on the spiritual exercises of ancient philosophy exemplifies this existential approach in two respects. First, he insists on the terminology "spiritual" (as opposed to "moral" or "intellectual") in describing these exercises in order to emphasize their existential significance. No other term, he insists, captures their force in effecting a complete transformation of subjectivity.[32] This transformation involves what Hadot calls a "universalization" of the self which transforms the subject of *askesis* from an egoistic, passion-ridden individual to a transcendent, moral self open to the universality and objectivity of thought: "This is a new way of being-in-the-world which consists in becoming aware of oneself as a part of nature, and a portion of universal reason."[33] Thus Hadot retains the ancient correlation between physics and ethics, and seems to hold that this correlation is essential to the transformative efficacy of *askesis*.

But Hadot's approach can also be considered "existential" in a second respect which signals his partial break with the cognitivist assumptions of the ancient model. This aspect of Hadot's account emerges in his somewhat surprising contention that ancient spiritual exercises can be retrieved in the present in abstraction from their original philosophical background. He writes, "I think modern man can practice the spiritual exercises of antiquity, at the same time separating them from the philosophical or mythic discourse which came along with them. It is therefore not necessary, in order to practice these exercises, to believe in the Stoics' nature or universal reason. Rather, as one practices them, one lives concretely according to reason."[34] Such statements seem to indicate that Hadot embraces the antitheorist assumption that concrete practices are prior to or separable from their philosophical or theoretical justification.[35] He supports this claim with evidence from ancient philosophy itself, which consistently held that "theory is never considered an end in itself; it is clearly and decidedly put in the service of practice."[36] In addition, he notes that the very form of ancient philosophical discourse testifies to the centrality of practice, since ancient treatises were patterned after oral expression, were often intended to be read aloud, and were meant to facilitate the activity of teaching and the philosophical direction of the soul.[37]

Yet Hadot's assertion that the contemporary practice of *askesis* is separable from its original theoretical background cannot, in my judgment, be accounted for solely by his appeal to the ancient philosophical evidence. Rather, it reveals a trace of his early training in existentialist philosophy at the Sorbonne, which exerted a strong influence on his conception of philosophy.[38] This influence can be seen at a crucial point, when Hadot characterizes the life of wisdom as a matter of choice rather than vision. The practice of spiritual exercises, he argues, represents an existential choice to follow a certain form of life, rather than an intellectual commitment to the dogmas of a philosophical system: "ethics—that is to say, choosing the good—is not the consequence of metaphysics, but metaphysics is the consequence of ethics . . . [I]t is one's choice of life which precedes metaphysical theories, and . . . we can make our choice of life, whether or not we justify it by improved or entirely new arguments."[39] Thus, in contrast to the strong cognitivism of the ancient model of *askesis*, which holds that metaphysics, or a vision of the cosmic order, is the condition for ethics, Hadot asserts that ethics is prior to any metaphysics.[40] In this respect, his existential approach to *askesis* weakens the cognitivism of the ancient account (which he otherwise seems to support) and displays a voluntaristic emphasis on the act of choice which seems to be in tension with the more naturalistic elements of his retrieval.

I turn now to the second type in my order of exposition, the "aesthetic" approach to *askesis*. This type, as I noted above, represents the farthest extreme from the ancient model in its rejection of both universalism and cognitivism. The purpose of spiritual exercises is not to train the self to live in accordance with the norm of nature, but rather to form the self as an ethical subject capable of recognizing itself as such. Further, the function of these practices is not so much to mediate a substantive body of ethical truth about the rational order of the universe; rather, their purpose is to allow one to shape oneself through a "stylistics of existence." *Askesis* thus represents an intensification of one's relation with oneself, rather than a conformity to a cosmic order. Accordingly, these practices are more appropriately described as "techniques of the self" whose primary purpose is to constitute the self as an ethical subject rather than to transform the self according to a universalist and naturalist norm of wisdom.

Foucault's approach to ancient philosophical practices exemplifies this "aesthetic" model of *askesis*. The term "aesthetic" is derived from his contention that ancient philosophy functioned as an "art of existence" or "style of life" guided by the principle that "one must take care of oneself."[41] This principle was a pervasive theme in Greek culture beginning with Socrates, but Foucault argues that in the first and second centuries it acquired the intensified form of what he calls the "cultivation of the self."[42] In this form, the goal of ancient techniques of the self was not primarily to connect the self up with a rational order of the universe, but rather to enact a conversion to self through various forms of self-examination and other exercises.[43] This conversion to self does not mean that "one must . . . devote oneself entirely and exclusively to oneself," Foucault writes; but "one had best keep in mind that the chief objective one should set for oneself is to be sought within oneself, in the relation of oneself to oneself."[44]

The purpose of this intensified attention to oneself is to escape external dependencies and the enslavement of the passions that are a threat to the soul's mastery of itself. This much it shares with the ancient model of *askesis*. However, Foucault describes this conversion in terms of an intensification of subjectivity rather than a universalization of subjectivity.[45]

That is, *askesis* brings about a relation to self that allows one not simply to master oneself as a passion-ridden ego and to recognize oneself as part of universal reason, as Hadot had argued; rather self-mastery also brings pleasure and delight in oneself. Foucault writes, "Access to self is capable of providing a form of pleasure that comes, in serenity and without fail, of the experience of oneself."[46] This self-pleasure results not from the awareness of one's connection to a cosmic whole, but "arises out of oneself and within ourselves."[47] *Askesis* is transformative, in other words, because it provides access to what Foucault (quoting Seneca) calls "the true good . . . your very self and the best part of you."[48]

The problem with Foucault's account of the cultivation of the self is that it seems to assume a notion of the good and of specifically ethical subjectivity that goes undefended.[49] It is not clear, for example, what normative conception of the good is implied in the above-mentioned contrast between "true" and "false," or 'better" and "worse" notions of subjectivity. This failure, I contend, is related to the "aesthetic" metaphor which guides his approach to *askesis*, and which signals certain antitheorist assumptions underlying his conception of ethics. For Foucault, "ethics" properly speaking is not primarily concerned with the system of rules or laws which regulate and constrain human behavior (nor with the normative justification of such prescriptions), but rather with "the elaboration of a form of relation to self that enables an individual to fashion himself into a subject of ethical conduct."[50] Ethics is about the constitution of oneself as an ethical subject through concrete practices of "subjectivation." This emphasis on the shaping or fashioning of subjectivity, on making one's life "into an *oeuvre* that carries certain aesthetic values and meets certain stylistic criteria,"[51] leads Foucault to focus on the *practice* of self-formation over its content, the *manner* of self-cultivation over its substance. In short, it leads him to conceive *askesis* primarily as an "aesthetics" or "stylistics" of existence, while neglecting the normative background on which his own account of conversion and self-cultivation depends.

The third and final type of approach to *askesis* is the therapeutic model. This type represents a complex alternative to both the existential and the aesthetic types in that it modifies universalism and cognitivism in a direction that might be called "pragmatic." The purpose of philosophical practices on this model (as on the other models) is to free the soul from the disturbances and distortions of the passions by cultivating certain types of detachment.[52] But the therapeutic model emphasizes the socio-political implications of *askesis* to a greater extent than the other types: it recognizes that the passions arise from errors of belief or opinion derived largely from society. Thus philosophical therapy involves social criticism as well as personal practices of self-training and self-examination.

In emphasizing this dual aim of *askesis*, the therapeutic model articulates an ideal of wisdom that qualifies both the universalism and the cognitivism of the ancient model. It preserves the naturalism of ancient forms of *askesis* by defining the ideal of wisdom as *eudaimonia*, translated as "human flourishing," and it correlates this ideal with an account of the kinds of creatures we are.[53] Yet in contrast to the ancient model, the therapeutic model weakens the sense in which *eudaimonia* includes the aspiration to live a "godlike" life, that is, one that transcends the passions altogether. In this respect, it minimizes the tension that some ancient forms of *askesis* posit between nature and divinity; between finite human life and a life lived according to reason. In a similar way, this model qualifies ancient cognitivism in holding that the truths needed to correct errors of belief are to be found within our human condition, rather than beyond or outside our condition.

Nussbaum's work exemplifies this therapeutic model of *askesis*. In keeping with the socio-political emphasis of this model, she contends that the aim of Hellenistic philosophy was to "deliver freedom from the tyranny of custom and social convention, creating a community of beings who can take charge of their own life story and their own thought."[54] This requires a form of radical social criticism whose commitment to reason, in her view, distinguishes philosophical therapy from other types of self-shaping practices prominent in the ancient world.[55] Accordingly, Nussbaum pays special attention to the educational practices of ancient philosophy and the distinctive style and structure of therapeutic arguments. These were intended to teach a new ideal of community that could reform existing society.

This emphasis on the socio-political dimensions of therapeutic *askesis* already signals the way in which Nussbaum's account will modify ancient universalist and cognitivist assumptions. With respect to universalism, she attempts to articulate a norm of ethical objectivity that combines "critical power" and "worldly immersion."[56] That is, she seeks a norm that will provide critical distance on the errors of belief which give rise to the passions, but she insists that this norm "must be found, if at all, from within ourselves and one another, as what answers to the deepest aspirations and wishes we have for ourselves and for one another."[57] In this sense, Nussbaum embraces a pragmatic notion of ethical truth which holds that "ethical reality is not independent of what human beings deeply wish, need, and (at some level) desire."[58] She qualifies ancient cognitivism in a similarly pragmatic direction. Ancient therapeutic practices teach us how to live a life committed to reason, but Nussbaum questions the extent to which this aim requires the total repudiation of the emotions that she finds in some ancient philosophical schools. For mortal beings like ourselves, this may be a "godlike" aim not worth seeking.[59] Thus Nussbaum retains the politico-therapeutic aim of Hellenistic *askesis*, while challenging this more radical aspect of its aspiration to divinity. If there remains a tension on this model between "the deepest layers of our own makeup and the true good,"[60] it can only be resolved by an appeal to something *within* human life.

In these respects, Nussbaum's position is ambiguously situated in relation to the other models with respect to the type of self-transcendence or transformation that is enacted in *askesis*. In agreement with both the ancient and existentialist models, she holds that the therapy of the passions involves transcending one's false beliefs, and to this extent it requires more than simply an immersion in or intensification of one's relation to oneself. But she seems to embrace a more "innerworldly" notion of transcendence than either the ancient or the existentialist models, stressing what she calls the "finitist" or "anti-transcendent" strain in Hellenistic philosophy.[61] This is perhaps not surprising, given the therapeutic, pragmatic, and ultimately political emphasis of her model of *askesis*. At the same time, however, Nussbaum faults Foucault's work on *askesis* for failing "to confront the fundamental commitment to reason" that she believes distinguishes philosophical *techniques du soi* from other such techniques circulating in the ancient world.[62] In contrast to what she regards as Foucault's antirational ethic of self-fashioning (which, as antirational, would seem to have little capacity for transcendence at all), Nussbaum contends that the therapeutic arguments of Hellenistic *askesis* achieve the kind of transcendence that comes with the exercise of critical reason in the service of compassion and truth.[63]

Having presented the typology, my final task in this section is to show that each of these approaches to *askesis* falls into one or another of the problematic tendencies noted earlier, as a result of assumptions that might be termed "antitheorist." In the case of Hadot, as we have already seen, the universalism of his approach to *askesis* is in the end undercut by his antitheorist assumption that these practices are prior to and separable from their conceptual or metaphysical background. If, as he argues, the efficacy of spiritual exercises lies in the transformation that results from the adoption of a cosmic perspective, how can the practices retain their transformative efficacy in the absence of the theoretical grounds for this perspective? In the end, Hadot's insistence that the universalizing effects of ancient spiritual exercises can be retrieved without their metaphysical background is rendered problematic by virtue of his own existentialist assumptions. By assuming the primacy of the will over any metaphysical conception of the world, his position exemplifies the danger of voluntarism.

Foucault's aesthetic approach to *askesis*, on the other hand, manifests an intensified attention to the shaping or fashioning of subjectivity without sufficient attention to the norm governing these techniques. In this respect, his position seems to take the antitheorist suspicion of universal principles to an extreme. As Hadot has observed, Foucault's interpretation of ancient philosophical exercises seems to exclude the cosmic dimension which Hadot believes is essential to their transformative power: "The feeling of belonging to a whole is an essential element. Such a cosmic perspective radically transforms the feeling one has of oneself."[64] Or as Arnold Davidson puts Hadot's criticism: "By not attending to that aspect of the care of the self that places the self within a cosmic dimension, whereby the self, in becoming aware of its belonging to the cosmic Whole, thus transforms itself, Foucault was not able to see the full scope of spiritual exercises."[65] More pointedly stated, Foucault's position seems to promote an ethic of self-shaping in the absence of any coherently articulated norm, and thus risks both subjectivism and voluntarism.

Finally, Nussbaum's concern with the formation of a rational community of freedom by means of a critical therapy of the passions seems to lose an element of *askesis* which is crucial to some ancient forms of philosophical therapy, the aspiration to "divinity."[66] As a result, she risks losing the critical power of Hellenistic *askesis* in favor of a worldly immersion in the fragile vulnerability of human life and a defense of the emotions in a life committed to reason.[67] The problem here is not really subjectivism or voluntarism, since Nussbaum's conception of *eudaimonia* is keyed not simply to the self's flourishing but to a more general naturalistic account of what all human beings need to flourish. Nevertheless, in challenging the notion that a "godlike" transcendence of the passions is integral to the therapeutic aim of ancient philosophical practices, Nussbaum may not fully appreciate the radical nature of the transformation they entail.

In sum, the central conclusion that has emerged from my critique of these contemporary approaches to *askesis* is that, by embracing assumptions I have termed "antitheorist," none of these models is able to provide an adequate account of the radical moral transformation necessary to resolve the central problem addressed by *askesis*, that is, the proper ordering and orientation of the human soul in relation to the good and to others. This, I contend, is the deeper moral issue at stake in the charges of subjectivism and voluntarism. Subjectivism and voluntarism are problematic not simply because they fall short of the epistemological presuppositions which made ancient forms of *askesis* possible and meaningful; they are also morally problematic in the sense that they do not provide a strong enough theory of moral transformation for *askesis* to accomplish its goal. What is really at stake in the idea of *askesis*, I am suggesting, is the question of what form of moral transformation is required to resolve the fundamental dilemma of human life, a question that drives to the deeper anthropological assumptions of each of the models.

In coming to this conclusion about the limitations of the three contemporary models of *askesis*, however, I do not mean to suggest that we must somehow return to ancient philosophical and cosmological assumptions in order to resolve these difficulties. Such a return is clearly impossible, for reasons that Charles Taylor has articulated perhaps more clearly than anyone in his analysis of the historical and cultural shifts underlying the transition to modernity. Granting this, the constructive question that remains to be addressed is the following: can we conceive of a contemporary approach to *askesis* which retains the transformative efficacy of the ancient model while avoiding the subjectivism and voluntarism associated with antitheorist assumptions?

## A "Reflexive" Model of *Askesis*

Based on the previous analysis, my claim in this final section of the paper is that an adequate contemporary model of *askesis* must take seriously the loss of ancient cosmological assumptions in the transition to modernity, while also providing a strong account of moral transformation that resists both subjectivism or voluntarism. Both of these conditions can be met, I contend, in what I will call a "reflexive" model of *askesis*, drawn in part from the work of the contemporary moral philosophers Charles Taylor and Iris Murdoch.

Taylor's analysis of modern identity in *Sources of the Self* provides crucial conceptual resources for my account by offering both an historical explanation and a constructive response to the loss of the ancient cosmos. In contrast to the ancient period, he contends, modern persons no longer understand themselves as participating in a universal order of reason which is thought to exist "outside" us in nature or the cosmos; rather, any sense of an objective moral order is understood to depend on our own powers of construction or our own activity of willing. Taylor describes this development as a process of "internalization" whereby the moral sources that were previously understood as situated in the rational order of the cosmos are now sought within. This shift away from the ancient conception of an "ontic logos," he contends, "gives rise to the notion of a subject in its modern sense . . . it involves a new localization, whereby we place 'within' the subject what was previously seen as existing, as it were, between knower/agent and world, linking them and making them inseparable."[68] As a result of this internalization, we now look for the good not in a publicly accessible order of meaning, but in ourselves.[69] "We are now in an age in which the publicly accessible cosmic order of meanings is an impossibility. The only way we can explore the order in which we are set with an aim to defining moral sources is through . . . personal resonance."[70] This is what Taylor refers to as the "reflexive" turn of thought, by which he means that our access to moral sources "outside" the self can only take place through language which resonates within the self; an objective moral order now comes "inseparably indexed to a personal vision."[71]

The three models of *askesis* analyzed in Part II can be seen as illustrating this internalizing trend of modern thought. Each model attempts to respond to the loss of the ancient cosmic order by locating the source of the moral good in some inner dimension or capacity of the self: for example, in the cultivation and enjoyment of the "best part" of oneself (Foucault); or the search for the norm of human flourishing in "the deepest layers of our own make-up" (Nussbaum). Even Hadot, who initially seems to resist this internalizing move by defending the ancient ideal of "universalization" and "cosmic consciousness," insists that achieving this cosmic perspective depends in the end on our own activity of willing rather than on a "metaphysical necessity." In every case, then, each of these authors challenges or qualifies ancient universalist assumptions by turning to some capacity of the human.[72]

By adopting this internalizing strategy, however, contemporary retrievals of *askesis* risk losing some of the self-transcending power of the ancient model, as I tried to show in my critique in Part II. In light of this, the question that my constructive account must address is whether the internalization of moral sources leads *inevitably* to this result. In other words, if the only access we now have to moral sources is through some type of "personal resonance," what is to prevent the reflexive turn from degenerating into subjectivism? Taylor himself acknowledges that the internalization of moral sources "can easily slide into a celebration of our creative powers, or the sources can be appropriated, interpreted as within us, and represented as the basis for 'liberation'."[73] But if the turn inward remains properly reflexive, Taylor insists, it is actually an attempt "to surmount subjectivism" rather than to capitulate to it.[74] In order to see how this might be the case, I want to use Taylor's insights to articulate a "reflexive" model of *askesis*. My claim is that the reflexive model succeeds in holding together the inward turn of modern thought and the objective force of the ancient model of *askesis* in a way that avoids both subjectivism and voluntarism.

On the reflexive model, the purpose of *askesis* is to cultivate moral sources that help to reorder the selfish desires and passions of the egoistic consciousness. As is the case with the ancient model, the goal is to achieve a moral condition in which one's desires and hence one's actions are properly oriented to an objective good, and thus to the self's fulfillment. However, the reflexive approach reconfigures the universalist and cognitivist assumptions of the ancient model by mediating them through the idea of personal resonance, that is, through the unique consciousness of the individual. Thus, instead of positing an ontological connection between human reason and the rational order of the cosmos, the reflexive model posits a correlation between consciousness and the good that can only be accessed through consciousness itself. In other words, the good is not conceived as existing solely outside us in the order of the cosmos; rather, it is located in the very texture of consciousness. Moreover, this universal good resonates in the consciousness of *individuals*, and thus is mediated through human particularity.

Iris Murdoch's moral thought exemplifies this reflexive model of *askesis*. The central problem of the moral life, on her view, is the egoism of the human psyche, which continually evades the truth about itself and others by fabricating a consoling veil of illusions designed to protect the psyche from pain. Accordingly, the purpose of *askesis* is to purify the naturally selfish energies of the psyche by orienting it towards a transcendent good. It is in and through these "techniques of unselfing" that Murdoch believes human beings gain access to and cultivate their ability to apprehend the good.[75] In keeping with this reflexive turn of thought, Murdoch conceives the good as the structuring principle of consciousness. That is, she contends that the idea of the good is implied in the activity of thinking itself, where it functions as the transcendental condition which makes thought possible, as well the inner standard of perfection by which we make qualitative judgments and distinctions between good and bad, better and worse, and so forth.[76] This process of moral reasoning depends on the particular vision and imaginative resources of the individual's consciousness; thus the good is "indexed to personal vision."[77]

The crucial question to be raised at this juncture is how the idea of a moral standard that is conceived as the structuring principle of consciousness can be "objective." In other words, if the good is located within the evaluative structure of consciousness, what is to prevent it from simply collapsing into the selfish desires and fantasies of the psyche? At stake in this question is the issue I raised earlier about whether this position can hold together both the inward turn of modern thought and the objectivity of the ancient model of *askesis*. Murdoch would respond that the location of the good within the structure of consciousness does not mean that the good is identifiable with the subjective preferences of the agent. This is because the reflexive model holds that consciousness or subjectivity is the inescapable *medium* for our access to moral sources, not that consciousness is identifiable with the source and content of the moral good. The claim of this model is that by turning inward, we discover not only our own powers but accede to a condition of thought that surpasses subjectivism. In this respect, Murdoch (as well as Taylor) can be understood as defending a form of "reflexive realism," which holds that the good is discovered through the medium of consciousness as it reflects on itself; yet at the same time, the act of reflexivity reveals the good to be a perfection or "higher condition" that transcends consciousness.[78]

This reflexive account of the relation of consciousness to an ideal standard allows us to return to the problem of moral transformation that is so central to the idea of *askesis*. I contend that the reflexive model requires a strong theory of moral transformation because of its deep anthropological assumptions about the moral being of the human. In Murdoch's view, human beings have a natural orientation to the good that is continually and obsessively distorted by the egoism of the psyche. The purpose of spiritual exercises is to purify the psyche of its selfish desire by reorienting its energies towards the world and others (hence the idea of "unselfing"). Through disciplined attention to the reality that exists outside the self, spiritual exercises break the hold of egoism and release the self to achieve a just and accurate perception of the world and of others. Thus *askesis* achieves a relation to a good which transcends the self by overcoming egoism; nevertheless, this good resonates within the self because *askesis* draws on the resources of the individual's own consciousness, imagination, and personal vision in order to perfect his or her natural orientation to the good.

This moral psychology and its correlative account of moral transformation offer, in my judgment, a more adequate analysis of the fundamental moral problematic of human life than the other three models of *askesis*. Demonstrating this will help to complete my argument. In relation to the existential approach, the reflexive model succeeds in retaining Hadot's emphasis on a radical transformation of consciousness, while rejecting his voluntarist separation of metaphysics from ethics. Murdoch's techniques of unselfing are intended to cultivate a truthful vision of reality which is devoid of egoism and is thus objective. In this respect, it shares much with Hadot's notion of "cosmic consciousness" as a liberation from the self's partial vision, which is distorted by the passions. But this objective vision of reality is, for Murdoch, part of a metaphysics of the good which is not simply "chosen" as it is for Hadot, but is rather the transcendental condition of consciousness from which acts of choice arise. In this respect, Murdoch's reflexive model affirms the ancient priority of metaphysics to ethics, and thus avoids the voluntarist tendency that undermines Hadot's approach.

In relation to Foucault's aesthetic approach to *askesis*, the reflexive model challenges the notion that the moral life is primarily an "art" or "stylistics of existence" whose purpose is to constitute the self as ethical subject, rather than to train the self to become a certain kind of person who conforms her consciousness to a vision of the good. Foucault's aesthetic approach acknowledges neither a natural orientation of human beings toward the good, nor a distortion in that orientation. Therefore, his "techniques of the self" are meant primarily to intensify the experience of subjectivity by effecting a conversion to the self, whereas Murdoch's "techniques of unselfing" effect a conversion to the real which purifies the self of egoism and makes a proper relation to the good and hence to others possible.

Finally, with respect to Nussbaum's therapeutic approach, Murdoch's reflexive model of *askesis* recognizes the need for a critical therapy of the passions, without denying the so-called divine element in *eudaimonia*. The reflexive model scrutinizes the relentless egoism of the psyche in order to purify it of selfish desire. In this respect it is a form of "therapy," which acknowledges (as Nussbaum's does) the central and inescapable role of *eros* in the moral life. But the reflexive model represents a radical "unselfing" which exceeds Nussbaum's construal of *eudaimonia*. This is because Murdoch is more wary of the distortive force of the psychic energies of *eros* in our relation to the good and to others. For her, it is not enough to say (as Nussbaum says in her qualified agreement with the Stoics), that there is little tension between "the deepest layers of our own makeup and the true good." Rather, the reflexive model requires that this tension remain a constant possibility within the moral life.

## Conclusion

This paper has presented an analysis of three recent philosophical retrievals of the idea of *askesis*, placing them against the background of the debate over "antitheory" in ethics. After clarifying the tensions involved in these retrievals through a critical typology, I have argued that a "reflexive" model of *askesis* can respond to these difficulties by providing an alternative account of our moral being as persons, grounded in the relation between consciousness and the good.

Theories of *askesis* address what is arguably the most basic aspect of ethics, the formation of persons as moral selves. The task for future work on this topic is to develop theoretical, conceptual, and historical resources for reflecting on the problem of moral formation in increasingly complex and diversified cultural circumstances. In this context, the current critique of "theory" must be taken seriously insofar as it is conceptually and ethically motivated by an authentic concern for the particularity of persons and cultures. Yet some form of theoretical reflection is necessary in order to judge what form of "therapy" human beings need, and to assess critically the processes of formation already underway. This paper is intended as an initial contribution to that broadly theoretical task.[79]

## Notes

[1]Pierre Hadot, *Philosophy as a Way of Life: Spiritual Exercises from Socrates to Foucault*, ed. and with an introduction by Arnold I. Davidson (Oxford and Cambridge, MA: Blackwell Publishers, 1995), 210.

[2]Ibid. The quotation is from the *Meditations*, 5, 1. Many other passages could be cited to illustrate Hadot's point, including the following: "When you are outraged by somebody's impudence, ask yourself at once, 'Can the world exist without impudent people?' It cannot; so do not ask for impossibilities. That man is simply one of the impudent whose existence is necessary to the world. Keep the same thought present, whenever you come across roguery, double-dealing or any other form of obliquity . . . and at once you will feel kindlier towards the individual" *(Meditations* 9, 42).

[3]Ibid., 202.

[4]Hadot takes this definition from K. Heussi; see *Philosophy as a Way of Life*, 128. Similar definitions of asceticism could be cited from other sources.

[5]See *Philosophy as a Way of Life*, 128, as well as Hadot's more lengthy catalogue of "Stoico-Platonic inspired philosophical therapeutics" drawn from two lists found in Philo of Alexandria, 84.

[6]The article on "Asceticism" in the *New Catholic Encyclopedia*, vol. I (New York: McGraw Hill, 1967), 939 defines *askesis* as "'exercise,' 'practice,' or 'training' for the purpose of obtaining something that is worth aspiring to, that represents an ideal."

[7]See for example the three volumes of *Christian Spirituality: Origins to the Twelfth Century*, edited by Bernard McGinn, John Meyendorff, and Jean Leclerq (New York: Crossroad, 1985) and the multi-volumed *World Spirituality: An Encyclopedic History of the Religious Quest*, gen. ed. Ewert Cousins (New York: Crossroad Publishing Company, 1984-1998).

[8]*Asceticism*, ed. Vincent L. Wimbush and Richard Valantasis (New York: Oxford University Press, 1995), xxix.

[9]To illustrate what may happen when critical, theoretical reflection on the processes of formation already occurring in contemporary culture is neglected, the authors cite the powerfully negative forces of formation operative in urban street gangs and hate groups: "Cities have become centers for formation in violence, as the member of any gang in the United States or racial supremacist group in Europe will attest, so that any young person willing to submit to the intense formative experience of entering a gang or a racist group will easily become capable of inflicting violence and acting out hatred. This constitutes an asceticism of violence, an ethics of destruction." Ibid., xxx.

[10]I have limited my analysis to philosophical treatments of *askesis* rather than focusing on theological appropriations of this notion, e.g., in the study of spirituality, asceticism, or mysticism. My reason for doing so, aside from space limitations, is that the philosophical work on *askesis* tends to address its ethical significance explicitly, while the theological work often neglects this dimension. My hope is that gaining some clarity on the normative dimensions of philosophical *askesis* may provide some of the conceptual tools needed to undertake an ethical analysis of religious forms of *askesis* in the future.

[11]On the latter see Edith Wyschogrod, *Saints and Postmodernism: Revisioning Moral Philosophy* (Chicago: University of Chicago Press, 1990) and her essay, "The Howl of Oedipus, the Cry of Eloise: From Asceticism to Postmodern Ethics," in *Asceticism, op. cit.*

[12]For an account of the debate over theory, See *Antitheory in Ethics and Moral Conservatism*, eds. Stanley G. Clarke and Evan Simpson (State University of New York Press, 1989), especially the editors' introduction, 1-26. The list of antitheorists cited in this account is too long to include in its entirety but includes Bernard Williams, Martha Nussbaum, Richard Rorty, Charles Taylor, Alasdair Machityre, and "a number of others who might be surprised to find themselves associated in this way." Theorists include Richard Brandt, David Gauthier, Alan

Gewirth, R. M. Hare, Thomas Nagel, and (with qualifications) John Rawls and Ronald Dworkin. See *Anti-Theory in Ethics*, 2.

[13]See Dwight Furrow, *Against Theory: Continental and Analytic Challenges in Moral Philosophy* (New York and London: Routledge, 1995), 2-3. Furrow traces the antitheorist position through the work of MacIntyre, Nussbaum, and Rorty in the analytic tradition, and Levinas and Lyotard in the continental.

[14]Ibid., xiii.

[15]Ibid., xii.

[16]This procedure, as Clarke and Simpson characterize it, "applies abstract principles to moral problems in an almost computational way, giving a procedure for deducing the morally correct answer in any given circumstances." *See Anti-Theory in Ethics*, 2.

[17]In the case of MacIntyre, moreover, the idea of practice has been appropriated by some thinkers in support of the turn to spirituality in religious thought. For example, Peter Van Ness has remarked that MacIntyre "has provided a theory of virtue that includes a notion of practice quite relevant to discussion of spiritual life." See the introduction to volume 22 of *World Spirituality*, titled *Spirituality and the Secular Quest*, ed. Peter H. Van Ness (New York: Crossroad, 1996), 5.

[18]*Anti-Theory in Ethics*, 2-3.

[19]On this point, some have conceived the contrast between theorists and antitheorists as a debate between those who favor 'system" and those who favor "story" as the dominant metaphor for ethical reflection. See Stanley Hauerwas and David Burrell, "From System to Story: An Alternative Pattern for Rationality in Ethics" in *Why Narrative? Readings in Narrative Theology*, eds. Stanley Hauerwas and L. Gregory Jones (Grand Rapids: William B. Eerdmans, 1989).

[20]Martha Nussbaum, *The Fragility of Goodness: Luck and Tragedy in Greek Ethics* (Cambridge: Cambridge University Press, 1986),13.

[21]See *Philosophy as a Way of Life*, 64, emphasis added.

[22]See Hadot's discussion of the relation between theory and practice in ancient philosophy, ibid., 60 ff.

[23]See Nussbaum's discussion of therapeutic arguments in the first chapter of *The Therapy of Desire: Theory and Practice in Hellenistic Ethics* (Princeton: Princeton University Press, 1994), 34-35.

[24]Ibid., 35.

[25]The claim is that theory necessarily relies on some general category (such as rationality) which mediates the reality of persons and hence reduces their unique particularity. Thus Edith Wyschogrod, for example, criticizes the scientific and universalizing pretensions of ethical theory as unable to do justice to the radical claim of the other without treating the other as "another myself." In response to this perceived limitation of theory, Wyschogrod turns to the resources of art and narrative as more appropriate media to portray the reality of the other and the nature of moral obligation. See her *Saints and Postmodernism*.

[26]See, for example, Katie Cannon's critique of dominant ethics (including theological ethics) in "Moral Wisdom in the Black Women's Literary Tradition," in *Weaving the Visions: New Patterns in Feminist Spirituality*, eds. Judith Plaskow and Carol P. Christ (San Francisco: Harper San Francisco, 1989), 281-92.

[27]I am acutely aware of the limitations of this approach in relation to works as historically and conceptually rich as these. For those who have not read these texts, it is important to emphasize that each covers a diverse range of philosophical practices across several centuries of antiquity in careful textual and historical detail. I am not able fully to represent this complexity here, but I hope my typology will be useful in provoking further constructive reflection on the larger issues at stake in these philosophical retrievals of *askesis*.

[28]See Charles Taylor, *Sources of the Self: The Making of the Modern Identity* (Cambridge: Harvard University Press, 1989), 125.

[29]Ibid., 278.

[30]Ibid., 56.

[31]Ibid., 126. Taylor's account of the loss in the modern period of ancient assumptions about an objective order of the good that provided the framework for notions of identity has informed many aspects of this paper. I will return to Taylor's account in Part III.

[32]See Hadot, 82 and also 127: "[T]hese exercises have as their goal the transformation of our vision of the world, and the metamorphosis of our being. They therefore have not merely a moral, but also an existential value. We are not just dealing here with a code of good moral conduct, but with a way of being, in the strongest sense of the term."

[33]Ibid., 211

[34]Ibid.

[35]Hadot writes that "the same spiritual exercises can, in fact, be justified by extremely diverse philosophical discourses. These latter are nothing but clumsy attempts, coming after the fact, to describe and justify inner experiences whose existential density is not, in the last analysis, susceptible of any attempt at theorization or systematization." Ibid., 212.

[36]Ibid., 61.

[37]Ibid., 61-66 on the form of ancient philosophical discourse and its relation to the practical goal of spiritual formation. Arnold Davidson places particular stress on this feature of Hadot's analysis. Quoting Hadot in part, he notes that "the philosophers of antiquity were concerned not with ready-made knowledge, but with imparting that training and education that would allow their disciples to 'orient themselves in thought, in the life of the city, or in the world . . . . [T]he written philosophical work, precisely because it is a direct or indirect echo of oral teaching now appears to us as a set of exercises, intended to make one practice a method, rather than as a doctrinal exposition."' See Ibid., 21.

[38]See his remarks in the interview published as the "Postscript" to *Philosophy as a Way of Life*, esp. 278.

[39]Ibid., 283.

[40]Ibid.

[41]Foucault defines the "arts of existence" as "those intentional and voluntary actions by which men not only set themselves rules of conduct, but also seek to transform themselves, to change themselves in their singular being, and to make their life into an *oeuvre* that carries certain aesthetic values and meets certain stylistic criteria." See *The History of Sexuality*, volume 2: *The Use of Pleasure* (New York: Random House, 1985), 10-11. For a discussion of the theme of the care of the self, see *The History of Sexuality*, volume 3: *The Care of the Self* (New York: Random House, 1986), esp. 43-68.

[42]On this theme, see *The Care of the Self*, 45-47. The successive volumes of *The History of Sexu*ality trace the "intensification" of the idea of the care of the self from the classical period of Greco-Roman antiquity through the growth of Christian sexual ethics.

[43]Foucault describes this conversion *ad se* as a "shift of one's attention" from "idle curiosity" in external things to a state of independence in which "one ultimately rejoins oneself." See *Care of the Self*, 64-65.

[44]Ibid.

[45]Foucault acknowledges the influence of Hadot in his work on ancient philosophical practices; see *The Use of Pleasure*, 8. Yet Hadot critiques Foucault on some of the same points I have been noting. For Hadot, the point of spiritual exercises is "to liberate oneself from one's individuality, in order to raise oneself up to universality." In contrast, he sees Foucault's account of these practices as "focused far too much on the 'self,' or at least on a specific conception of the self," and thus "*too* aesthetic." What has dropped out of Foucault's account is the dimension of universalization. It is not the case, Hadot writes, that the ancient practitioner of *askesis* finds joy and delight in his "self"; rather, he finds it "by discovering that there is within him—within all human beings, that is, and within the cosmos itself—a reason which is a part of universal reason." The conversion effected by spiritual exercises "contains a universalist, cosmic dimension upon which, it seems to me, M. Foucault did not sufficiently insist. Interiorization [that is, conversion to self] is a going beyond oneself; it is a universalization." For the full text of these remarks, see Hadot's "Reflections on the Idea of the 'Cultivation of the Self"' in *Philosophy as a Way of Life*, 206-213.

[46]*Care of the Self,* 66. Foucault understands pleasure in this context in relation to the Senecan terms *gaudium* or *laetitia*, "a state that is neither accompanied nor followed by any form of disturbance in the body or the mind." He contrasts this with *voluptas*, also drawn from Seneca, which denotes "a pleasure whose origin is to be placed outside us and in objects whose presence we cannot be sure of: a pleasure, therefore, which is precarious in itself, undermined by the fear of loss, and to which we are drawn by the force of a desire that may or may not find satisfaction." For a critique of Foucault's use of Seneca on this point, see Hadot's essay noted above.

[47]*Care of the Self,* 66.

[48]Seneca, *Letters to Lucilius*; quoted in *Care of the Self,* 66-67.

[49]I am indebted to an anonymous reviewer for helping me to clarify this criticism.

[50]See *The Use of Pleasure*, 251, and especially chapter 3 of the introduction, "Morality and the Practice of the Self," 25-32. Although Foucault acknowledges that every morality contains both "codes of behavior and forms of subjectivation" and that these essential elements can never be entirely dissociated, he argues that ancient moralities were "much more oriented towards practices of the self." See 29-30.

[51]Ibid., 10-11.

[52]The therapeutic model as I am outlining it here might also be called the "medical" model in that it takes the analogy between philosophy and medicine as its central guiding motif. In this respect, it picks up on a theme noted by all three authors, that is, the way in which ancient philosophy served as a therapy or cure for the disturbance and suffering of the soul analogous to medicine's cure of the ills of the body. This analogy between philosophy and therapy or medicine is already implicit in both the existential and aesthetic models. For example, Foucault notes that the cultivation of the self in antiquity exists "in close connection with medical thought and practice" and draws on a "shared set of notions" as "a common guide for the medicine of the body and the therapeutics of the soul." See *The Care of the Self,* 54-55. And Hadot notes that ancient philosophy was first and foremost a "therapeutic of the passions." See *Philosophy as a Way of Life*, 83.

[53]This ideal includes both individual and social health, since the errors represented by the passions are understood as arising from deformed social conditions.

[54]*Therapy of Desire*, 5.

[55]Ibid. See Nussbaum's critique of Foucault on this point here, and on 353.

[56]Ibid., 32. In developing this pragmatic, "medical" view of truth, Nussbaum is seeking to combine the strengths and avoid the deficiencies of two other approaches to ethics: the "Platonic approach" and the "ordinary-belief" approach often ascribed to Aristotle. See her discussion on 16-29.

[57]Ibid., 22-23.

[58]Ibid., 23.

[59]Thus, for example Nussbaum rejects the Stoic aspiration to extirpate the passions as essentially "inhuman," that is, as completely transcending our nature as finite, mortal human beings. "It seems to me a major contribution of Hellenistic ethics to have urged us to think humanly, like the finite beings we are. I believe that this insight should have moved the argument, in some cases, away from *apatheia* and toward both *eros* and compassion." Ibid., 499, and see also her concluding comment on 510.

[60]Ibid., 499.

[61]See especially her discussion of Epicureanism and Stoicism on this point, ibid., 497-99. William Schweiker has recently noted that on Nussbaum's view, "the only transcendence we can and ought to seek is an 'inner-worldly' one. But this 'transcending' is defined in a specific way. We ought to reach beyond our moral limitations, to extend the bonds of the human world, to deepen our capacity to care for others in all their fragility and folly. Any other view of human transcending is seen as 'other-worldly' and religious; it is trapped in what Nietzsche called 'slave-morality' and will rob us of the only world we have or that matters." See his "The Required Voice and Sacred Whispers: Reflections on Literature and Ethics," unpublished paper circulated for a panel discussion at the American Academy of Religion in November 1997.

[62]*Therapy*, 5-6. And as she notes on 353: "[W]hat [Foucault's] emphasis on habits and *techniques du soi* too often obscures is the dignity of reason. Many forms of life in the ancient

world purveyed *techniques du soi.* What sets philosophy apart from popular religion, dream--interpretation, and astrology is its commitment to rational argument."

[63]For a valuable discussion of the issue of transcendence in Nussbaum's thought, see her essay responding to Charles Taylor, "Transcending Humanity," in *Love's Knowledge: Essays on Philosophy and Literature* (New York: Oxford University Press, 1990), 365-91.

[64]*Philosophy as a Way of Life*, 208.

[65]See Davidson's introduction to *Philosophy as a Way of Life*, 24-25.

[66]Diskin Clay has articulated this criticism of Nussbaum in his review of *The Therapy of Desire*. "The problem of representing the Greek concept of happiness (*eudaimonia* literally being favored by divinity) by the current term 'flourishing' is that it expunges from the record of ancient philosophy the aspiration—shared by Platonists, Aristotle, Epicureans, and Stoics (and indeed some Hellenistic kings)—to come to resemble the divine . . . [I]t does not capture the aspirations of the Epicureans and Stoics, who were determined to become 'godlike,' according to their own conceptions of divinity. These puzzlements are not merely philological; they point to themes in the unargued argument of this book that require, I think, more justification." See Clay's review, titled "Deep Therapy," in *Philosophy and Literature* 20 (1996): 501-505.

[67]Nussbaum herself acknowledges this as a problem facing Hellenistic philosophy generally, and her own account by implication: "Philosophy in the hands of the Hellenistic thinkers no longer calmly contemplates the world: it plunges into the world, and becomes a part of it. And this changes philosophy. We must wonder whether it will, in gaining engagement, lose something of philosophy's reflective power." See *Therapy*, 36-37.

[68]Taylor, *Sources of the Self*, 188.

[69]For example, in our own inner motivation and sense of dignity (as in Kant); or in the discovery of the creative powers of the imagination, or a sense of nature as an inner source of feeling (as in Romanticism), or in the power of language as a medium of poetic or epiphanic insight (as in literary Modernism).

[70]Ibid., 512.

[71]Ibid., 510.

[72]An antitheorist might argue that this internalizing move is not unrelated to these authors' attempts to take moral particularism seriously, e.g. by affirming the freedom of the individual to choose her own moral destiny over the constraints of metaphysics (Hadot); the creative ability of human beings to engage in diverse forms of self-creation and self-fashioning (Foucault); and the emotional capacity for the deep attachments that bind particular human beings to one another in friendship, compassion, and love (Nussbaum).

[73]Ibid., 510.

[74]Ibid.

[75]These techniques include such exercises as the contemplation of beauty in nature and art, the mental discipline of academic work, and especially, attention to the reality of others. See Murdoch's discussion of these techniques in *The Sovereignty of Good* (London: Routledge & Kegan Paul, 1970), esp. 84 ff., and also in *Metaphysics as a Guide to Morals* (New York: Allen Lane/The Penguin Press, 1992). For a suggestive analysis of Murdoch's thought in the context of the current retrieval of spiritual exercises, see David Tracy's essay, "The Many Faces of Platonism" in *Iris Murdoch and the Search for Human Goodness*, eds. Maria Antonaccio and William Schweiker (Chicago: The University of Chicago Press, 1996), 54-75.

[76]I cannot do justice here to Murdoch's complex argument for a correlation between consciousness and the good, which she justifies, ultimately, by an appeal to the ontological proof. For a comprehensive treatment and exposition of Murdoch's position, see my dissertation, "Moral Identity and the Good in the Thought of Iris Murdoch," (University of Chicago, 1996), esp. chapters 2 and 5. For a briefer discussion of some of the same themes, see my "Imagining the Good: Iris Murdoch's Godless Theology," *The Annual of the Society of Christian Ethics* (1996): 223-42.

[77]For Murdoch's well-known philosophical example demonstrating this process of moral reasoning and its dependence on the idea of the individual, see the story of M and D in *The Sovereignty of Good*, 17-28.

[78]I have defended this interpretation of Murdoch in my dissertation, see esp. chapter 5. The term "reflexive realism" is William Schweiker's, whose work on this subject has deeply informed my own thinking. See his *Responsibility and Christian Ethics* (Cambridge: Cambridge University Press, 1995) for an articulation and defense of this position in relation to current debates over realism and antirealism in ethics.

[79]I have an unusually large number of people to thank for criticism and support on this paper. I am especially grateful to the editors of *The Annual*, John Kelsay and Sumner Twiss, and the two anonymous reviewers, for the quality of their criticisms and constructive suggestions. I am indebted to Jeffrey S. Turner for discussions of Hadot's work, which led to my interest in this topic, and to William Schweiker for comments on several drafts of this paper. I thank the members of the audience in Atlanta who heard and responded to the paper, as well as Gerald McKenny, Douglas Sturm, and Janet Nelson for providing written comments in the months following. The process of revision was considerably aided by my colleagues in the Institute for the Advanced Study of Religion at the University of Chicago Divinity School during Spring 1998. Finally, I recognize the support of Bucknell University in granting me the research leave during which this paper was written.

# Schleiermacher's Christian Ethics in Relation to His Philosophical Ethics

*John Crossley*

## Abstract

The paper argues that while Schleiermacher intends to base Christian ethics on the Christian principle of a supra-rational knowledge of God's will communicated solely through Christ, and not available to human reason, Schleiermacher nevertheless borrows for his Christian ethics from his philosophical ethics. He is able to do this because his philosophical ethics, as distinct from Kant's, incorporates insights from religious feeling. Schleiermacher's Christian ethics, therefore, is more a theory of Christian, reformative action in the church and the state than a full-blown religious ethics.

Schleiermacher's discovery of what he regards to be the basis for a new Christian dogmatic theology necessitates a decision on his part as to how he will handle Christian ethics. On pragmatic grounds, he rejects, as we will show below, the inclusion of Christian ethics in his *Glaubenslehre*, even though he believes dogmatics is incomplete without ethics. Therefore, the writing of his Christian ethics is a project separate from the writing of his dogmatics in the narrow sense, but linked to it as "the other half" of a complete dogmatics.

At the time he began to lecture on Christian ethics, he had already lectured extensively on philosophical ethics. Unwilling, on the one hand, to concede that philosophical ethics, proceeding from a rational basis, can say what needs to be said in a Christian ethics proceeding from an evangelical basis, he is also unwilling to concede that Christian ethics can contradict rational ethics. The dilemma is posed: What is distinctive about Christian ethics?

Joseph Fuchs, S.J., in his seminal essay, "Is There a Christian Morality?" concludes that there is a common, human morality which Christian morality in content does not go beyond.[1] "The newness that Christ brings," he writes, " is not really a new (material) morality, but the new creature of grace and of the Kingdom of God, the man [sic] of divinely self-giving love."[2] Schleiermacher would agree with Fuchs that Christ brings "the new creature of grace and of the Kingdom of God"; whether he would also agree with Fuchs that there is in Christian morality no new (material) morality is part of the subject of this paper. I will argue that Schleiermacher's Christian ethics is more dependent on his philosophical ethics than he intends it to be.

Schleiermacher stands as the first modern theologian to think through the relationship between Christian and philosophical ethics. Whether contemporary Christian ethicists are obliged to present, as he does, two different ethics, one philosophical, one theological, is an open question; we can be grateful, however, that he does it, because this enables us to see and learn from the moves he makes. We will begin with the way in which he conceives of the relation between Christian dogmatics in the narrow sense and Christian ethics, move from there to a brief overview of his philosophical ethics, then to an examination of how he understands the relation between his Christian and his philosophical ethics. From these analyses, we will draw some critical conclusions.

## The Relation between Dogmatics and Ethics

From the publication of his *Brief Outline on the Study of Theology* in 1811 through both editions of *The Christian Faith* in 1821/22 and 1830/31, respectively, Schleiermacher maintained that the particular division of historical theology he calls dogmatic theology consists of both dogmatics in the narrow sense and Christian ethics.[3] While Schleiermacher chooses to treat dogmatics in the narrow sense separately from ethics for purposes of expedience, he is clear that only the two together form a complete Christian dogmatics. He goes so far as to say, "It will always remain desirable that the undivided treatment should regain currency from time to time."[4]

Furthermore, the dogmatics and the ethics are organized similarly. Both begin with a long introduction consisting of propositions borrowed from philosophy and designed to situate Christian dogmatics and ethics in the total, intellectual scheme of things.[5] All of the safeguards for dogmatics in the narrow sense which Schleiermacher lays out in paragraphs 196-216 of the *Brief Outline* are also, he tells us, applicable to Christian ethics.[6] We can safely assume, therefore, that the entire Introduction in *Christian Faith* is as applicable to Christian *Sittenlehre* as to *Glaubenslehre*.

Both the dogmatics and the ethics proceed from the religious affections of Christians, that is, from the Christian consciousness of Jesus Christ as redeemer, and from membership in the community formed by him.[7] This Christian consciousness tends to express itself in two distinct but analogous ways, once as thought, resulting in beliefs or doctrines, and again as action, resulting in moral propositions.[8] This distinction between thought and action goes back to Schleiermacher's discussion of piety in *Christian Faith* when he says, in a proposition borrowed from philosophical ethics, ". . . The stirred-up Feeling sometimes comes to rest in a thinking which fixes it, sometimes discharges itself in an action which expresses it.'"[9]

It is the same piety that expresses itself in both dogmatic and moral propositions. This is an important point because it shows that Christian ethics is not dependent on Christian dogmatics in the narrow sense. As Schleiermacher puts it in introducing his Christian ethics, "Christian faith is indeed assumed, but only in the form of the primordial consciousness, not dogmatic development.[10] Schleiermacher goes so far as to say, "The same morals can even be linked to different dogmatic systems,"[11] although this statement has to be taken as something of a one-sided, dramatic flourish, as he takes great pains in his lectures on Christian ethics to make sure that they are in line with the *Glaubenslehre*.[12] And, as we have seen, only dogmatics in the narrow sense and ethics taken together comprise a complete dogmatic system. Nevertheless, the fact that Christian ethics is not tied to any specific dogmatic system leaves it somewhat unprotected from encroachment by philosophical ethics.

## Philosophical Ethics: Brief Overview

### *1. Locating Ethics in Dialectics*

Even though Schleiermacher gave the first of his lectures on philosophical ethics in 1804/05 (in Halle), and the first of his lectures on dialectics (*Dialektik*[13]) not until 1811 (in Berlin), he presupposed from the outset of his lectures on philosophical ethics that the task of situating philosophical ethics in the total scheme of scientific knowledge of being is a task for dialectics. In the lectures on dialectics of 1811, he divides human knowing, in its role as constructing concepts, into the domains, physics and ethics.[14] These two together, physics as the formation of concepts about natural being, and ethics as the formation of concepts about rational being, comprise the sum total of all conceptual knowledge of being.[15]As he puts it, ". . . All existing forms must be contained in this system of concept formation."[16]

The existing forms of being, however, present themselves to the mind, not only as concepts, but for observation of "kinds" (*Arten*).[17] Kinds are not individual entities, but generalizations into which all individual artifacts, natural or reasonable, fit.[18] Conceptual thinking forms kinds into types; at the same time, however, the formation of kinds from individual artifacts of history, natural or reasonable, is dependent on concepts.[19] Observation and concept formation as the two modes of thinking which result in the knowing of being interpenetrate each other. Observation of kinds implies that there are intellectual disciplines underlying, in a predominantly empirical deployment of thinking, the predominantly conceptual disciplines of physics and ethics.

In his lectures on dialectics of 1814/15, Schleiermacher identifies these predominantly empirical disciplines as natural history and history proper (that is, historiography).[20] There is a relative contrast between "judgments" (*Urteilen*) about both natural being and reasonable being, on the one hand, and "concepts" (*Begriffen*) about both types of being, on the other hand.[21]

Schleiermacher says "relative" contrast because there is no true knowledge of being in either empirical judgments alone or in speculative concepts alone, and the two types of knowing interpenetrate one another to the extent that ethics or physics can become empirical, and natural history or history, become speculative.[22]

In summary, as thinking is deployed to know being, there are four intellectual disciplines that interpenetrate one another. Physics is reason knowing natural being from a predominantly speculative or intellectual standpoint. Natural history is reason knowing natural being from a predominantly empirical standpoint. Ethics is reason knowing reasonable (human) being from a predominantly speculative or intellectual standpoint. History is reason knowing reasonable being from a predominantly empirical standpoint. All four are interrelated, and knowledge of being in one discipline cannot rise any higher than knowledge of being in the others. As Schleiermacher says in both his dialectics and his ethics, "Ethics is at no time better than physics; the two are always in parallel."[23]

In identifying ethics as the predominantly speculative or intellectual knowing of predominantly reasonable being, it is important always to keep in mind that it never stands in isolation from the disciplines which surround it. The whole system of judgments and concepts of being is in a constant state of flux (*Fluss*), and there can never be fixed judgments or concepts of being.[24] This means that ethics, even though it is predominantly a speculative or intellectual knowing of predominantly reasonable being is dependent for its level of development at any given moment in history on the constantly changing levels of knowing being in physics or in the predominantly empirical disciplines which underly ethics and physics.

## 2. *Philosophical Ethics Proper*

**a. Definition of Ethics.** Ethics is a descriptive science, directly analogous to physics; the task of ethics is ". . . to embrace and report all true human action."[25] Schleiermacher presupposes that reason is found in nature; therefore ethics does not represent an action by which it enters the scene from without, but represents the power of reason to shape and disseminate extensively the unity of reason with nature.[26] The original interpenetration of reason and nature is the unity of and antithesis between soul and body in the human personality.[27] The human organism is considered to be a part of nature in general, in which a potential unity with reason is presupposed.[28] In its broadest sense, ethics as the representation of the joining (*Zusammensein*) of reason with nature is the philosophy (*Wissenschaft*) of history, inclusive of a philosophy of culture and life in society.[29] If the unity of reason and nature were complete, there would be no more history and therefore no ethics.[30] Ethics presupposes both an original unity of reason and nature in the transcendental idea of God, and a final unity of reason and nature in the transcendental idea of the world, but these transcendental ideas are available only in feeling, not in real history.[31] Ethics itself is a process, viz., the process of nature's becoming the organ and symbol of reason.[32] In this process there is no distinction between what is and what ought to be, as what is is not an empirical but an ideal description, and what ought to be is merely the form such an ideal ethical description takes.[33] Ethics can be contrasted with physics, which also describes the ideal unity of nature and reason, but from the side of reason's being shaped by the power of nature.[34] Only ethics utilizes the imperative form.[35]

Ethics divides itself into the concepts of the good, virtue, and duty.[36] The concept of the highest good is the overarching concept, and the concepts of virtue and duty always refer back to the highest good, and are necessarily incomplete in themselves.[37] As Schleiermacher says, "The objective representation of the ethical is at the same time the representation of the highest good."[38] He also says, ". . . The representations of the concepts of virtue and of duty refer back to [the representation of the concept of the highest good] and are incomplete in themselves."[39] This should not be taken to mean that the concepts of virtue and duty in themselves are not important; Schleiermacher lectured on them frequently, albeit incompletely, and strove always to bring them into harmony with his overall conception of ethics as the process of nature becoming an organ and symbol of reason which he develops in his concept of the highest good. The highest good itself is not any one thing, but the complete organizing (*organisirend*), knowing (*erkennend*), and symbolizing (*symbolisirend*) of nature by reason.[40]

The concept of duty is particularly important for the purposes of this paper because Schleiermacher notes in his *Brief Outline* that ". . . Christian ethics can draw for the most part only from discussions about duty in philosophical ethics."[41] In his *Introduction to Christian Ethics*, he says, "The comparison of . . . Christian ethics with philosophical ethics of duty presupposes an identity of subject and method and, since we do not equate the two, also a difference."[42] We will reserve till later an analysis of the exact relation between a philosophical ethics of duty and Christian ethics, but wish to note here that Schleiermacher himself acknowledges that Christian ethics touches philosophical ethics most closely in the latter's concept of duty.

**b. Antitheses in Ethics and the Four Spheres.** In the ethical process of reason shaping nature to make nature its own organ and symbol, Schleiermacher identifies two pairs of antitheses in reason which cross each other to form four quadrants, and relates these quadrants to four major forms of human activity.[43] The first antithesis in reason is between its organizing or shaping function and its knowing or symbolizing function.[44] To organize nature, one starts with organizing all one's faculties (*Sinne*) and talents, that is, one's embodied self, by bringing it under the control of reason in a process Schleiermacher calls "gymnastics," in the widest sense of the word.[45] The same process extended to organic nature is "agriculture," and to inorganic nature, "mechanics."[46] In general, the organizing function of reason is a civilizing function, shaping all of nature in accord with reason.

The knowing or symbolizing function of reason differs from the organizing or shaping function in that while the latter represents the act of taking possession of nature and virtually penetrating it, the former represents the act through which reason is in nature and manifests itself in it.[47] The knowing or symbolizing function of reason is, in a sense, more passive and receptive than the organizing or shaping function in that the knowing function is open to the impression nature makes on reason, and senses the absolute, transcendental unity which lies behind the manifold of experiences of nature.[48] Even more important than the distinction between the two functions of reason, however, is the fact that they never operate in isolation from each other, but are bound together in every instance of reasoning about nature.[49]

The antithesis that crosses the antithesis between the organizing and knowing functions of reason is that between the identical (*Identität*) and the particular (*Eigentümlichkeit*).[50] By the identical, Schleiermacher means to refer to reason in its focus on the formation of a just, universal community.[51] By the particular, he means, not the reason of each individual person, but reason in its focus on the formation of ethical individuals.[52] Schleiermacher has in mind different temperaments and different talents.[53] Each individual is to express the identical in his or her own way.[54] As in the case of the antithesis between the organizing and knowing functions of reason, however, neither the identical nor the particular can stand alone; every formative activity oscillates between the identical and the particular.[55]

As Schleiermacher identifies the four spheres of human activity and their corresponding societal institutions which relate primarily to the four quadrants formed by the crossed antitheses, we need to keep in mind that these four spheres and institutions are never isolated from one another, just as formative reason itself is never isolated as organizing or knowing, or as identical or particular. Corresponding to the organizing/identical quadrant is the human sphere of work, earning of money, and exchange of money and goods.[56] Schleiermacher views as ethical a system of exchange that is fair, and in which every individual has enough money and influence to be a full participant in his or her own moral development and in the development of an ethical society.[57]

The societal institution that has the responsibility to maintain and enhance such an ethical society is the state, primarily through just legislation.[58] Schleiermacher recognizes, however, that the state can only do so much to insure ethical exchange, and that there is an area of organizing reason that takes place in the sphere of particularity, where the state has no role to play other than to insure that such a sphere continues to exist.[59] The principal role of the state, however, is to bring organization to the original, unformed mass of human families in such a way as to enhance the ethical process already at work in them.[60] Thus the state cannot be totalitarian, as if it had a foundation of its own apart from the ethical process, or so weak that it loses all authority to assist in the ethical process.[61]

The sphere corresponding to the organizing/particular quadrant is the sphere of personal assets (talents, or one's home, for examples), and finds its full ethical development in the give and take of friendship free from commercial business.[62] The ideal is a complete harmony within oneself and with friends in exchanges that result in mutual self-development.[63] Of course this inner and outer harmony carries over into the organizing/identical sphere, and there can be no moral development in one sphere without development in the other.[64] Nevertheless, it is clear to Schleiermacher that there is a sphere of "free fellowship" (*freie Geselligkeit*) that is separate and distinct from the sphere of the state.[65] Free fellowship serves the development of the individual through social life with others, as distinct from the state's emphasis on the development of a universal ethical community.

The sphere which corresponds to the knowing/identical quadrant is the sphere of learning and transmission of knowledge, that is, the sphere of tradition, which is both in process of being ever newly formed and communicated to a people at the same time.[66] The vehicle for this process is language.[67] Schleiermacher has in mind in this sphere the entire, complex process of learning and disseminating knowledge from earliest childhood through mature adulthood to old age.[68] Language and memory are reciprocal aspects of a process that leads ultimately to knowledge that is identical for all people, albeit expressed in different ways, and in different degrees of completeness at different stages of a person's development.[69] For such a process to succeed requires national organization, and Schleiermacher sketches out in his ethics his conception of an organized, scientific community of research and schooling.[70]

Knowing or symbolizing also takes place in a particular way that differs from the knowing or symbolizing which expresses itself primarily universally. The sphere that corresponds to the knowing/particular quadrant is the sphere of feeling (*Gefühl*).[71] The community (*Gemeinschaft*) of the knowing or symbolizing of particularity is more unmediated and inner than the organizing social life (*Geselligkeit*) of particularity.[72] Any particular excitation of feeling is accompanied by bursting into song or a change in countenance (*Geberde*, or *Gebärde* in modern spelling) as the natural expressions of an inner event.[73] At the root of feeling is direct, unmediated self-consciousness, and, while each moment of feeling combines a sense of four moments (quantitativeness: mathematical, joy: physical, conscientiousness: ethical, religion: dialectical), feeling reaches its culmination in religion.[74]

Religious feeling naturally establishes itself in religious communities or churches complete with their own artistic expressions.[75] There are two main classes of religious communities, ethical and naturalistic, and many more temperamental distinctions.[76] Churches tend to be organized through a division of clerical and lay, corresponding to the division of ruler and subject in the state, and of teacher and audience in the educational community.[77] A church, when it most fully embodies the religious feeling that brings it into being, is a repository of art, both in the sense of visual art which expresses religious feeling, and in the sense of the art of the self-development of religious feeling in each individual in community with others of the same religious sensibility.[78] It is the latter sense that distinguishes the sphere of religious feeling from the knowing/identical sphere of the state, on the one hand, and from the organizing/particular sphere of free fellowship, on the other hand. Religious feeling and the churches serve the development of individuals, not of everyone identically, yet draw those who share the same religious sensibility into a tighter fellowship than those motivated by the spirit of free fellowship.

All four spheres formed by the four quadrants of the antitheses between organizing and knowing or symbolizing, on the one hand, and between the identical and the personal, on the other hand, are anticipated in the family.[79] The family contains the seed (*Keim*) of moral legislation in the sphere of work and exchange, the seed of friendship and personal development in the sphere of free fellowship, the seed of scientific inquiry in the sphere of education, and the seed of religion in the sphere of unmediated feeling.[80] It is in the family where the ethical process of personality formation begins, that is, where the unity of soul and body, which itself is the seed of the intuited unity of reason and nature, commences to become reality.[81]

In a complete overview of Schleiermacher's philosophical ethics, we would at this point indicate how his theories of virtue and duty relate to the four spheres. For our purposes here, however, we need only to indicate that virtue is an empowering aspect of ethics. That is, virtue theory attempts to highlight those qualities of character necessary for the realization of the highest good in the spheres of life. Analogously, duty is a guiding aspect of ethics. That is, a theory of duty attempts to establish the principles of action necessary for the realization of the highest good in the spheres.

This summary of Schleiermacher's philosophical ethics reveals clearly, I believe, that his ethics is a form of what I would call critical, objective idealism. The ideal is the unity of nature with reason as nature becomes, progressively, the organ and symbol of reason. This process is at once necessary and free, necessary because the potential for this unity is built into the structure of nature imbued with rationality (that is, human nature), free because the furtherance of the process depends upon the compliance of each individual to nurture the virtues and perform the duties necessary to achieve the goal. "Evil" or "sin" has no substantial place in the ethical process other than as a name for the failure to comply.

Contemporary philosophical ethics has little patience with objective idealism, even when presented as critically as Schleiermacher presents it. (His is critical because, in his notion that thought works only in antitheses, he has no sanguine notion that reason can make nature its own organ or become the symbol of the unity of reason and nature at all easily or anytime in the near future.) Schleiermacher knows nothing of the contemporary criticism of "reason" that associates it with male or class privilege and thereby undermines its universality. However, his fundamental notion of ethics is not to privilege reason (indeed, all his life he resisted Kant's privileging of pure practical reason as a way to bypass human desires, talents, and intuitions, and go straight to the universal concept of duty) but to establish a basic human ethics prior to and apart from any historical revelation. Had he not been able to do this through critical reason, he would have to have found some other way to do it, for his idea of a universal feeling of dependence that expresses itself in both intellectual and moral propositions is the heart and soul of his philosophy. And, as we shall argue later, his Christian ethics, based on the historical revelation of Jesus Christ, is dependent on having as its underlayment, a universal, human ethic.

## Christian Ethics in Relation to Dogmatics and Philosophical Ethics

### *1. An Overview of Christian Ethics*

**a. Definition of Christian Ethics.** It is easy to empathize with the remark of Martin Redeker made at the interstice between his analyses of Schleiermacher's philosophical and Christian ethics, to wit: "Were one to consider only the philosophical ethics he might well believe that no specific Christian ethics is possible for Schleiermacher."[82] Indeed, in view of the comprehensiveness of the philosophical ethics in its description of the process of the unifying of reason and nature, what more is there to say? Schleiermacher says, in a passage from his Christian ethics we quoted earlier, that "The comparison of . . . Christian ethics with philosophical ethics of duty presupposes an identity of subject and procedure (*Verfahrens*) and, since we do not equate the two, also a difference."[83] To make the meaning of this statement clear, Schleiermacher draws an analogy between the relation of rational theology to Christian theology, on the one hand, and the relation of philosophical (rational) ethics to Christian ethics, on the other hand.[84] Rational theology is true for all human beings; Christian theology is true only for Christians.[85] Rational theology produces the consciousness of God purely from universal human reason; Christian theology is dependent on Jesus Christ and the specifically Christian consciousness introduced by him.[86] Schleiermacher then says, "This is also the relationship between Christian ethics and the philosophical ethics of duty."[87]

There is a problem with this analogy which is at the heart of the argument of this paper, but we shall defer the problem for a moment and take first from the analogy what Schleiermacher intends to prove by it. The first and decisive thing to be said is that Christian ethics takes its rise from faith in the redemption made manifest in Jesus Christ in time and history, while philosophical ethics proceeds purely from human reason.[88] In Schleiermacher's own words,

> If we begin with Christ himself, he lays the most certain claim to the fact that he has knowledge of God that can be communicated only through him, and that he sets forth a knowledge of God's will that did not exist before him. . . . [I]f one says that with the person of Christ and through Christ something real has entered human nature, that something has appeared that was not previously there and that even now can come forth only insofar as the union with Christ persists, then one must concede that human reason does not yet have that on its own. *Therefore the existence of a special Christian ethics stands or falls with the superhuman conception of the person of Christ.*[89]

As I have pointed out in the above cited article, Schleiermacher's view of Jesus Christ is superhuman in one respect, viz., in the sense in which he has introduced into human nature something that was not there before him and would not be there without him, but natural in another sense, that is, in the sense that the very possibility of human being's recognizing in Jesus Christ what it needs reveals that the something new he brings is already present in human nature, at least in the form of the recognition of need.[90] Schleiermacher also recognizes that ". . . it is impossible always to distinguish, even in the same individual, between what is effected by the divine Spirit and what is effected by the human reason."[91] Nevertheless, the working of reason and the working of the divine Spirit cannot be conflated because, as he puts it, ". . . everything experiential is supra-rational. For there is an inner experience to which [Christian dogmas] may all be traced: they rest upon a *given*; and apart from this they could not have arisen, by deduction or synthesis, from universally recognized and communicable propositions."[92]

The "given" on which Christian ethics rests is the Christian consciousness, that is, the consciousness that stems from "the impression of the divinity of the redeemer."[93] This consciousness, collectively, is the Christian church, and Christian ethics, unlike philosophical ethics, which is universally binding, is binding only on the particular community, the church.[94] Schleiermacher recognizes that if reason were able to reach the point of developing a universal, ethical, human community, the Christian church and Christian ethics would be superfluous.[95] He also says that ". . . [Christ] alone is destined gradually to quicken the whole human race into higher life."[96] When that process is complete, there will also be no need for a specifically Christian ethics. Meanwhile, since the rational process of unifying reason and nature is incomplete (if it were complete there would be no philosophical ethics, let alone Christian ethics), and the evangelical process of quickening the whole human race is likewise incomplete, there must be a Christian ethics alongside philosophical ethics.

While Christian ethics is binding only for Christians, its subject matter is identical to the subject matter of philosophical ethics; both encompass the whole of human life.[97] They differ in that Christian ethics covers the whole of human life, not from the perspective of reason, as does philosophical ethics, but from the perspective of the Christian principle.[98] Schleiermacher recognizes that in the actual doing of ethics, the two disciplines are often jumbled together in ways that do a disservice to both. As he puts it, ". . . many things pass for rational ethics of duty that are nothing more than elements of Christian ethics."[99] By the same token, there is a strong tendency, even in the church, ". . . to subsume Christian morality under the morality of reason . . . ."[100] Schleiermacher considers it his task as both a scientific philosopher and theologian to keep the two forms of ethics as conceptually true to their respective starting points as is humanly possible.

As I mentioned much earlier in the paper, the concept of duty is common to both philosophical and Christian ethics. This does not mean that the concept of duty is the point at which the two forms of ethics forget their respective guiding principles and converge; rather, it means that because Christian ethics is concerned with *action*, Christian ethics will take the philosophical form of duty, and not that of the good or virtue.[101] Indeed, one of the most noteworthy features of Schleiermacher's Christian ethics is that it contains no doctrine of the good, which plays the leading role in his philosophical ethics, or of virtue: the whole Christian ethics is an analysis of different types of action. In Schleiermacher's words, "We regard Christian ethics as the description of those ways of acting that have evolved in the Christian church from the effect of the Christian principle."[102] The Christian does not have to be given reasons as to why he or she should act in such and such a way: "Whoever is in the Christian church knows [them]."[103] In his Christian ethics, Schleiermacher substitutes for the concept of the highest good the concept of "the highest essence" under which a person ". . . in harmony with God cannot behave otherwise than [in accord with] the divine will."[104] In other words, what in philosophical ethics has to be explicated as the highest good in order to establish the aim of all duty and virtue simply enters Christian consciousness at the outset under the form of the highest essence, viz., communion with God.[105] Thus, there is no place in Christian ethics for a doctrine of the highest good separable from the will of God to establish the kingdom of God on earth.[106]

The exclusion of a doctrine of virtue from Christian ethics by Schleiermacher is handled in much the same way as the exclusion of a doctrine of the good. Virtue has to do with moral capacity. In the Christian church, moral capacity is grounded, not in the individual, but in the active power of the divine Spirit, which is the power given to Christians in and with Christian consciousness.[107] The answer to the person who complains of a lack of capacity to act in harmony with God is a pastoral answer: stay in the community of grace; let the power of the Spirit strengthen you.[108] There is no answer in Christian ethics itself to the question of a lack of moral capacity because Christian ethics assumes that the capacity is a constituent part of Christian consciousness.[109] Thus, there can be no Christian concept of virtue separable from the power that is communicated to the Christian by the divine Spirit.

**b. The Organization of Christian Ethics.** If Christian ethics is then essentially a theory of Christian action, how is that theory of action to be organized? Proceeding in his usual manner of identifying antitheses, Schleiermacher perceives in the doctrine of the church, the doctrine from which Christian ethics takes its rise, a fundamental antithesis in the action of the Christian between effective or efficacious action (*wirksame Handeln*) and representative or performative action (*darstellende Handeln*).[110] By efficacious action, Schleiermacher has in mind the action of the church militant, that is, the church as we find it now on earth facing the discrepancy between the ideal and the actual.[111] By representative action, he has in mind the action of the church perfected.[112] "These [standpoints], however, are not merely two different situations, but two different relationships already in the present situation."[113] That is, the antithesis is not absolute; the two poles interpenetrate one another in every action of the Christian, and the two types of action can never contradict each other.[114]

Efficacious action gives rise to a subordinate antithesis within itself, depending on whether it is predominantly corrective (*correctiv*) action,[115] on the one hand, or predominantly disseminating (*verbreitend*) action, on the other hand.[116] These two poles take their respective rise from the Christian's consciousness of pain or pleasure.[117] When the Christian consciousness perceives the pain of the world occasioned by the fact that the world is as yet "passed over" for inclusion in the Christian church as the earthly representative of the Kingdom of God, Christian consciousness acts out of this "perception of deficiency" to correct the problem, conscious of the fact that it has the power to do so.[118] On the other hand, when the Christian consciousness is predominantly conscious of its power, without an accompanying perception of deficiency, its action simply disseminates its own power without a conscious effort to effect an external change.[119] Disseminating action might also be compared to representative action except that in the former, the Christian, operating from the standpoint of the church militant, is still conscious of the dichotomy between pleasure and pain, and therefore not yet in a full state of happiness, while in the latter, the Christian is operating beyond the dichotomy between pain and pleasure, and is in a full state of happiness.[120] In disseminating action, the incomplete union of Christian consciousness with consciousness in general is extended and increased, while in representative action, the union is already complete.[121]

Schleiermacher's usual antithesis between the universal and the particular is also present in the Christian ethics,[122] but it is not nearly as prominent as another antithesis, viz., that between action which is directed inward and action that is directed outward.[123] By inward action, Schleiermacher means action that has to do primarily with the development of the Christian community. By outward action, he means action that has to do primarily with the Christian's action in the state and in the other spheres of societal life. Schleiermacher's Christian ethics is structured so as to provide for a description of both representative and efficacious action (the latter as both corrective and disseminating) in both inner and outer spheres.[124]

The four quadrants which result when the two major antitheses, efficacious and representative action, on the one hand, and action in inner and outer spheres, on the other hand, appear as follows and form the skeletal structure of the Christian ethics: The first quadrant, as formed by efficacious action as corrective action in the inner sphere, is the realm of church education and church reformation.[125] As formed by efficacious action as disseminating action in the inner sphere, this quadrant describes the nature of community in the family and in the church.[126] The second quadrant, as formed by efficacious action as corrective action in the outer sphere, describes the Christian's role in the state's system of civil justice, the reformation of the state, and conflict between national states.[127] As formed by efficacious action as disseminating action in the outer sphere, this quadrant describes the Christian's role in relation to the state's function of organizing people into a political entity.[128]

The third quadrant, formed by representative action in the inner sphere, is the realm of Christian worship, both in the church and in the wider sense.[129] The fourth quadrant, formed by representative action in the outer sphere, is the realm of Christian action in the general social sphere, including art and play.[130] It is apparent just from the number of pages Schleiermacher devotes to these various quadrants that the two issues which interest him most are Christian action in church education and reformation (over 200 pages, under the rubric of effective-corrective/inner) and Christian action in reforming the state and in inter-state conflict (nearly 300 pages, under the rubric of effective-corrective/outer). All told, Schleiermacher devotes nearly 500 pages to effective action (inner and outer) and 200 pages to representative action (inner and outer).

Schleiermacher expresses a certain arbitrariness about the order in which he chooses to treat efficacious and representative action.[131] Both types of action are present in any actual action of the Christian.[132] Schleiermacher begins with efficacious action in the form of corrective action simply because that type of action marks the temporal beginning point of the Christian life.[133]

### *2. Comparison of the Structure of Christian Ethics with the Structure of Philosophical Ethics*

Schleiermacher intends that the structure of his Christian ethics should be determined purely by the Christian consciousness and not by the general human reason, as is the case in philosophical ethics. Nevertheless, as he himself indicates, the relation between efficacious action and representative action in the Christian ethics is proportionate to the relation between organ and symbol in the philosophical ethics.[134] As we noted in our overview of philosophical ethics, the organizing function of reason is the more active, and the knowing or symbolizing function, the more passive. The same is true with respect to the difference between efficacious action and representative action in that the former, proceeding from the standpoint of the church militant and the consciousness of the antithesis between pain and pleasure, exhibits a restless energy to reform or extend, and in that the latter, proceeding from the standpoint of the church triumphant and the consciousness of the overcoming of the antithesis in a state of happiness or contentment, soaks up its joy and infuses it into human society. In sum, while Schleiermacher prefers to use words in his Christian ethics such as efficacious and representative which can be more readily tied to Christian consciousness than organizing and symbolizing, he could have used the philosophical terms had he so chosen without distorting the structure of his Christian ethics.

The soft-pedaling in Christian ethics of the antithesis in philosophical ethics between the identical or universal and the particular or individual, and the virtual substitution for it of the antithesis between the inward and outward action of the Christian consciousness, is not so easily dealt with as the substitution of efficacious/representative for organizing/symbolizing. For one thing, there is no correlation between universal/particular and inward/outward (or even outward/inward). The two antitheses are different in kind. Inward/outward is peculiar to the church in relation to the other spheres of society. There can be no inward/outward in philosophical ethics since it has the whole human community in view at all times; there is no special community in view which could turn its attention either inward or outward. Therefore, the soft-pedaling of the universal/particular antithesis in the Christian ethics appears to be unrelated to the appearance of the inward/outward antithesis.

Then why does the universal/particular antithesis play such a small role in Christian ethics? The answer has to be that in his Christian ethics, Schleiermacher is not as interested in the moral development of the individual Christian as he is in the general Christian consciousness expressed in the various types of action, in relation to the church first, and then in relation to the state and the other spheres of society. He speaks of the individual (*die einzelne Persönlichkeit*) as the *Durchgangspunkt* by means of which the Christian consciousness is disseminated in the church and the world.[135] Hans-Joachim Birkner cites Wilhelm Dilthey as correct when he says of Schleiermacher in his Christian ethics that no one has foreclosed on the value of the individual will in attaining the goal of humankind more successfully than this man of feeling and individuality![136] Schleiermacher's philosophical ethics, as we have seen, is also not concerned with the individual will *per se*, but it is concerned with the way reason deploys itself to create moral personality. There is no such emphasis in the Christian ethics; therefore, the antithesis between the universal and the particular is extremely subdued.

This lack of emphasis in the Christian ethics on the will of the individual should not be taken to mean that the church performs its actions through its leadership or general assemblies rather than through individual Christians, only that Schleiermacher's emphasis is on the actions of the Christian consciousness taken as a whole. Individual Christians express their own wills only insofar as the

Christian principle indwells them and expresses itself through them. There is room in Schleiermacher's treatment of corrective action in the church for the individual to lead reform in the church, but even in this case, the individual is operating, not out of his or her own will, but out of a more nearly pure Christian consciousness than that dominant in the particular church being reformed.[137]

Thus, for Schleiermacher, the development of Christian personality falls out of Christian ethics in much the same way that a doctrine of virtue falls out of it. The consciousness of Christ and the power of the Holy Spirit operating through it supply all that Schleiermacher feels is needed for the new moral power of the Christian.[138] The closest he comes in the Christian ethics to a concern with the moral development of the individual is in his two formulae for individual action, "Act such that your behavior always resembles the behavior of Christ," and "Above all, act in such a way that you allow yourself to be governed exclusively by the divine Spirit."[139] These two formulae have the same meaning for Schleiermacher and serve to document the point that he sees no need to introduce any further discussion of the moral development of the individual. Hence, there is no need in the Christian ethics for the antithesis between the universal and the particular. The "universal" in the form of Christian consciousness dominates throughout.

## Conclusions

As we now attempt to pinpoint those aspects of Schleiermacher's Christian ethics that lead us to think it is more dependent on his philosophical ethics than he would have us believe, the place to begin is with the antithesis between inward and outward action which is not found in the philosophical ethics at all, yet forms one of the two major antitheses which structure the Christian ethics. This antithesis raises an issue that bears on our argument. Birkner points out that in distinguishing an inner sphere from an outer sphere in the action of the Christian consciousness, Schleiermacher fails to consider the outer sphere widely enough, viz., as the church as the earthly expression of the universal Kingdom of God.[140] This wider sphere is at the core of Schleiermacher's doctrine of the Christian church and is the basis of his contention that the Christian faith is destined to quicken the whole of humanity into the higher life.[141] On this basis, one might expect that the Christian ethics would be a full description of the Kingdom of God as the Christian life in the same sense that the philosophical ethics is a full description of the process of unifying reason and nature as the life of reason. It is not, or, more accurately, it is only partially this. Representative action in the outer sphere might have been intended this way (Schleiermacher says that representative action precedes and is the means of efficacious action[142]), but as Schleiermacher actually works it out, representative action is not fully developed and relinquishes pride of place to efficacious action. Birkner characterizes efficacious action in the inner sphere as essentially a theory of churchly action that succeeds in being a close neighbor to practical theology.[143] I would add that efficacious action in the outer sphere is essentially a theory of the church's impact on societal structures that are already given to it by philosophical ethical analysis. Thus, the Christian ethics is constrained by the philosophical ethics in a way that Schleiermacher does not directly intend, and is thereby hemmed in and prevented from sprouting its own wings, as Schleiermacher does intend, judging from his attention to developing a distinctive Christian ethical methodology.

A second observation is closely related to this judgment. If we ask the question, does Schleiermacher's Christian ethics actually express the Christian consciousness in action, as he intends, the answer is yes within the constraints he has placed upon the Christian consciousness through the structure of his ethics. The constraints, however, are considerable. In his dogmatics, the Christian consciousness is free to express itself through doctrines that best conform to the Christian God-consciousness itself, and free to reject any formulations that do not so conform. Any "constraints," such as those posed by tradition or particular biblical texts, can either be acknowledged or ignored on the basis of political judgment in the church, but do not essentially constrain the Christian consciousness.

Is the idea of the church itself a constraint on dogmatics? In a sense, yes, because the "church," as a religious community called into being by the feeling of absolute dependence prior to any historical modification of it, pre-exists the Christian church and is its external foundation. However, when Jesus Christ founds his church historically, the major aspects of it which carry forward into it from the prior philosophical establishment of the church are the idea of religious community itself and the sense that the primordial feeling of absolute dependence is enhanced in this community. The elements that would be philosophically excluded from Christian faith are a purely individualistic Christianity and a Christianity without feeling. Since, however, the church of Jesus Christ also excludes both possibilities on its own internal grounds, the philosophical constraints on Christian faith are negligible. All other aspects of Christian faith—that it is monotheistic, teleological, and determined by the redemption wrought in Christ—are supplied by the Christian consciousness of Christ as redeemer.[144]

In Schleiermacher's Christian ethics, however, the spheres of human society already identified in philosophical ethics prior to Christian ethics mean that from the outset of Christian ethics, there is already something "there" to modify. Each of these spheres already contains its own ideal within itself, a just state, for example, or freedom of association in social life. Christian ethics has no chance to create its own moral propositions free from the given structures of society it must impact. That is, Schleiermacher makes no attempt in his Christian ethics to describe the universal Kingdom of God in itself, apart from the spheres of life given to Christian ethics by philosophical ethics. This is not necessarily bad, as I will show below, but it does mean that Christian ethics does not take its rise solely from the Christian consciousness without prior constraint. Earlier I drew attention to a problem with the analogy Schleiermacher makes when he says that Christian ethics is related to philosophical ethics as Christian dogmatics is related to rational theology. The problem is that philosophical ethics brings more baggage into Christian ethics than rational theology brings into Christian dogmatics.

Third, if we ask the question, can there be such a thing as a Christian ethics which is completely independent of a prior philosophical ethics, the answer is, probably not, unless one wishes to spin out a purely utopian vision unrelated to common life, or, in theological language, separate redemption completely from creation. Schleiermacher's intuition that Christian ethics cannot contradict an ethics given in and with creation seems correct. Dietrich Bonhoeffer and Karl Barth pushed the idea of a thoroughgoing, christologically based ethics about as far as it can go, and both retreated from a completely independent Christian ethics. Bonhoeffer developed his concepts of "the natural," "the right to bodily life," and "the mandates," which, though ultimately grounded in the Gospel, present themselves to all human beings prior to these concepts' modification by the Gospel. Barth in his doctrine of creation developed his concept of the *analogia relationis*, which gives to human life a structure analogous to the structure of the Godhead, and which provides the external skeleton for Christian ethics to flesh out. The correct question to Schleiermacher, then, would seem to be, to what extent and in what ways does his Christian ethics add to or go beyond his philosophical ethics? That it does so is undeniable, in two ways.

A. Christian consciousness provides the motivation to act in whichever ways ethical analysis determines it should act. Schleiermacher writes, "The recognition of what is pleasing to God is independent of the fact of redemption through Christ, but in this fact Christianity has given assistance, which is not found outside of Christianity, for realizing the God-pleasing action."[145] While Schleiermacher does not say that there is no motivation in philosophical ethics to achieve the good that it describes, he does say that only in and through Christianity will the ideal be realized. Whether Schleiermacher would agree with Joseph Fuchs that Christ does not bring a new, material morality into the world—Schleiermacher says that Christ does bring a new morality into the world, but gives no evidence of what its material content is—he would certainly agree that Christ brings a motivation to attain the ethical ideal that is not present in the world.

B. Schleiermacher's Christian ethics is much more practically oriented than his philosophical ethics. In the philosophical ethics, he establishes, fairly abstractly, a picture of the four (or five) spheres of social life, and a corresponding abstract picture of the perfect equilibrium necessary for making nature the organ and symbol of reason. In the Christian ethics, he has in mind, not only the abstract picture of equilibrium in each sphere, but also the actual ways in which life in the spheres falls short of the ideal. If one were to ask, which specific society does he have in mind, any answer has to be fairly speculative. Of course he has in mind his own Prussian society with its controversy over whether the state should be an absolute or constitutional monarchy (he favored a constitutional monarchy and suffered the consequences for a short period), the Prussian view of the family, the educational system, and so on. But he is never specifically German in his judgments, and I would conclude that his picture of concrete society is inclusive of the Western societies he knows best, viz., his own, French, British, and even American societies. One could conclude without much fear of contradiction that he has in mind post-revolutionary Western society.

It is this picture of actual society that enables him to focus his Christian ethics on actual abuses and actual reforms in civil society. He advocates the abolition of the death penalty.[146] While opposed to wars of aggression as immoral, he allows for defensive war.[147] He rejects violent revolution against an unjust state, but condones gradual reform.[148] There is nothing like this in the philosophical ethics. The question is, could there be? That is, if Schleiermacher had chosen to extend his philosophical ethics to deal with actual situations of abuses in the spheres of society, is there anything other than his personal proclivities which would have prevented him from doing so? The answer appears to be no. Had he so chosen, he could have pulled his philosophical ethics down from the level of abstraction he selected to concrete abuses in the spheres he describes. Why he left it to Christian ethics to deal with such concrete violations of the norms he describes in the philosophical ethics is not easy to understand. The only explanation that seems to make sense is that he did not trust ordinary human reason to muster the power to address the potential abuses it could and did identify. That power, in his view, comes into play only through the advent of Christianity into the world and the creation of new persons guided by the divine Spirit. There appears to be no theoretical reason, however, to prevent philosophical ethics from being as concrete as Christian ethics.

The issues of pacifism and conscientious objection to war deserve a special comment. Schleiermacher, after an extended discussion of the immorality of war, nevertheless finally rejects both pacifism and conscientious objection.[149] There is no need here to comment on the merits of his argument except to say that when faced with the issue of whether to follow the lead of philosophical ethics in explicating justice in the state, or the teachings of Jesus in the Sermon on the Mount, Schleiermacher subordinates the pacifist teachings of Jesus to a conception of justice in the state which he has previously developed in his philosophical ethics. Even while agreeing with Schleiermacher's conclusion that war may sometimes be just, I cannot help but notice the extent to which the philosophical conception of justice overrides the explicit teaching of Jesus to turn the other cheek. Philosophical ethics does indeed infiltrate and influence Christian ethics.

Fourth, I would like to hazard a judgment about Schleiermacher's Christian ethics that has to do with his ongoing wrestling with the ethics of Immanuel Kant. Kant rejects any possibility of a religiously-based ethics on the grounds that in the last analysis religion, with its penchants for fanaticism, superstition, illumination, and thaumaturgy, cannot be brought under the control of reason and is therefore a danger to ethics.[150] Any religious ethics to be valid must essentially be a philosophical ethics expressed in religious language. Schleiermacher, on the other hand, holds to the view that religion as feeling is a distinct category of human thought independent of reason and philosophical ethics.[151] Therefore, there can and must be a religious ethics alongside but distinct from a philosophical ethics. Schleiermacher himself never wrote a general religious ethics, and probably could not have, because he believes that real religion manifests itself only in positive, historical religions, and not directly in reason.[152] The best of the historical religions is Christianity, and it contains within itself an all-encompassing ethics.[153]

Therefore, Schleiermacher's Christian ethics is his main (but not his only) answer to the Kantian contention that there can be no such thing as a religious ethics, Christian or otherwise. How adequately does his Christian ethics meet the Kantian objection? I would say, not especially well, because, as I have attempted to demonstrate, he allows philosophical ethics inordinate intrusion into his Christian ethics. This would have suited Kant fine: the more intrusion, the better. But it does not bode well for Schleiermacher's project to construct a Christian ethics free from philosophical influences. I am not suggesting that Schleiermacher's ethics could be or should be completely free of philosophical underpinnings. As I said earlier, not even Bonhoeffer's or Barth's is, and no Christian ethics can or should be. I am suggesting that Schleiermacher gives away too much to philosophical ethics, and thereby curtails Christian ethics at the outset from establishing its own societal structures.

To put the same criticism in a different way, it could be that in establishing such structures philosophically prior to Christian ethics, he is allowing philosophical ethics to commandeer what belongs essentially to Christian ethics, a possibility he himself foresaw as a real danger.[154] As we said in the first major section of the paper, primordial feeling in its tendency to express itself in action is as much the presupposition of his philosophical ethics as of his Christian ethics. Christian ethics, basing itself on the now more fully developed primordial feeling as modified by Christ to become Christian consciousness, could have encompassed philosophical ethics in such a way as to reveal and demonstrate the primordial religious basis of all ethics.

As the matter stands, however, Schleiermacher uses his philosophical ethics, especially through his understanding of reason, as a vehicle for a partial development of the primordial religious feeling that is the presupposition of both rational ethics and religious ethics. In other words, his philosophical ethics is already partially a religious ethics insofar as Schleiermacher's view of reason is one controlled by his understanding of the idea of God as the *terminus a quo* of all thought and action. This is what makes his rational ethics so different from Kant's rational ethics. There is a softness or flexibility in Schleiermacher's view of reason that does not allow it any privileged access to the *Dinge-an-sich*, as in Kant's ethics. Access to the Real is through feeling, not reason. This is what I meant above when I said Schleiermacher's Christian ethics is not his only answer to Kant's dismissal of religious ethics. Schleiermacher's philosophical ethics is also an answer, for the conception of reason that is operative there already bears the impress of religious feeling even though Schleiermacher has no intention of turning his philosophical ethics directly into a religious ethics.

When he does turn to religious ethics, however, in his Christian ethics, some of his own thunder has already been stolen by his philosophical ethics. The reason which controls his philosophical ethics is a reason both humbled and empowered by the religious feeling that stands as the presupposition of reason. Consequently, it is not surprising that his Christian ethics borrows as heavily as it does from his philosophical ethics since the philosophical ethics already contains elements that belong to a religious ethics.

This mutual interlacing of philosophical ethics and religious ethics seems to me to strengthen philosophical ethics, but weaken Christian ethics. It strengthens philosophical ethics by providing it with a more realistic concept of reason than is usual in rationalistic ethics; it weakens Christian ethics by depriving it of its own claim to present a complete picture of the Christian life, individual and communal, on the basis of primordial religious feeling, now fully developed.

Contemporary Christian ethicists who seek to learn from Schleiermacher's experiment in balancing Christian and philosophical ethics would do well to heed his intuition that the "two" ethics cannot contradict each other. If, as we have suggested, he himself privileged philosophical ethics at the expense of Christian ethics, contemporary ethicists should avoid the opposite mistake, viz., to overload Christian ethics while denigrating "mere" philosophical ethics. Furthermore, in a religiously pluralistic age wherein Christian ethics can no longer be assumed to be the universal ethics of the future, the way is open for the development of a religious ethics based on insights from the several traditions. Even so, the philosophical underpinnings of any such religious ethics should be neither overblown nor under-appreciated.

## Notes

[1]In *Readings in Moral Theology No. 2: The Distinctiveness of Christian Ethics*, ed. Charles E. Curran and Richard A. McCormick (New York/Ramsey: Paulist Press, 1980), 11.

[2]Ibid., 12.

[3]See *Kurze Darstellung des theologischen Studiums zum Behuf einleitender Vorlesungen*, kritische Ausgabe, ed. Heinrich Scholz (Leipzig: A. Deichert, 1910), para. 223. ET *Brief Outline on the Study of Theology*, trans. & ed. Terrence N. Tice, Richmond, Va.: John Knox, 1966. See also the two editions of *Der christliche Glaube nach den Grundsätzen der evangelischen Kirche im Zusammenhange dargestelt* (Berlin: G. Reimer, 1821/22, Studienausgabe, herausgegeben Hermann Peiter, Berlin/New York: Walter de Gruyter, 1984), para. 32, and siebente Auflage, auf Grund der zweiten Auflage, ed. Martin Redeker (Berlin: Walter de Gruyter, 1960), para. 26. ET of second edition *The Christian Faith*, trans. and ed. H. R. Mackintosh & J. S. Stewart

(Edinburgh: T. & T. Clark, 1928), para. 26. Unless otherwise noted, all quotations from the *Brief Outline* and the *Christian Faith* are from the English translations.

[4]*Brief Outline*, para. 231, p. 82. See also *Christian Faith*, para. 29, 2, p. 124.

[5]The theological sciences in general, including dogmatic theology in the broad sense as encompassing both dogmatics proper and ethics, are organized by Schleiermacher under philosophical ethics, which is the category that encompasses all the human sciences. Dogmatics is therefore dependent on philosophical ethics for its terminology, dogmatics proper on the terminology of "rational theology," and ethics on the terminology of a philosophical ethics of duty. See *Brief Outline*, para. 226, pp. 80-81. (Schleiermacher is clear, however, that the use of philosophical, dialectical terminology and strict, systematic arrangement of the subject by dogmatic theology is purely external to the fundamental, Christian principle which drives it. See *Christian Faith*, para. 28, 3, p. 122.)

[6]*Brief Outline*, para. 230, pp. 81-82.

[7]*Christian Faith*, para. 11, 3, p.56; para. 26, 1, p. 111.

[8]Friedrich Schleiermacher, *Christliche Sittenlehre Einleitung: Wintersemester 1826/27*, herausgegeben und eingeleitet Hermann Peiter (Stuttgart/Berlin/Köln/Mainz: W. Kohlhammer, 1983), 20. ET Friedrich Schleiermacher, *Introduction to Christian Ethics*, trans. John C. Shelley (Nashville: Abingdon, 1989), 47. Subsequent references are to the ET unless otherwise specified.

[9]Para. 3, 4, pp. 10-11. The adjective "stirred-up" (*erregte*) signals that Schleiermacher is talking about a feeling that has entered human consciousness, that is, a determinate feeling, and not about the feeling that underlies human consciousness. See para. 4, 3, p. 16.

[10]*Introduction to Christian Ethics*, 46.

[11]Ibid.

[12]". . . The propositions of one discipline must be analogous and homogeneous with those of the other," ibid., 45.

[13]At this point there appears to be no consensus on whether to translate *Dialektik* dialectics or dialectic. Both are standard English words with identical dictionary meanings. I prefer the plural form, dialectics, because it parallels the translation of *Ethik* as ethics, *Physik* as physics, *Poetik* as poetics, *Hermeneutik* as hermeneutics, and so on.

[14]F.D.E. Schleiermacher, *Dialektik (1811)*, herausgegeben Andreas Arndt, Hamburg: Feliz Meiner, 1986, 24. ET of the Jonas text on which Arndt's is based, Friedrich Schleiermacher, *Dialectic or, The Art of Doing Philosophy*, trans. Terrence N. Tice (Atlanta: Scholars Press, 1996), 30. Subsequent references are to the ET unless otherwise noted.

[15]Ibid.

[16]Ibid.

[17]Ibid. *Arten* are contrasted with *Gattungen* (types). The formation of types is a result of knowing employed in its role of concept formation. The formation of kinds is a result of knowing employed in its role of observing. From one perspective, observation and the formation of kinds is prior to concept formation and the formation of types, because a type is created only through kinds. From the opposite perspective, no kinds can be discerned through observation without the concept of types. In "pure knowing," construction and observation belong together, although one can still distinguish between knowing that is predominantly "philosophical," and knowing that is predominantly "historical." Cf. pp. 30-31.

[18]Ibid., 30.

[19]Ibid., 30-31.

[20]F.D.E. Schleiermacher, *Dialektik (1814/15) [und] Einleitung zur Dialektik (1833)*, ed. Andreas Arndt (Hamburg: Felix Meiner, 1988), 54-55.

[21]Ibid.

[22]Ibid., 55.

[23]Friedrich Daniel Ernst Schleiermacher, *Ethik (1812/13)*, herausgegeben Hans-Joachim Birkner (Hamburg: Felix Meiner, 1981), 9. Schleiermacher often uses just physics and ethics to encompass all four disciplines. See also *Dialectic*, 30.

[24]*Dialektik (1814/15)*, 53-54.

[25]*Ethik (1812/13)*, 6. "Die Ethik muss also alles wahrhaft menschliche Handeln umfassen and verzeichnen."

[26]Ibid., 9-10.
[27]Ibid., 31-32.
[28]Ibid., 10.
[29]Ibid., 11.
[30]Ibid., 9.
[31]*Dialektik (1814/15)*, 67-71.
[32]*Ethik (1812/13)*, 14.
[33]Ibid., 6.
[34]Ibid.
[35]Ibid., 6.
[36]Ibid., 16.
[37]Ibid. Schleiermacher's first scientific work on ethics, *Grundlinien einer Kritik der bisherigen Sittenlehre* (Berlin: Realschulbuchhandlung, 1903), deals with the failure of most previous treatments of ethics (especially those of Aristotle and Kant) to integrate successfully the good, virtue, and duty. The putative failure is not just a failure of harmony, but a failure to place virtue and duty under the control of an overall image of the good.
[38]Ibid.
[39]Ibid.
[40]Ibid., 19.
[41]*Brief Outline*, para. 226, p. 81.
[42]*Introduction to Christian Ethics*, 42.
[43]Schleiermacher first spelled out this structure of his ethics in *Brouillon zur Ethic (1805/06)*, herausgegeben und eingeleitet von Hans-Joachim Birkner (Hamburg: Feliz Meiner, 1981).
[44]Ibid., 16.
[45]*Ethics (1812/13)*, 36.
[46]Ibid.
[47]Ibid., 53.
[48]Ibid., 55.
[49]Ibid., 53.
[50]Ibid., 40.
[51]Ibid., 39-40.
[52]Ibid., 46-47.
[53]Ibid., 47.
[54]Ibid., 49.
[55]Ibid.
[56]Ibid., 40-43.
[57]Ibid., 43, 44.
[58]Ibid., 45.
[59]Ibid.
[60]Ibid., 94-107.
[61]Ibid., 95-96.
[62]Ibid., 46-49.
[63]Ibid.
[64]Ibid.
[65]Ibid., 127. Schleiermacher held steadfastly throughout his adult life to the idea of a sphere of pure sociality free from state regulation, yet still a *Gesellschaft*, not a *Gemeinschaft*, as in the church. See, for example, his 1799 essay, "Versuch einer Theorie des geselligen Betragens," which has been translated recently by Jeffrey Hoover as "Toward a Theory of Sociable Conduct," in *Friedrich Schleiermacher's "Toward a Theory of Sociable Conduct" and Essays on Its Intellectual-Cultural Context*, ed. Ruth Drucilla Richardson (Lewiston/Queenston/Lampeter: Edwin Mellen Press, 1995).
[66]Ibid., 64.
[67]Ibid., 65.
[68]Ibid., 69.

[69]Ibid., 67.

[70]Ibid., 107-116.

[71]Ibid., 70.

[72]Ibid.

[73]Ibid., 71.

[74]Ibid., 71-72.

[75]Ibid., 120.

[76]Ibid., 120. Schleiermacher associates temperamental characteristics with different religious communities as follows: Indian: phlegmatic, Greek: sanguine, Jewish: choleric, and Christian: melancholic.

[77]Ibid., 119.

[78]Ibid., 122-123.

[79]Ibid., 33.

[80]Ibid., 33, 31.

[81]Ibid., 32. See also Schleiermacher's extended treatment of sexual differentiation and the family, with which he begins his discussion of the ethical spheres, 81-93.

[82]Redeker, 168.

[83]*Introduction to Christian Ethics*, 42. I prefer "procedure" to the ET's "method" as a translation of *Verfahren* because "method" implies a similarity in methodology which is not present between the two treatments of ethics, while "procedure" implies a similarity of extension and precision that is present in both treatments.

[84]Ibid., 39.

[85]Ibid.

[86]Ibid., 42-43.

[87]Ibid., 42.

[88]Ibid., 52-53.

[89]Ibid. Emphasis mine. I have dealt elsewhere ("Christ's Consciousness and the Christian's Consciousness of Christ in the Ethics of Schleiermacher," *Understanding Schleiermacher: From Translation to Interpretation: A Festschrift in Honor of Terrence N. Tice*, ed. Ruth Drucilla Richardson and Edwina Lawler (Lewiston/Queenston/Lampeter: Edwin Mellen Press, 1997) with the problem of Schleiermacher's ascribing to Jesus Christ perfect God consciousness in the light of Strauss's criticism, and pointed the way to how Schleiermacher's assertion might yet hold up.

[90]The definitive passage in all of Schleiermacher's work regarding the matter of the extent to which he regards the advent of Jesus Christ into the world as a supernatural fact, on the one hand, and the redemption wrought by him as something supra-rational, on the other hand, occurs in *The Christian Faith*, par. 13. An excerpt from pp. 64-66 reads as follows: ". . . [E]ven the most rigorous view of the difference between [Christ] and all other men does not hinder us from saying that His appearance, even regarded as the incarnation of the Son of God, is a natural fact. For in the first place: as certainly as Christ was a man, there must reside in human nature the possibility of taking up the divine into itself, just as did happen in Christ. So that the idea that the divine revelation in Christ must in this respect be something absolutely supernatural will simply not stand the test. . . . But secondly: even if only the *possibility* of this resides in human nature, so that the actual implanting therein of the divine element must be purely a divine and therefore an eternal act, nevertheless the temporal appearance of this act in one particular Person must at the same time be regarded as an action of human nature, grounded in its original constitution and prepared for by all its past history, and accordingly as the highest development of its spiritual power (even if we grant that we could never penetrate so deep into those innermost secrets of the universal spiritual life as to be able to develop this general conviction into a definite perception). Otherwise it could only be explained as an arbitrary divine act that the restorative divine element made its appearance precisely in Jesus, and not in some other person.

[91]Ibid., 65.

[92]Ibid., 67.

[93]*Introduction to Christian Ethics*, 41, 47.

[94]Ibid., 53.

[95]Ibid., 54.

[96]*The Christian Faith*, 63.
[97]*Introduction to Christian Ethics*, 43.
[98]Ibid., 81.
[99]Ibid., 44.
[100]Ibid., 55.
[101]Ibid., 42.
[102]Ibid., 87.
[103]Ibid.
[104]Ibid., 88.
[105]Ibid.
[106]*Brouillon zur Ethik,* 17. Schleiermacher does indeed equate the highest good in philosophical ethics with the Kingdom of God in Christian ethics. This equation is one more way of saying what Schleiermacher repeats often, viz., that through Christian consciousness the union of reason and nature is destined to become complete.
[107]*Introduction to Christian Ethics*, 88-89.
[108]Ibid., 89.
[109]Ibid.
[110]Ibid., 95. How best to translate these two adjectives and the noun *Handeln* is an ongoing, unsettled problem. With *wirksam*, any difference between effective and efficacious (the ET uses efficacious) seems relatively benign. *Darstellend* poses a more difficult problem. Schleiermacher has in mind the action of the church when viewed from the standpoint of the mission of the church fulfilled. Such action "represents" the church in its fullness (one could even say "presents"); it is also "performative," in the sense that the church and the Christian have now left behind reforming action and are expressing the Christian life in its own fullness. The ET uses "self-expressive." The prefix "self" could be attached to any of these words providing it is understood to refer to the church as a whole, as well as to the individual Christian. For the time being, I will use "efficacious" for *wirksam* and "representative" for *darstellend.*
[111]Ibid.
[112]Ibid.
[113]Ibid.
[114]Ibid., 101-103.
[115]Schleiermacher uses two other adjectives (for the most part indiscriminately) to describe corrective action, viz., purifying (*reinigend*) and restorative (*wiederherstellend*).
[116]Ibid., 101-102.
[117]Ibid., 101-102. See also 73-74.
[118]Ibid., 74.
[119]Ibid.
[120]Ibid. See also 102.
[121]Ibid., 102.
[122]Ibid., 78-79. See also 86.
[123]Ibid., 72.
[124]Friedrich Schleiermacher, *Die christliche Sitte nach den Grundsätzen der evangelischen Kirche im Zusammenhange dargestelt*, ed. L. Jonas (Berlin: G. Reimer, 1884).
[125]*Die christliche Sitte*, 97-290.
[126]Ibid., 330-440.
[127]Ibid., 217-290.
[128]Ibid., 440-501.
[129]Ibid., 516-620.
[130]Ibid., 620-705.
[131]Ibid., 107-108.
[132]Ibid., 108.
[133]Ibid.
[134]*Die christliche Sitte*, Beilage A, 63. In this passage, Schleiermacher uses disseminating as a synonym for efficacious, which he often does since philosophical ethics makes no distinction between corrective and disseminating action.

[135]Ibid., 457.

[136]*Schleiermachers christliche Sittenlehre in zusammenhang seines philophisch-theologischen Systems* (Berlin: Verlag Alfred Töpelmann, 1964), 137.

[137]*Die christliche Sitte*, 121 ff.

[138]*Introduction to Christian Ethics*, 91.

[139]Ibid.

[140]*Schleiermachers christliche Sittenlehre*, 111.

[141]*The Christian Faith*, par. 13, 63.

[142]*Introduction to Christian Ethics*, 100.

[143]*Schleiermachers christliche Sittenlehre*, 111.

[144]*The Christian Faith*, par. 11, pp. 52-60.

[145]*Introduction to Christian Ethics*, 51.

[146]*Die christliche Sitte*, 249.

[147]Ibid., 454, 484.

[148]Ibid., 267-269.

[149]Ibid., 280-285.

[150]Immanuel Kant, *Religion within the Limits of Reason Alone*, trans. by Theodore M. Greene and Hoyt H. Hudson (New York/ Hagerstown/San Francisco/London: Harper and Row, 1934), 48.

[151]*On Religion: Speeches to Its Cultured Despisers*, trans. by Richard Crouter (New York/New Rochelle/Melbourne/Sydney: Cambridge University Press, 1988), 101-102.

[152]Ibid., 195.

[153]Ibid., 213ff.

[154]*Introduction to Christian Ethics*, 44.

# SOCIAL ETHICS

# Church Talk in Christian Ethics: Lessons from the Writing of Tex Sample and Robert Wuthnow

*Peter D. Browning*

## Abstract

Christian ethicists writing about the church need to take the contributions of sociology of religion more clearly into account when they develop their theories. Using the work of Tex Sample and Robert Wuthnow, the author criticizes the image of the church as "colony" adopted by Stanley Hauerwas and William Willimon, as well as the model of church as "discipleship of equals" supported by feminist biblical scholar Elisabeth Schüssler-Fiorenza. Neither model of the church attends adequately to various sociological realities in the church, in particular, to the influences of class and social location on church communities and their members.

In his 1990 study, *U.S. Lifestyles and Mainline Churches*, Tex Sample offers a contemporary version of H. Richard Niebuhr's *The Social Sources of Denominationalism* by exploring American church life as it is expressed within the "cultural left," the "cultural right," and the "cultural middle."[1] In Robert Wuthnow's recent work, the diverse cultural locations and practices of public religious life also receive significant attention. Unfortunately, many Christian ethicists writing about ethics from within the perspective of the church frequently write about "the church" as if it were a singular reality. Consequently, they fail to recognize the range of needs, concerns, and issues faced by persons from within these varying sociological classifications. As a result, the adequacy of the Christian ethical visions that they create is significantly reduced.

To offer an illustration of this problem, I wish to explore the church as "Christian colony" vision of Stanley Hauerwas and William Willimon and the church as "discipleship of equals" vision in Elisabeth Schüssler-Fiorenza's recent scholarship. I will contend that, in Hauerwas' and Willimon's case, an understanding of the church standing over and against society is problematic because it tries to create a disconnection from social embeddedness which is neither possible nor entirely appropriate. I will also argue that Schüssler-Fiorenza's vision of church as "liberator" can be problematic when it assumes that all aspects of the church should understand "liberation" in a similar manner.

My contention is that contemporary Christian ethics will be more fruitful if it discusses "the church" in a manner that attends to the kind of sociological classification suggested by the recent work of Sample and Wuthnow. Christian ethics will benefit in at least two ways: a) it will be forced to recognize the concrete challenges that particular communities of faith face as they attempt to embody a Christian vision of the moral life; and b) it will be more attentive to the way in which the language of a theological ethical vision is interpreted differently by particular Christians in distinctive social contexts.

The project is indebted to James Gustafson's sociological study of the church, *Treasure in Earthen Vessels*.[2] In that work Gustafson insisted that the church could not be discussed adequately by giving exclusive attention to doctrines and beliefs. One could understand the church only if one also attended to the church's existence as a human institution located in various human communities. Following Gustafson's concern that theological ethicists write about ethics in the context of actual church life, I wish to contend that Hauerwas and Willimon, on the one hand, and Schüssler-Fiorenza on the other, would contribute more constructively to Christian ethical discourse if their writings focused more on the social locations of churches and church members. When the ecclesiology at the base of a Christian ethic conflicts with sociological knowledge of the ways in which Christians actually live communally, then that ecclesiology and the ethic it articulates should be questioned.

## Illustrating the Dilemma

To begin my discussion, I wish to illustrate the dilemma of social context and the church through reflection on an experience that I had nearly ten years ago. In the late eighties and early nineties, I served in an administrative position at a theological foundation associated with the University of Chicago Divinity School and the Christian Church (Disciples of Christ). As part of my responsibilities, I was a resource person in ethics to the Senate of the College of Ministers in the Illinois-Wisconsin region of the Christian Church (Disciples of Christ). At the time, the Senate was engaged in a study of sexuality. The catalyst for the inquiry was a debate over the appropriateness of ordaining gay and lesbian candidates for ministry.

I attended and helped to lead some of the Senate's discussions of sexuality at meetings that were held around the state. The responses from clergy were wide ranging. Indeed, Illinois Disciples seemed to reflect the full spectrum of the national denomination on the matter of sexuality, in particular, homosexuality. For instance, the congregation where I was a member, University Church, was considered the most liberal church in the Disciples communion and was in support of gay ordination. Located near the University of Chicago, it was an activist congregation which was "open and affirming" on the matter of homosexuality, had a "No Nukes" sign placed above the entrance to the church, and offered sanctuary to an illegally resident Guatemalan family.

Also in the state was the congregationally based office of the conservative renewal movement within the Disciples of Christ denomination, "Disciple Renewal." It was committed to a "Christian Coalition" type of social and political agenda, a campaign to reaffirm the inerrant and inspired authority of scripture, and a renewal of the Disciples denomination through a proposal to assure that all Disciples accepted the theological concept that salvation came through "Jesus Christ *alone*."[3] After attending a meeting in southern Illinois with Senate members, many of whom were rural preachers with more conservative views, a Chicago-area minister and I drove back through the farm roads on our way home. Chatting about the debates while driving through a small town, our eyes were caught by the view of an Amish farmer plowing his field with a team of five horses. We felt as if we had been thrown back momentarily into the last century. And then we saw a town sign. "Lovington," it said, and we smiled, recognizing that it was the headquarters of Disciple Renewal.

The world of Lovington, where the majority of the population knew no one who was openly gay, and the world of academic Hyde Park, where Gay and Lesbian Affirming Disciples (GLAD) had held national meetings, were barely in the same universe. Yet, rural, almost pre-industrial Lovington and urban Hyde Park were all connected through the web of relations called "the church." This experience symbolized for me the incredible power which social location plays in determining how we function as a church and how we function in moral discourse as Christians. When ethicists discuss "the church" as if it were a monolithic reality, I am reminded of the great chasm that separated Lovington and Hyde Park. Moreover, I am convinced that the kind of Christian ethic which they articulate, however creative and insightful, cannot be fully adequate.

While many sociologists of religion and experts in church studies could be relied upon to make the case, I turn to Sample and Wuthnow because their particular contributions have been focussed specifically on the interface between morality and social/cultural analysis. In the commentary which follows, I will begin with the provocative book, *Resident Aliens* and its sequel *Where Resident Aliens Live*, co-authored by Hauerwas and Willimon, and then turn to Schüssler-Fiorenza's study, *Discipleship of Equals: A Critical Feminist Ekklesia-logy of Liberation*.[4] In both cases, it will be suggested that the vision of the church and the approach taken to Christian ethics within the church could benefit from the lessons of Sample and Wuthnow.

## The Addresses of "Resident Aliens"

Few academic books have had the impact that *Resident Aliens* has experienced since its publication in 1989. Hauerwas and Willimon struck a chord with their appeal for a church standing as a "Christian colony" in relation to a world corrupted by materialism, individualism, and relativism. The central thesis of the book is a critique of the accommodationist tendencies of the church in relation to the modern world, together with a call for the church to separate itself from the world for the purpose of training Christians to embody practices of Christian community. The authors condemn the "Constantinian" assumptions that encourage the church to support the state. They also take aim at the church's modernist agenda of striving to make faith language credible to a world ruled by Enlightenment reason. But their greatest wrath is reserved for the church's tendency to support the individualistic ideological assumptions of liberal democracy. Rejecting the efforts of liberal theologians such as Rudolf Bultmann and Paul Tillich to make Christianity intelligible to an unbelieving world, Hauerwas and Willimon insist that Christians should abandon such efforts and instead celebrate the radical alternative to the world's ways which may be found in following the message and practices of Jesus Christ.[5]

The Christian colony they envision is associated with John Howard Yoder's "confessing church" type, which is a third option transcending both liberal "activist" churches and conservative "conversionist" churches.[6] For Hauerwas and Willimon, both the "activist church" tradition of the liberal University Church and the "conversionist church" illustrated by conservative Disciple Renewal are intellectually weak options since they both accommodate reigning ideologies in the democratic state. Liberal activism fails because it reduces the radical message of Christ to a transformation of the secular world via leftist politics, while conversionism is inadequate because it makes faith too privatized and otherworldly.[7]

By contrast, the confessing church, "finds its main political task to lie, not in the personal transformation of individual hearts or the modification of society, but rather in the congregation's determination to worship Christ in all things."[8] By living as a worshipping community, Christians can model a radical alternative to a culture which worships individual choice, power and wealth, and which maintains the status quo through violence. Just as Dietrich Bonhoeffer's Confessing Church community modeled Christian community at a time when the "German Christians" accommodated the ideology of the Nazi state, so the contemporary church must be a worshipping body that models the practices of Christian discipleship and does not give in to the secular and individualistic assumptions of American liberal democracy.[9]

Hauerwas and Willimon call Christians, especially mainline Protestant communities, to reinterpret the meaning of church so that it becomes a radical alternative to an unbelieving world.

> The death of Christendom (still alive in our culture but terminally ill with no hope of recovery) forces each congregation to reexamination. What does it mean for us to live in a culture of unbelief, a culture which does not even know it does not believe because it still lives on the residue of Christian civilization? What does it mean for the pastor to have as his or her job description, not the sustenance of a service club within a generally Christian culture but the survival of a colony within an alien society?[10]

They conclude that it means establishing a Christian community with distinctive disciplines and practices based on faith.

Given their argument, which is intended to transcend and criticize conservatives and liberals, one must ask why attention to sociological distinctions would take anything away from their central message about the church as a Christian colony. Are not all churches in America faced with the same basic choice of living as a Christian community in a world that does not share many of their values (although it might share some)? It is at this juncture that Robert Wuthnow and Tex Sample are helpful. From them I find resources to question the idea of a church as a colony separate from the world. Consideration of their sociological analysis suggests that the colony model fails to take seriously the diversity which emerges from the socially embedded character of all church communities.

Beginning with Wuthnow, two important lessons emerge. They are: 1) the observation that churches "produce the sacred" in a public setting and thus, cannot be disassociated practically or theoretically from that public realm, that is, that members of congregations are so deeply shaped by the visions, practices, tasks and challenges of modern culture that their way of being a church will always in some way embody the larger cultural context in which they find themselves; and 2) that "the western world" from which Hauerwas and Willimon wish the church to distinguish itself is imbued so deeply with values that emerge out of Christian culture that the language of the world as "enemy" used in *Where Resident Aliens Live* is itself an exercise in self-deception.

## Producing the Sacred

First, let us explore the import of the church as a "producer of culture." In his 1994 volume, *Producing the Sacred: An Essay on Public Religion*, Wuthnow makes a claim crucial for understanding the failing in Hauerwas and Wuthnow's thesis. All culture is "produced." The sociological theory of "cultural production" claims that "culture does not simply happen or merely exist but is the outcome of deliberate human activity."[11] Religious culture is no exception. When the church produces the sacred in congregations, denominational hierarchies, special interest groups, the academy, and public rituals, it does so in a public context.[12] As Wuthnow suggests, the environment of the public can be seen through this theory as having only so many resources available to support cultural products, especially when they are embodied in the form of organizations. Thus, there is always an element of competition between religious organizations for the participation of individuals, and that reality unavoidably influences churches to engage in practices that will be accepted, at least minimally, by members and potential members. The church, by definition, must produce its religious culture in some type of public realm to continue as an organization.[13]

In turn, each organizing element of the church interacts with the public in a way that makes discourse about the church far more "residential" than Hauerwas and Willimon's church talk would suggest. For instance, when Wuthnow looks at a congregation, he finds that the worshipping community's size influences its practices and traditions. The small church of less than 100 can more easily function with agreed upon disciplines and with high levels of personal interaction consistent with the colony images that one finds in *Resident Aliens*. When the church reaches 200 to 300 members, it tends to become a family or "program church" with a wider array of educational programs offered and with greater diversity in theological views and social locations. The "mega-church" of 1000 or more members tends to be associated with ministries that target a spectrum of age groups, cultural locations, and particular life problems. Wuthnow notes a statistical likelihood as well for such churches to "[speak] out in ways that may challenge taken for granted social and political norms."[14]

While the church may strive to be a colony, at the very least there will be many different kinds of colonies with distinctive challenges. Small churches are more likely to establish a set of practices that gain the consent and affirmation of the community. When one turns to the mega-church, levels of personal interaction often drop, or, at the very least, become focused into particular sub-groups that then reinforce particular faith practices.

One of Wuthnow's most important points is that, regardless of size or organizational pattern, all churches are faced to some degree with growing plurality within their membership. Wuthnow points to "geographic mobility, the intermixing of ethnic groups, new bases of social differentiation (such as education), changes in the occupational structure, and the effects of mass consumerism and the mass media" as examples of factors that make plurality a given for all Christian worshipping communities in America.[15] Even if Christians train themselves to see with the distinctive eyes of Christian discipleship, they will bring with them such an array of prior cultural experiences and expectations that their very understanding of what constitutes proper discipleship will vary markedly.

When Wuthnow examines the denominational sector of churches, he also sees evidence for a close interrelationship with public life. In *The Restructuring of American Religion*, Wuthnow traces the decline of denominationalism in response to several features of modern society.[16] First, higher education has introduced denominational members to differing social, political, and religious perspectives. One concrete result has been a greater likelihood of the college graduate to marry a person from another denomination.[17] Second, the growth of professionalization has moved persons away from their communities of birth into new religious communities. Third, the tendency for various denominations to be associated with particular classes has diminished as general levels of education between the denominations have become similar. Finally, the ecumenical movement's support of greater dialogue between denominations has led to a greater sense of comfort with and acceptance of other faiths.[18] The sharp borders of denominations have begun to fade.

It is illuminating that in Hauerwas's and Willimon's sequel to *Resident Aliens*, entitled *Where Resident Aliens Live*, they are appreciative of their own roots as Methodists, and yet implicitly encourage other Christians to turn to the resources within their own traditions to obtain "skills of resistance against the powers of our day."[19] At the very least, the non-triumphalist way in which they look at their own Methodist heritage suggests that there are differing Christian colonies in the church and that those differences should, on some level, be respected.

## The "Churchly" Character of the "World"

The other contribution that Wuthnow makes is a richer discussion of the interplay between Christians and "the world" as it emerges in American society's actual values. In *Poor Richard's Principle*, subtitled "Recovering the American Dream Through the Moral Dimension of Work, Business and Money," Wuthnow demonstrates that two primary American attitudes toward work and money emerge directly out of traditions within Christianity.[20] Those attitudes he characterizes as "ascetic moralism" and "expressive moralism."

Ascetic moralism is associated with the Calvinist tradition. It emphasizes obedience to the absolute commandments of God, self-denial for the purpose of glorifying God in the world, and, as Max Weber noted, a "worldly asceticism."[21] In his study, Wuthnow emphasizes that "much of the moralists' concern was directed against the economic consequences of undercommitment, or idleness as it was commonly called."[22] The idolatrous view of work which Hauerwas and Willimon associate with "the world" has its origin connected at least in part to the public embodiment of an historic theological concern.

The same is true of expressive moralism, suggests Wuthnow. A more romantic vision of life, which emphasizes the importance of happiness and self-fulfillment, this view is often associated with the generation of the baby boomers. Instead of pursuing more and more wealth through hard work, it suggests that one fulfill the divine intentions for one's life through self-development and attention to non-economic practices. As Horace Bushnell stated, "We are to conceive that the highest and complete state of man, that which his nature endeavors after, and in which only it fulfills its sublime instinct, is the state of play."[23] Wuthnow sees this expressive commitment as central to the growth of voluntary support groups in American culture, groups that have a tendency to be highly spiritually focused but often directed most to the nurturing of the individual's sense of flourishing and inner peace.[24]

The import of Wuthnow's analysis for our discussion is a suspicion about any difference between the church and the world that is too sharply drawn. The very elements of the American "world" from which Hauerwas and Willimon wish to separate the church grow, in no small part, out of interaction with Christian theological traditions. Cultural reality can never be as separate from the church as the colony model suggests.

## The Cultures of Left, Right, and Middle

If one takes Wuthnow seriously and concludes that all churches will function in the midst of society and that the society in which churches function is not as separate from Christianity in its own practices and ideologies as the "church as colony" metaphor would suggest, then one is left asking the next question. How does the cultural location of particular churches, whether left, middle, or right, affect the claim that the church should be a colony?

At this point, our argument must turn to the writings of Tex Sample. In his volume, *U.S. Lifestyles and Mainline Churches: A Key to Reaching People in the 90's*, Sample suggests that the very theology of Christians is shaped significantly by the social contexts in which those Christians are located. The churches of the cultural left practice what Sample labels a "journey theology." The churches of the cultural right tend to embody "popular religion and folk theology" while the churches of the cultural middle are characterized by an "explanatory theology."[25] Persons in the cultural left tend to see life more in terms of self-fulfillment than self-denial. It is a pattern typical of many baby boomers, who "reacted sharply to the conformism they witnessed in their parents as they grew up" and who tend to be more inner-directed in their life goals.[26] Sample notes that the cultural left has incomes and levels of education above the national average, values tolerance and personal freedom, and generally identifies with political liberalism.[27] The journey theology that they espouse sees Christian faith as a process open to change and development. There is a "persistent mystical, therapeutic, and experimental character of the spirituality."[28] These persons wish to transform the world, but they are especially interested in making sense out of their own lives often characterized by highly tentative commitments.

*Resident Aliens* seems to have this group more in mind than any other cultural identity. For instance, the emphasis on personal freedom and the fear of commitment associated with the cultural left are skewered when Hauerwas and Willimon paraphrase Bernard Shaw to caricature the modern, western world: "Hell is where you must do what you want to do."[29] They are disgusted by the "unquestioned assumption that every human person has the 'right' to develop his or her own potential to the greatest possible extent" because they see such a view as utterly selfish.[30] The result of this modern commitment, according to them, is that we become our own despots.

But the "church as colony" model stumbles ironically precisely because the message that it directs largely against the cultural left and the cultural middle does not encompass all Christians. Indeed, Tex Sample's research into the "cultural right" and the American working class creates a picture of social location not consistent with the implied enemy of *Resident Aliens*. As Sample's research indicates, one of the key components of the working class culture is a "belief in a God who is highly providential and immediately involved in the events of the world."[31] The cultural right does not assume a world of unbelief. Even more important, the cultural right does not embrace the individualism so strongly associated with "the world" that the Christian colony is to condemn. While Hauerwas and Willimon are right to conclude that "modern people usually seek individuality through the severance of restraints and commitments," working class Americans see lack of restraint and failure to maintain commitments as immediate threats to survival.[32]

In Sample's book, *Blue-Collar Ministry*, he outlines the belief system of the working class people he dubs the "Respectables."[33] Individuality and inner-directedness, the values of the cultural left, do not function well in an economic world where one is far more likely to be taking orders than giving them. Moral permissiveness and non-conformity are also shunned because they prove so economically and socially dangerous. Blue-collar respectables tend to be church-going, civic-minded, and respectful of authority because they are aware of how thin the line is between "making it" and not. While *Resident Aliens* and its sequel, *Where Resident Aliens Live*, stress the virtue of obedience and the submersion of the individual ego, the social location of the lower classes in a world that they do not control is one, arguably, where the virtues of disobedience and non-conformity might be far more appropriately taught.

Blue-collar religion, as Sample contends, also embodies a deeper general sense of religious commitment than is the norm among middle-class Christians. While *Resident Aliens* chastises Christians in America for not seeing themselves as "alien" enough, blue-collar and lower-class Christians in this country frequently know just how alien they are. They live in a "winner culture" based on success, and their lives frequently tell them that they are failures. As Sample reminds us, these Americans are often drawn to churches that see themselves as colonies over against culture because it is the one place where they may find themselves affirmed as "on God's side."[34]

At the very least, the virtues which such persons would need to learn and practice in the Christian colony would be different from those that would challenge middle and upper class Christians. Gloria Albrecht makes this point in a more direct fashion in her study, *The Character of our Communities: Toward an Ethic of Liberation for the Church*.[35] In her analysis of Stanley Hauerwas' writings, she finds sin described as the "active and willful attempt to overreach our power."[36] The problem, she contends, is that Hauerwas's ethic

> suggests no distinction in the nature of sin based on the very different historical contexts of a black Christian in a racist United States, or of white affluent men in the United States, or of Christians in the base communities of Central America or in the black churches of South Africa, or of abused women."[37]

Indeed, in her judgment, *Resident Aliens* largely presupposes a white, male, middle class audience. She even contends that the emphasis on self-denial, submission to community authority, and the virtue of obedience is an example of what Sharon Welch describes as "the erotics of domination."[38] "In this form of eroticism, a powerful group satisfies its own emotional needs by humbling itself to an absolute authority."[39]

While Albrecht may be right, Sample's analysis of the middle class leads me to conclude that its social location may not be well represented by the Christian colony model either. In *U.S. Lifestyles and Mainline Churches*, Sample describes cultural-middle religion as a "theodicy of good fortune" which allows the middle class to associate their own social and economic success with God's favor.[40] The message that successful, but also anxious and insecure, middle class Christians yearn to hear is that they are accepted, that their worth is not entirely dependent on their ability to win. But, as Sample contends,

> It is not enough to tell cultural-middle people that they are accepted. Too often they have heard the simplisms of a preacher or teacher that do not move into the texture of their lives and name the demons. The task of explanatory theology is to describe the landscape of career life and then to point the gospel at the place where it can be heard afresh.[41]

When explanatory theology is done well, cultural middle Christians not only feel an interior release from their anxiety; they are also called to reinterpret God's calling for their lives and to develop the disciplines that will allow them to see how they can participate in God's reign within the world.[42] That is, they can move beyond inner healing to a commitment to justice.

The problem with the colony metaphor, when taken to an extreme, is that it does not equip this group to function in the world where they must live and work. Hauerwas and Willimon may contend that this is good; that Christians need to see how odd they really are and how alien the practices of modern society are. Yet one wonders whether the model of a separate colony will be effective in accomplishing its goals when it suggests that the Christian's vocational life lies in a fundamentally separate realm. Indeed, one must ask whether the colony model can be sustained at all in the kind of interactive societal existence that characterizes life for almost all Christians in technological societies.

Summarizing the lessons from Wuthnow and Sample in regard to the "Christian colony," we find, first, that congregations are embedded in diverse cultures reflected within the congregants themselves; second, that the world from which *Resident Aliens* wishes to distinguish the church is imbued with values that have Christian influences; third, that cultural locations of Christians in America create differing needs and theological concerns that make the united colony image questionable; and fourth, that Hauerwas' and Willimon's colony has a middle class social location that does not attend to the differing dynamics of Christians in the "cultural right" and the working class. By describing the church colony as a singular reality, these authors give inadequate attention to the differing church dynamics that emerge from differing sociological influences.

Supporters of Hauerwas and Willimon may suggest that sociological differences among churches really do not matter. Christians will always have to distance themselves from some type of cultural pattern in order to be faithful followers of Jesus. Yet, as this analysis has demonstrated, such a strategy ultimately makes the church as the Body of Christ an overly abstract theological concept. The resulting ecclesiology is inconsistent with the very nature of embodiment that constitutes the church community both in the New Testament and in the lived experiences of congregations. It also contradicts Gustafson's thesis that all discussion of church must include both doctrinal reflection as well as attention to social location and practice.

## Elisabeth Schüssler-Fiorenza and the Discipleship of Equals

Turning our attention to the "Discipleship of Equals" ekklesia-logy articulated by Elisabeth Schussler Fiorenza, it is striking to see how Fiorenza also makes use of the image of a resident alien.[43] As a female Catholic and a German emigrant to the United States, she sees herself as someone living in a church and a society not entirely her own. This alien quality, she believes, conveys the experience of all women within the Roman Catholic community and patriarchal society.

Espousing a feminist ekklesia-logy grounded in a critical theology of liberation, Schüssler-Fiorenza calls for an "emancipatory ecclesial and theological praxis" to transform Catholicism.[44] She distinguishes her ecclesiology from reformist efforts that integrate women into the ecclesial hierarchy without getting rid of it, and she founds the discipleship of equals on Paul's teaching in Galatians 3:27-29 that all are one in Jesus Christ. The neologism "ekklesia-logy" is created because the "ekklesia," or "assembly of the people" includes a fundamentally democratic vision of Christian community which may be contrasted with the hierarchical concept of Lordship communicated in the etymology of the word, "ecclesiology."[45]

At the heart of this ekklesia-logy is a call for an ethics of solidarity to unite women of all classes, races, ethnic identities, and cultural locations. To her credit, Schüssler-Fiorenza recognizes that there is some danger in understanding an ekklesia-logy grounded in solidarity among women. Two traps are to be avoided. One trap is focusing so strongly on solidarity among women as to fail to "problematize but reinscribe the patriarchal divisions of race, class, religion, ethnicity, or sexuality among women."[46] That is, a feminist ecclesiology could create an artificial union among Catholic women which does not attend to the structural patterns of inequality which are not dependent on gender. The second danger is to create an "essentialist equality" that unites women in Christian community but fails to recognize that there will continue to be debate among women in regard to various practical and theoretical concerns.[47] In short, all feminists should not be expected to think alike.

Given this sensitivity to the danger of creating a monolithic "discipleship of equals," one must ask how it is possible to suggest that Schüssler-Fiorenza describes the church as a singular reality and fails to recognize the distinctiveness it has in relation to varying sociological patterns. Certainly, her work is much less vulnerable to such a critique than the writing of Hauerwas and Willimon.

## The Lessons of Wuthnow and Sample

While neither Wuthnow nor Sample has given significant attention to the Catholic communion, their understandings of church sociology and class analysis do make a contribution. In particular, Wuthnow's analysis of special interest groups and Sample's reflection on the division among the cultural groups suggest two vulnerabilities which Schüssler-Fiorenza does not address adequately.

First, Wuthnow's analysis of special purpose groups as a contemporary phenomenon in church and society raises a concern. In *Producing the Sacred*, he explores three consequences of the growth in church organizations which are primarily directed to particular interests. "One of the clearest connotations they contribute to public understanding," he writes, "is that the sacred is fundamentally associated with conflict rather than with compromise, consensus, or reconciliation."[48] Secondly, the disparate agendas of special interest or purpose groups contribute to a sense that the divine realm is "scarcely any different from the rational, means-end, purposive logic that governs other realms of modern society."[49] Finally, Wuthnow notes the tendency for special interest groups to associate the divine with "great causes rather than with other aspects of life."[50] The point one might draw from Wuthnow is not that a feminist ekklesia-logy is lacking in coherence or integrity. It is rather that there is always an internal tension in a special agenda that focuses on one particular group of people while at the same time being designed to speak to all people. Schüssler-Fiorenza would probably respond that the point of a critical feminist theology of liberation is the restructuring of the church in a way which will liberate all persons, yet Wuthnow's concern remains as an important issue to be addressed by any particular ecclesiology of liberation.[51]

Tex Sample's analysis of social location also raises questions for Schüssler-Fiorenza to consider. Sample would locate the discourse of "solidarity" in the discipleship of equals in the context of the cultural left. Taking Sample's research into consideration, one can locate two potential forms of exclusivity in Schüssler-Fiorenza's image of the feminist discipleship of equals. First is the problem that her feminist ethic of solidarity does not clearly attend to the lived experience of the "cultural right" and the working and lower classes. Second is the problem of exclusivity which emerges from the intellectual discourse itself.

As Sample notes in his study, *White Soul*, working class women in America are often highly suspicious of feminism because of their lived experience. Sample is convinced that the reason for this suspicion is

> because [feminism] seems so distant from their lives. She has a better chance of finding the right man who can solve her problems (as unlikely as that may be) than she has to correct the way the system works. She may know far more about this in her bones, in the lived practices of everyday life than anyone else. The very idea that she is going to get work that pays enough for the kids, for housing, for health care, for food, for clothes seems to be the impossible dream. To think that her pay will equal that of a high-paying, traditionally male job is like believing that she could land on the other side of the moon.[52]

Schüssler-Fiorenza believes that a movement of solidarity among women will help such persons become empowered and see new possibilities.[53] Sample's point is that women in the working class do not trust larger movements to free them. If given the choice between the stability, order, and comfort of a patriarchal church tradition, on the one hand, and radical change, on the other, they will tend to accept tradition because their lived experience shows that radical changes are often destabilizing and threatening to their already precarious positions.[54]

The second part of Schüssler-Fiorenza's "discipleship of equals" church model which is problematic for the working class is the rhetoric on which it is based. Feminist discourse operates at a level of intellectual critique which is almost completely foreign to the working class experience. Sample's point is that this alienation cannot be explained solely through the structures of patriarchy, although a critique of patriarchy is entirely appropriate. In *Ministry in an Oral Culture*, Sample offers an insight into the self-understanding of persons in the "traditional/oral culture." Those women and men who are intended beneficiaries of Schüssler-Fiorenza's feminist theology often view feminist discourse with suspicion if not contempt. Sample's research may be used to suggest three recommendations for the kind of rethinking that is required of Schüssler-Fiorenza if her model of church is to be embraced by persons other than members of the "cultural left."

First, Sample reminds us that faith and moral reflection among traditional/oral people is normally "non-critical" in perspective.[55] Oral/traditional persons think in "proverbs, stories, and relationships"; generally, they do not think through "theory, propositions, and discourse."[56] Secondly, oral persons associate critical theories with "experts," and they have learned to distrust experts and to view them as outsiders. Finally, says Sample, "to traditional people there are as many opinions as experts, and they suspect that the reason for such diversity grows from the variety of interests they represent. They know, too, that many experts can't make up their own minds."[57] Schüssler-Fiorenza's ethic of solidarity will require more attention to this very different way of thinking about matters of faith, gender and the church.

Sample's next point is a strategic recommendation. Traditional/oral persons do not want to have their traditions assaulted. Schüssler-Fiorenza makes highly persuasive arguments for ending patriarchy in the Roman Catholic communion. If all persons are children of God, and scriptures themselves can be read to support the inclusion of all persons into ministry, then the continuation of a ministerial tradition which rejects the gifts of some members of the body of Christ is not consistent with a proper understanding of discipleship. However, the fundamental shift in authority and tradition that her model supports would be considered a threat to most working class women.

While Sample does not want to argue that traditional/oral persons will reject all fundamental change, he does want to contend that there is an approach to change which will be different from the model more accepted among the middle class and the highly educated. Change is far more likely to be embraced within oral/traditional culture when it is seen less as a condemnation of past tradition than as an "adding-on" to the tradition.[58] For Schüssler-Fiorenza's discipleship of equals to function, the presentation of the ecclesial change and its implementation will have to be altered dramatically for this group.

Finally, Sample recommends that efforts to communicate issues of justice, such as Schüssler-Fiorenza's church model of equality, be accomplished through the strategies of story telling and through the attitude of loyalty. Traditional/oral thinkers are most likely to change when they can connect a story to their personal lives. To illustrate this idea, Sample recalls a congregational debate he witnessed in a working class community over the issue of homosexuality. While theoretical discourse was going nowhere, from Sample's perspective, the entire discussion changed when a young gay man stood up and asked to give a "testimony." This use of coded language gave him the church members' immediate attention. He went on to tell the story of how his father, upon learning that he was gay, walked to the closet, got out a gun, loaded it, set it down on the lamp table next to his son and then said to the young man's mother, "Come, dear, let's give our son some time by himself" and walked out of the room.[59] The tenor of the congregational debate about this controversial issue changed dramatically after that testimony. The story hit home with their own experiences of troubled relationships between parents and children. For Schüssler-Fiorenza's ethics of solidarity to become a reality, she will need to attend more explicitly to the distinctive ways in which women of different classes think about faith and morality.

Finally, a reading of Sample's study suggests for Schüssler-Fiorenza that her feminist discourse will be persuasive among the working class only if it communicates loyalty to the church. Traditional/oral peoples have a pattern of biblical literalism and unquestioning acceptance of church authority structures attributed to a deep conviction that loyalty is an essential value for integrity. For the blue-collar worker and the lower class, traditions are frequently the only realities and practices which allow persons to cope and survive. Survival is often dependent on loyalties to church, extended family networks and employers. If Schüssler-Fiorenza is to embody a "critical feminist ekklesia-logy of liberation," then she will need to come to terms very explicitly with the persons in the Christian right who are often grounded in the lower-middle and lower classes. For, far from simply being "the enemy," they are the ones who embody a traditional/oral cultural context that must be heard and taken seriously before it can be liberated.

## Conclusion

In conclusion, both images of church explored in this paper have been demonstrated to have limitations when viewed from the perspective of sociologists of religion Robert Wuthnow and Tex Sample. Evidence has been presented to suggest in the case of the church as "Christian colony" metaphor that it fails to attend adequately to the social embeddedness of all Christian communities. Wuthnow's theory of cultural production was used to suggest how such embeddedness in public life occurs, and his theory of the Christian origins of much ideology and practice was explored to give further evidence of the interrelationship between church and society. Sample's cultural analysis was also employed to show how the virtues emphasized in *Resident Aliens* and *Where Resident Aliens Live* are more appropriately directed to the middle class and the cultural left than to the working class and the cultural right.

In the analysis of Schüssler-Fiorenza's "discipleship of equals" church model, concerns were raised about the applicability of this ecclesiology to all persons, regardless of class, in spite of Schüssler-Fiorenza's clear effort to consider class differences. Wuthnow's analysis of the patterns associated with special interest groups was examined to suggest an inner tension between her ecclesiology's focus on women and her goal of including all persons. In addition, Sample's arguments about the approach to faith and morality exhibited by Christians within traditional/oral culture also suggested the need for a differing discourse about feminism among the working class.

The result of this investigation is the conclusion that the visions of church in the theology and ethics of *Resident Aliens* and *Discipleship of Equals* would be enhanced by attending more precisely to the role of social location among Christian communities. While both the "colony" and the "discipleship of equals" metaphors for the church have power, they face difficulties when they are examined in light of studies in the sociology of religion.

In his 1966 study, "Man - In Light of Social Science and Christian Faith," James Gustafson reflected on the unavoidable influences of society on Christian behavior. As he warned,

> Christians are often likely to assume that their behavior is governed by their trust and loyalty to Jesus Christ, when the larger part of it is actually determined by their relationships to parents and to social groups. They are likely to assume that in faith they are freed from bondage to their personal histories, to ideologies and groups, when in actual behavior they are not.[60]

Gustafson's warning is just as relevant today for Christian ethicists and theologians who would create a vision of the church which fails to take seriously the inherent embeddedness of all church communities in cultures. A Christian colony metaphor can be a powerful source of renewed identity yet it can also be an invitation to drape one's own cultural assumptions in the cloth of the sacred. Similarly, the rhetoric of liberation and equality may be the occasion for blindness to the ways in which one's own theological commitments represent a particular cultural and class location.

Noting these limitations is not to dismiss or denigrate the richness of the theological insights represented by Hauerwas and Willimon and Schüssler-Fiorenza. Rather, they are offered for the purpose of aiding those theologians in re-examining and refining their models. In volume one of *Ethics from a Theocentric Perspective*, Gustafson articulates his conviction that "human experience" must have a priority in theological ethics.[61] Reflecting on the powerful influence of communities on the lives of all Christians, he claims that "there is no point at which one leaps to a fictive community of persons and ideas that are not in part determined by any community."[62] It is precisely this message which needs to be remembered. For the colony or the discipleship of equals to embody the lived world in which all Christians must make moral decisions, these images of the church must move from the realm of "fictive community" to the reality of actual churches struggling to give faithful witness *in* the world. As the opening narrative of this essay suggests, the social locations of Lovington and Hyde Park will always have dramatic consequences for the practices and visions which their church communities sustain. Any ecclesiologies which fail to acknowledge or allow an account of such influences will be the worse for the omission.

## Notes

[1]Tex Sample, *U.S. Lifestyles and Mainline Churches* (Louisville, Westminster/John Knox Press, 1990) and H. Richard Niebuhr, *The Social Sources of Denominationalism* (New York: Meridian Books, 1957).

[2]James M. Gustafson, *Treasure in Earthen Vessels* (Chicago: The University of Chicago, 1961). Originally published by Harper & Brothers.

[3]This final theological issue was of great concern to the region since it was the centerpiece of a stormy conflict at one of the regional assemblies during this period. While advocates did not win their battle at the regional assembly, Disciple Renewal became a very well known group and launched a conservative renewal campaign across the Disciples denomination.

[4]Stanley Hauerwas and William Willimon, *Resident Aliens* (Nashville: Abingdon Press, 1989) and *Where Resident Aliens Live* (Nashville: Abingdon Press, 1996); Elisabeth Schüssler-Fiorenza, *Discipleship of Equals: A Critical Feminist Ekklesia-logy of Liberation* (New York: Crossroad Publishing Company, 1993).

[5]Hauerwas and Willimon, *Resident Aliens*, 19-24.

[6]Ibid., 45-46. For Yoder, see John Howard Yoder, "A People in the World: Theological Interpretations," *The Concept of the Believers' Church*, ed. James Leo Garrett, Jr. (Scottsdale, PA: Herald Press, 1969), 252-83.

[7] Ibid., 45.

[8]Hauerwas and Willimon, *Resident Aliens*, ibid.

[9]For a more complete analysis of the role which worship plays in Hauerwas's theory of Christian ethics, see *In Good Company: the Church as Polis* (Notre Dame: University of Notre Dame Press, 1995), "The Liturgical Shape of the Christian Life: Teaching Christian Ethics as Worship," 153-68.

[10]Hauerwas and Willimon, *Resident Aliens*, 115.

[11]Robert Wuthnow, *Producing the Sacred: An Essay on Public Religion* (Urbana and Chicago: University of Illinois Press, 1994), 21.

[12] Ibid. These six categories are each given chapter length analysis in Wuthnow's study.

[13]For a detailed account of the struggles which many churches face as attendance shrinks and donations do not keep up with inflation, see Robert Wuthnow, *The Crisis in the Churches: Spiritual Malaise, Fiscal Woe* (New York: Oxford University Press, 1997).

[14]Ibid., 52. For a discussion of these three forms of congregational life, see 50-53.

[15]Ibid., 65.

[16]Robert Wuthnow, *The Restructuring of American Religion* (Princeton: Princeton University Press, 1988).

[17]Ibid., 90.

[18]Ibid., 93.

[19]Hauerwas and Willimon, *Where Resident Aliens Live*, 106. I see this implicit acceptance of other approaches in the reference to the existence of traditions beyond Methodism that could provide the resources necessary to develop skills to live faithfully and to resist modern culture.

[20]Robert Wuthnow, *Poor Richard's Principle* (Princeton: Princeton University Press, 1996).

[21]Max Weber, *The Protestant Ethic and the Spirit of Capitalism*, trans. by Talcott Parsons (London: Unwinn Paperbacks, 1985) [originally published in 1904-5], 95.

[22] Wuthnow, *Poor Richard's Principle*, 64.

[23]Ibid., 71. See Horace Bushnell, *Work and Play* (London: Alexander Strahan, 1864), 7.

[24]For an in-depth analysis of support groups, which now have the participation of 40% of American society, see Robert Wuthnow, *Sharing the Journey: Support Groups and America's New Quest for Community* (New York: The Free Press, 1994).

[25]Sample, *U.S. Lifestyles and Mainline Religion*. For a discussion of "journey theology" see 45-56; for an analysis of "popular religion and folk theology" among the cultural right, see 83-98 and for an analysis of "explanatory theology" see 123-138.

[26]Ibid., 9.

[27]Ibid., 25-28.

[28]Ibid., 47-48.

[29]Hauerwas and Willimon, *Resident Aliens*, 33.

[30]Ibid.

[31]Ibid., 85.

[32]Ibid., 64.

[33]Tex Sample, *Blue-Collar Ministry* (Valley Forge: Judson Press, 1984), 71-83.

[34]Tex Sample, *U.S. Lifestyles and Mainline Religion*, p. 90.

[35]Gloria Albrecht, *The Character of our Communities: Toward an Ethic of Liberation for the Church* (Nashville: Abingdon Press, 1995).

[36]Ibid., 99.

[37]Ibid.

[38]See Sharon Welch, *A Feminist Ethic of Risk* (Minneapolis: Fortress Press, 1990), 112.

[39]Albrecht, *The Character of Our Communities*, 128.

[40]Sample, *U.S. Lifestyles and Mainline Religion*, 13.

[41]Ibid., 133.

[42]Ibid., 134.

[43]Elisabeth Schüssler-Fiorenza, *Discipleship of Equals: A Critical Feminist Ekklesia-logy of Liberation* (New York: Crossroad Publishing Company, 1993), p. 335.

[44]Ibid., 63.

[45]Ibid., 196.

[46]Ibid., 345.

[47]Ibid.

[48]Wuthnow, *Producing the Sacred*, 98.

[49]Ibid., 99.

[50]Ibid., 100.

[51]For an exploration of the way in which Catholic feminist and progressive special interest groups function, see Kathleen M. Joyce, "The Long Loneliness: Liberal Catholics and the Conservative Church," *"I Come Away Stronger:" How Small Groups are Shaping American Religion*, ed. Robert Wuthnow. (Grand Rapids: William B. Eerdmans Publishing Company, 1994), 55-76.

[52]Sample, *White Soul: Country Music, the Church, and Working Americans* (Nashville: Abingdon Press, 1996), 105.

[53]Schüssler-Fiorenza, *Discipleship of Equals*, 314.

[54]Tex Sample, *Ministry in an Oral Culture: Will Rogers, Uncle Remus, and Minnie Pearl* (Louisville: Westminster/John Knox, 1994), 7.

[55]Ibid., 30.

[56]Ibid.

[57]Ibid., 33.

[58]Ibid., p. 55.

[59]Ibid., 63.

[60]James Gustafson, "Man-In Light of Social Science and Christian Faith," reprinted in Gustafson's collected volume, *Theology and Christian Ethics* (Philadelphia: United Church Press, 1974), 205.

[61]James Gustafson, *Ethics from a Theocentric Perspective: Volume One: Theology and Ethics* (Chicago: The University of Chicago Press, 1981), 115-29.

[62]Ibid., 128.

# Ebonics as an Ethically Sound Discourse: A Solution, Not a Problem

*Cheryl A. Kirk-Duggan*

## Abstract

During 1996-1997, between the OJ Simpson criminal and civil trials, the media needed a sensational topic. They discovered "Ebonics." The Oakland, California School Board's resolution declaring "Ebonics" a language triggered controversy and condemnation. This essay explores ethical implications for the pedagogical use of Ebonics from a Womanist perspective, as a vehicle of empowerment. After defining Womanist thought, I explore: (1) the history of Ebonics and the Oakland School Board's concerns; (2) the impact of Ebonics on student and teacher authority; (3) the hermeneutics and ethical issues surrounding Ebonics; and (4) how using Ebonics empowers or marginalizes teacher and student.

During the 1996-1997 school year, between the O.J. Simpson criminal verdict and the O.J. Simpson civil trial, the media needed a new and sensational African American topic. The media discovered "Ebonics." The Oakland, California School Board had adopted a political resolution declaring "Ebonics," an inner city African American speech system, to be a separate language, and sought bilingual treatment for those students versed in Ebonics who were not fluent in Anglo-American [Standard] English. The Oakland School Board's act triggered an immediate nationwide controversy and the school board's action was castigated by people who had never heard of Oakland, California, or Ebonics.

We use language to empower or to undermine, to communicate, using sounds, words, gestures, signs, and symbols. We inform, compliment, and educate, or we kill, annihilate, and destroy, via language. Pedagogues do not own Uzis or AK 47s, but they have the means to assassinate people's character, malign their ideas, and destroy their self-esteem, through an accessible, dangerous weapon: language. But language does not have to be used as a weapon; it can also be used as a tool of empowerment. The pedagogical use of the language of Ebonics is a political question that raises questions pertaining to issues of authority, culture, accountability, and power.

From a *Womanist* perspective, this essay explores ethical implications of the pedagogical use of Ebonics as a vehicle of empowerment. Womanist ethics, a constructive praxis, analyzes and critiques human individual and social behavior and aims at discerning the good. In particular, it investigates the ramifications of injustice and malaise due to the triple oppressions of racism, classism, sexism, and moves for change, balance, and promise. A Womanist emancipatory ethic behooves us to make accurate assessments of the facts regarding the Ebonics controversy.[1] After defining Womanist thought, I explore the issues and views of advocates and opponents related to: (1) the history of Ebonics and the Oakland Unified District School Board's concerns; (2) the impact of Ebonics on student and teacher authority; (3) the hermeneutics and ethical issues surrounding Ebonics; and (4) how using Ebonics empowers or marginalizes teacher and student.

*Womanist*, derived by Alice Walker from the term "womanish,"[2] refers to women of African descent who are audacious, outrageous, in charge, and responsible. The term Womanist refers to a Black feminist who takes seriously the dynamics of gender, race, and class. Womanist Theory focuses on these multiple oppressions and the use of power in American society amid personal and societal fragmentation. Womanist Thought intentionally creates forums where one makes visible African American women's experience. Womanists expose the cruelty they encounter in society and commit to the survival, wholeness, and health of all people. I am a Christian Womanist: I am a Womanist story teller and performer with faith in the Christian story, who is ethically concerned about creating new avenues of possibility and communal solidarity. Consequently, my use of Womanist Theory embodies reformation. This view of reformation confronts the many complex ethical issues of individual and communal daily life and social justice issues in forwarding a vision of life that champions immediacy and inclusivity. A Womanist vision searches for a way to champion the freedom, dignity, and justice of *all* people.

## Ebonics Defined

The term Ebonics was coined by a group of African American scholars, led by psychologist Robert L. Williams, at a conference, "Language and the Urban Children," in St. Louis, Missouri, in January, 1973. Ebonics is a concatenation of two terms, **Ebony** (black) and **Phonics** (sounds). Ebonics pertains to Black sounds: the linguistic, verbal and non-verbal (e.g., sounds, gestures, cues, rhythms) features that blend the communicative capability of the West African, Caribbean, and United States slave descendants of African ancestry, including varied idioms, *patois*, and social dialects of Black people, in response to slavery and colonialism.[3] The terms African American Vernacular English, Black English, Black English Vernacular, Black Vernacular English, and Ebonics, are synonyms. As Geneva Smitherman notes, Ebonics allows "for [the] decolonization of the African American mind . . . repairing the psycholinguistically maimed psyche of Blacks in America."[4] Ebonics is spoken in various forms and comes out of the African American Oral Tradition (hereafter AAOT). This oral tradition is a synthesis of African, particularly West African, and European, particularly English, language-cultural traditions. While the words used in AAOT can often be identified as words of Standard English or the Language of Wider Communication in the United States, the *meanings* of the words in AAOT are often different. The distinctiveness of Ebonics, or Black Language, derives from certain word combinations that form grammatical constructions and particular AAOT idioms of speech.[5]

This AAOT language system shapes the home linguistic environment of many Black children, where Standard English is not dominant. Noted scholars such as Carter G. Woodson (1933), Melville Herskovits (1940), Lorenzo Turner (1973), and Aisha Blackshire-Belay and Karen Crozier (both in 1996) posit that Ebonics is not an English dialect. Ebonics advocates claim that Ebonics is an African language system that has adopted European words and has retained a canonical shape of using Niger-Congo African language nuances. For some opponents, Ebonics is thought to encompass poor enunciation or grammar, including the apparent non-use of the verb form, *to be*. For Africologists, such constructions are not the result of an omission, dropping, deletion, or reduction. Final consonants, the patterns of double consonants or consonants with many vowels, and the use of the verb *to be* do not exist in African language systems. As opposed to noun and verb phrases, African language systems tend to have topic and comment components. Thus "That teacher she ugly!" in Ebonics is correct: the topic is "teacher," the comment is "she ugly." In Ebonics, the implied verb form "be" has an existential and ontological setting, that is, an essential mode of being and acting in the present, past, and future time. In Ebonics, "be" also connotes a habitual or recurring state of affairs.[6]

Ebonics is a different language system and thus, the use of it is not indicative of a cognitive disorder. Dialectal variances of English are functional, effective forms of English that serve as vehicles of communication and social solidarity, maintaining an interactive network and social fabric of the community of speakers who employ these language systems. Difference is not synonymous with pathology or disorder. A Latino who uses Spanish words or phraseology or sentence structure in an Anglo-American setting is not suffering from a cognitive disorder. Language use is disordered or defective when one's skills register lower than one's peers. Students with disorders need competent assessment and compassionate attention. Students without disorders should not be placed in speech therapy or special education, for such a placement marks these children for system-wide educational failure, and lowers their self-esteem.[7]

Ebonics celebrates respect and honor, and uses patterns and speech acts that include but are not limited to (1) a *Call and Response* strategy of antiphonal rhythmic speech acts; (2) *Signifying or Signification*, where speakers either use exaggeration, indirection, or irony to evoke ritualized insults or coded messages; and (3) the *Dozens*, a species of signifying wherein the one signified usually is a person's mother, for example, "yo' mamma so ugly Animal Control use her face to capture strays." Signifying can focus on a person, thing, or action either for fun or for corrective critique. Signifying avoids giving a direct answer and is useful, for example, as a way of telling someone to mind their own business; it involves humor, spontaneity, creativity, and exaggeration. Both Jesse Jackson and Maya Angelou, who derided the Oakland school board for its Resolution to use Ebonics, have skillfully used Ebonics—Jackson in sermons, and Angelou in her poetry, particularly her 1971 poem, "The Thirteens Black."[8]

Many studies have documented the existence, systematic tenets, and dynamics of Ebonics, including James A. Harrison's study on "Negro English" and Lorenzo Dow Turner's *Africanisms in the Gullah Dialect*.[9] Turner reported 6,000 words of direct African origin, for example, the familiar American English words, "gorilla," "gumbo," "jazz," "tote," and "cola."[10] Ebonics analysis continued with the efforts of White scholars, particularly William Labov, in his "The Study of NonStandard English," 1972. Simpkins and Simpkins began a research project, "Bridge," to take students from Black Vernacular to Standard English. The project involved 14 teachers, 27 classes, and 540 students, in the form of control and experimental groups in five areas (Macon County, Alabama; Phoenix, Arizona; Washington, D.C.; Chicago, Illinois; and Memphis, Tennessee) over four months. The results showed an increase of 6.2 months in student-reading ability, whereas the control non-Bridge group only gained 1.6 months in their reading ability. Bridge was never implemented because many Black leaders opposed the idea.[11]

If one establishes language kinship systems based on vocabulary, grammar rules, and historical origins, and defines grammar as the semantic, morphological, phonological, phonetic, and syntactic systems of a language, then as Janheninz Jahn notes, "[t]hose who believe that Black America's language is a dialect of 'English' have not documented the existence of a single Black dialect in the African Diaspora that has been formed on an English grammar base."[12] Since there is no hybrid dialect, etymology, or vocabulary invented by English-speaking European peoples based on Niger-Congo African languages grammar systems, so-called Black English has never existed. Though the etymology for Standard English stems from Romance or Latin language families, Standard English is classified as a West Germanic language. Since the English lexicon largely comes out of Latin and French, the logical dialect of Africans in America is more accurately Black French or Black Latin.[13] Whatever the origins, African American children are taught that they have a public and a private face; and different languages help animate the two distinct personas. The metaphors of "quiet grace," "invisible dignity," and "unshouted courage" that Katie Cannon uses to critique the life and work of Zora Neal Hurston embrace the visible yet invisible, the spoken yet silent, and the present yet hidden experiences of many African American children as they negotiate public and private sectors.[14]

Public and private discourse often converge in the home communal experience. Students learn about responsibility and the interrelationship of language, power, and identity. They learn, for example, that mastering Standard English language may transform the lived reality of Black folk.[15] Coming out of environments where the entire Black community wanted children to receive an education, many African American students, growing up in segregated America, with segregated schools, prior to the 1960s Civil Rights Movement, knew that mastery of Standard English language would transform their unpleasant reality. African Americans learned to cope with the hardships associated with living in segregated America, and they began to recreate themselves. But such adaptations did not entail giving up their home language or their culture. Ebonics is a medium of artistic and creative expression for African Americans. The Oakland School Board's decision to recognize Ebonics as such a language and culture points to the School Board's concern for its African American children, who constitute over 50% of the children in the Oakland School District.[16] Many speakers who use Ebonics and Standard English bidialectically need to justify their choice; many who are uncomfortable speaking Ebonics are defensive and protective of who they are as members of the African American community.[17] The Oakland School Board's decision gives African American students flexibility in communicating in both public and private spheres.

Earl Ofari Hutchinson argues that championing the introduction of Ebonics into the classroom is a counter-productive measure that assumes that Black students cannot learn like White students, and which becomes a self-fulfilling prophecy, putting many Black students at risk.[18] He says that to posit that Ebonics is the home language of most Blacks is to accept unsubstantiated cultural and educational assumptions and stereotypes. The notion that Ebonics will assist Black students in learning Standard English, he further suggests, is an absurd and dubious one, supported only by anecdotal evidence and inconclusive studies of other bilingual educational practices. Conversely, he notes that African Americans, like Anglo ethnic groups in Appalachia, New England, and Texas, use a continuum of language communication styles. Hutchinson refutes the notion that conclusive proof exists for positing Ebonics as a distinct language system. He contends that no credible study has been cited by Ebonics advocates to justify their premise that the use of Ebonics occurs among 80 percent of the Black population. Hutchinson maintains that Ebonics supporters fail to explain how generations of Black students have mastered Standard English without Ebonics as a second language instruction. Hutchinson suggests that the greatest irony is that if any persons of European decent had devised an Ebonics program they would have been dubbed racists.[19] Hutchinson's rationale can lead to enhancing the public's belief in the mental and social inferiority of African Americans, as well as the public's belief in instability of African Americans and their tendency to be uneducated, uncooperative, and crime-prone.[20] While Hutchinson's argument may seem persuasive, the Oakland School Board did not assume that Black children cannot learn, nor did it assume that Black students are chronic failures. In fact, many elementary school teachers have successfully used Ebonics in their classrooms. Further, Hutchinson does not offer an alternative plan for transforming the troubled school system. Hutchinson is not alone.

John McWorter, a linguist, argues that to name Black English as a barrier that prohibits children learning Standard English is a misidentification, because Standard English and Ebonics are not different enough from one another. McWorter attributes the substandard education and the mental poverty of the Oakland students to inner city chaos, ill-prepared students, under-funded American schools, and abysmal pedagogical efforts. He argues against giving much credence to the African influence on Ebonics and argues that even if such a program were adopted, the outcome would barely make a dent in the plight of African American children. McWorter posits that most of the non-structured features of Black English can be traced to the exposure of African slaves in America to the dialects spoken by the British settlers. He critiques the poor composition of the Resolution, and argues that a Black Nationalist sentiment, which embraces an anti-intellectual spirit, fuels the Oakland School Board's Resolution. Consequently, money should not be funneled into an Ebonics program, "[f]or this brand of pernicious nonsense to be extended to seven-year-olds should be chilling to all thinking people."[21]

Womanist ethics can assist in understanding and unpacking this issue. In view of the oppressions of race, class, and gender, it is an ethic that desires emancipation: a call to women and men together to mentor and to provide hope for all marginalized people. The Oakland School Board's agenda was to create an emancipatory pedagogy around language for the students they were charged to teach. The fortitude to take on such a challenge embodies the Womanist ethical commitment to a new moral vision, one that identifies the concrete moments of oppression, analyzes the context and the lived dynamics of the oppressed, and clarifies options for solidarity and strategies for action.[22]

## The Oakland School Board's Concerns

Thirty African American task force participants and teachers, community activists, and school board members met for about six months to wrestle with the problem of the low performance and under-achievement of their African American students. African American students scored a 1.8 grade point average, while the mean was 2.4 for the District. They comprised 71% of the special needs cases, and 80% of the suspensions, but only 53% of the actual student population.

The task force was also intrigued by the above-average performance of the African American Prescott Elementary School students, the only Oakland district school where most of the teachers voluntarily chose to take part in the Standard English Proficiency Program (SEP). SEP "acknowledges the systematic, rule-governed nature of Black English" and assumes the use of language "to help children learn to read and write in Standard English."[23] The SEP model, based on culture, literacy, and language, sees Ebonics as a respected second language, not as a dialect or as bad English. The focus on content, speech, and culture in the Oakland SEP program helps teachers and students to enhance their reading achievement, featuring nine components of African American life experience: spirituality, resilience, humanism, communalism, verbal and oral expressiveness, personal uniqueness and style, emotional vitality, rhythm and musicality, and realness. The primary aim is to experience and respect Ebonics as many students' home language, and in the process to use techniques and strategies that will move them to competent skills using the English language.

On Dec. 21, 1996, the Oakland School Board unanimously passed an Ebonics Resolution, accompanied by the "Policy Statement of Oakland School Board," which required all district schools to participate in SEP as one part of a broad strategy to improve African American students' performance.[24] The Oakland Resolution on Ebonics claimed that "persuasive evidence" confirms the existence of "genetically based" patterned grammatical African American speech. Some states, unlike California, have recognized the beneficial "unique language structure of African American pupils," especially the *Federal Bilingual Education Act* (20 U.S.C. 1402 et seq.), which orders local educational agencies to develop programs for students with "limited [Standard] English proficiency."[25] Such a project was warranted because the Oakland School District wanted to provide equal opportunities for all students with limited English proficiency, to remedy the low standardized test scores of African American students in language arts and reading, and to certify and adequately compensate teachers and aides in these programs. The action taken included: (1) recognizing the cultural basis of Ebonics; (2) adopting the report and policy statement; (3) designing the "best possible academic program for teaching" African American students "in their primary language;"[26] (4) funding; and (5) monthly assessment procedures. The Policy Statement recommended that all African American children master the reading, writing, and speaking of Standard English as an outcome. The Board adopted the Resolution on January 21, 1997.[27]

Twenty years earlier, Michigan had faced a similar challenge. In the 1979 "Black English Case" in Ann Arbor, Federal Judge Charles Joiner ruled for the plaintiffs and noted that "the school had an obligation to teach Standard English reading and writing skills using approaches that would "take into account [students'] indigenous language patterns."[28] As in the Oakland debate, the justification for this ruling rested on Judge Joiner's consideration of the way in which people actually hear, interpret, and communicate. As in Ann Arbor, in

Oakland the objective was to increase student proficiency in speaking Standard English. As a result of misunderstandings and poor media reporting, however, the issue of whether or not Ebonics was appropriate to use in the classroom overshadowed the more important issue of how best to develop students' Standard English speaking skills. In response to the Ann Arbor ruling and the Oakland Resolution, there was tremendous resistance by whites, and even more resistance by those African Americans who did not want to accept the notion that African American children were not capable of learning to speak correctly and read like other children. Ebonics opponents were concerned that the sanctioning of Ebonics would indicate to Black children that they would not be expected to learn Standard English. What opponents of both the Ann Arbor ruling and the Oakland resolution do not acknowledge is the value of teachers becoming sensitive to the role that Ebonics plays in many African American students' ability to communicate. Opponents of these measures fail to consider the possibility that the retention of Ebonics might be conducive to African American students becoming more fluent in Standard English.

The first step under the Oakland Black Language/Ebonics Resolution was to sensitize teachers so that they could learn how "to use the rich and varied linguistic abilities of African American children to help them become fluent readers and writers."[29] Despite the difference in demographics and time, the Oakland initiative closely paralleled the Ann Arbor School Board case, where 66% of the African American children, in an affluent, liberal, college town, were categorized as special needs cases.[30] In response to the dire situation, Carolyn Getridge, the President of the Oakland School Board, argued that the School Board ought to develop potent instructional pedagogical strategies to make sure that every child had the chance to achieve Standard English language proficiency. The disproportionately low numbers of African American students in Gifted And Talented Programs compared to the high numbers of African American students in special education programs, in addition to the dismal statistics regarding African American student graduation, were "mind-numbing" and a cause for "moral outrage."[31] A more constructive attitude towards reform was desperately needed.

An attitude of embracing Ebonics would create a healthy sense of identity and self-esteem, which could move students toward being proficient in Standard English, a goal that most educators and their critics would agree is desirable. If the goal of education is to impart knowledge, then it makes sense to use Ebonics as part of the strategy to speak to children so that they can listen well and make them proficient in Standard English. This common goal of helping the children, with the goal of increasing the numbers of African American children in the Gifted and Talented Programs and reducing the numbers assigned to Special Education classes was lost amid the controversy. Part of the difficulty concerned those African Americans who are ashamed of their own Ebonics heritage, who regard Ebonics as a mark of inferiority. Another difficulty pertained to student resistance by other African Americans who perceive speaking Standard English as a betrayal or "steppin' up." Whereas "stepping up," in Standard English, means to advance or improve, in Ebonics, "steppin' up" describes someone who is disrespectful and challenging to one's peers. The Ebonics Resolution was deemed a way to advance and empower African American students by using the home language familiar to most of them to enhance their experience and celebrate both modes of communication, providing a well-rounded education.[32] One Oakland teacher avoids the "fix-the-something-that-was-wrong" approach, and works on difficult issues with the entire group.

Oakland teacher Carol Street explains to her students when it is appropriate to use Ebonics and when it is appropriate to use Standard English. She has students read something written in Ebonics by Langston Hughes or Paul Laurence Dunbar, and then has them read different pieces by the same authors, written in Standard English. She reads to the children to help train their ears so that they can begin to tell the difference between the two languages. Street also uses oral recitation of poetry and singing to engage the students. Her teaching style explicitly acknowledges their various backgrounds. As a result of her pedagogical strategy, she has created a learning dynamic in which students have come to trust and mutually respect one another. This has a positive effect on their families and communities and helps them to fortify their self-esteem and cultural awareness. Parents who were once embarrassed and ashamed to come to school have begun to lose their fears. One parent exclaimed, "You know, Carrie, I wish I had only known I had to learn [Standard] English better, and that it wasn't [simply that I was] using bad English."[33]

Dismissing or devaluing the way in which students talk is not only disrespectful, it thwarts their identity and self-worth. Many adult African Americans "code-switch" between Ebonics and Standard English in order to feel like they can identify with the larger population. Code-switching enables them overcome the psychological drain of living in oppression, while allowing them to communicate with Whites who have little exposure to the realities of African American culture. But just as adult African Americans need to use standard English to be persuasive among Whites, many adult African Americans often rely upon Ebonics to mobilize support within their own communities. They sometimes use statements like "I know you know bettuh;" or "Don't make me act ugly;" as a way of letting younger African Americans know that they are loved, valued, and respected; and, that they must be accountable to their community, be able to read between the lines, exercise logic, and possess self-respect. If students have an opportunity to read books by European and African American authors from a broad spectrum, they will see the similarities and differences between "Black talk" and "book talk." This will enhance children's awareness of metalinguistics: the development of one's self-consciousness about the personal and communal use of language, which helps students in adjusting to switching between language styles needed for different reasons and audiences.[34]

Teachers who are not familiar with Ebonics often assume that the child who speaks it is dumb, retarded, or a troublemaker, and that as a result, he or she is likely to fail. Many students in special education are there for "being disruptive," a designation often aligned with language deficiency problems. Unfortunately, every year that most inner-city African American pupils remain in school in the United States, the worse they do relative to other populations. Many of the failing students speak Ebonics fluently. Along with poor teacher salaries, inadequate facilities and supplies, and oppressive attitudes that prevail within the dominant culture, language remains a major factor contributing to the phenomenon of poor academic performance among African American students. To handle some of these issues, teachers need to adopt discerning pedagogical strategies that treat seriously the problems of communication which those who speak Ebonics as a first language experience.[35] Some of these strategies have been put into place in Oakland's Prescott Elementary School system.

Contrary to the deficiencies in some elementary school children, Prescott Elementary students, *who come from public housing*, read well, exhibit proper diction, and have good reasoning skills by the third grade. School Board member Toni Cook notes that many children come from extreme poverty and have little parental guidance. Most of them have not learned to adopt the duality of speaking the home language and the standard language. Not all African Americans speak Ebonics: some are good at code-switching and do not use Ebonics in a more public setting, while some have become comfortable with Standard English and are embarrassed about the home language. Cook warns that the "English Only Campaign" is so sophisticated that it is "anti-anything that's not [Evangelical] Christian": anti-Black, [anti-Catholic,] anti-Jewish, anti-immigrant . . . anti-urban, anti-female."[36] At the very least, such a campaign alienates many African Americans from their roots, dismissing altogether any benefit to incorporating Ebonics into an academic curriculum.

Rather than have a fruitful public forum that would explore the pedagogical possibilities of Ebonics, there was chaos in the Oakland community. Misrepresentation, ridicule, and a national debate about race, including speculation about the moral and mental health and capacities of African Americans, fascinated the nation. The national conversation failed to see the relationship between Ebonics and the way Black preachers and novelists use the musicality, complexity, and techniques of Ebonics. There were no interviews with the thousands of bidialectical African Americans, who grew up speaking and skillfully articulating both Ebonics and Standard English. There were no substantive discussions about the impact and function of literacy and oral skills in the Black community. In the process, we all lost. The debate reiterated the acceptance of particular Black writers and philosophers like Alice Walker, Gwendolyn Brooks, August Wilson, Toni Morrison, Maya Angelou, Cornel West, and Henry Louis Gates, Jr., while it left rejected and repulsed the culture, people, language, and history of the people and traditions commodified by these scholars, who were lauded with Pulitzers and liberal White sanction. The Whiteness pervasive in the Oakland situation, following social historian David Roediger's definition, was "that complex admixture of longing and hate that [some] white people have for African Americans, their cultural formations, and their cultural products."[37]

The rampantly irrational, racist and classist dialogue that ensued made it impossible to have a non-acrimonious conversation about critical linguistic, political, and educational issues that were necessary for a resolution to the problem.[38] Several factors shaped the public's reaction to the Oakland situation: (1) the White community's hegemonic discourse about schooling; (2) the absence of a response to the dominant discourse by African American educators, socio-political activists and scholars; (3) the successful camouflage of many oppressive forces related to demographics, which set off subtle and not-so subtle racist violence in some schools; (4) the media's exaggerated focus on African American students, especially Black males speaking Black slang in reference to the Oakland resolution; and finally, (5) the ambivalence of many African Americans about Ebonics, caused by the media's narrow understanding of the issue.[39] Each of these factors had an impact on shaping the public's negative perception—even among many African Americans—of the appropriateness of using Ebonics in the Oakland school system.

Persons from various political backgrounds, often ignorant of theories about educational reform, hurled invectives at the Oakland School Board members. From long term Civil Rights activists to right-wing talk show hosts, persons of widely varying political persuasions lambasted the School Board. Sound bites, distortions of the original resolution, and sentences taken out of context flooded the airways.[40] Such critics did not consider the abysmal statistics that had led the Oakland School Board to take action. They did not consider the degree to which students who speak only Ebonics were discriminated against by the very institutions supposedly devoted to educating them. In desperate circumstances, the Oakland School Board determined that Ebonics "was a legitimate, rule-based, systematic language, . . . and that Ebonics, the home/community language of African American children, should not be stigmatized, and that this language should be affirmed, maintained, and used to help African American children acquire fluency in the standard code."[41] Ebonics advocates were concerned that teachers respect students when communicating with them. Unfortunately, critics of Ebonics saw the Oakland School Board's resolution primarily as a way of avoiding the task of pressing African American students to learn Standard English. The issue of relationship between student and teacher, and in particular the issue of the authority of the teacher, was being raised implicitly.

## Ebonics: Student and Teacher Authority

Ebonics advocates who seek to empower their students contend that using Ebonics with students who use this non-standard form of English at home and outside of the school setting is critical because it allows children to see themselves and their own experiences as ones which are reflected in the language and literature used in the classroom. Lessons in African American literature and history give children the opportunity to be exposed to a myriad of characters and themes from their heritage, which can help them to improve their vocabulary and instill in them the feeling that their educational and personal lives comprise a unity. How better to do this than by showing children the puissant, potent linguistic models coming out of their own cultural heritage? Toni Morrison asserts that Ebonics is "the thing black people love so much - the saying of words, holding them on the tongue, experimenting with them, playing with them. It's a love, a passion . . . . The worst of all possible things that could happen would be to lose that language. There are certain things I cannot say without recourse to my language."[42] People must be free to determine their language. Oakland was deluged with rhetoric introduced by vocal White politicians, the same politicians who had in the past often remained silent about the deplorable conditions of African American inner-city schools.[43] The allies of these politicians consisted of two sorts: (1) a well-meaning, but often ill-informed African American bourgeoisie and (2) the media, which reveled in black censure. These opponents of Ebonics failed to recognize the extent to which Ebonics is celebratory of African American life. They failed to acknowledge its distinctive fluidity, the way in which its speakers use intonational, stylistic, and often indirect methods in order to make a point. Ebonics forms a standard of excellence that celebrates the rich heritage of African American oral and literary ways of communicating.[44]

Language is artistic, communicates the beautiful, and reflects the ability to create. Margo Jefferson illustrates the beauty, power, and economics of Ebonics. [45] Stolen from Africa, shackled and chained in the bowels of ships through the Middle Passage, slaves were deprived of dignity, safety, and home. Despite the laws and customs of the slave owners, which deliberately and intentionally separated slaves from family members and from others who spoke the same language, slaves ingeniously merged their languages with English to form an early species of Ebonics. The use of Ebonics became a lavish and profitable business in nineteenth-century minstrel shows, where people were pleased to regard this Black vernacular comically, as a series of malapropisms and syntactical mishaps. This style of Ebonics was a mixture of numerous influences, from British archaisms to mock Latin constructions, and it was intended to communicate cheerful, intentional ignorance and "hilariously inept delusions of grandeur."[46] One such example is the 1874 minstrel version of "Othello," entitled *Desdemonum*:

> OTELLER: Wake Desdemonum, see de risin' moon,
> Ebrybody's snorin', nightingale's in tune . . .
> DESDEMONUM: 'Tel, my duck, I hear you: daddy's gone to bed.
> Fotch along your ladderum, I'm de gal to wed! . . .

BOTH: De hour am propitious—come, my darlin' flame!
Dey say dat in de dark all cullers am de same.[47]

Many people utilize Ebonics, from anthropologists, linguists and writers, to blues, jazz, and vocal and instrumental gospel musicians. Black language systems are rife with rhythm, melody, and relationships between speech, song, and pure sound. The power and popularity of Black language systems brought fame and fortune to Elvis Presley, who learned from Bo Diddly, and the Beatles, who studied with Little Richard. Paul Simon acknowledges his reliance on Black language and music forms. Bing Crosby recorded pop-jazz numbers with Paul Whiteman's Orchestra and took pleasure in the musical resources of Black language, switching from Black English to White English. The all African American musical of 1943, *Cabin in the Sky*, featured Louis Armstrong, dancer John Bubbles, Ethel Waters, and Lena Horne. When Armstrong intones "I've got an idea – it's terrifical," combining "terrific" and "magical," it works. When Bubbles dances, sings, or speaks his rural Southern intonation and fast urban pacing, he mixes Standard English and Black English. Countless performers of European heritage appropriated the African American language systems and styles without acknowledging their sources. How can we teach children about creativity, that they can be who they want to be, and claim that the language these children use, Ebonics, is bad? How can we do this while White and Black consumers are spending millions to buy Ebonics' lyrics (e.g., Skat, Rap, Rock 'n Roll), often sung by a White face, set to music? The economic advantage does not mitigate the fact that Ebonics has been exploited for years.

Several studies reveal that African American children form their own self-identity through use of language in stylized and sophisticated ways by the time they reach kindergarten.[48] Pre-schoolers have established their own sense of authority linguistically and have received acknowledgment for their language competencies by the time they have demonstrated their ability to negotiate in the world through verbal gymnastics of rap, rhyme games, signifying, and navigating in and out of trouble. In her 1996 study,[49] Vernon-Feagans demonstrates that African American kindergarten pupils may not perform as well on a paraphrasing task as their White mainstream counterparts because African American kindergarten pupils use language in more creative ways and have distinctive story-telling abilities. Terry Meier explains that when African American children are asked to paraphrase, they often embellish a story and usually end up creating a "different but often more interesting vignette . . . , excluding elements of the original vignette, for which they [are] penalized when their performance on the paraphrasing task [is] evaluated . . . . Studies consistently show that teachers commonly underestimate or fail to recognize many of the verbal abilities nurtured in African American communities."[50] Educators of language must try to get African Americans to use these abilities in connection with the task of becoming literate in Standard English. All of society, especially teachers and students, are affected by literacy incompetence. Illiterate children who do not learn to read become illiterate adults. Parents and societal institutions must become proactive rather than reactive concerning the process of education. Ebonics can become a vehicle of transformation from non-literacy to literacy if the myths surrounding its viability as a language are dispelled.

## Hermeneutics and the Ethics of Ebonics

Ebonics advocates suggest that there are in fact several myths about Ebonics, each of which affect the way in which Ebonics is likely to be used in the classroom and publicly received. The first myth is that Ebonics is simply poor grammar, lazy pronunciation, and slang; the second myth is that the ties between Ebonics and education have not been researched; the third myth is that parents are the primary reason for African American children's literacy difficulties; and the fourth myth is that the Ebonics debate itself is useless. These myths can be dispelled one by one. First, Ebonics has a grammar system that uses an habitual verb style; involves semantics where word meanings are often inverted; employs an intonation, especially an extended vowel enunciation that identifies one as African American; favors genres of drama, proverbs, and poetry/rap; includes sociolinguistic rules where certain terms are eschewed; and engages a particular rhythmic speaking style and a learning/teaching method that embraces a technique of audience participation and structure. Second, linguists have studied Ebonics for thirty years; when Ebonics speakers have difficulty reading Standard English, the problem is usually a function of not using Standard English phonics. Third, while the parents are vital and necessary to the educational process, the schools that are primarily responsible for teaching, and the school administrations in particular, are in a position to lead the cause for beneficial changes. Fourth, Ebonics pedagogy includes literacy methods geared toward improving teacher attitudes, a critical move to solving the problem of Black illiteracy. The research supporting this fourth claim has been in place since 1967.[51]

Although the wording of part of the Oakland Resolution was problematic, especially the unsupported conclusion that Ebonics was inherited and genetic (linguists use the term "genetic" to infer a language's linguistic family tree, non-linguists inferred that Ebonics is inherited via bloodline or RNA/DNA) Frank Heynick, a scholar in applied linguistics, addressed those objections. Heynick noted that the genetically based Standard English language, although classified, artificially, as belonging to the Germanic linguistic family, had borrowed a great deal from other language systems.[52] Similarly, Ebonics was linguistically genetically tied to 17th century pidgin English and the Niger-Congo family of languages spoken by the ancestors and distant cousins of today's African Americans. Some of the resistance to Ebonics was related to race and class issues. Apparently, many Afrocentrics and Black nationalists upheld the dedicated, if not exclusive, use of Ebonics in the elementary and middle classrooms, while Black middle-class professionals tended to oppose the Oakland School Board's action on the grounds that classroom use of Ebonics would handicap all of those students who needed Standard English to survive in a Standard English society. Other participants in the debate felt that it made no sense to take sides, while still others took a middle position.[53]

Language relates to human behavior. Studying human behavior to determine what is the good, and what the values of a particular society are, is ethics. Morals involve putting ethics into practice. What then, is our ethical basis for relying on language for communication? What is our job as educators? At least, it requires that we be committed to procuring justice in the classroom, that we emphasize the value of respecting one another, and that we try to avoid practices that are oppressive and manipulative.

If we are to teach and communicate ethically and justly, we must question the commotion over Ebonics. If a child comes to school and speaks French or Spanish and the teacher speaks Standard English only, the two cannot communicate effectively until and unless a common means of communication is established. To teach a child Math, the teacher will need to learn some French or Spanish to get the child thinking and speaking in Standard English. If children come to school speaking Ebonics, and our goal is to have them speak Standard English, we need to speak to them in Ebonics to explain what Standard English is. We need to communicate with them without making them feel stupid and without stereotyping them as ignorant and/or lazy. The burden of communication falls on the teacher's shoulders: she or he must communicate with their student in a way that the student can hear and grow. The teacher cannot simply refuse to communicate with the student. If Ebonics has been used to engage children in their home environment, then justice dictates that we must take this into account when addressing them. Parents and the community must also do their part. In any educational system, our job is to begin with where students are and bring them to where we want them, with the goal that everyone learns in the process.

Listening requires that, as a professor, I accord students some authority and power. The use of language, specifically Standard English, becomes the vehicle for sharing that power. When difference of style or thought emerges, a dominant culture often feels threatened by what it does not know or understand. In traditional African settings, and traditional African American communities, God or the gods, language and music are an integral part of daily life. Such activities allow speakers certain liberties, for communication through these media is free, fluid. Spoken Ebonics embraces many of the same liberties. Like singers of African American music, for example, Ebonics speakers make use of musical vowels. Music psychologist Carl Seashore, as early as 1938, recognized this musical pattern. [54] Slaves knew what every voice teacher knows, it is easier to sing on vowels rather than on consonants because vowels carry the sound. There is beauty and artistry in Black song and Black talk.

## Ebonics: A Vehicle of Empowerment or Marginalization

Teaching students in a culturally responsible manner mandates that a teacher make Standard English accessible while simultaneously working to understand and appreciate the home/community language of African American children. Our knowledge of Standard English in and of itself is not the sole criterion by which we become capable, intelligent caretakers of the future. The ease with which many of us communicate in Standard English does not by itself make us good teachers. We must be compassionate and sensitive by realizing the harm that can occur in the classroom when we expect those who do not share our privilege to have the same skills that we have.

Excessive correction of students during oral presentations produces silence and affects both the students' attitudes toward the teacher and the teacher's attitude towards the students. In one experiment with Ph.D. candidates, language researcher Robert Berdan created a language, had students read orally, and interrupted them, following the pedagogical pattern he had observed in elementary school classrooms. The graduate students lost their intonation, subvocalized or pronounced words to themselves before saying them out aloud, guessed at pronunciations, stumbled, repeated words, switched letters around, fidgeted, and bit their fingernails. These "mature adults" whispered, wadded up their papers, and some refused to continue.[55] In a different study, researchers found that fourth graders who had attained competence in Standard English during grades 1-3 chose to gravitate toward their home/community language system. Students made this choice because their home/community language was key to their group membership and well-being. They may have sensed negativity at school, directed towards their home community, and may have reacted by choosing their first language, the language closely tied to personal, family, and community identity. Telling students that their language use is wrong is to say that something is bad or wrong with the students themselves and/or their families, and it impugns their way of telling stories.

Harvard University researchers analyzed a session of children's story telling, in which African American students, especially girls, told episodic narratives.[56] The stories of the African American students included longer, shifting scenes, while White students told topic-centered narratives that relayed a single event. When African American adults heard the stories of African American children and were asked to respond to them, they understood the stories to be written by children who were well developed, understandable, and interesting; they recognized the shifts and associations but did not find them distracting. Black adults viewed the story-shifting (African American) child as bright, highly communicative, and successful in school. White adults regarded these same students as incoherent and incapable and felt that the children would have difficulty in reading. They surmised that these African American children probably came from homes with family and emotional problems. Consequently, White teachers developed lower expectations for the African American child who utilized Ebonic rhythms.[57]

In order to empower and give a sense of community to Black students who speak Ebonics fluently, teachers must help their students by affirming that speaking Standard English does not dismiss their Blackness or their African heritage. Some advocates suggest that using Ebonics to teach literacy is effective because, unlike Standard English, Ebonics is spelled the way one speaks the language. Using metaphors, rap, and body kinesthetics to help children interpret poems and stories involves cognitive, affective, and psychomotor experiences in which children come to participate in their own learning.[58]

Charles DeBose, who crafted the preamble of the "Declaration of the Committee of Linguists of African Descent on Language Issues concerning the Education of African American Children," notes that while there may be disagreement about the Oakland School Board Resolution, all can agree on the urgent need for coherent educational policies and strategies that keep in view the rich diversity and dignity of language varieties spoken in these United States.[59] This Declaration defines Ebonics as a continuum of pronunciation and grammar, based on region and social class. Ebonics is here not taken to be incorrect or substandard Standard English, for all American English speakers speak a dialect and, according to the Declaration, "all dialects are equal." Ebonics is expressive of Black culture, its artistic, spiritual, and literary development; and is also a mixture of English and African languages. An Ebonics curriculum demands the insights of professional pedagogues. The stigma presently attached to Ebonics makes it important to carefully develop ways to "remove artificial barriers caused by lack of knowledge of the children's precious language gifts."[60]

DeBose argues that, according to the Bilingual Education Act of 1968, as amended in 1974, Americans who have trouble speaking English have a right to an equal opportunity for an education, a right that applies to students who speak Ebonics as well as other first languages. Consequently, African American students with Limited-(Standard)-English-Proficiency (LEP) ought to be treated with the same care as Native Americans, Asian Americans, Hispanic Americans, and others for whom Standard English is not the dominant language. To strip African American students of this right is to deny them the empowerment that comes with their education.[61] The difficulties many African Americans have speaking Standard English is not a problem that will easily disappear. As long as the barriers of classism and racism exist and the outward and upward mobility of African Americans is hindered, every new generation of Black youth will acquire a slightly different variety of Black English from that of their parents. As long as ghettos and inner city blight continue to exist, varieties of Ebonics will continue to flourish as the mother tongue of African Americans living in segregated inner city areas. Because children continue to come to school speaking a variety of Ebonics, teachers must be sensitive to their experiences and attain the enhanced qualifications that will allow them to nurture their students as well as oversee their academic progress.[62]

One twenty-seven year old African American female educator laments the "painful silencing" of her identity as she gave up and masked her Blackness to embody a "quality education."[63] She moved from acculturation to appropriation to almost complete assimilation, in the private, suburban education systems of Boston. She successfully mastered Standard English and could at will "blur, blend, dismiss" her Blackness. The collapsing of her double-consciousness transformed her passion for education into rage and eventually indifference. However, this painful chaos ultimately had a productive effect, leading her to return to her home community as an educator for children. She did not "want any children to suffer, as [she] had, from feelings of inferiority and self-hate, separation from [her] culture, and loss of the love of learning."[64]

Hannah Arendt claims that knowing ourselves is the one task we cannot do alone.[65] We know ourselves by the feedback we get from others. Since we rely on others to tell us who we are, that act is political. Being political involves being a citizen, having power, making rules, determining status, or, more negatively, it involves being shrewd, manipulating, and oppressing another. To deny a child the right to an education because we will not talk to him or her in a language that he or she can understand is unethical, demoralizing, and politically negative. To refuse to talk to a person in a language that she or he can understand while doing so in the supposed service of their own benefit is tantamount to educational sharecropping. After the end of the Civil War, the newly freed slaves were promised 40 acres and a mule, which they never received. How often do we fail to deliver on the promises to educate our youth?

The issues underlying the use of Ebonics are complex. They include everything from racism, to the poor quality of public education, to the debate over private education, to questions of vouchers and single gender education. What is our ethics of education? To whom do we accord the right to have an education? Do we assume that children are uneducable because we do not want them to think or function in society, but rather wish to control their destinies? Why is it that we quibble over welfare taking 2% of the national budget, fudge on paying teachers adequately, and cut back the support services in our schools, while spending billions on spy satellites and defense budgets? How can we hire principals, teachers, and staff that have no clue as how to communicate with the souls they have been charged to nurture?

Ebonics, like all languages, is a living, diverse, vibrant, constantly changing phenomenon. I am not suggesting that we replace Standard English with Ebonics. I am suggesting that it is ethically and politically astute to regard Ebonics *as an appropriate means of communication in the classroom* and acknowledge that this cultural artifact is a means of assisting children to become self-confident students who are proud of their racial and cultural heritage. Such an acknowledgment does not preclude them from articulating in, writing in, singing in, and playing with

Standard English. Quite the contrary, the use of Ebonics may in fact help those non-fluent African American students to become more capable users of the dominant language.

If we fail to communicate with our children as students, we cannot blame them when they fail to learn to read and write and eventually do not finish school, all because someone berated them when they came to school speaking a different tongue. America is a country of many tongues. We must not let false pride and greed cause us to cut out the tongues of beautiful Blackness, and cripple Black children for life, putting yet another burden on them and on the system. We did not penalize Al Jolson, Bing Crosby, Elvis Presley, or Paul Simon for exploiting Ebonics: we paid them well to use Ebonics. Let us not penalize the children, the progeny from whom those entertainers learned their skills. Let us respect and love our children well.

## Notes

[1]Katie G. Cannon, *Katie's Canon: Womanism and the Soul of the Black Community* (New York: Continuum, 1995.

[2]Alice Walker, *In Search of our Mother's Gardens: Womanist Prose* (New York: Harcourt Brace Jovanovich, 1983), xi.

[3]Robert Williams, *Ebonics: The True Language of Black Folks* (St. Louis: Institute of Black Studies, 1975), 100.

[4]Geneva Smitherman, "Black English/ Ebonics: What It Be Like?" in "The Real Ebonics Debate: Power, Language, and the Education of African American Children," *Rethinking Schools: An Urban Educational Journal* 12 (Fall 1997): 8.

[5]Smitherman, "Black English/ *Ebonics*," 8-9; See R.L. Williams, ed., *Ebonics: The True Language of Black Folks* (St. Louis: Institute of Black Studies, 1975).

[6]Smitherman, "Black English/ *Ebonics*," 8.

[7]Jean E. van Keulen, Gloria Toliver Weddington, Charles E. DeBose, *Speech, Language, Learning, and the African American Child* (Boston: Allyn & Bacon, 1998), 89-90, 133. Conclusions according to the American Speech-Language-Hearing Association (ASHA).

[8]Smitherman, "Black English/ Ebonics," 8-9.

[9]Geneva Smitherman, "Black Language and the Education of Black Children: One Mo Once," *The Black Scholar: "Ebonics,"* 27 (1997): 31. See also J. A. Harrison, "Negro English," *Anglia* 7 (1884): 232-279; Lorenzo D. Turner, *Africanisms in the Gullah Dialect* (Chicago: University of Chicago Press, 1949). Turner was the first African American linguist, and he wrote this work based on twenty years of researching Ebonics. Beryl Bailey, the first woman of African descent to be a linguist also did extensive research on Ebonics.

[10]Smitherman, "Black Language and the Education of Black Children," 31-32.

[11]Ibid., 32-34; G. Simpkins and C. Simpkins, "Cross-Cultural Approach to Curriculum Development," 212-240, in *Black English and the Education of Black Children and Youth*, Geneva Smitherman, ed. (Detroit: Wayne State University Center for Black Studies, 1981). See also William Labov, *The Study of NonStandard English* (Champaign, Illinois: National Council of Teachers of English, 1970); William Labov, *Language in the Inner City: Studies in the Black English Vernacular* (Philadelphia: The University of Pennsylvania Press, Inc.).

[12]Janheninz Jahn, *Muntu: The New African Culture* (New York: Grove Press, 1961), 194.

[13]Ernie Smith, "What is Black English? What is *Ebonics*?" in "The Real Ebonics Debate: Power, Language, and the Education of African American Children," *Rethinking Schools: An Urban Educational Journal* 12 (Fall 1997): 14.

[14]Katie Cannon, *Black Womanist Ethics*, (Atlanta: Scholars Press, 1988), 105-124.

[15]Joyce Hope Scott, "Official Language; Unofficial Reality: Acquiring Bilingual/Bicultural Fluency in a Segregated Southern Community," in "The Real Ebonics Debate: Power, Language, and the Education of African American Children," *Rethinking Schools: An Urban Educational Journal* 12 (Fall 1997): 30-31. This article originally appeared in the *San Francisco Chronicle*, January 19, 1997.

[16]Charles DeBose, "Academic Perspective on African American English," Unpublished paper, Ebonics Forum, California State University Hayward, February 13, 1997.

[17]Rosina Lippi-Green, "What We Talk About When We Talk About *Ebonics*: Why Definitions Matter," *The Black Scholar: "Ebonics II"* 27 (1997): 7, 11.

[18]Earl Ofari Hutchinson has a doctorate in social studies and is a writer and frequent guest on radio and television programs.

[19]Earl Ofari Hutchinson, "The Fallacy of Ebonics," *The Black Scholar: "Ebonics"* 27 (1997): 36-37

[20]Ibid., 37.

[21]John H. McWorter, "Wasting Energy on an Illusion" *The Black Scholar: "Ebonics"* 27 (1997): 9.

[22]Marcia Y. Riggs, *Awake, Arise, & Act: A Womanist Call for Black Liberation* (Cleveland, OH: The Pilgrim Press, 1994), ix-xi.

[23]Theresa Perry and Lisa Delpit, "An Introduction From the Guest Editors," in "The Real Ebonics Debate: Power, Language, and the Education of African American Children," *Rethinking Schools: An Urban Educational Journal* 12 (Fall 1997): 3.

[24]Ibid.

[25]"The Oakland Ebonics Resolution," reprinted in "The Real Ebonics Debate: Power, Language, and the Education of African American Children," *Rethinking Schools: An Urban Educational Journal* 12 (Fall 1997): 25.

[26]Ibid.

[27]Ibid. The empirical evidence for validating a unique patterned grammatical African American linguistic structure or language; the push of equality and inclusivity in policies by the Oakland Unified School District, towards creating an environment "where a language other than English is dominant," [whether Asian, Latin, Native or African - American] . . . African American pupils shall not, because of their race, be subtly dehumanized, stigmatized, discriminated against or denied."; the appropriation of adequate general funds as in bilingual education, following Title VIII; faculty support; parental assurance; option for African American parents to choose to have their child's "limited English proficiency," that is, "speech disorders and English Language deficits addressed by special education and/or other district programs."

[28]Perry A. Hall, "The *Ebonics* Debate: Are We Speaking the Same Language?" *The Black Scholar: "Ebonics II"* 27 (1997): 12.

[29]Theresa Perry, "Reflections on the Ebonics Debate: "I 'on Know why They be Trippin'" in "The Real Ebonics Debate: Power, Language, and the Education of African American Children," *Rethinking Schools: An Urban Educational Journal* 12 (Fall 1997): 3.

[30]Ibid.

[31]Carolyn Getridge, "Oakland Superintendent Responds to Critics of the Ebonics Policy," in "The Real Ebonics Debate: Power, Language, and the Education of African American Children," *Rethinking Schools: An Urban Educational Journal* 12 (Fall 1997): 27.

[32]"Embracing Ebonics and Teaching Standard English: An Interview with Oakland Teacher Carrie Secret," in "The Real Ebonics Debate: Power, Language, and the Education of African American Children," *Rethinking Schools: An Urban Educational Journal* 12 (Fall 1997). 18-19, 24, 34; Terry Meier, "Teaching Teachers About Black Communications," in "The Real Ebonics Debate: Power, Language, and the Education of African American Children," *Rethinking Schools: An Urban Educational Journal* 12 (Fall 1997): 23.

[33]"Embracing Ebonics," with Carrie Secret," 34.

[34]Meier, "Teaching Teachers," 23.

[35]Nanette Asimov with Toni Cook, "Opening Pandora's Box: An Interview with Oakland School Board Member Toni Cook," in "The Real Ebonics Debate: Power, Language, and the Education of African American Children," *Rethinking Schools: An Urban Educational Journal* 12 (Fall 1997): 28. This article originally appeared in the *San Francisco Chronicle*, January 19, 1997; Charles Johnson, "An Interview with Linguist John Rickford - Holding On to A Language of Our Own," in "The Real Ebonics Debate: Power, Language, and the Education of African American Children," *Rethinking Schools: An Urban Educational Journal* 12 (Fall 1997): 12.

[36]Asimov with Cook, "Opening Pandora's Box," 28.

[37]Theresa Perry, "Reflections on the Ebonics Debate: "I 'on Know why They be Trippin'" in "The Real Ebonics Debate: Power, Language, and the Education of African American Children," *Rethinking Schools: An Urban Educational Journal* 12 (Fall 1997): 5; David Roediger, *The Wages of Whiteness*, (London, New York: Verso, 1991).

[38]Theresa Perry and Lisa Delpit, "An Introduction From the Guest Editors," in "The Real Ebonics Debate: Power, Language, and the Education of African American Children," *Rethinking Schools: An Urban Educational Journal* 12 (Fall 1997): 3.

[39]Theresa Perry, "Reflections on the Ebonics Debate: "I 'on Know why They be Trippin'" in "The Real Ebonics Debate: Power, Language, and the Education of African American Children," *Rethinking Schools: An Urban Educational Journal* 12 (Fall 1997): 4-5.

[40]Ibid., 3.

[41]Ibid.

[42]Terry Meier, "Kitchen Poets and Classroom Books: Literature from Children's Roots," in "The Real Ebonics Debate: Power, Language, and the Education of African American Children," *Rethinking Schools: An Urban Educational Journal* 12 (Fall 1997): 20; T. Leclair, "'The Language Must Not Sweat:' A Conversation with Toni Morrison," in *The New Republic*, March 21, 1981, 27.

[43]Mumia Abu-Jamal, "The Mother Tongue: Black English Revisited," *The Black Scholar* 27 (1997): 27.

[44]Meier, "Kitchen Poets," 20-21.

[45]Margo Jefferson, *Wall Street Journal*, January 15, 1997, B1

[46]Abraham Lincoln was attending just such a stage performance, *Our American Cousin*, the night that he was assassinated by an actor, John Wilkes Booth, whose specialty was the Standard English of Shakespeare.

[47]Jefferson, *Wall Street Journal*, B1.

[48]Janice Hale-Benson, *Black Children: Their Roots, Culture and Learning Styles* (New York: Johns Hopkins University Press, 1982); Shirley Heath, *Ways with Words* (New York: Cambridge University Press, 1983); M. H. Goodwin, *He-Said-She-Said: Talk as Social Organization Among Black Children* (Bloomington: Indiana University Press, 1990); William Labov, *Language in the Inner City: Studies in the Black English Vernacular* (Philadelphia: University of Pennsylvania press, 1972); D. Taylor and C. Dorsey-Gaines, *Growing Up Literate* (London: Heineman, 1988); Lynn Vernon-Feagans, *Children's Talk in Communities and Classrooms* (Cambridge: Blackwell Publishers, 1996).

[49]Lynn Vernon-Feagans, *Children's Talk in Communities and Classrooms* (Cambridge: Blackwell Publishers, 1996).

[50]Meier, "Teaching Teachers," 23.

[51]Mary Rhodes Hoover, "Ebonics: Myths and Realities," in "The Real Ebonics Debate: Power, Language, and the Education of African American Children," *Rethinking Schools: An Urban Educational Journal* 12 (Fall 1997): 17.

[52]Herb Boyd, "Been Dere, Done Dat!," *The Black Scholar: Ebonics* 27 (1997)15-16.

[53]Ibid., 15-17.

[54]Carl Seashore, *Psychology of Music* (N.p: 1938; repr. New York: Dover, 1967).

[55]See Robert Berdan, "Knowledge into Practice: Delivering Research to Teachers," in M.F. Whiteman, ed., *Reactions to Ann Arbor Vernacular Black English and Education* (Arlington, VA: Center for Applied Linguistics, 1980).

[56]C.B. Cazden, Classroom Discourse (Portsmouth, NH: Heinemann, 1988) in Lisa D. Delpit, "What Should Teachers Do? Ebonics and Cultural Response Instruction" in "The Real Ebonics Debate: Power, Language, and the Education of African American Children," *Rethinking Schools: An Urban Educational Journal* 12 (Fall 1997): 7.

[57]Ibid., 6-7.

[58]Jacobsen, Eggen, Kauchak, 1989 in Brinson Monique Brinson, "Removing the Mask: Roots of Oppression Through Omission," in "The Real Ebonics Debate: Power, Language, and the Education of African American Children," *Rethinking Schools: An Urban Educational Journal* 12 (Fall 1997): 24.

[59]Charles DeBose, "Declaration of the Committee of Linguists of African Descent on Language Issues Concerning the Education of African American Children," Sept. 18, 1997. Unpublished.

[60]Ibid. For a broader discussion see also Van Keulen, Weddington, DeBose, *Speech, Language, Learning* (see also note #7).

[61]Ernie Smith, "What is Black English? What is Ebonics?" in "The Real Ebonics Debate: Power, Language, and the Education of African American Children," *Rethinking Schools: An Urban Educational Journal* 12 (Fall 1997): 15.

[62]"Language Planning in the United States: The Status of Black English, Conference on Theoretical Orientations in Creole Studies," St. Thomas, Virgin Islands, March 28-April 1, 1979, Unpublished.

[63]Monique Brinson, "Removing the Mask: Roots of Oppression Through Omission," in "The Real Ebonics Debate: Power, Language, and the Education of African American Children," *Rethinking Schools: An Urban Educational Journal* 12 (Fall 1997): 24.

[64]Ibid.

[65]See Hannah Arendt, *The Human Condition* (Chicago: University of Chicago Press, 1958).

# Babel's Children: Reconstructing the Common Good

*William O'Neill, S.J.*

## Abstract

In this essay, I consider the rival liberal and communitarian accounts of justice emerging in complex, pluralist societies. I argue that we err in posing the question of human rights as a Hobson's choice between a formal, universal metanarrative, as envisioned in philosophical liberalism, or as a merely local, ethnocentric narrative of the western bourgeoisie, as in the communitarian critique. For human rights are best viewed rhetorically, as establishing the possibility of rationally persuasive argument across our varied narrative traditions. The essay concludes by attending to the role of religious belief in the public reason of a postmodern society.

In a memorable passage, Paul upbraids the Corinthian Christians for the "jealousy and rivalry" in their midst: "every one of you is declaring, 'I belong to Paul,' or 'I belong to Apollos,' or 'I belong to Cephas,' or 'I belong to Christ'" (1 Cor. 1:11-12, 3:3). Such uncivil strife, Paul laments, belies the Gospel: "Has Christ been split up? Was it Paul that was crucified for you, or was it in Paul's name that you were baptized?" (1 Cor. 1:12-13). For the philosophers of this age, communion (*koinōnia*) in the crucified Christ is mere folly (1 Cor. 17-26). Yet in a world divided against itself in enmity and casual slaughter, one wonders if the "wisdom of the wise" (1 Cor. 1:19) does not finally prevail.

To the worldly wise, indeed, Paul's exhortation to unity seems but "fragments shored against our ruin" to which even our assessments of modernity's discontents succumb.[1] We prove ourselves Babel's worthy children, differing not only in our national, ethnic, racial, and religious loyalties, but in the very meaning we attribute to such differences in our conceptions of justice.[2] In these pages, I will first consider the rival liberal and communitarian accounts of justice in complex, pluralist societies. I will then offer an interpretation of rights rhetoric that seeks to reconcile our multiple loyalties with a reconstruction of the ethical ideal of the common good. I will conclude by attending to the role of religious belief in the public reason of a postmodern society.

## Genealogies of Justice

Modernity bequeaths us the rhetoric of natural rights in a "godless and prophetless time." The "ultimate and most sublime values have retreated from public life," writes Max Weber, while the fragmented values of a demystified polytheism succeed to the "grandiose moral fervor of Christian ethics."[3] With the eclipse of the traditional, eudaimonistic ideal of the common good, technical reason (*Zweckrationalität*) reigns supreme. In our disenchanted world, Grotius's modern heirs thus speak not of the divine finality of natural *law* ordered to the *bonum commune* (the *jus naturale* of the medievals), but of the "natural, inalienable and sacred *Rights* of Man."[4]

For liberalism as a philosophic doctrine, the very irreconcilability of our particular ends or conceptions of the good leads us to cherish the "liberties of the moderns" as our foremost rights.[5] "The only freedom which deserves the name," writes J. S. Mill in a justly memorable phrase, "is that of pursuing our own good in our own way." Our liberty, in turn, is parsed as our several immunities or negative rights, limited principally by duties of forbearance; for we must, says Mill, respect others' like liberty, neither depriving them of their own good, nor impeding "their efforts to obtain it."[6] Under the banner of negative freedom, heirs of the liberal tradition extol their individual liberties, while relegating positive delimitations of liberty, for example, claim-rights to adequate nutrition, to an inferior sphere, if not dismissing them as mere rhetorical license. Our negative liberties, says Robert Nozick, "fill up the space of rights."[7]

With the apotheosis of the sovereign self, social bonds, once derived from the ethical ideal of the common good (the positive determination of freedom or *libertas*) must now be "constructed" through exercise of individual will (*liberum arbitrium*), whether of Locke's fiduciary contract or the imperious fiat of Hobbes's Leviathan. Many, to be sure, dispute the nominalistic view of society as a grand artifice of interest, but our liberal heritage has yet to cede the stage in Anglo-American political philosophy. In his magisterial account of justice as fairness, for instance, John Rawls recurs to the heuristic device of a social contract in which mutually disinterested agents select the principles of justice under a "veil of ignorance."[8] Fairness is achieved by bracketing agents' knowledge of their particular cultural roles, economic status, natural and acquired abilities, desires, and goals. In Rawls's thought experiment, self-interested choice under the veil of ignorance is thus tantamount to fairness or impartiality once the veil is lifted. So reflecting modernity's skepticism regarding a comprehensive conception of the common good, what Hans-Georg Gadamer describes as our "prejudice against prejudice,"[9] perfectly prudential agents, says Rawls, would prefer an increment of liberty (immunity from interference) to that of any other social good.

In Rawls's earlier treatise, such recognition obtains *sub species aeternitatis*, so that our natural rights are "established independently from social conventions and legal norms."[10] Yet in his later writings, the justification of rights defers to "the public political culture of a democratic society," that is, "the political institutions of a constitutional regime and the public traditions of their interpretation."[11] Rawls's revised theory, though more modest in import, thus commends itself precisely as a resolution of the distinctively modern problem of establishing fair conditions of co-existence for citizens with differing, even incommensurable conceptions of the good. Such citizens may, of course, pursue their private religious beliefs, but their public world, as Weber foresaw, remains disenchanted.

Communitarian critics as diverse as Charles Taylor, Alasdair MacIntyre, and Michael Sandel take issue with Rawls, demurring that the liberal appeal to an abstract, "essentially unencumbered" self, "given prior to its ends," is far from perspicuous.[12] Harking back to the Romantic critique of the empty formalism of Kantian morality (*Moralität*), such communitarian theorists envision the self as constituted in the ensemble of social relations, the distinctive mores of Hegelian ethics (*Sittlichkeit*), albeit bereft of "Reason's cunning."[13] Not only, say his critics, is Rawls's agent deprived of sufficiently determinate motives for rational choice under the veil of ignorance, but the formal constraints of choice, including the veil itself, depend for their justification upon a richer conception of the good.[14] Rawls's belated gambit of reasoning from within a certain political tradition redeems the incoherence of the original theory, but at the price of adequacy, that is, the putative sublimation of our particular social conventions and legal norms; for finally Rawls has not bracketed agents' cultural horizon so much as tacitly assumed the cultural horizon of the postmodern, liberal bourgeoisie.

For Richard Rorty, such historicization of liberal theory is the fitting *denouement* of Rawls's thought experiment. Philosophy holds a mirror, not to nature or natural rights, but to our cultural mores, characterizing, in Rawls's words, "a democratic society under modern conditions."[15] To the "thoroughly enlightened" postmodernist, indeed, the "natural, inalienable, and sacred rights" of the individual are a supreme fiction. Rorty's "post-modernist bourgeois liberalism" is "one in which no trace of divinity remained, either in the form of a divinized world or a divinized self," that is, a self endowed with "objective moral values" or human rights.[16] In Rorty's agnostic piety, rights are redeemed, not as self-evident or sacred verities, but as "local and ethnocentric" customs—"the tradition of a particular community, the consensus of a particular culture."[17] Rights talk, like edifying discourse generally, would be "relative to the group to which we think it is necessary to justify ourselves—to the body of shared belief which determines the reference of the word 'we'."[18] Rorty's demystification of rights, echoed by Alasdair MacIntyre, recalls Jeremy Bentham's dismissal of natural law in the *Déclaration des droits de l'homme et du citoyen* as an "imaginary" law which could beget only "imaginary rights."[19] For Rorty, as for Bentham, rights are the progeny of positive law—what Edmund Burke termed the prejudices or "latent wisdom" of Englishmen.[20]

Our world, for such postmodern critics, is utterly disenchanted. Far from serving as a universal ideal language, that is, a neutral "metanarrative" in adjudicating cultural narratives, the discourse of human rights is revealed to be but one of many "local narratives," the cultural legacy of the western bourgeoisie.[21] Rooted in our local narratives, the "politics of the common good" supersedes the "politics of [human] rights,"[22] belief in which, says MacIntyre, is but "one with belief in witches and in unicorns."[23] One wonders, then, if the Roman Catholic Church, in embracing the rhetoric of human rights in interpreting the common good,[24] has read the "signs of the times" aright, or if its belated rapprochement with the traces of divinity in modernity is, in Rorty's words, merely "quaint." For we seem fated to founder on the Scylla of an empty formalism, a universal metanarrative divested of determinate material content, or on the Charybdis of an ethical relativism and its postmodern fragmentation of value.

## A Rhetorical Riposte

It would be quixotic, indeed, to seek to chart a *via media* between these doctrinal extremes. I wish to argue, rather, that we err in thus posing the question of human rights as a Hobson's choice between a formal, universal metanarrative and the local, ethnocentric narrative of the western bourgeoisie. For such rights are best viewed rhetorically, that is, as limning the possibility of rationally persuasive argument across our varied narrative traditions. Let me put forth the following theses as a modest proposal: 1. As a form of persuasive speech or rhetoric, the practice of rational claim-making presumes the mutual respect of practically rational agents. 2. Deriving their backing from the principle of mutual respect, human rights serve as warrants in our "reasoned speech." 3. The justification of basic human rights derives from the internal relation of what is explicitly "said" in particular rights claims and what is tacitly "shown" in the saying. 4. Interpreted discursively, the common good signifies the regime of basic rights presupposed in reasoned speech within and across our narrative traditions.

### *1. As a form of persuasive speech or rhetoric, the practice of rational claim-making presumes the mutual respect of practically rational agents.*

In the practical domain, rhetoric, we may say, aims at persuading a rational agent that she do or refrain from doing X (where X is fittingly described in terms of her intentions or reasons for acting). My locution may be strategic in form, a stylistic, productive art in which, indifferent to her own best reasons, I seek to tailor my interlocutor's intentions to fit my own. Over against such a technical reduction of rhetoric as "perfectly manipulated information,"[25] Chaim Perelman proposes a "new rhetoric" as the art of redeeming practical validity claims in argument.[26] Hans-Georg Gadamer writes in a similar vein of Plato's dialectical foundation of rhetoric: "The task is to master the faculty of speaking in such an effectively persuasive way that the arguments brought forward are always appropriate to the specific receptivity of the souls to which they are directed." One must accordingly have "a grasp of the truth (that is, the ideas)," and second, "one must have a profound knowledge of the souls of those one wishes to persuade."[27]

In formal, analytical terms, the judgment of the practically rational agent $S_1$ that "$S_2$ ought to do (or refrain from doing) X" where X is done intentionally, presumes not only $S_1$'s interest in the redemption of her claim, but in its redemption precisely *as* a practical validity-claim (in Gadamer's terms, one's "grasp of the truth"). Now the claim of $S_1$ is *rationally* persuasive if it satisfies the best reasons (conative attitudes and beliefs) of her respondents, all things considered (implying, thus, one's "profound knowledge of the souls of those one wishes to persuade").[28] Claim-rights, for instance, define a subset of practical prescriptive judgments, "$S_{1,\ 2,\ 3,\dots n}$ ought to do, or forbear from doing, X," the validity of which depends upon the fitting ascription to $S_{1,\ 2,\ 3,\dots n}$ of reasons that vindicate or verify the "ought" judgment. As Bernard Williams observes, "in the practical or deliberative sense," the judgment that $S_2$ ought to do X is "relativised to the *agent's* set of aims, projects, objectives, etc. (including of course moral and other constraints that [she] may recognize)."[29]

In the rhetorical practice of claim-making, my judgment that "$S_{1,2,3,\dots n}$ ought to do X" generates a practical validity claim if, and only if, it implies my belief that X is fittingly described in terms of $S_{1,2,3,\dots n}$'s best reason(s) for acting, all things considered, and my interest in $S_{1,2,3,\dots n}$ doing X thus described. In the practical or deliberative sense, that is, my judgment (that "$S_{1,2,3,\dots n}$ ought to do X") displays my interest in "$S_{1,2,3,\dots n}$ acting in accordance with their best reasons, all things considered," or inasmuch as they are semantically (intensionally) equivalent action descriptions, my interest in the "rationally autonomous action of $S_{1,2,3,\dots n}$" or "$S_{1,2,3,\dots n}$ acting autonomously."[30] The *practice* of redeeming practical validity claims thus presupposes the formally generalized interest of practically rational agents in $S_{1,2,3,\dots n}$ acting autonomously or, *pari passu*, their *respect* for $S_{1,2,3,\dots n}$ as practically rational (autonomous) agents (where respect signifies regard, in the sense of both recognition of, and interest in, $S_{1,2,3,\dots n}$ acting autonomously).

Just as for Kant, practically rational agents are self-existent ends (*selbständiger*), so my generalized interest in $S_{1,2,3,\dots n}$ acting autonomously is logically antecedent to $S_{1,2,3,\dots n}$'s contingent (*bewirkender*) ends or particular reasons for acting.[31] Yet whereas Kant recurs to a transcendental epistemology, that is, a formal "metanarrative" of noumenal agency, we turn rather to the pragmatic, discursive (intersubjective) conditions of practically rational judgment.[32] Our practical rhetoric thus exhibits "what *we* do"[33] when, forsaking merely strategic interaction, we engage in what Aristotle termed "reasoned speech" in the public realm.[34]

We need not proceed *more geometrico*; indeed, in a manner analogous to Aristotle's distinction of practical wisdom (*phronēsis*) from technical reason (*technē*), $S_1$'s respect for $S_{1,2,3,...n}$ exhibits the affinity of the one judging ($S_1$) to the object domain (the practically rational actions of $S_{1,2,3,...n}$).[35] I forsake the language game of "reasoned speech," conversely, if I revert to a merely strategic or technical use of rhetoric. Let us say, for instance, that through deceptive advertising, I seek to entice you to start smoking against your own best judgment. Saying "you ought to smoke Camels" expresses *my* contingent interest in your performance of X (in this case, your starting to smoke). Yet if, *ex hypothesi*, your starting to smoke is contrary to your own best judgment (that is, a judgment made in light of all available, relevant reasons), my locution would fail to generate a practical validity claim, since it is not only not relativised, but contrary to *your* aims, projects, objectives, or the moral constraints you may recognize.[36]

*2. Deriving their backing from the principle of mutual respect, human rights serve as warrants in our "reasoned speech."*

Claim-rights, we observed above, define a subset of practical prescriptive judgments, "$S_{1,\ 2,\ 3,...n}$ ought to do, or forbear from doing, X," the validity of which depends upon the fitting ascription to $S_{1,\ 2,\ 3,...n}$ of reasons that vindicate the judgment. Such claim-rights, we might say, are distinguished from practical validity claims in general by their putative reason-giving force. To say that I have a claim-right to X is not merely to say that I have an interest in X or that X is a benefit due me, but rather that my claim is internally justifiable to my potential interlocutors, those, that is, for whom such claim-making serves as a persuasive, rhetorical practice.[37] My claim that I not be tortured, for instance, rests on my belief that my interest in not being tortured corresponds to the "moral constraints" recognized implicitly by my interlocutors. The assignment of rights, as in Rawls's original position, is best viewed, then, not as expressing the singular interests of abstract, mutually disinterested agents, much less, of a single, representative individual, but, *pace* Bentham, as "discourse that aims at persuasion and conviction."[38] For although rights, in general, may express our interests, it is as practical rhetoric that our interests acquire the sense of rights, that is, as commonly recognized warrants in suasive speech.[39]

Such warrants may be constituted for a given polity by positive legislative enactment, constitutional arrangement, or juridical decision. We assume, for instance, that citizens will respect the regime of property rights. The question posed by *human* rights rhetoric, conversely, is whether we may speak of general warrants whose backing is logically antecedent to such "positive" measures; the generation of claims, that is, that derive their reason-giving force from moral constraints commonly recognized in the practice of rational claim-making. The question is not entirely adventitious, for as we argued in our initial thesis, our "reasoned speech" is tempered by the mutual respect due practically rational agents as such. Might such respect serve as backing for warrants described by human rights?

The principal instruments of international positive law, for example, the International Bill of Rights, presume as much. The initial clause of the Preamble of United Nations' *Universal Declaration of Human Rights* (1948) solemnly recognizes "the inherent dignity" and "equal and inalienable rights of all members of the human family."[40] In a similar vein, the rights assigned in Rawls's thought experiment are not finally conjured of the contracting parties' disinterested rationality in a feat of conceptual legerdemain.[41] Attaining and sustaining a rational consensus (as a discursive finality) presumes, rather, that Rawls's parties adopt a practical attitude of mutual respect, that is, each regards the other as a worthy interlocutor, equally entitled to representation, who must be persuaded through the force of better argument. The rhetoric of rational claim-making in the contracting parties' deliberation (and implicitly, their foregoing merely strategic interaction) thus *shows forth* the status of the parties *as* moral persons, constituting, implicitly, a universal audience.[42]

*3. The justification of basic human rights derives from the internal relation of what is explicitly "said" in particular rights claims and what is tacitly "shown" in the saying.*

I have argued thus far that the discursive redemption of practical validity claims presupposes the mutual respect of practically rational agents, which, in turn, serves as implicit backing for claim-rights as warrants in suasive speech. Yet in the legal sphere, as we have seen, the scope and limits of such warrants remain elusive. If our regnant liberal theory cedes pride of place to negative claims or immunities, nonwestern usage favors positive "second generation" economic, social, and cultural rights, and even "third generation" rights of peoples to self-determination and development. The various covenants, conventions, and declarations elaborated in international law offer us a veritable bouillabaisse of putative rights, yet fail to establish their relative significance or urgency.

Here, too, I believe the rhetorical construal is illuminating. For the relation between what is shown (the latent wisdom of respect for claimants as backing for rights) in making a rights claim, and what is said (the assignment of a particular rights claim as a warrant) serves to specify the content of human rights.[43] Our rights claims, that is, exhibit, in a performative or illocutionary fashion, the interest of practically rational agents in being respected as such. As R. J. Vincent observes,

> Not only are [human] rights an important part of the language of morals, but they have, too, a unique role within that language. It is to denote a

> particular moral attitude. The demeanour of someone claiming his or her rights is not that of begging or pleading, and the response if the claim is met is not one of gratitude. Equally, if the claim is not met, the response is not one of disappointment but of indignation. This is because rights are insisted on as part of one's status as a person. They are not favours done by the holders of power to those beholden to it.[44]

Rawls's thought experiment illumines the latent wisdom of respect, displayed in the rhetorical practice of claim-making.[45] Human rights, that is, express our moral self-knowledge as dignified subjects (as well as objects) of narration.[46] Where such respect is denied, as in Hutu or Serbian supremacist narratives, or the enduring racism or gender discrimination in our own midst, the appropriate response is indignation, for at issue is not merely this or that subjective end, but our very status as moral interlocutors, that is, as free and equal moral agents. Such a view of human rights is supported, I believe, in the rights rhetoric of such nonwestern advocates as Rigoberta Menchú, Daw Aung San Suu Kyi, Adolfo Pérez Esquivel, Desmond Tutu, et al. For their rhetoric testifies they will no longer passively acquiesce in servitude. Indeed, as Paulin Hountondji of Benin remarks, it is here that the discursive reference of the word "we" is extended in its concrete universality:

> What varies, not only from one culture to another,...but also within one culture from one period to another and from one class or social group to another, are the forms of this indignation, the modes of expression of this universal demand for respect and, consequently, the details of the rights considered to be essential and inalienable. But in no society is awareness of dignity truly absent, perhaps because in no society, alas, has this dignity ever been fully respected.[47]

Our preceding remarks do not, of course, offer a knockdown justification of rights discourse; yet they illumine the meaning of human rights in our varied local narratives. The rhetoric of human rights exhibits what we might call "the banality of goodness," that is, the intrinsic worth or value of persons which Rawls himself acknowledges as "beyond all price."[48] Indeed, even the immunities from coercion or interference recognized by Rawls's original choosers acquire their moral salience from their antecedent entitlement to respect. For in ascribing worth, rather than mere price, to persons as agents, we implicitly valorize the prerequisites of their exercising agency, that is, the realization of their basic agential capabilities.[49] The maxim of respect thus underwrites agents' claim-rights not only to such civil liberties, but to security from torture or intimidation, and subsistence, including adequate nutrition, basic health care, education, and the like.

Alan Gewirth terms these "the generic goods of agency," inasmuch as they are presupposed in any reasonable conception of flourishing.[50] Claim-rights to such goods, embracing both liberties and positive "agency needs" are mutually implicatory, for they constitute the moral minima of respect presumed in one's status as a claimant.[51] What Rawls terms the "fair value" of liberty is imperiled if persons' basic right to adequate nutrition or security is denied.[52] And so too, one's right to security is threatened if, as in pre-genocidal Rwanda, liberties of effective participation are systemically suppressed.[53] In the rhetoric of claim-making, such basic human rights (and the complex, correlative duties they imply) assume lexical priority over other, less exigent claims, for example, private property rights, permitting us to distinguish the graduated urgency of differing human rights claims, as well as the differing material entitlements presumed for the satisfaction of agency needs, for example, the greater nutritional requirements of pregnant women. Aptly described by Gustavo Gutiérrez as the preemptory "rights of the poor,"[54] these basic claim-rights constitute a moral template or "independent standard for formulating, interpreting, and criticizing law."[55]

*4. Interpreted discursively, the common good signifies the regime of basic rights presupposed in reasoned speech within and across our narrative traditions.*

Conceived rhetorically, human rights discourse is neither an abstract metanarrative or metavocabulary, as in Rawls's thought experiment, nor merely one of innumerable local narratives or "*petits recits*."[56] For the rhetoric of our basic human rights figures not only in the discursive constitution of social goods (as in the Rawlsian contract), but in the constitutive goods of discourse itself, that is, the social conditions presumed for the practical discourse of free and equal moral agents. In exhibiting the banality of goodness (rather than "the ultimate and most sublime values" distinguishing our particular narratives), basic rights function as a "depth *grammar*" specifying the discursive constants of reasoned speech or narration in the public realm.[57] Denial of these rights, conversely, as in the supremacist suppression of basic civil liberties or security rights, undermines the practice of rational claim-making and imperils the common good of civic discourse itself.

In defining the moral minima of our reasoned speech, rights rhetoric thus illumines what Habermas terms "systematic distortions" of our civic discourse, for example, the "effacing" of the other.[58] The supremacist may, of course, counter that his merely local and ethnocentric narrative of justice justifies torture in the interest of apartheid or "ethnic cleansing." Yet time and again, the narrator *does* appeal, implicitly, to a universal audience for vindication, as when Serbian or Hutu supremacists or homegrown racists deny their complicity in injustice or defend their atrocities in the name of past injustice visited upon them. In either case, their apologies employ the very grammar of dissent, that is, the goods of reasoned speech, they would deny their victims. "By degrading the victim to a state where only 'cries and whispers'—or groans and screams—are possible," writes David

Hollenbach, "the torturer seeks to destroy the commonality among persons that is born with the birth of language."[59]

In playing such a critical, hermeneutical role, rights rhetoric does not so much suppress our native tongues in a grand metanarrative, as ensure that all may speak. For our rights are not ascribed to an abstract, "generalized other," as in the "formal" construal of Kant's categorical imperative which bids us "abstract from the individuality and concrete identity of the other."[60] On the contrary, our rights rhetoric schematizes the "material" maxim which, in demanding indiscriminate respect, enjoins a discriminate response to the "concrete other."[61] What Kierkegaard says of Christian *agapē* as embracing "everyone in particular but no one in partiality," pertains no less to the concrete universality of respect, for dignity is always clothed in local garb.[62] Like rules of Wittgensteinian "language games," rights admit of differing narrative interpretations, so that the *universal* maxim of respect for the "concrete other" bids us attend to its *particular* narrative embodiment.[63]

Such narratives comprise a "family of language-games," which, as such, are not rigidly limited but open-textured.[64] We may, indeed, speak not only of varied narratives, but of varied voices within a common narrative tradition. Yet just as family resemblance is not infinitely malleable, so what is "said" in our narratives must be consistent with what is "shown" in the narration of free and equal moral persons. Only narrative claims consistent with "what we *do*" in our reasoned speech *as* (practically rational) narrators can be fittingly entertained as rights. In so reconfiguring our narrative imagination, rights belie the myth of a hermetic "we" for whom justification remains, perforce, merely local and ethnocentric.[65]

Mercy Amba Oduyoye's critique of the "socio-cultural norms" which "demand submissive and subordinate behavior of women," for instance, rests on the very hermeneutical premises that enjoin respect for particular cultural systems:[66]

> Now we have come to realize that a theology appropriate for Europe is not necessarily appropriate for Africa. Similarly, the theology deemed appropriate for African men is not always appropriate for women. An Akan proverb says *Nea oda ne gya na onim senea ehyehye fa* ("it is the person sleeping by the fire who knows the intensity of the heat").[67]

In a similar vein, respect for women's moral agency permits us to condemn the practice of genital mutilation as "female circumcision" is properly described. And yet as Oduyoye sagely observes, the "politics of rights" cannot be abstracted from the hermeneutical spiral of narrative interpretation and transmission. "African women who are studying or challenging such practices [as female genital mutilation] tread lightly in their desire to learn and to participate in what they see as a necessary transformation of the practice."[68]

## Conclusions

In adumbrating a rhetorical theory of rights, I contended that human rights discourse does not descend from Nietzsche's empyrean as an abstract metanarrative; nor is it of local and ethnocentric provenance, merely one of innumerable "*petits recits*." Attaining a formal, normative consensus as in the Kantian constructivism of Rawls or the discourse ethics of Habermas is funded by a richer, discursive *telos* of the common good, that is, the finality of establishing a regime of basic rights commensurate with the respect due moral persons. Such a discursive teleology illumines the moral (*moralisch*) grammar of our ethical (*sittlich)* traditions, including our distinctively religious traditions, permitting a significant, if still limited, degree of narrative inter-translatability. For "[i]f language is to be a means of communication," as Wittgenstein famously observed, "there must be agreement not only in definitions but also (queer as they may sound) in judgments."[69] Such an agreement, I argued, extends to our practical judgments—not merely in the "construction" of validity claims through formal procedures of attaining rational consensus, but likewise, and more fundamentally, in displaying the normative consensus always, already at play in our claim-making, that is, the moral grammar of respect (and of the rights that give it force) as "the commonality among persons that is born with the birth of language." *Pace* Rorty, it is not we who have nothing to say to the torturers of the innocent "of the form 'there is something within you which you are betraying'"; but the torturer who, in effacing the other, forsakes reasoned speech.[70]

What *we* say in international human rights law, conversely, attests to our implicit agreement or original consensus regarding the moral priority of "the inherent dignity" and "equal and inalienable rights of all members of the human family." One may, of course, play the skeptic; the burden of my argument is not to show that one *must*, on pain of logical contradiction, opt into the language game of "reasoned speech," but rather to elucidate the conditions of our practical claims being valid or "true for us," that is, "what we do" in the rhetorical practice of human rights. As with other linguistic practices, it may be that, in Wittgenstein's words, "I have exhausted the justifications," and having "reached bedrock . . . am inclined to say: 'This is simply what I do'."[71] Yet saying this is not finally to acquiesce in rhetorical anomie, for rights retain their persuasive, reason-giving force, even if they are not logically "self-evident" verities.

Such philosophical modesty permits us to reassess the role of religious belief with respect to the justification, application, and reception of (or compliance with) a regime of basic rights. For if we need not recur to an abstract metanarrative in deriving our theory of rights, neither need we methodologically abstract from the *ultimate* justificatory role of our religious narratives in grounding such rights.[72] On the contrary, far from enjoining a vacuous tolerance regarding religion,[73] our explicit consensus (regarding our "grasp of the truth" of a universal rights claim) may rest upon our understanding of differing religious traditions ("knowledge of the souls of those one wishes to persuade").[74]

Just as our *distinctive* religious beliefs may provide backing for the *universal* scope and categorical (apodictic) modality of our practical rhetoric (precisely where our philosophical or legal justifications, in Wittgenstein's words, "give out"[75]), so the application of rights in our particular historical contexts presumes our rich narrative repertories. For as we remarked above, the essential dignity of persons is always clothed in native garb; rights grammar is always the grammar of a particular narrative, tempering our moral imagination, for example, how we view the "resident alien" or stranger in our midst (Lev. 19:33-34). Such narrative embodiment, moreover, comports with our derivation of rights from the conditions of exercising agency. For while the abstract universality of Rawls's metanarrative requires a thin theory of primary, social goods;[76] the concrete universality of our rights claims bids us attend to the distinctive manner in which agential capabilities are fulfilled in varied cultural and religious settings, for example, how, for Oduyoye, African women's agency must be nourished by "traditional matriarchal values."[77]

Our religious traditions, finally, contribute to the public reception of rights talk, as in the vexed issue of compliance in neo-Kantian moral theories.[78] The heritage of modern Roman Catholic social teaching or the exhortations of the Dalai Lama enrich our civic *paideia* (what Martha Nussbaum calls our "civic imagination"[79]), just as they remind us of lacunae in our own practices, for example, the relative denigration of subsistence rights in philosophical liberalism. Religious belief may even inspire deeds that attest to the claims of justice in transcending them, for example, the martyrdom of Archbishop Oscar Romero or Bishop Juan José Gerardi in defense of human rights. In times of uncivil strife, civic rapprochement (*koinōnia*) and compliance with a regime of rights may, indeed, depend upon such supererogatory *evangelical* inspiration. And here, perhaps, in faith costing "not less than everything," the promise of rights is redeemed[80]—that a prophet in Israel can be heard, even by the children of Babel; for these, too, "belong to Christ and Christ to God" (1 Cor. 3:23).

## Notes

[1]The allusion is to T.S. Eliot's "The Waste Land," in T.S. Eliot, *The Complete Poems and Plays* (New York: Harcourt, Brace and World, 1962), 50.

[2]See Cornel West's remarks on differing interpretations of the moral significance of race in *Race Matters*, especially chap. 2, "The Pitfalls of Racial Reasoning" (New York: Vintage Books, 1993), 35-49.

[3]Max Weber, "Science as a Vocation," in *From Max Weber: Essays in Sociology*, trans. and ed. H. H. Gerth and C. Wright Mills (New York: Oxford University Press, 1946), 148-55.

[4]"Déclaration des droits de l'homme et du citoyen," in David G. Ritchie, *Natural Rights*, 3d ed. (London: George Allen and Unwin, 1916), 290-94.

[5]Benjamin Constant, "De la Liberté des anciens comparée à celle des modernes," in *Oeuvres politiques de Benjamin Constant*, ed. C. Louandre (Paris: Charpentier, 1874).

[6]J. S. Mill, *On Liberty*, ed. Gertrude Himmelfarb (New York: Penguin Books, 1974), 72.

[7]Robert Nozick, *Anarchy, State, and Utopia* (Oxford: Basil Blackwell, 1974), 238.

[8]John Rawls, *A Theory of Justice* (Cambridge, Massachusetts: The Belknap Press of Harvard University Press, 1971), 587, 505-6, n 30; idem, *Political Liberalism* (New York: Columbia University Press, 1993), 13-14.

[9]See Hans-Georg Gadamer, *Truth and Method*, rev. 2d. ed., trans. Joel Weinsheimer and Donald Marshall (New York: The Crossroad Publishing Company, 1991), 270.

[10]Rawls, *A Theory of Justice*, 587, 505-6, n. 30.

[11]Idem, *Political Liberalism*, 13-14.

[12]Michael Sandel, *Liberalism and the Limits of Justice* (Cambridge: Cambridge University Press, 1982), 54, 94. Cf. Michael Walzer, *Thick and Thin: Moral Argument at Home and Abroad* (Notre Dame: University of Notre Dame Press, 1994), 21-25.

[13]Cf. Hegel's criticism of Kantian *Moralität* in the *Philosophy of Right: Hegel's Philosophy of Right*, trans. T. M. Knox (Oxford: Oxford University Press, 1952), par. 135.

[14]See Charles Taylor, *Sources of the Self: The Making of the Modern Identity* (Cambridge, Massachusetts: Harvard University Press, 1989), 88-90.

[15]John Rawls, "Kantian Constructivism in Moral Theory," *Journal of Philosophy* 77 (September 1980): 518.

[16]Richard Rorty, *Contingency, Irony, and Solidarity* (Cambridge: Cambridge University Press, 1989), 45.

[17]Idem, "The Priority of Democracy to Philosophy," in Merrill D. Peterson and Robert C. Vaughan, eds., *The Virginia Statute for Religious Freedom: Its Evolution and Consequences in American History* (New York/Cambridge: Cambridge University Press, 1988), 259.

[18]Ibid.

[19]Jeremy Bentham, *Anarchical Fallacies*, in *Works*, vol. 2 (Edinburgh: William Tait, 1843), 523.

[20]Edmund Burke, *Reflections on the Revolution in France*, 1700, in *Works*, vol. 2 (Bohn's British Classics, London, 1872), 305-306, 412; cf., Burleigh Taylor Wilkins, *The Problem of Burke's Political Philosophy* (Oxford: Clarendon Press, 1967), 59-60, 109-110.

[21]Rorty, *Contingency, Irony and Solidarity*, 73.

[22]Michael Sandel, "Introduction," in *Liberalism and Its Critics*, ed. Michael Sandel (New York: New York University Press, 1984), 4, 6, 10.

[23]Alasdair MacIntyre, *After Virtue* 2d ed. (Notre Dame, Indiana: University of Notre Dame Press, 1984), 69.

[24]Even within modern Roman Catholic social teaching, one observes a shift from the perfectionist teleology of *Mater et magistra*, no. 65 which depicts the common good as "the sum total of those conditions of social living, whereby [we] are enabled more fully and more readily to achieve [our] own perfection," to an invocation of dignity and rights in *Pacem in terris*, no. 60; cf. *Gaudium et spes*, no. 26, and *Dignitatis humanae*, no. 6.

[25]Hans-Georg Gadamer, "On the Scope and Function of Hermeneutical Reflection," trans. G. B. Hess and R. E. Palmer, in *Philosophical Hermeneutics* (Berkeley: University of California Press, 1976), 25.

[26]Chaim Perelman, *The Realm of Rhetoric*, trans. William Kluback (Notre Dame: University of Notre Dame Press, 1982), 1-8. Cf. Chaim Perelman and L. Olbrechts-Tyteca, *The New Rhetoric: A Treatise on Argumentation*, trans. John Wilkinson and Purcell Weaver (Notre Dame: University of Notre Dame Press, 1969), 13-62.

[27]Gadamer, "On the Scope and Function of Hermeneutical Reflection," 22.

[28]Cf. Donald Davidson, "Actions, Reasons, and Causes," and "Intending" in *Essays on Actions and Events* (Oxford: Clarendon, 1980), 3-19, 83-102 respectively.

[29]Bernard Williams, "Ought and Moral Obligation," in *Moral Luck* (New York: Cambridge University Press, 1981), 120 (emphasis added).

[30]I act rationally or autonomously if, and only if, my intentional action X is governed by my best reasons for acting, all things considered. My action, conversely, would be heteronomous if, say through rashness or incontinence, I act intentionally, albeit not from my best reasons, all things considered. Cf. Donald Davidson, "Reply to Essays I-X," in *Essays on Davidson: Actions and Events*, ed. Bruce Vermazen and Merrill B. Hintikka (Oxford: Oxford University Press, 1985), 195-229.

[31]Immanuel Kant, *Groundwork of the Metaphysic of Morals*, trans. H. J. Paton (New York: Harper and Row, 1964), 427-29 (pagination is that of the *Preussische Akademie der Wissenschaften* edition [Berlin, 1902-1938], Vol. IV]).

[32]In offering an intersubjective (discursive) and pragmatic account of what Kant describes as the "fact of pure reason," that is, the practically rational sense of "ought" (*sollen*), my analysis recalls Jürgen Habermas's discourse ethics; cf. Jürgen Habermas, *Moral Consciousness and Communicative Action*, trans. Christian Lenhardt and Shierry Weber Nicholsen (Cambridge: MIT Press, 1990), and *Justification and Application: Remarks on Discourse Ethics*, trans. Ciaran P. Cronin (Cambridge: MIT Press, 1993). Yet my interpretation differs in several salient respects: Habermas proceeds from a general theory of communicative speech acts, while I analyze a particular class of locutions, that is, practically rational judgments. Habermas, moreover, proposes a formal, procedural conception of justice, drawing upon a discursive reformulation of Kant's "formal" formula of the Categorical Imperative. My analysis, conversely, is grounded in a substantive conception of respect for rationally autonomous agents, deriving from a discursive reconstruction of the "material" formula of respect for persons (a formula by no means coextensive with, or necessarily entailed by, the formal formulation). As I argue in section 3, the primacy of respect serves as backing for an interpretation of basic human rights presumed for the discourse of free and equal moral persons.

[33]Cf. Ludwig Wittgenstein, *Philosophical Investigations*, third edition, trans. G. E. M. Anscombe (New York: Macmillan Publishing Co., 1958), pt. 1, par. 217.

[34]Aristotle, *Politics* 1253a9ff.

[35]I have developed this analysis in greater length in *The Ethics of Our Climate: Hermeneutics and Ethical Theory* (Washington, D.C.: Georgetown University Press, 1994).

[36]Since validity claims govern intentional action, the description of which is satisfied by my best reasons for acting, a validity claim would not be redeemed if I act, through weakness of will (*akrasia*), for example, due to addiction, or contrary to my own best reasons, for example, due to deceptive advertising. Cf. Davidson, "How is Weakness of the Will Possible?" in *Essays on Actions and Events*, 21-42.

[37]For an elaboration of the interest and benefit theories of rights, see Jeremy Waldron, *The Right to Private Property* (Oxford: Clarendon Press, 1988), 62-105.

[38]Perelman, *The Realm of Rhetoric*, 5.

[39]Cf. Stephen E. Toulmin, *The Uses of Argument* (Cambridge: Cambridge University Press, 1958), 94-145.

[40]*United Nations Declaration of Human Rights*, U.N.G.A. Res. 217A (III), 3(1)U.N. GAOR Res. 71, U.N. Doc. A/810 (1948). The *Convention against Torture and Other Cruel, Inhuman or Degrading Treatment or Punishment*, A/Res/39/46, 10 Dec., 1984, recognizes explicitly that "the equal and inalienable rights of all members of the human family. . . derive from the inherent dignity of the human person."

[41]Cf. Rawls, *A Theory of Justice*, 585-87.

[42]See Perelman, *The Realm of Rhetoric*, 14, 17-18. Since my interest in practically rational agents acting autonomously is unaffected by the mere numerical distinction of agents, the scope of my respect for persons is coextensive with Perelman's "universal audience." Although the modality of reasoning remains practical, the maxim of respect, in Perelman's terms, carries conviction as a matter "not of fact, but of right." Perelman and Olbrechts-Tyteca, *The New Rhetoric*, 31.

[43]For the distinction between saying and showing, cf. Ludwig Wittgenstein, *Tractatus Logico-Philosophicus*, trans. D. F. Pears and B. F. McGuinnes (Routledge and Kegan Paul, 1922), 6.1-6.12; idem, *On Certainty*, trans. Denis Paul and G. E. M. Anscombe (New York: Harper and Row, 1969), par. 618.

[44]R. J. Vincent, *Human Rights and International Relations* (Cambridge: Cambridge University Press, 1986), 17. Cf. Alexis de Tocqueville's observation, "There is nothing which, generally speaking, elevates and sustains the human spirit more than the idea of rights. There is something great and virile in the idea of right which removes from any request its suppliant character, and places the one who claims it on the same level as the one who grants it." Quoted in K. R. Minogue, "Natural Rights, Ideology and the Game of Life," in Eugene Kamenka and Alice Ehr-Soon Tay, eds., *Human Rights* (London: Duckworth, 1977), 34.

[45]I have argued in *The Ethics of our Climate*, 67-75, that the practical attitude of respect functions as a "prejudice" in Gadamer's sense, that is, a pre-judgment of our practical understanding, in the design of Rawls's original position. As such, it is disclosed rather than constructed in rational choice. Cf. Gadamer, *Truth and Method*, 265-307.

[46]Cf. Joel Feinberg, *Social Philosophy* (Englewood Cliffs, N.J.: Prentice-Hall, 1973), 58-59. In exhibiting agents' moral self-knowledge, rights rhetoric recalls the distinctive Aristotelian understanding of practical wisdom or *phronēsis*.

[47]Paulin J. Hountondji, "The Master's Voice—Remarks on the Problem of Human Rights in Africa," in *Philosophical Foundations of Human Rights*, intro. Paul Ricoeur (UNESCO: Paris, 1986), 325.

[48]Rawls, *A Theory of Justice*, 586.

[49]Cf. the refined understanding of needs, capabilities, and functionings as defining the moral minima of agency in the analyses of Amartya Sen and Martha C. Nussbaum in *Women , Culture and Development*, ed. Nussbaum and Jonathan Glover (Oxford: Clarendon Press, 1995), 259-73, and 61-115, 360-95 respectively.

[50]Alan Gewirth, *Human Rights* (Chicago: University of Chicago Press, 1982), 41-78. Cf. idem, *The Community of Rights* (Chicago: University of Chicago Press, 1996), 1-30, 135. By "reasonable" I understand a conception of flourishing consistent with the status of the agent as a "dignified object of respect." Cf. Rawls, *Political Liberalism*, 58-66.

[51]Alan Gewirth, *The Community of Rights*, 32. Cf. Henry Shue, *Basic Rights: Subsistence, Affluence, and U.S. Foreign Policy* (Princeton, New Jersey: Princeton University Press, 1980), 18-34.

[52]Rawls, *A Theory of Justice*, 204-5, 224-27; idem, *Political Liberalism*, 6-7, 166-67, 324-31.

[53]See Gérard Prunier, *The Rwanda Crisis: History of a Genocide* (New York: Columbia University Press, 1995).

[54]See Gustavo Gutiérrez, *The Power of the Poor in History*, trans. Robert R. Barr (Maryknoll, N.Y.: Orbis Books, 1983), 87-88; see likewise Jon Sobrino, *Spirituality of Liberation: Toward Political Holiness*, trans. Robert R. Barr (Maryknoll, N.Y.: Orbis Books, 1988), 103-14.

[55]David Little, "The Nature and Basis of Human Rights," in *Prospects for a Common Morality*, ed. Gene Outka and John P. Reeder, Jr. (Princeton: Princeton University Press, 1993), 75.

[56]See Jean-François Lyotard, *The Postmodern Condition: A Report on Knowledge*, trans. G. Bennington and B. Massouri (Minneapolis: University of Minnesota Press, 1984), 27.

[57]See Weber, "Science as a Vocation," 155; Wittgenstein, *Philosophical Investigations*, pt. 1, pars. 497, 664.

[58]See Jürgen Habermas, "The Hermeneutic Claim to Universality," in Joseph Bleicher, *Contemporary Hermeneutics* (London: Routledge and Kegan Paul, 1980), 190-203. Cf. Ralph Ellison's eloquent depiction of our "national tendency to deny the common humanity shared by my character and those who might happen to read of his experience," in *Invisible Man* (New York: Random House, 1992), xxvi.

[59]David Hollenbach, "A Communitarian Reconstruction of Human Rights: Contributions from Catholic Tradition," in *Catholicism and Liberalism*, ed. R. Bruce Douglass and David Hollenbach (Cambridge: Cambridge University Press, 1994), 145.

[60]Seyla Benhabib, "The Generalized and the Concrete Other: The Kohlberg-Gilligan Controversy and Feminist Theory," in *Feminism as Critique*, ed. Benhabib and Drucilla Cornell, (Minneapolis: University of Minnesota Press, 1987), 87; cf. George Herbert Mead, *Mind, Self,*

*and Society from the Standpoint of a Social Behaviorist*, ed. Charles W. Morris (Chicago: University of Chicago Press, 1962), 152-64, 379-89.

[61]Cf. Kant, *Groundwork of the Metaphysic of Morals*, 436-37, where Kant distinguishes the form of the moral imperative which prescribes that "Maxims must be chosen as if they had to hold as universal laws of nature," from the matter which prescribes that "A rational being, as by his very nature an end and consequently an end in himself, must serve for every maxim as a condition limiting all merely relative and arbitrary ends." Matter and form are united in a complete determination such that "all maxims as proceeding from our own making of law ought to harmonize with a possible kingdom of ends as a kingdom of nature."

[62]Søren Kierkegaard, *Works of Love*, trans. Howard and Edna Hong (New York: Harper and Brothers, 1962), 10. Cf. Gene Outka, *Agape: An Ethical Analysis* (New Haven: Yale University Press, 1972), 20.

[63]Wittgenstein, *Philosophical Investigations*, pt. 1, pars. 7, 66ff.

[64]Ibid., pars. 68, 179.

[65]Cf. Rorty, "The Priority of Democracy to Philosophy," 259. As Martha Nussbaum argues, cultural narratives typically "contain argument, resistance, and contestation of norms." *Cultivating Humanity: A Classical Defense of Reform in Liberal Education* (Cambridge, Massachusetts: Harvard University Press, 1997), 127; cf. chap. 4, "The Study of Non-Western Cultures," *passim*.

[66]Mercy Amba Oduyoye, *Daughters of Anowa: African Women and Patriarchy* (Maryknoll, N.Y.: Orbis, 1995), 164.

[67]Idem, "Christian Feminism and African Culture: The 'Hearth' of the Matter," in *The Future of Liberation Theology: Essays in Honor of Gustavo Gutiérrez*, ed. Marc H. Ellis and Otto Maduro (Maryknoll, N.Y.: Orbis, 1989), 442.

[68]Idem, *Daughters of Anowa*, 165.

[69]Wittgenstein, *Philosophical Investigations*, pt. 1, par. 242.

[70] Richard Rorty, *Consequences of Pragmatism* (Minneapolis: University of Minnesota Press, 1982), xlii.

[71]Wittgenstein, *Philosophical Investigations*, pt. 1, par. 217.

[72]Cf. David Little and Sumner B. Twiss, *Comparative Religious Ethics: A New Method* (San Francisco: Harper & Row, 1978); Sumner B. Twiss, "Comparative Ethics and Intercultural Human-Rights Dialogues: A Programmatic Inquiry," in *Christian Ethics: Problems and Prospects*, ed. Lisa Sowle Cahill and James F. Childress (Cleveland: The Pilgrim Press, 1996), 357-78. Robert Traer, *Faith in Human Rights: Support in Religious Traditions for a Global Struggle* (Washington, D.C.: Georgetown University Press, 1991); and Hans Küng, ed. *Yes to a Global Ethic* (New York: Continuum, 1996) in support of an ecumenical and interreligious consensus on the rhetoric of dignity and human rights.

[73]See John Rawls, *Political Liberalism*, 4-11; 212-54.

[74]Gadamer, "On the Scope and Function of Hermeneutical Reflection," 22.

[75]Wittgenstein, *Philosophical Investigations*, pt. 1, par. 211, cf. pars. 217ff.

[76]Cf. Amartya Sen, "Well-Being, Agency and Freedom: The Dewey Lectures 1984," *Journal of Philosophy* 82:195-202. Unlike the mere distribution of primary goods, the realization of basic capabilities depends upon our distinctive cultural resources. Subsistence rights imply not only provision of culturally appropriate food, but of culturally pertinent means of protecting the most vulnerable (typically women and children) against deprivation, for example, employment opportunities, extension of land tenure and credit, etc. Rawls concedes the force of Sen's criticism that "basic capabilities are of first importance and that the use of primary goods is always to be assessed in the light of assumptions about those capabilities." *Political Liberalism*, 183.

[77]Mercy Amba Oduyoye, "Feminist Theology in an African Perspective," in *Paths of African Theology*, ed., Rosino Gibellini (Maryknoll, N.Y.: Orbis, 1994), 176.

[78]Cf. Rawls, *Political Liberalism*, 81-88; 133-44.

[79]Nussbaum, *Cultivating Humanity*, 88.

[80]T. S. Eliot, "Four Quartets," in *The Complete Poems and Plays*, 145.

# Passionate Mothering: Toward an Ethic of Appropriate Mother-Child Intimacy[1]

*Cristina L. H. Traina*

## Abstract

Women's informal accounts of their experience, news reports, and psychological and endocrinological studies concur that maternal-infant relations are inevitably erotic, if not explicitly sexually charged. In a culture that both affirms pursuit of "natural" pleasure and condemns overt eroticism in any relationship between unequals, maternal erotic experience is problematic. This essay gathers insights from the literatures of psychoanalysis, naturalism, maternal practice, and victim advocacy, as well as the Christian theological ethics of Lisa Sowle Cahill, Christine E. Gudorf, and Bonnie J. Miller-McLemore, to construct a tentative descriptive and prescriptive account of maternal eroticism.

> Nothing, to be sure, had prepared me for the intensity of relationship already existing between me and a creature I had carried in my body and now held in my arms and fed from my breasts . . . . No one mentions the strangeness of an attraction--which can be as single-minded and overwhelming as the early days of a love affair—to a being so tiny, so dependent, so folded-in to itself--who is, and yet is not, part of oneself.[2]

For Adrienne Rich the ardor of maternity is intensely physical: the "passion" of the infant gaze, the "pleasure of having [her] full breast suckled."[3] Noelle Oxenhandler calls this "intense physicality" "the eros of parenthood: an upswelling of tenderness, often with a tinge of amazement, that expresses itself primarily through touch."[4] How many of us have been bodily in love with our children, have been gripped by this unexpected and mysterious longing for "direct sensuous congress" with them?[5]

The explicit eroticism of maternity is not news. Medieval women's accounts of mystical drinking from the side of the adult Christ or luxurious nursing of the infant Jesus contain erotic language no less powerful than that of their descriptions of mystical bridal union with Christ.[6] Recent and contemporary authors—Sheila Kitzinger, Helene Deutsch, Sara Ruddick, Ashley Montagu, Marie Langer, Alice Rossi, and Toni Morrison, to name a few—also treat maternal eroticism frankly. Yet in an age still overshadowed by Freud, talk of this experience is dangerous. For although the medieval church does not appear to have reduced maternal eroticism to adult genital pleasure, Freud makes it hard for us to read any instance of eroticism in any but a sexual way. Thus women of northern cultures in this generation--especially nursing mothers—at times experience their contact with their children as sexually pleasurable. This is not merely a case of "seeing as." Almost fifty years ago, Niles Newton provided biological evidence of such a link: nursing releases into women's bodies the hormones of sexual arousal and orgasm.[7] Hence the urgency of paying special attention to the nursing relationship. Although not every woman experiences breastfeeding as an erotic exchange, if maternal eroticism is destined to be interpreted as sexual pleasure, nursing will fall under suspicion first.

We do not reflect ethically on this brand of eroticism. But we must think hard about it, for in a culture fixated on adult sexual release even the term "maternal eroticism" puts two moral dogmas on a collision course. One is the belief—now so widely accepted that even conservative Catholics and evangelical Protestants hold it—that the pleasure of erotic touch is a good worth experiencing, or even worth seeking, in the proper context. If for many women it is hard *not* to read nursing—a practice that doctors and parenting literature enjoin—as sexually pleasurable, then sexual enjoyment of nursing is good. The conflicting dogma is the moral conviction that relationships between persons of unequal power—and who is more vulnerable than an infant in the care of its mother?—must be free from even the slightest taint of sexual eroticism. Hence the "strange unease" Oxenhandler feels when she describes the physical rapture of parent-child love. How do we deal ethically with the conflict between the apparent naturalness and goodness of maternal erotic pleasure on the one hand, and the seemingly necessary proscription of it on the other?

This is not a purely theoretical question. The confusion of perspectives is already wrecking the lives of families and confounding the tasks of child welfare workers. Oxenhandler tells

> of a young mother outside Syracuse whose two-year-old daughter was taken away from her after she naïvely confided to an uninformed stranger that she had become aroused while breast-feeding. She had called a community volunteer center to find out how to contact the local

> chapter of the La Leche League support group. Anyone at La Leche could have assured her that such feelings were utterly normal. Instead, the community volunteer center referred her to a rape crisis center, which in turn reported her to a child abuse hotline. She was arrested and subjected to a five-hour interrogation, and was separated from her daughter for an entire year.[8]

In a less clear-cut case, child welfare workers began a sexual abuse investigation when a six-year-old girl mentioned breastfeeding. On learning, among other things, that the parents slept unclothed and that their daughter sometimes cuddled in bed with them, a judge supported the welfare workers' removal of the girl from her home.[9] Social workers and family courts should not bear the blame in these cases; their mandate is to protect children from likely abuse, and they must err on the side of caution. Yet in order to minimize damage to the children they are to protect they must distinguish more subtly between abnormal, incestuous behavior and normal parental eroticism. And they can hardly be expected to apply a distinction no one has articulated.

This essay is a first effort to disentangle these categories, and like most first efforts it builds its tentative conclusions on an artificial but necessary simplification of the issues. First, it asks an explicitly feminist question: "How does serious reflection on women's experience unsettle traditional modes of moral thought on sexuality?" There is not space to answer this query comprehensively, let alone pose the other questions that deserve exploration. Second, therefore, the "toward" in the title is meant seriously. The following review of cultural and theological resources for such a distinction is not comprehensive--notably absent is literature on pedophilia, for instance--and my conclusions are provisional. Challenges, additions, and refinements are necessary and welcome. Third, I focus on mothers nursing infants to whom they have given birth. I start here not because other adult-child relations are derivative or unimportant but because, rightly or not, we tend to consider experiences that have verifiable biological causes to be less voluntary, more inexorable, more "natural." The breastfeeding relationship may then be the safest place to begin working out the distinctions between healthy and perverse maternal eroticism and, eventually, between appropriate and condemnable eroticism between unequals in general. Finally, I take the experience for granted and look for interpretive guidance from two sorts of literatures: secular psychology and ethics, and theological ethics.

## Secular Psychology and Ethics

Each of the schools of thought below contributes something essential to the task of analyzing maternal eroticism, but each on its own is inadequate. I do not address social constructionism and critical theory directly—not because they are unimportant, but because their singularly helpful message is the indispensable reminder to watch for ideological dragons, to avoid reducing women to mothers, and to resist any assumptions that we have defined maternity or sexuality once for all.

*Freudianism*

Freudian appreciation for the crucial and fragile process of psychological development in infants and children is an element of all the other categories of thought below, especially contemporary naturalism. Freud and his intellectual descendants insist that we approach children with great thought, care, and respect, that we understand the weight of even our earliest patterns of interaction with them.[10] In particular, infants are already sexual subjects, and failure to respond appropriately to the needs posed by their sexual developmental stages can lead to sexual, social, and psychological problems later.[11] Thus, although Freud and those who came after him may have erred by seeming to reduce everything to sex, they at least integrated sex psychologically with other human emotions and desires and so humanized and domesticated it.

Freud's pupils, Marie Langer and Helene Deutsch, went on to acknowledge the sexual eroticism that breast-feeding arouses in mothers, gave it a place in the psychological system, recognized the conflicts and ambivalences it posed, and put limits on its appropriate fulfillment.[12] In addition, 25 years before Kristeva, Langer decried the western dissociation of maternity and sexuality in the asexual ideal of the Virgin Mary, that "maximum symbol of motherhood for Western man."[13] Langer at times listened so hard to women's maternal experiences that she turned Freud's psychoanalytic focus upon "adjusting" women to their cultural circumstances upside down: internal psychological tensions revealed points of external cultural conflict, rather than the reverse.

Yet the Freudian revolutionary integration of sexuality with human emotional and developmental life was achieved at a significant cost. In the end it resembles Ptolemaic astronomy: it correlates observed events brilliantly, but the explanation it gives—the unconscious—ends up obscuring rather than illuminating their true connections. Mothers' anxiety over the conflict between maternity and outside work evolves not just from unresolved tensions with their parents but also from social and economic pressures. Similarly, not just remembered orality, but hormones, make breast-feeding erotic. Nipple-biting may sometimes be an attack on the mother,[14] but teething pain is an important and usual cause. Although for a psychologically conflicted mother cracked nipples may be a welcome excuse to stop nursing, fissures themselves are not, as Langer suggested, the result of unconscious emotional sabotage[15] but a consequence of poor nursing technique. As Eli Sagan concludes, Freud never could decide whether we should integrate the mind and the body or leave the body as far as possible behind,[16] and that ambivalence—as far as it endures in western psychology—ensures ambivalence toward the *conscious* eroticism of nursing.

*Naturalism*

One antidote to Freudian anxiety about the body is what might be called bioevolutionary naturalism. It is fashionable to say that sexuality is a cultural construct.[17] But naturalism's first point is that sexuality is embodied and therefore, to an important extent, given. For example, Alice Rossi argued recently that sexuality is not simply a plastic idea but also an embodied experience encompassing "physical and chemical processes" laid down in us over millennia,[18] processes that resist "dramatic changes in social and economic circumstances" and the new ideals and practices of sexuality these changes generate: "The most ardent feminist and the tenderest of men carry residues of the old traditional ways, and we cannot yet know to what extent our cognitive reformulations can control and redirect the quite different messages that stem from earlier emotional layers of our personalities, resist the pressures imposed by external roles we need to fill in society, or cope with opposing predispositions laid down in the biology we have inherited."[19] Rossi believes that we may be unable to wish away gender differences in such things as mate selection criteria, verbal and spatial intelligence, levels of comfort with casual sex, or styles of love. This does not mean that we must simply resign ourselves to following our archaic tendencies,[20] but it does dictate that if our new, more egalitarian constructions of sexuality are not to be self-defeating, we must compensate for the bodies and psyches that evolved in eras in which men's and women's social roles differed radically.[21]

It is not necessary to accept Rossi's list of potential non-negotiables in order to see what her thesis might yield for this discussion. Our task is to identify and learn to live with the less malleable dimensions of our sexuality. Maternal eroticism may be an evolutionary adaptation that motivates women to nurse their children and, like sex,[22] inspires caretaking behavior. Now that we have other perfectly good feeding methods, not to mention religious and social inducements to care for our children, this unavoidable eroticism is superfluous. The challenge is dealing justly with it today. The answer, Rossi argued 25 years ago, lies in the context: twentieth-century western culture is marked by western male desire to control women's sexuality and hence by the submergence of maternal eroticism. Here the appropriately rebellious feminist response is to embrace maternal eroticism and speak publicly about it.[23]

Rossi bases her argument on women's bodily experience and social standing. Ashley Montagu, although cognizant of both the eroticism of nursing for women and the physical benefits for both mother and baby of breastfeeding, points toward a slightly different use of naturalism. He makes what amounts to a moral case for meeting children's developmental social, emotional, and psychological needs for touch, supporting his thesis with descriptive studies of touch-deprived primates and hospitalized and orphaned children.[24] Relaxed breastfeeding—the perfect medium of nurturing touch—is also the infant's earliest and possibly most influential sexual education.[25] Love and caress, and the baby will grow up happy, healthy, and capable of sexual affection; deny its need for touch, and it will grow up stiff and rather uncomfortable with people.[26] Muses Montagu, "Freud himself was a bit of a cold fish, and one cannot avoid the suspicion that he was insufficiently fondled when he was an infant."[27] Yet Montagu's naturalism is not rigid. As his primary concern is the baby's social, sexual, and psychological welfare, the *manner* in which the baby is cuddled and talked to is much more important than the *mode* of feeding; better a gentle, nurturing bottle-feeding than a cold, impatient breast-feeding, he implies.[28]

Rossi and Montagu explore from the mother's and the child's perspectives, respectively, the naturalist maxim that the body makes moral claims. Yet they and other naturalists sometimes fail to consider the interpersonal and social dynamic of touching. This problem—evident in both Montagu and Rossi—finds its way into childbirth and baby care literature, much of which is breezily dismissive of—even blind to—the genuine psychological conflict that may accompany the intense tactile pleasures of mothering an infant. As Sheila Kitzinger at least points out, some women experience considerable conflict, even revulsion, at experiences of arousal during breast-feeding, or even at sharing their breasts—which had been for them organs of sexual display or pleasure—with an infant.[29]

Yet Kitzinger, like most naturalists, naïvely fails to ruminate on the social, experiential roots of these conflicts. For instance, Elaine Westerlund found that the female victims of childhood incest whom she interviewed, if they nursed at all, often felt betrayed by their own unsought erotic responses to their children and said that the pleasure of nursing felt incestuous. That many victims of incest find it difficult to *associate* love and sexual intimacy[30] may further complicate the issue. Conversely, Niles Newton found that women who are comfortable with their own sexuality tend to succeed at breastfeeding;[31] presumably they are also less anxious about its erotic dimensions. How "natural" following "nature" is depends upon whether our experience permits us to trust it.

Naturalism presents a number of other dangers against which it can be protected only by an additional philosophical overlay. First, even when naturalism exerts itself mightily against the tendency to equate description with prescription, the lines it draws often seem arbitrary. One leaves Rossi, for instance, wondering whether men's tendency to desire attractive mates is *really* ingrained. It may be ubiquitous, but is it biological? Naturalism also easily casts women in the "barefoot and pregnant" role. Second, Montagu and the childbirth and parenting literature especially assume that although *others* may have a wounded or perverse sense of the body, the *reader* will not go wrong if she simply attunes herself to her own and others' "biopsychosocial" needs. An important warning against this assumption is Edward Brongersma's two-volume work on man-boy love, which draws upon primate studies, developmental arguments, and accounts of man-boy relationships to argue that man-boy love is a natural and even superior way of meeting boys' needs for affection.[32] So although naturalism deals seriously with the body and with developmental requirements, it is not a sufficient basis for an ethic of intimacy.

*Maternal practice*

Brongersma's arguments could lead us—as he unabashedly admits—toward full-fledged incest: mothers seeking out their infants explicitly for sexual gratification. Brongersma sees no difficulty here, but we should, and that is where the collection of authors we might call "maternal practice thinkers" can be particularly helpful: in distinguishing, as he refuses to, between the eroticism (for example) of nursing an infant and the eroticism of initiating a full-fledged sexual affair with one's 15-year-old son.[33] Adrienne Rich, Sara Ruddick, Noelle Oxenhandler, and Julia Kristeva work not solely from psychological, sociological, and evolutionary studies but also from their own experience of concrete, embodied maternal practice.

Oxenhandler helps us begin to grasp the distinction between maternal and romantic eroticism:

> In its intense physicality, it partakes of the love that also exists between grownup lovers—but it is different in some absolutely crucial ways. For healthy parental love is a sheltering, protective love that respects the radical inequality—in size, in power, in maturity—between parent and child. Though it sometimes flares into wild playfulness, its predominant rhythm is serene and relaxed, and it does not approach the driving, climactic movement of adult sexuality.[34]

Parental eros, for Oxenhandler, motivates and rewards the "hard work, exhausting and unceasing labor" of parenting and inspires an intense awareness of the infant's needs for protective nurture.[35]

A second distinction, the distinction between erotic connection to one's own infant and erotic relationship with another child, applies especially to biological mothers and their babies. My infant—physically, at least—has been me. We have already heard Rich marvel at "a being so tiny, so dependent, so folded-in to itself—who is, and yet is not, part of oneself."[36] Julia Kristeva adds, "There is him, however, his own flesh, which was mine yesterday."[37] No wonder mothers treat infants with passionate and meticulous interest! Yet, as Rich hints, this passion is not self-perpetuating. It meets the developmental needs of both mother and child: it lays the groundwork for and looks toward separation.[38] Ruddick observes:

> Regarded in the light of hope rather than suspicion, the entangling of self and other in birth—physical union in metaphysical separateness—is a

> crystallizing symbol not of self-loss but of a kind of self-restructuring. The birthing woman is actively herself and her activity is a giving to, a creating of another who could not live without her. Her creation fails unless the infant takes up the singular life, breathing, crying, kicking, sucking her or his own way into the world.[39]

Adult sexual union is the passionate catalytic reaction of two bodies that were formerly not only distinct but unrelated. The ardor of maternity is the opposite: a *weakening* of a formerly almost boundaryless connection, a stage in the long process of *separation* of the infant from the mother: "a nursing infant and mother hint at a union *past*."[40]

Finally, these authors are content to live with the ambiguity of an eroticism that, impossibly, seems sexual but is not genital; they even insist that the truth of parenting cannot be told without it. Oxenhandler ties parental eros to "exhausting and unceasing labor"; Kristeva muses that "a mother is always branded by pain," and yet she returns us to a calm "that finally hovers over pain."[41] Rich finds it impossible to remember the overwhelming wave of contentment that comes from snuggling a new life against her breast without also recalling the equally overwhelming emotional and practical strain of trying to meet the needs of several children, spouse, and self.[42] Ruddick reflects on the unique "conjunction of erotic excitement, physical pain, and social promise" in birth, as well as the need to combine a "welcoming maternal eros" with "sexual restraint."[43] Oxenhandler articulates the inadequacy of available modes of ethical analysis: "And there I feel the gaze again—the gaze that cannot see that two things can share similarities without being identical. For this mentality must have its boundaries in black-and-white; it cannot tolerate gradations or continuums. At the heart of it lies a sense of great moral fragility. Precisely because the soul is so likely to plummet to the abyss, it must be carefully protected by walls of prohibition."[44]

Maternal practice thinkers simply resist defining their experiences in the singular categories with which ethicists are used to dealing. They can distinguish but not divide pleasure from pain, sexuality from maternity, mental labor from physical labor.[45] Nor do subcategories created by adjectives convey the truth that they are struggling to express. "Painful pleasure" and "pleasurable pain" sound perverse or masochistic; "maternal eroticism" and "erotic maternity" make one dimension of the experience ascendant over the other. What they are describing is pleasure-pain or maternity-sexuality, genuinely multivalent experiences created by the overlay of two or several simpler categories and radically different from any of them.

What are the drawbacks of the maternal practice approach? First, we must exercise caution. Used carelessly, it risks an epistemological matricentrism that ultimately would disqualify all non-mothers from participating in discussions of appropriate maternal touch. In addition, we must not ignore the care with which all four authors examine the effects of social institutions and political ideologies on the experience and moral practice of mothering. Failure to reincorporate these would produce a naïve, culturally bound, and unself-critical vision of mothering.

But two more serious drawbacks also plague maternal practice ethics. To begin with, it is not enough to acknowledge maternal eroticism and notice the necessity of establishing a boundary between it and perversion; we must also explain precisely where the boundary—or at least the danger zone—lies. Brongersma's vision of man-boy love illuminates this need because it ostensibly fulfills all but one of the marks of healthy maternal eroticism mentioned so far: the bodily, biological connection between mother and infant. Plainly this criterion is no protection against abuse. So while the poetic truths of these mothers' writings set us on the path, we must hone our descriptions still further. We also tend to hide our vices under the cloak of virtue. We may not be about to "plummet to the abyss," but we must balance a trust in our maternal wisdom with a healthy skepticism about our intentions. We can misread, err, and ignore. Otherwise there would not be child sexual abuse.[46] Here advocacy literature steps in.

*Advocacy*

Among the most powerful writings condemning sexual abuse is the work of Marie Fortune. Fortune demonstrates that our visions of ideal social relations, however vital to our moral and spiritual lives, do not protect the vulnerable from individuals and systems that now fall short of these ideals. We must be able to set boundaries and identify violations. In professional relationships, which are the focus of most of her writing,[47]

> The purpose of clear boundaries is not to preserve some cache of patriarchal power on the part of the professional. Boundaries used appropriately create a safe place where an individual can reflect on her own experiences and learn from them without having to deal with the personal needs of the professional. In any relationship, boundaries provide the structure within which a relationship can grow and mature. Boundaries, like lane markers or guardrails at the edge of the road, give guidance and direction and recommend necessary caution. Living without relational boundaries is like driving on the freeway in a snowstorm: very dangerous to all concerned.[48]

These limits are indispensable in a culture in which gross imbalance—for instance, "the absolute powerlessness and vulnerability of a child"—is a sexual turn-on, a culture that has not yet learned that "equality can be very erotic."[49]

Two premises lie behind Fortune's convictions: all sexual activity must be governed by the principle "do no harm," and a relationship may become explicitly sexual only by mutual, genuine consent. The latter criterion has to do with power relationships between partners: the choice of a peer as sexual partner, and authentic and informed consent. Fortune elaborates it:

> 1. Is my choice of intimate partner a peer, that is, someone whose power is relatively equal to mine? We must limit our sexual interaction to our peers and recognize that those who are vulnerable to us, that is, who have less power than we do, are off limits for our sexual interests.
> 2. Are both my partner and I authentically consenting to our sexual interaction? Both of us must have information, awareness, equal power, and the option to say "no" without being punished as well as the option to say "yes."[50]

Student-teacher, congregant-minister, client-therapist, and employee-employer relationships are all fundamentally unequal and so preclude genuinely free consent.[51] The parent-child relationship is analogous: a bond between unequals in which the parent, possessing nearly absolute authority and social power, is entrusted with benevolent care for the vulnerable child. For the parent to admit sexual activity into the relationship—even if it is the child who "sexualizes" the bond initially—is wrong.[52]

The usefulness of Fortune's criteria for judging maternal eroticism depends on the completeness of this analogy. Although the similarities are real and compelling, two subtle refinements must be made. First, Fortune seems to assume that there is no middle ground between suppressing eroticism on one hand and acknowledging and acting on it in full-blown, adult genitality on the other. But this either/or, on/off dictum does not quite reflect the experience of erotic interaction, either maternal or adult. Ruddick, for example, combines acknowledgment and enjoyment of maternal eros with disciplined, protective restraint—an eros of a different quality than Fortune's, somewhere on or above a continuum between suppression and abandon. Even relationships between adults admit degrees of eroticism. How many of us can honestly say that we never engage in not-quite-subconscious flirtations with others—perhaps subordinates or superiors—with whom we would never dream of having an affair? So while Fortune's proscription of full-blown adult genitality in parent-child relations may hold, it is not clear that she has the language to deal with maternal eroticism as I have described it.

Second, for Fortune the inegalitarianism of parental and professional relationships, and the prohibition of eroticism within them, seems to be fundamental and therefore constant. Carter Heyward objects that all relationships are dynamic and should move self-consciously toward egalitarian mutuality, with its potential for erotic intimacy.[53] Their disagreement is rooted partly in a philosophical difference: Fortune holds that status differences are benign if the powerful either voluntarily abdicate their power or use it to create justice; Heyward sees status differences as inherently oppressive.[54] But relationships between unequals—therapy, teaching, parenting--are more subtle and complex than either author admits. For instance, the mother-child bond is dynamic but may be permanently unequal without being dysfunctional.[55] Eventual, full parent-child mutuality is a fine hope but a rare accomplishment and a presumptuous and unfair expectation. In this dynamic but unequal relationship, my overriding maternal task is developmental: to nurture my children in such a way that they learn to create mutual relationships with others.[56] I cannot complete this charge without a frightening degree of intimacy, tenderness, and its accompanying eroticism. In short, eroticism cannot simply be excised from this unequal relation. A glimmer of an acknowledgment arises in Fortune as a negative criterion for the adult-child connection: "children and adults do . . . have intimate or deeply meaningful relationships. But adults should not be asking children to meet their emotional and sexual needs *in the same way* that they ask their adult partners to do so."[57] Still lacking is a more explicit description of adult-child relationships and the likewise unique place of a healthy eroticism in them.

What materials for an ethic of maternal eroticism have we gleaned so far? None of the approaches examined so far is adequate, but cumulatively their wisdom is impressive.

1. Maternal eroticism is widely acknowledged, as are its connections to evolutionary biological factors. The capacity for maternal eroticism is universal, not merely in the human mind, but also in the physical and emotional "wiring" of the evolved female body. It is both "natural" and commonplace, although social constructions have a say in its articulation; so although not all contemporary mothers experience it as sexual, a large proportion of them inevitably do.

2. Although attentive affection, including loving touch, is a universal condition of thriving, it is a prerequisite especially for children's normal emotional, physical, and social development. The eroticism of maternal touch, especially breast-feeding, tends to make this task an attractive one. Yet its developmental character also seems to dictate a gradual tempering of intense physical contact in response to the child's changing needs--for instance, as a child begins to wean. This separation meets maternal needs as well.

3. Mothers tend to describe mothering experiences multivalently rather than reducing them to singular categories. Thus even when maternal eroticism is experienced as sexual, it is not typically experienced as identical to full-blown adult sexual passion. Similarly, adult-child relationships can be intense, even to a degree mutual, but unlike adult friendships. "Overlay" or "multivalence" may help us to articulate the ethical import of these similarities and differences.

4. Gauged by the apparent holistic benefits of early, intensely physical mothering for mother, child, and their relationship, maternal eroticism seems at least morally acceptable, and possibly morally good, as long as it is alert to and remains within the bounds of the child's developmental needs.

## Theology

To this point we have explored a phenomenon and have begun to articulate some guidelines for interpreting and evaluating it. The figures discussed even anticipate many theological insights into parental experience. But a Christian religious ethic must still provide an explicitly theological frame for maternal eroticism, and here the insights of Lisa Sowle Cahill, Bonnie J. Miller-McLemore, and Christine E. Gudorf are instructive. What follows should be taken as groundwork only, for probing their theologies deeply enough to enumerate all their contributions, or to resolve the tensions among them, is not possible in a small space. I limit myself to one dimension of each writer's work and caution that each point can in fact be found in two—or in some cases all—of the authors.

### *Lisa Sowle Cahill and Natural Law*

The feminist dilemma is that, while to ignore women's particular embodiment has been to accept an unattractively sterile rationalism (or a social constructionism equally ungrounded in physical reality), to embrace embodiment—especially the maternal body—has been to risk an equally unpalatable reductionism. In the first case bodies do not matter, so women are not-mothers and perhaps not-women; in the second, *all* the elements of their character and experience are determined by their potential maternity.

Lisa Sowle Cahill is notable for walking a path between these extremes. In an era given to assuming that society constructs bodies, Cahill contends that bodies ground society. Sexed bodies, she insists, are "relatively invariant over space and time."[58] Women and men do differ fundamentally and universally, and these differences ground sexual reproduction and whole systems of social-biological kinship, none of which Cahill thinks we should dismiss lightly.[59] Yet these differences are not absolute. Not only are women and men also united by their even more fundamental common humanity, but also their sexed bodies underdetermine moral norms, setting boundaries and conditioning possibilities rather than dictating hard-and-fast roles: "Biological sex differences and male and female parenthood . . . are more opportunity than limit."[60]

So like Rossi and Montagu, Cahill takes embodiment seriously and yet refuses to map instinct directly onto moral norms: "It is neither true that what biological drives suggest, moral expectations must accept; nor that every bodily tendency which must be rearranged, sublimated, or even curtailed to accomplish moral excellence is an outlaw to humanity's true nature."[61] But as we have seen, this affirmation alone can lead to arbitrary and opportunistic reasoning. If one inclination is as obsolete as an appendix, and the next is a signpost to be followed, what criterion supports this judgment?

Although, as I will show, Cahill's conclusions on adult sexuality provide an analogue for a credible ethic of maternal eroticism, what is invaluable is her method of making ethical use of physical givens: systematic criteria and theological backing for a consistent method of identifying the type, scope, and specificity of the body's authority in moral reflection. Cahill fills the gap between bodily description and moral prescription with a version of natural law. She begins with Thomas Aquinas, "for whom the natural law [is] the inclination of every creature to the proper ends and actions intended for it by God; in human beings this inclination is not just physical or instinctual, but also intellectual and rational."[62] Moral knowledge—as it has to do with interdependent, integral human flourishing—is empirical and social.[63] Experience sets bodily drives and gender differences within a substrate of profound similarities in human social and physical functioning, as well as principles of justice and right, and virtues of prudential reasoning, without which neither societies nor individuals function smoothly.[64] Bodies and embodied experience have voices, but they do not have absolute power, for they are subordinate to the integral (physical, intellectual, and spiritual) human telos.[65] Therefore we must begin our reflection with this integral end.

Cahill's concrete conclusions are instructive in a different way. When she reflects on adult genital intimacy in light of this integral end, a marital ideal emerges: a God-given, interpersonal pleasure within an equally God-given, inherently parental-reproductive context. An alternative vision of the human end would produce a different ideal. Yet it is essential to notice that even this highly traditional norm, when rooted in Cahill's vision of the body as the ground of possibility of sexuality, suggests maternal eroticism as an analogue to the gift of marital sexuality, *for in a parental-reproductive context* both could be seen as ontic goods. Like all other goods, maternal eroticism would have to be probed for trustworthiness, tested for empirical success, and related prudently to all the other goods and ends before us.[66] We need not apologize for its inherent "femininity"—its potential distinction from male parental experience—but neither must we accept it as evidence of a divine sanction for reduction of women to their potential maternal function.[67]

### *Christine E. Gudorf and Self-interested Love*

Christine Gudorf's powerful writing on sexuality and parenting develops most of the themes discussed under naturalism and maternal practice. Gudorf sees bodily pleasure as an experience to be trusted and a good to be pursued, as well as the primary criterion and indicator of morally good sex.[68] Like Cahill, she holds that a critically reconceived natural law is the most promising foundation for an ethic of sexuality that takes embodied pleasure seriously.[69] But among her indispensable theological contributions is an experientially inspired, critical reconsideration of parental love. As Gudorf points out, western Christianity ratifies an agapic model of parental love. Parent is to child as God is to parent: a font of limitless, disinterested, selfless energy and affection poured out ceaselessly, her children's welfare her only thought,[70] her only morally approved gratification a distant and intellectual satisfaction in a job well done. A feminist ethic of adult mutuality does not necessarily disrupt this model of parenting.

Yet Gudorf does overturn it. Not only is genuine parental love thoroughly partial and passionate, but also its task is to push parental relationships with children toward greater mutuality and interdependence.[71] The further, essential characteristic of Gudorf's parenthood is her unabashed self-interest. Except in cases of children with severe mental disabilities, we give one-sidedly to children in anticipation of later reciprocity. Even shorter-term self-interest is common.[72] Few of us can honestly say, when we plead with an eight-year-old for the hundredth time to close her mouth when she chews, that our immediate concern is that she make a good impression in future job interviews; we are also hoping for a more pleasant dinner hour. The same is true for toilet training, or finally getting an infant to sleep through a night of reasonable adult length without nursing.

Gudorf develops two important consequences. First, in the family, as in society at large, Christian love is a love that at least considers mutual self-interest, even when it admits that win-win solutions are not always possible.[73] This vision echoes the natural law vision of the common good, in which the genuine good of the whole generally benefits the individual, and conversely. Second, until we can face honestly our tendencies to describe our love as agape while actually functioning out of self-interest, we not only will be liars but also will often fail to meet both our children's needs and our own.

> When we assume that to do the hard, self-sacrificing thing is to do the loving thing, we have, in fact, defined the interest of the other in terms of ourselves, and not in terms of the person and conditions of the other.
>
> *****
>
> When we overemphasize the Gift-love in our loving and deemphasize the Need-love, we end up disguising our needs by calling them gifts for others. This can seriously damage the other, distorting his/her real needs and desires.[74]

Gudorf's rejection of agape yields us a God who loves us in the particular, who delights in us, who has more than our own flourishing in mind when she sets the goal and means of moral virtue before us, who in moments of genuine self-sacrifice anticipates our eventual loving response.[75] We are to imitate God in acknowledging and admitting to the pleasures we receive, not just *from* meeting the needs of others, but *in* meeting them.[76]

What does this yield for maternal eroticism? Gudorf does not deal with maternal erotic experience, or even generally distinguish maternal from parental experience. But when we combine her writings on sexual pleasure, sexual victimization, and parenting, it seems to me that they point in the following direction: It would be an unnatural and deluded mother who never admitted to seeking her own pleasure in her relationship with her children. The physical pleasures of maternity are worth desiring, and on reflection may also be worth pursuing, alongside and in balance with our other parental ends.[77] If we obscure these pleasures with claims like "I've continued to nurse only for the baby's sake," we hypocritically misplace our motives and so end up pursuing a self-sacrificial ideal we know we cannot fulfill. At the same time, Gudorf cautions us that our needs do not always coincide with others'; specifically, we must scrupulously respect children's bodyright.[78]

*Bonnie J. Miller-McLemore and Demonic Distortion*

The central claims of Bonnie Miller-McLemore's writing on maternity corroborate Gudorf's and Cahill's. Her "mother as speaking subject" is theologically subversive in the same way as Gudorf's parental self-interest; she likewise concurs with Cahill's different-and-good-but-equal-and-not-determinative evaluation of sexual biology.[79] Her unique theological contribution is her sense of the profound ambiguity and fragility of human practices. As we have seen, Gudorf transforms the vice of self-love into a virtue, diagnosing one root of maternal sinfulness along the way: the desire to disguise fulfillment of one's own needs as sacrifice for another. In the midst of her celebration of the richness and trustworthiness of maternal experience, Miller-McLemore too reminds us that without serious attention to sin our paeans to maternal moral intelligence risk baroque excess or demonic distortion.

Miller-McLemore alludes to two kids of maternal sin. The first arises out of the practice of lactation and what she calls "fleshly" knowing: "circular bodily reasoning, interweaving physical sensation, momentary cognition, behavioral reaction, and a physical sensing and intellectual reading of the results—a trial and error, hit-and-miss strategy." When this cycle fails (as it tends to do, late on the umpteenth or even the first night of failing to comfort a wailing newborn) we "must master a physical desire to retaliate in stormy, mindless abuse"; hence the "immense power for misuse" of maternal knowing.[80] This observation invites us to add a second caution: if we trace a circle of bodily reasoning that is misshapen or off-center, we and the child will wear a path the perversity of which familiarity may make it easier for both of us to deny. Again, it is easy to think of both trivial and grave examples. Then we have not only temptations to abuse but—worse—a habit of it.

Second, Miller-McLemore is not romantic when it comes to desire: "In the goodness of the human capacity 'to desire' lies the penchant not just to desire, but to doubt, worry, covet, crave, envy, and forever increase what is desired. Desire for the rich goodness of created life gives way to a disregard for divinely ordered limits on creation and a drive for invincibility."[81] The problem is not desire *per se* but the human tendency to ignore human limitations. When we reach for too much, we turn "being into having, sharing into owning, growing into getting,"[82] eclipsing and forgetting our community in God, the ultimate source of good and love. Miller-McLemore has in mind the excessive self-extension of American professional women, a frantic fragmentation (made nearly inevitable by inequities in the gendered division of labor) that turns some desires into obsessions and completely thwarts others.[83] But her point is more widely applicable. Any attentive, delighted participation in a created good can become an insatiable desire to possess and control it. On the wrong side of this line maternal erotic enjoyment is quite clearly sinful.

## Concluding Remarks

The strategy of this essay has simply been to assemble a collage of descriptions, prescriptions, and theological ruminations with an eye to formulating a coherent ethical response to the oddly hidden experience of maternal eroticism. I have suggested 1) that maternal eroticism is a normal, predictable experience that, while different from full-blown genital sexuality, has pleasures that are at face value no more or less laudable than adult sexual pleasures; 2) that children require the sort of attentive, affectionate, intimate touch that a restrained eroticism inspires; 3) that this mode of relating is appropriate to a relationship of progressive maturation and separation, not ever more intense physical involvement; and 4) that the experience can be truthfully described only multivalently ("really sexual" or "primarily maternal" is inadequate, just as green is not "really yellow" or "truly blue"). Maternal eroticism also requires a theology in which the body and its goods and pleasures are dimensions of an integral human good, in which relationships between unequals can appropriately incorporate self-love, and in which we are made profoundly aware of our own capacities to misread and abuse these goods and loves. Finally, as this essay has assumed but not argued, "what is learned from biological motherhood has parallels in other persons":[84] maternal eroticism has analogues outside the bounds of mother-infant relations, in other relationships of unequal power, and a careful analysis of it can both illumine and be illumined by them.

These suggestions cumulatively confirm that the solution to the problem posed at the beginning—how to negotiate between the affirmation of the goodness and appropriateness of the erotic pleasures that arise in maternity and the imperative to protect our children from abuse—must be not only methodological or practical but theological. For underlying this problem there is a conflict between two visions: an optimistic picture of the human inclination to know the good and do it, and soberly recounted statistics revealing endlessly rationalized, unrepented sexual exploitation. In the first case we have a profound confidence (reminiscent of natural law) in the goodness of the female body and the appropriateness of its desires to immediate and ultimate human ends; and in the second we have a pessimistic account of a depravity—also frequently connected with the body—that destroys knowledge, reason, and will. The constellation of insights that accommodates the colliding trends of contemporary sexual ethics seems theologically inconsistent.

Yet an honest assessment of the evidence suggests that the theological truth lies precisely in the tension between the two claims: our capacities for moral virtue and perversity are equally real. The key to resolving the tension may lie in an ecclesiology and epistemology of communal grace. In her discussion of sin, Miller-McLemore points out that failed generative knowing results in the temptation to abuse only when no one else relieves the burden, helps her rethink, or distracts her temporarily.[85] *Isolated* reflection on isolated maternity quickly loses perspective and grows demonic. When other people share the task of caring, thinking, or even laughing, equilibrium is restored. The lesson is that the power to discern and negotiate among goods is a communal power. If moral reflection is truly inclusive and comprehensive, the community becomes a channel of a grace that empowers us collectively to develop criteria for distinguishing between the perverse and the good.

What are the implications for maternal eroticism? First, we can trust, value, and even pursue maternal erotic pleasure within or alongside motherly caretaking. At the same time, we must confess to our capacity to deceive ourselves; I cannot trust myself absolutely to know when I have crossed the line into obsession or abuse. The Syracuse mother's questions—is this normal? should I worry about it?—reflect an appropriate caution. But not until parental experience and reasoning become topics of wide public moral reflection will descriptions of appropriate maternal eroticism acquire the richness and ethical nuance that will allay fears of abuse by aiding us to articulate the boundaries between love and mistreatment. Such a communal debate—challenging and endless—is the only way to authenticate isolated moral experience.

## Notes

---

[1]I thank the reviewers at the SCE *Annual*, as well as all present at the lecture, for their helpful comments on this essay. Remaining errors are mine.

[2]Adrienne Rich, *Of Woman Born: Motherhood as Experience and Institution*, tenth anniversary edition (New York: W.W. Norton, 1986), 35-36.

[3]Ibid., 31.

[4]Noelle Oxenhandler, "The Eros of Parenthood," *The New Yorker* (19 February 1996): 47.

[5]Sara Ruddick quotes Walker's unpublished paper. See Sara Ruddick, *Maternal Thinking: Towards a Politics of Peace* (Boston: Beacon Press, 1989), 212.

[6]Cristina L.H. Traina, "Set Afire: Images of Maternity in Medieval 'Theoeroticism,'" American Academy of Religion Annual Meeting, San Francisco, CA, November 23, 1997.

[7]Niles Newton, *Maternal Emotions* (New York: Hoeber, 1955); idem., "Psychologic Differences between Breast and Bottle Feeding," *American Journal of Clinical Nutrition* 24 (1971):993-1004; for a summary of many of her findings, see Niles Newton, "Interrelationships between Sexual Responsiveness, Birth, and Breast Feeding," in *Contemporary Sexual Behavior:*

*Critical Issues in the 1970s*, ed. Joseph Zubin and John Money (Baltimore: The Johns Hopkins University Press, 1973), 77-98.

[8]Oxenhandler, "The Eros of Parenthood," 48. See also Peggy O'Mara, "Breastfeeding and Arousal," *Natural Health* (September/October 1992): 102, 106.

[9]Observation by the author.

[10]Here my estimate of the literature follows Sidney Callahan, "The Psychology of Family Relationships," in Lisa Sowle Cahill and Dietmar Mieth, eds., *The Family*, Concilium 1995/4, 26-36 (Maryknoll: Orbis Books, 1995), 29-30.

[11]D.W. Winnicott, *The Child and the Outside World: Studies in Developing Relationships*, ed. Janet Hardenberg (London: Tavistock, 1957), 157.

[12]See Helene Deutsch, *Psychoanalysis of the Sexual Functions of Women*, ed. and intro. by Paul Roazen, trans. Eric Mosbacher (London: Karnac Books, 1991; original edition, 1924), 100-101; idem, *The Psychology of Women: A Psychoanalytic Interpretation*, 2 vols. (New York: Grune and Stratton, 1944-45), 2:290-91; Marie Langer, *Motherhood and Sexuality*, trans. and intro by Nancy Caro Hollander (New York: The Guilford Press, 1992; original edition, 1951), 230, 233.

[13]Langer, *Motherhood and Sexuality*, 238.

[14]Deutsch, *Psychoanalysis*, 101; Langer, *Motherhood*, 233-34.

[15]Langer, *Motherhood*, 230-326; Deutsch, *Psychology*, 2:281; idem, *Psychoanalysis*, 101.

[16]Eli Sagan, *Freud, Women, and Morality: The Psychology of Good and Evil* (New York: Basic Books, 1988), 137-38.

[17]See Michel Foucault, *Histoire de la Sexualité* (Paris: Gallimard, 1976-84); and Judith Butler, *Bodies that Matter: On the Discursive Limits of "Sex"* (New York and London: Routledge, 1993).

[18]Alice S. Rossi, "Eros and Caritas: A Biopsychosocial Approach to Human Sexuality and Reproduction," in *Sexuality Across the Life Course*, ed. Alice S. Rossi, *Studies on Successful Midlife Development*, 3-36 (Chicago: University of Chicago Press, 1994), 4-6.

[19]Ibid., 25.

[20]Ibid., 19-30.

[21]Ibid., 18-19.

[22]Newton, "Interrelationships," 77.

[23]Alice S. Rossi, "Maternalism, Sexuality, and the New Feminism," in *Contemporary Sexual Behavior: Critical Issues in the 1970s*, ed. Joseph Zubin and John Money (Baltimore: The Johns Hopkins University Press, 1973), 145-73, especially 165-70.

[24]Ashley Montagu, *Touching: The Human Significance of the Skin*, 3rd ed. (San Francisco: Harper and Row, 1986), 81-82, 97-99.

[25]Ibid., 92-3 (see 95 for an even more baroque paean to the breast); 206-7.

[26]Ibid., 263-5, 284-5.

[27]Ibid., 363.

[28]Ibid., 88-89.

[29]E.g., Sheila Kitzinger, *Woman's Experience of Sex* (New York: Penguin, 1983), 159, 225-230.

[30]Elaine Westerlund, *Women's Sexuality after Childhood Incest* (New York: W.W. Norton, 1992), 53-54; 59; 51, 70.

[31]Newton noted that women who were enthusiastic toward breastfeeding seem to be more comfortable with their own sexuality and with sexuality in general than those who were not; see Newton, *Maternal Emotions*, and Newton, "Interrelationships," 83-84.

[32]Edward Brongersma, *Loving Boys: A Multidisciplinary Study of Sexual Relations Between Adult and Minor Males*, 2 vols., intro. by Vern. L. Bullough (Elmhurst, NY: Global Academic Publishers, 1986-1990).

[33]Brongersma, 2:47-50.

[34]Oxenhandler, "The Eros of Parenthood," 47.

[35]Ibid.

[36]Rich, *Of Woman Born*, 36.

[37]Julia Kristeva, "Stabat Mater," trans León S. Roudiez, *The Kristeva Reader*, ed. Toril Moi, 160-186 (New York: Columbia University Press, 1986), 169.

[38]Winnicott, *The Child*, 7-8.

[39]Ruddick, *Maternal Thinking*, 210.

[40]Ibid. See also Rich, Of Woman Born, 36.

[41]Kristeva, "Stabat Mater," 167-69.

[42]Rich, *Of Woman Born*, 31-33.

[43]Ruddick, *Maternal Thinking*, 212-14.

[44]Oxenhandler, "The Eros of Parenthood," 49.

[45]On the latter see Ruddick, *Maternal Thinking*, 206.

[46]Carter Heyward and Marie M. Fortune, "An Exchange: Boundaries or Barriers?" *Christian Century* 111, no. 18 (June 1-8, 1994): 581. The point is Fortune's.

[47]See especially Marie M. Fortune, *Is Nothing Sacred? When Sex Invades the Pastoral Relationship* (San Francisco: Harper and Row, 1989).

[48]Marie M. Fortune, "Therapy and Intimacy: Confused about Boundaries" [review of Carter Heyward, *When Boundaries Betray Us: Beyond Illusions of What is Ethical in Therapy and Life*] *The Christian Century* 111, no. 17 (May 18-25, 1994): 525.

[49]Marie M. Fortune, *Love Does No Harm: Sexual Ethics for the Rest of Us*, foreword by M. Joycelyn Elders, preface by James B. Nelson (New York: Continuum, 1995), 77, 79.

[50]Fortune, *Love Does No Harm*, 38-39.

[51]Ibid., 83.

[52]Analogues taken from Fortune, "Is Nothing Sacred?" 353-4. See also Fortune, "Therapy," 525.

[53] Heyward, "Exchange," 579-80.

[54]See Fortune, "Therapy" and "Exchange."

[55]Cf. Carter Heyward, *Touching our Strength: The Erotic as Power and the Love of God* (San Francisco: Harper San Francisco, 1989), 34-35.

[56]See Christine E. Gudorf, "Parenting, Mutual Love, and Sacrifice," in *Women's Consciousness, Women's Conscience: A Reader in Feminist Ethics*, ed. Barbara Hilkert Andolsen, Christine E. Gudorf, and Mary D. Pellauer, 175-91 (San Francisco: Harper and Row, 1985), 185.

[57]Fortune, "Therapy," 525, italics added.

[58]Lisa Sowle Cahill, *Sex, Gender, and Christian Ethics, New Studies In Christian Ethics*, no. 9 (Cambridge: Cambridge University Press, 1996), 79.

[59]Ibid., 102-7.

[60]Ibid., 89.

[61]Ibid., 97.

[62]Ibid. 46-47; see also Thomas Aquinas, *Summa Theologiae*, I-II 91.2 and 94.

[63]Cahill, *Sex*, 49.

[64]See e.g. ibid., 236.

[65]See also Cristina L. H. Traina, *Undoing Anathemas* (working title), forthcoming; and Pamela M. Hall, *Narrative and the Natural Law: An Interpretation of Thomistic Ethics* (Notre Dame: University of Notre Dame Press, 1994), 37.

[66]On marital sexuality see Cahill, *Sex*, 60-61, 108-120; on the ethics of adult sexuality see also Lisa Sowle Cahill, *Between the Sexes* (Minneapolis: Fortress Press, 1985).

[67]See, e.g., Cahill, *Sex*, 97; this is not to be a call to fulfill our "true nature."

[68]Christine E. Gudorf, *Body, Sex, and Pleasure: Reconstructing Christian Sexual Ethics* (Cleveland: The Pilgrim Press, 1994), 97, 114.

[69]Ibid., 63.

[70]Gudorf, "Parenting," 182. Many of Gudorf's reflections have been inspired by her adoptive children, for whom she did not care in their infancies; the language of "parenting," quite important to the essay, also signifies this distinction.

[71]Ibid., 181-86.

[72]Ibid., 183. On the self-interested dimension of mutuality in general, see also Heyward, *Touching Our Strength*.

[73]Gudorf, "Parenting," 184, 186-7.

[74]Ibid., 184, 185.

[75]On the latter, see ibid., 187-88, 190.

[76]See Gudorf, Body, 98, 115.

[77]Ibid., 90.

[78]On bodyright, see ibid., chapter 6, and Christine E. Gudorf, "Western Religion and the Patriarchal Family," in *Feminist Ethics and the Catholic Moral Tradition, Readings in Moral Theology* No. 9, ed. Charles E. Curran, Margaret A. Farley, and Richard A. McCormick, S.J., 251-77 (New York: Paulist Press, 1996), 268-72.

[79]Bonnie J. Miller-McLemore, *Also a Mother: Work and Family as a Theological Dilemma* (Nashville: Abingdon, 1994), 94; for examples see 92, 129, 135-36.

[80]Ibid., 147-48.

[81]Bonnie Miller-McLemore, "Family and Work: Can Anyone 'Have It All?'" in *Religion, Feminism, and the Family*, ed. Anne Carr and Mary Stewart Van Leeuwen, 275-93 (Louisville: Westminster/John Knox, 1996), 289.

[82]Ibid.

[83]See Bonnie Miller-McLemore, "What's a Feminist Mother to Do?" in *Setting the Table: Women in Theological Conversation*, ed. Rita Nakashima Brock, et al., 185-204 (St. Louis: Chalice Press, 1995), 192; and Miller-McLemore, "Family and Work."

[84]Miller-McLemore, *Also a Mother*, 136.

[85]Ibid., 148.

# JUST WAR TRADITION

# Applied Just War Theory: Moral Implications of New Weapons for Air War[1]

*Martin L. Cook*

## Abstract

More than any other dimension of modern war, strategic use of air power has systematically violated the moral principle of non-combatant immunity to direct military attack that lies at the heart of the idea of just war. This paper will argue that new air weapons and tactics, such as those used in the Gulf War, mark a real change in that moral reality of war. Further, the paper explores directions in which weapons procurement, tactics, and military doctrine should continue to evolve if the military forces of the United States are to continue to improve their capabilities to conduct stragetic bombing campaigns in future wars within the limits of just war.

## Introduction

John Howard Yoder consistently held non-pacifists to a high standard of sincerity. Throughout his life he pointedly reminded just war thinkers that their just war language and categories have all too often been employed to mask the national interest of war.[2] Often, the categories of just war thought are not applied with consistency and clarity. Often, they do not serve to make strong judgments about morally legitimate war. This is a criticism that any morally sincere just war thinker must take seriously and address. This paper is an effort to apply just war thinking precisely and clearly to one area of modern war: aerial bombing.

For the purposes of this paper, I will be making two assumptions: a) that just war tradition (JWT) is an effort to instrumentalize and make practical the Christian concern that the use of force and violence always bears a "burden of proof" and must be given legitimation, and b) that international law and the restrictions of humanitarian law are important attempts to give practical force and specificity to this concern. This paper attempts to push JWT to its limits in a specific area of modern war in order to identify its limitations and its benefits. I believe this approach is preferable to the more general and abstract debate between pacifism and JWT. This detailed application allows us to see whether or not JWT can generate substantive moral judgments that respond to practical military realities, on the one hand, and yet preserve the fundamental Christian impulse to restrain and limit violence, on the other. For the sake of argument, this paper will take for granted the fundamental legitimacy of JWT and of international law as an instrumentalization of JWT's essential principles.

## Historical Perspective

From its origins, air war has been subject to peculiarly and dramatically bifurcated ways of thinking. In its ability to leap across borders and attack virtually anywhere, air power has threatened to undo the last shreds of JWT's effort to confine fighting among soldiers and its insistence on the immunity of noncombatants from direct and deliberate attack. The combatant/noncombatant distinction had been under pressure from the industrialization of war for some time before airpower's advent, of course, but the prospect of air war's deliberate attack on urban centers seemed likely to render it permanently moot. At the same time, especially in the immediate aftermath of World War I, air power offered a much-desired possibility of moving beyond costly, stagnant wars of attrition and defensive lines. Direct attack on enemy vital centers promised a new era of quick, humane war which would target the industrial and logistical support of the war effort directly, and only secondarily human beings, whether in or out of uniform. This prospect, early enthusiasts of air power suggested, would enormously reduce the length and carnage of war by focusing violence on the economic and industrial bases necessary to sustain conflict.

As matters evolved in practice through World War II and beyond, it began to appear that the prophecy of the obliteration of the combatant/noncombatant distinction would be fulfilled while precision targeting of vital centers was far more a rhetorical than a real possibility. Amid all the variations of targeting strategy for nuclear weapons in the Cold War, it seemed increasingly clear that the moral restraints on war that lay at the core of the just war tradition were archaic, at least in regard to air war conducted by well-equipped air forces. It did not require a subtle mind to determine that a full-scale conventional war between NATO and the Warsaw Pact would, in any credible scenario, inevitably evolve into at least a theater-wide total war with nuclear weapons. Almost equally certainly, it would cascade to global total war. In either case, noncombatant immunity would certainly not be respected, to put it mildly.

Some shreds of just war thinking might remain in the law books, and occasionally in practice in small-scale wars such as the Falklands conflict. For direct conflict between the U.S. and the Soviet Union, however, the probability that war would be conducted within meaningful restraints of the just war was essentially nil. This was true most especially, perhaps, in regard to air war. Strategic bombing would inevitably lead to bombing of targets in major population centers. Such bombing would, either by design or in fact (due to the limitations of the targeting mechanisms and weaponry available) be tantamount to World War II-style area bombing. Whatever the claims, bombing would inevitably involve huge numbers of direct civilian deaths due to inaccurate weapons and navigation.

The use of air power in the recent Persian Gulf War, however, potentially challenges this apparently inevitable historical progression. In that conflict, a vast application of air power was made with very little destruction of civilian life and property, even in the bombing of targets in highly urbanized environments. For the first time in the history of air power, it looked as though the promise of precision strategic bombing might, at last, be fulfilled.

Of course there were many characteristics unique to the Gulf War that give pause in drawing too sweeping conclusions about the future of air war generally. Yes, the new technologies of the F-117, cruise missile, and various kinds of precision munitions made a dramatic debut in that conflict,[3] presaging whole new classes of precision weapons in future air war. On the other hand, the desert environment in which front line troops met allowed the use of inherently indiscriminate weapons such as "dumb bombs" (the vast majority of the weapons discharged in the war) without endangering civilian lives. Further, the total air supremacy of Coalition forces in the theater was an element that may not be assumed in future conflicts.

Still, the emergence of precision weapons and new tactics for their use marks a distinctive turn in the attempt to assimilate air war to the laws and moral principles of just war. It is a turn which marks very good news indeed in the prospect of at last bringing air war under the umbrella of the central moral principles of just war. But it also points to novel areas for moral reflection on the use of such new weapons.[4] Before turning to these novel considerations, however, I briefly set their historical context.

From its very beginning, air power has been as much the subject of fantasy as of careful rational thought about its military potential. As Michael Sherry observed in *The Rise of American Air Power*, "Never viewed solely as a weapon, the airplane was the instrument of flight, of a whole new dimension in human activity. Therefore it was uniquely capable of stimulating fantasies of peacetime possibilities for lifting worldly burdens, transforming man's sense of time and space, transcending geography, knitting together nations and peoples, releasing humankind from its biological limits."[5]

From the first moments after its invention, the laws of war rushed to accommodate and attempt to regulate the new possibilities for the conduct of war the airplane made possible. In the Hague Conference of 1907, prohibition was placed on "bombardment, by whatever means" of "undefended" cities.[6] Such efforts seem quaint given the subsequent history of the use of air power. But it is important to note that early on there was the recognition that the indiscriminate attacks on cities made possible by aerial bombardment would be legally and morally unacceptable. Further, the Hague Conference recognized that such attacks, if they ever were to be accepted as means of legitimate warfare, would obliterate the prohibition on the deliberate attack on civilians that lay at the heart of just war restrictions.

Speculation about the practical military uses of air power consistently traded on the ambiguity of two quite different targeting ideas. On the one hand, early theorists such as Billy Mitchell imagined strategic uses of air power to attack the "vital centers" of an enemy, thereby avoiding the need to confront line armies in the field.[7] In this use, ideal targets would be those essential facilities of production of war materiel, and of command, control and communication, which made it possible to sustain a fighting force in the field. On the other hand, air power made it possible to entertain the possibility of direct strikes at enemy civilian populations in hope of sapping the *will to fight*. This possibility was explicitly laid out and advocated by the Italian theorist by Douhet in 1921. Douhet's idea was not that air power should destroy targets of direct and demonstrable relation to the capabilities of fielded military forces. Instead, direct, wholesale bombing of urban populations would serve to end war quickly due less to the physical destruction of the enemy's weapons and communications systems and more to the collapse of the civil society that sustained and fielded those forces. As Douhet wrote, "How could a country go on living and working under this constant threat, oppressed by the nightmare of imminent destruction and death? How indeed!"[8] The efficacy of such attacks was, apparently, deemed to be so obvious that further argument was unnecessary. When Douhet-inspired thinkers such as Britain's Trenchard wrote to address the moral justification of such a plan of attack, they were, of course, aware that intentionally bombing civilian populations would obliterate the noncombatant immunity principle. Thus, with tortured logic Trenchard insisted that bombing whole urban areas was not "for the sole purpose of terrorising [sic] the civilian population" but rather that it had its legitimate military purpose in bombing "to terrorise [sic] munitions workers (men and women) into absenting themselves from work"[9] The very illogic of such a "distinction" bears tribute to the strongly felt need to find a moral defense of the suggestion.

The point is the ambiguity in strategic thinking, and the consequent confusion about the most efficacious (never mind, morally preferable) use of strategic bombing. On one interpretation, the purpose of strategic bombing is to destroy specific identifiable targets. These targets are selected because intelligence indicates that they are the sources of production or distribution of specific items essential to the conduct of military operations or are the crucial points of command, control, intelligence coordination, and other important military functions. On the other, however, so-called strategic bombing is really a euphemism for deliberate attacks on populated areas with the intended purpose of demoralizing the population. The rationale for this mode of attack is the belief that the consequent demoralization and disorientation of the civilian population would force enemy political and military leadership to capitulate. Of course, the limited accuracy of the technology of bombardment through the Second World War made the distinction largely moot in practice. Still, it remained an important conceptual distinction, and one that would have practical consequence as the technology of air war evolved.

Although it is too complex to rehearse in detail here, in many ways the history of the use of air power in WW II can be mapped as a complex interplay between these two fundamental ideas. The differing opinions of the British and American air arms regarding the preferred method of bombing Germany early in the war illustrate this doctrinal dispute. American doctrine argued for "precision daylight" bombing. American theorists argued for careful targeting of key nodes in the enemy's economic and military system, partly as a consequence of their repugnance at wholesale terror bombing, and partly because they believed careful targeting would be more militarily effective. Sherry writes, "[Precision bombing] promised victory independent of the other branches of the armed forces, with minimal demands on and risks for Americans, employing the bomber as an instrument of surgical precision rather than indiscriminate horror, laying its high explosives (not gas or incendiaries) on its targets with pinpoint accuracy, incapacitating the enemy without slaughter."[10] In contrast the British advocated forthrightly bombing built-up areas for the purpose of terrorization, believing that this would cause German society to collapse and quickly end the war.

Despite these theoretical differences, in practice American technology was only slightly more able than British to deliver on the promise of precision bombing for the whole of the war. This became even more the case as German air defense improved and forced the bombers to higher altitudes for their bomb-runs. American and British decision-makers perceived the need to show some means of bringing home the war, first to the German and then to the Japanese public, which pushed in the direction of terror bombing. Altogether, these factors combined made area bombing the actual practice of the Allied air forces throughout the war.[11] Indeed, by the end of the war American bombing was directed away from strategic operations such as minelaying in the sea lanes (which might well have had a direct impact on the enemy's ability to wage war) *in favor of* a policy of incendiary bombing of Japanese cites.[12] But for bombing in urban areas, to repeat the point, the debate regarding pinpoint versus area bombing was pretty much a distinction without a difference. Even in 1941, close analysis of the effect of a hundred air raids into Germany revealed that "not one bomb in three had hit within five miles of its designated target, and there were extreme errors of up to a hundred miles."[13] Given these realities, area bombing was clearly the reality, regardless of the intent.

Again, the historical record of World War II is well known and well documented, and for our purposes here does not require rehearsing in detail. What is clear is that it was not technically feasible to engage in pinpoint strategic bombing given the technology available at the time. But *neither was it generally deemed desirable* to refrain from area bombing or to attempt to restrict civilian deaths to the category of reasonable collateral damage within the framework of such a careful bombing campaign.

It is only with the wisdom of hindsight after World War II that American Air Force doctrine on this point emerged into relative clarity. Current official Air Force doctrine identifies "two basic target sets" for strategic bombing: "those that would affect enemy capability to conduct military operations and those that would affect enemy will to continue fighting."[14] Even this formulation, of course, begs the question of which targets might affect "enemy will"—targets that demoralize combatants, or direct attacks on civilian populations? But clearly the possibility of targeting civilians is under consideration, since the Air Force's manual notes that the strategy rarely works: "Strategic attack has rarely affected enemy morale to the degree anticipated by early air power enthusiasts."[15] Further, in a footnote:

> Early air power theorists assumed that civilian populations would be more vulnerable and susceptible to the psychological impact of massed air power than would military personnel in combat. Ironically, history appears to demonstrate that civilian resistance tends to stiffen under persistent strategic air attacks, while the morale of soldiers on the battlefield has often been totally shattered by relatively small strikes.[16]

Increasingly after World War II it was apparent that the use of area bombing campaigns with the intent to terrorize civilian populations and demoralize enemy citizens was a dubious use of military resources. Compared to the efficacy of attack on targets that directly affected the enemy's capability to conduct military operations, the civilian target strategy was almost always ineffective.

Although recognized in theory, this realization had little opportunity for large-scale testing in Korea and Vietnam, where much of the use of air power was the air support mission to ground troops rather than engaging strategic targets. When strategic bombing was attempted, the inaccuracy of weapons made such pinpoint targets notoriously difficult to destroy until laser-guided munitions became available toward the end of the Vietnam War. Furthermore, when strategic bombing was conducted in Vietnam in the Linebacker II operation, even though exclusively military targets were selected, collateral damage was extensive. This damage was due partly to the inaccuracy of unguided munitions dropped from B-52s, and partly to Vietnamese air defense weapons which, having missed their targets, returned to earth and exploded.

In this period, thinking about truly strategic air war was relegated to the planning of the use of nuclear weapons. Even in nuclear planning, however, the counterforce vs. countervalue (i.e., counter-military capacity vs. counter population) targeting debate and issues of the prudence of thinking about a "winnable" nuclear war failed to truly help the discussion. And needless to say, the enormous destructive force of the weapons themselves made it difficult to distinguish pinpoint from area bombing in practice, regardless of the targeting theory.

Only in the Persian Gulf War did technology, political circumstance, and the nature of the enemy social organization combine to provide a new "experiment" in the efficacy of pinpoint strategic bombing. In its aftermath it was apparent that air war had entered a genuinely new phase in its history. The experience of the Gulf War suggested that the prophecies of early air war visionaries may finally be possible to a large degree.[17] Still, the very success of the air campaign points to new issues for exploration in the ongoing dialogue on international law and the law of nations regarding just conduct in war.

## International Legal Issues

In 1922-23, legal experts convened at The Hague to draft rules for air war that would, at a minimum, prohibit avoidable killing of civilians. Although these rules were never ratified by any state, many air forces did incorporate the gist of the rules into operational manuals[18] and leaders still spoke of using airpower within the restraints of just war. For example, in 1938, in an address to the House of Commons, the British Prime Minister said,

> In the first place, it is against international law to make deliberate attacks upon civilian populations. In the second place, targets that are aimed at from the air must be legitimate military objects and must be capable of identification. In the third place, reasonable care must be taken in attacking those military objects so that by carelessness a civilian population in the neighbourhood is not bombed.[19]

Despite this appearance of agreement prior to WWII, the course of the war evolved a style of air war where all pretense of maintaining this moral line was erased. Deliberate "area" or "carpet" bombing of cities became the standard of practice, especially for the Allies. Partly, this was a result of technological and operational constraints on the aircraft, targeting, and navigation systems available at the time. Partly it was a result of an explicit attempt to make civilian morale a direct object of attack. And partly it was an emotionally driven response to the German use of grossly indiscriminate weapons such as the V-1 and V-2 rockets.

This common practice did not in any way alter the legal understanding that direct attacks on civilian populations were prohibited. At the close of the war, the Nuremberg Tribunals were chartered to consider "wanton destruction of cities, towns, and villages, or devastation not justified by military necessity."[20]

Nuremberg declined to prosecute cases involving air war on the part of Axis powers, at least partially in recognition that Allied practice would be subject to precisely the same strictures.

The major shift in international law on point is marked by the passage of Additional Protocol I to the Geneva Convention in 1977. Although unratified by the U.S. and most other major powers, it nonetheless establishes a binding understanding of the customary law of war in the minds of United States military officials.[21] Additional Protocol I, Article 48 clearly codifies what (arguably) had been unclearly stated previously:

> The basic rule requires that a distinction must be made at all times between the civilian population and combatants and between civilian objects and military objectives, and that operations must accordingly be directed only against military objectives.[22]

Furthermore, the Protocol states that attackers must take "every precaution" to minimize incidental civilian losses and to insure that such losses and/or damage not be excessive in relation to the concrete and direct military advantage sought.[23]

In his comprehensive review of international law as it bears on air war, W. Hayes Parks writes,

> Article 48 states the fundamental principle of discrimination, a principle on which there should be no disagreement. Indeed, military efficiency calls for discrimination to the extent that it is reasonably possible, and the United States historically has used its technological superiority to endeavor to gain increased accuracy in order to be as discriminate as possible in placing munitions on the target.[24]

However one judges the morality and legality of the kind of air war the Allies conducted in World War II,[25] a similar pattern of targeting and target selection would clearly be illegal in the contemporary context. This is codified as the official Air Force interpretation of international law. After reviewing the conduct of air operations in World War II, the official United States Air Force interpretation of the laws of war states:

> The civilian population as such, as well as individual civilians shall not be made the object of attack. Acts or threats of violence which have the primary object of spreading terror among the civilian population are prohibited.[26]

As I will argue later, this understanding of the legal situation dovetails nicely with an improved understanding of the militarily efficacious uses of air power. Further, technological developments now permit the application of air power in ways largely congruent with such principles.[27]

## Contemporary Doctrine of the United States Air Force

Understandings of international law regarding armed conflict have practical force only insofar as they are incorporated in the doctrinal statements, the operational planning and training, and even the weapons acquisition pattern of the armed forces of nations. Only insofar as military forces incorporate these legal principles into the routines of "how we do business" do they have real action-guiding force. It is appropriate, therefore, to survey the official articulations of doctrine and theory regarding the application of air power in contemporary U.S. Air Force thinking.

The most influential thinker regarding strategic bombing in the contemporary Air Force is John A. Warden III. His book, *The Air Campaign: Planning for Combat* has been incorporated into the teaching at the United States Air Force Academy and at the various levels of Professional Military Education—the various professional schools officers attend as they advance through the ranks. To a great extent, the air campaign executed in the Persian Gulf War was the product of Warden's theories, and was actually planned by his close associates. Author Rick Atkinson wrote in *Crusade*, his history of the Gulf War, "In war no less than in peace, success has a thousand fathers, and paternity claims in the Persian Gulf War would mount in direct proportion to allied achievements. Yet no claim is stronger than Warden's."[28]

Warden's book begins with the assertion that planning for effective air war has been hampered by the lack of coherent thinking about the *operational* level of war planning. By "operational" Warden means the middle level, lying between the grand strategic plan for the overall conduct of the war and the *tactical* level, which concerns achieving reasonably discrete and identifiable objectives in battle. The operational level "is primarily concerned with how to achieve the strategic ends of the war with the forces allotted," and is generally the responsibility of the theater commander (rather than, say, of the Joint Chiefs of Staff).[29] In short, Warden's theory purports to guide the theater planner in finding the right "fit" between the overall goals of the war, on the one hand, and the panoply of resources available in theater for accomplishing those goals, on the other.

Warden argues strenuously that the Air Force has historically been crippled by an excessively narrow, "tactical" kind of thinking about the proper application of air power. Modern weapons make possible (at last) the fulfillment of much of the over-promised capability of air power from its inception: the direct attack on enemy "centers of gravity."[30] This requires more careful thought about the operational level of planning, above the tactical level.

Warden schematizes his theory in terms of five concentric circles of increasing radius, representing the five "centers of gravity" in an enemy state. The central and smallest circle represents enemy leadership. The second represents infrastructure and supplies essential to military operations such as petroleum and electrical power. The third includes other elements of infrastructure such as transportation. Fourth is the enemy population, and fifth the fielded military forces of the enemy. In a dramatic statement of his theory, Warden writes, "Strategic warfare is only indirectly concerned with what is happening on some distant battlefield"; instead, it should aim at vital centers usually far behind the lines.[31]

Warden's theoretical ideas, articulated in *The Air Campaign*, received their baptism of fire in the planning for the air campaign in Desert Storm. Although Warden's strategic campaign plan was initially dismissed by senior officers as the raving of an "Air power airhead," the essential framework of Warden's staff at the Pentagon (known as "Checkmate") survived in the plan for opening phase of the Desert Storm air campaign.[32]

Warden's views are thoroughly reflected in official U.S. Air Force doctrinal statements.[33] Regarding strategic targeting, for example, official Air Force guidance states:

> In large measure, successful strategic attack operations depend on proper identification of the enemy's major vulnerabilities—centers of gravity. Against a modern industrialized opponent . . . a center of gravity may be discerned by a careful analysis of the enemy's industrial infrastructure, logistics system, population centers, and command and control apparatus.[34]

Further, it notes "The capability to put any asset an enemy possesses at extreme risk, at any time, largely fulfills the theory of strategic air power expressed by aviation's pioneers and visionaries."[35]

Unfortunately, neither Warden's own work nor Air Force manuals are as clear on the issue of deliberate targeting of civilians as one would wish, or as international law would require. Warden, for example, writes,

> The theater commander should consider all kinds of operations that might have an influence on the campaign. If the will of the enemy people is vulnerable, the theater commander may want to concentrate efforts against that target.[36]

Similarly, volume 2 of the *Air Force Manual* 1-1 states,

> A basic premise of early air power theorists was that political and industrial targets deep behind enemy lines presented the most vulnerable and lucrative areas for attack and provided the greatest leverage for a favorable outcome to a war. The advent of air power made possible direct strikes against such targets, thus presenting the prospect of ending

> a conflict quickly by destroying an enemy's ability to wage war or by convincing him to desist without first having to fight and defeat his military forces. In the development of these theories, two basic target sets emerged: those that would affect enemy capability to conduct military operations and those that would affect enemy will to continue fighting.[37]

On the issue of deliberate attack on enemy civilian morale, however, the manual comments only weakly and with understatement: "[S]trategic attack has rarely affected enemy morale to the degree anticipated by early air power enthusiasts."[38] Only buried in a footnote do we find the more precise statement I cited earlier:

> Early air power theorists assumed that civilian populations would be more vulnerable and susceptible to the psychological impact of massed air power than would military personnel in combat. Ironically, history appears to demonstrate that civilian resistance tends to stiffen under persistent strategic air attacks . . ."[39]

At the level of official doctrine, therefore, contemporary Air Force writing and thinking is still somewhat ambiguous. On the one hand, the legal guidance is quite clear regarding deliberate attacks on civilians and civilian objects. On the other, both Warden's writing and Air Force policy statements allow for the possibility that, in some particular set of military circumstances, World War II-style direct attacks on civilians, with the hope of undermining enemy morale, *might* be a center of gravity. In such a case, they suggest that civilians would be the correct target set for a particular theater commander. Rather than noting the legal *prohibition* of such attacks, both content themselves with the pragmatic observation that attacks on civilians are rarely effective. This is an area where future editions of official air power doctrine manuals can and ought to be improved to bring the guidance more unambiguously under the legal and moral constraints of JWT.

## The Gulf War—"Lessons Learned"

Despite the somewhat ambiguous statements of doctrine, in practice planners of the air campaign in the Gulf War were extremely careful in target selection to minimize civilian casualties. Very self-consciously they avoided any hint of deliberate targeting of civilians. Further, they were extremely cautious to minimize even foreseeable collateral damage to civilians and civilian objects that might result from targeting of clearly military targets.

Both at the level of political leadership, and as implemented at the level of the targeting staff, the language and constraints of JWT were extensively employed in planning the Gulf War air campaign. Legal advisors were assigned to the targeting staff to insure that the bombing campaign conformed to the requirements of international law.[40] Obviously the motives for this were mixed. Among the mix of reasons were a real growth in understanding of the legal and moral constraints required in air war, the availability of weapons of sufficient precision to make constrained conflict possible and, of course, a political concern with public opinion and avoiding adverse press coverage.

However multivariate the causes, however, the air campaign in the Persian Gulf War marks a "revolution in warfare."[41] Although an extremely large number of weapons were delivered, many in built-up urban areas, for the first time in the history of air war non-combatant injuries and deaths as a result of direct discharge of weapons were remarkably few. Apart from clear mistakes (such as the Ameriyya shelter), civilian casualties seem largely to have been proportionate collateral damage, secondary to attacks on legitimate military targets. Furthermore, air power's long-promised and never delivered abilities to destroy pinpoint targets and thereby to disable enemy air defense, command, control communications, intelligence, and logistic operations were fulfilled to a truly remarkable degree.

The study of civilian casualties in Iraq conducted by Middle East Watch, although dramatically titled *Needless Deaths in the Gulf War: Civilian Casualties During the Air Campaign and Violations of the Laws of War*, is remarkably thin in actual cases. Disposed to be highly critical, even this study admits, "[I]n many if not most respects the allies' conduct was consistent with their stated intent to take all feasible precautions to avoid civilian casualties."[42] Indeed the "violations of the laws of war" they cite rest almost entirely on dubious interpretations of the provisions of Additional Protocol I to the Geneva conventions. For example, they suggest that bombing legitimate military targets in civilian areas should have been conducted exclusively at night, rather than during the day when civilians were more likely to be near them—a nice idea when technically possible, but hardly a requirement of the laws of war. Furthermore, the study cites very likely self-serving Iraqi official accounts of large numbers of civilian casualties and then notes that their own interviews with Iraqi physicians yielded a far lower set of casualty figures. It arrives at the conclusion that, apart from the single significant loss of life in the bombing of Ameriyya shelter, civilian casualties as a direct result of Coalition bombing were very low indeed.[43]

Clearly, for the first time in the history of the use of military aviation, there were few or no deaths of civilians due to *direct and deliberate* targeting of them or of civilian structures. Inherently inaccurate weapons (so-called "dumb bombs") were not used in tactical situations where large numbers of civilian deaths were foreseeable, and direct civilian deaths were reduced to very low numbers indeed. It is too strong, of course, to claim that the air war in the Gulf achieved perfection in bringing air war into conformity with the principles of non-combatant immunity. But it certainly is not an exaggeration to say that the combination of new weapons and platforms, combined with improvements in Air Force doctrine, hold out the promise of future air war which would go far toward abiding by those rules and limitations.

To say they hold out promise is, of course, not to claim that those promises have been fulfilled. As the Government Accounting Office evaluation of the air war noted, despite its obvious success, the air war was hampered in its desired effectiveness by a number of factors.[44] Deficiencies of timely Bomb Damage Assessment (BDA) were marked, and such deficiencies necessitated restriking targets (BDA attempts to determine the success of a given airstrike in destroying a target. If it is doubtful whether the strike was successful, another strike will generally be ordered). Obviously, restrikes put both civilians and pilots at additional and, in principle, unnecessary risks. Further, an understandable emphasis on pilot and aircraft survivability resulted in delivery of weapons from much higher altitudes than were used in training.[45] Such tactics degraded considerably the accuracy of some weapons, increasing the risk of civilian death due to missing of targets which would have been reduced had lower altitude releases been possible. Bad weather, smoke, and the deliberate firing of oil wells by Iraqi forces further degraded weapon accuracy for these weapons that depended on optical sensors or on pilot laser designation of targets. Clearly, these difficulties indicate the need for enhanced sensor capability in the next generation of such weapons.[46]

Still, I wish to argue that the experience of the Gulf War points to an area where further thought needs to be given in order to enhance the salutary direction in which air war is evolving. In particular, the conduct of air war needs to be brought into greater conformity with JWT. The most pressing and difficult issue is the moral status of dual use targets—targets whose destruction is reasonably believed to afford a real military advantage but the destruction of which has clearly foreseeable and significant impact on civilian health, well-being, and even survival. This problem is by no means unprecedented in earlier air war. But it achieves a much sharper focus in light of the development of weapons, weapons platforms, and tactics after Desert Storm. In the pursuit of the asymptotic goal of "one bomb, one target"[47] it is foreseeable that in future war there can be less and less direct destruction of civilian life and property as a result of deliberate targeting.[48] This goal is asymptotic, rather than realistic, of course, due to inevitable equipment failures, intelligence failures in target identification, and simple human error. But there can be no question that, from a legal and moral perspective, further development in these directions should be applauded and pursued.[49]

Even in an imagined "one bomb, one target" environment, with the benefit of perfect intelligence as to the nature of the targets selected, the moral concern to protect civilian life and property to the greatest extent possible points to an area where considerable further thought is indicated. In any reasonably modern society, the complex web of technical infrastructure necessary to maintain the life and health of the population is enormously interdependent. Modern urban life for civilians depends on available clean water, electrical power, sanitation, and garbage removal. Further, in the wartime context, the treatment of casualties as well as the routine aspects of civilian health care depend on electrical power for refrigeration of medicines and foodstuffs and for use of technical equipment for health care provision. Even an imagined "perfect" air war might avoid all *direct* civilian casualties and still, in its destruction of dual use targets, create huge numbers of civilian deaths and injuries—all, of course, of the "bomb now, die later" variety, rather than direct casualties of bombing.

Ramsey Clark's provocative book, *The Fire This Time: U.S. War Crimes in the Gulf*, documents in detail the effects of sanctions on the civilian population of Iraq. Clearly, the deliberate targeting of aspects of the civilian infrastructure, while it does not involve immediate and direct destruction of civilian life, exacerbated to a large degree the suffering and death of the civilian population.[50] Further, *it was intended to do so* in the hope that Iraq would perceive the need to seek external help to restore infrastructural elements such as electrical power, and be motivated to shorten the war.[51]

To some degree these issues are addressed (at least in principle) under the classical rubric of proportionality. One assesses the "distinct military advantage offered at the time" (Additional Protocol I, Geneva Convention) of targets in relation to these foreseen effects on civilians. But the concept of proportionality here is highly elastic and imprecise, especially in the determination of the relevant span of time within which proportionality is to be assessed.

I do not mean to suggest that morally and legally conscientious targeteers are oblivious to this issue. In the Gulf War, for example, there was a serious, if largely ineffective, effort to take such matters into consideration. *The Gulf War Air Power Survey, Summary Report* writes that in response to written directives of Brig. Gen. Buster C. Glosson,

> Planners wished to minimize long-term damage to Iraq's economic infrastructure, even as they provided for attacks against both electricity and oil targets. This constraint led air planners and targeting specialists to try to restrict attacks on Iraqi electric power to strikes on transformer/switching yards and control buildings rather than on generator halls, boilers, and turbines in order to minimize recuperation time after the conflict ended. Similarly, attacks on oil production were supposed to concentrate on refined-product storage; distillation and other refining areas were to be aimpoints only if they produced military fuels.[52]

For a variety of technical reasons (primarily the inability of pilots to distinguish among the buildings at plants due to smoke, haze, and the stress of combat) these attempts to restrict targets were ineffective. Attacks on electrical power

> rapidly shut down the generation and distribution of commercial electric power throughout most of Iraq, forcing the Iraqi leadership and military

> onto back-up power. Ultimately, almost eighty-eight percent of Iraq's installed generation capacity was sufficiently damaged or destroyed by direct attack, or else isolated from the national grid through strikes on associated transformers and switching facilities, to render it unavailable. The remaining twelve percent, mainly resident in numerous smaller plants that were not attacked, was probably only available locally because of damage inflicted on transformers and switching yards.[53]

Similar points could be made regarding the destruction of petroleum products, transportation systems and other dual use targets. As a result of the bombing of electrical power, for example, "the Harvard Study Team reported sharply increased levels of gastroenteritis, cholera, typhoid, and malnutrition in Iraqi children due to the delayed effects of the Gulf War."[54] William M. Arkin, of Greenpeace, estimates 111,000 civilian deaths as a result of the indirect detrimental health effects of the war.[55] These effects occurred despite the fact that the "Iraqis restored commercial power considerably faster then anticipated."[56] Another study claimed that "bombing of electrical power 'contributed to' 70,000-90,000 *postwar* civilian deaths above normal mortality rates over the period April-December 1991—principally because of the lack of electricity in Iraq for water purification and sewage treatment following the cease-fire."[57]

I do not wish to make the argument here turn on the *de facto* questions of the precise numbers of "bomb now, die later" deaths in this particular conflict. Nor is it essential to assess the rapidity with which the Iraqis did, or did not, manage to restore a reasonable level of civilian infrastructure. Regardless of the details of these matters, the Gulf War experience points to the following considerations:

1) Competent militaries will certainly have anticipated disruption of basic infrastructure such as power grids and prepared work-around solutions to them. Given that reality, how do we make a reasonable assessment of the military "value at the time" of such dual use targets as electrical power in planning future air campaigns? The mere fact that it is reasonable to think that attack on such targets will achieve *some* military effect is not sufficient to relieve the burden of proof that the civilian consequences are acceptable, legally and morally. The fact that coping with disruptions to normal services and infrastructure certainly will require diversion of personnel and resources from other military activities to some indeterminate degree is not, by itself, sufficient justification either.

A calculation of proportionality requires at least a rough degree of quantification of these matters. We know pretty clearly the significant costs on the civilian side of the equation. It is important to ask for some equal attention to quantifying the military side of the ledger. For example, it is true that Iraqi air defenses were effectively neutralized early in the conflict. But it is also true that the absence of grid electrical power made a minor contribution at best to that neutralization. Far more important was the direct suppression of enemy air defenses by direct missile attack on targeting radars whenever they were engaged.

2) W. Hayes Parks is certainly correct when he suggests that Additional Protocol I to the Geneva Conventions errs on the side of assigning too much—indeed nearly absolute—moral and legal responsibility for the welfare of civilians to the *attacker*. Clearly, there is a correlative responsibility *of the defender* to take reasonable precautions to separate civilian populations as much as possible from obvious military targets.[58] Certainly when an adversary such as Iraq routinely attempts to use civilian population, civilian structures, and foreign nationals and prisoners of war to shield military equipment and activity, such efforts cannot be given the permission of international law.[59]

But destruction of basic civilian *infrastructural elements* is indeed primarily the responsibility of the attacker. A defender sincerely concerned with the welfare of its civilian populations might take care to segregate infrastructural elements into military and civilian categories. It might declare (and in good faith, *insure*, perhaps even inviting in neutral observers to verify) that some essential infrastructural elements are solely for civilian use in an effort to spare its population. Still, it is unreasonable to ask that defenders segregate, say, civilian power grids from military ones. Indeed, in the absence of mutually trusted observers to verify such segregation, a defender's claim that it is doing so would hardly be credible!

But it is reasonable to require *a good-faith effort on the part of the attacker* to determine the genuine military necessity of attacks on targets with significant civilian value and use. Such a good-faith effort is necessary if one is to make a proportionality judgment of the "military value at the time" of attacks on such targets that err on the side of protecting civilian infrastructure.

3) Insofar as we wish to take the moral basis of non-combatant immunity seriously, how might we instrumentalize the above considerations sufficiently to provide practical action-guidance to targeting staffs in future air war? At a minimum, might it not be worthwhile to collect and analyze a series of real cases of difficult targeting decisions for use in the training of targeteers? Targeting staff officers should train routinely in making moral and legal as well as technical military judgments in war-gaming air campaigns. For example, Warden's core ideas are already incorporated into the war-gaming simulations at the Air Force Academy and, presumably, at the Air War College. It is not unreasonable to insist that the restraints of international law be incorporated as constraints within those war-gaming scenarios.

## Directions for the Future

I have argued throughout this paper that, with the Persian Gulf War, the use of air power within reasonable understanding of JWT is now imaginable and, to a degree not previously thought possible, has been demonstrated. This experience points to directions for further moral and legal thought of the sort I have just enumerated. It is also possible, on the basis of these considerations, to point to technical and procurement directions indicated by the attempt to conduct air war within the constraints of JWT. I wish to conclude by highlighting a few of these points, intended as practical suggestions that will make morally conscientious air war an ever-greater possibility.

First, our reflections indicate clear directions for future procurement. Precision bombing in the Gulf was seriously hampered by limitations of the existing inventory. Many existing weapons platforms were not prepared to deliver laser-guided munitions, placing an enormous burden operationally on those that were. Insofar as we envision the future of air war in terms of precision "centers of gravity" for targeting, future inventory mixes must attend more closely to this operational need. While it is economically unfeasible to acquire an inventory that is one hundred percent precision capable in the near future, the Gulf War clearly indicates the need for a higher percentage of such weapons platforms.

Second, there are important cost-effectiveness considerations. Although only eight percent of the delivered munitions of the Gulf War were guided, they represented eighty-four percent of the total munitions cost.[60] Although these weapons were used to great effect, the experience of Desert Storm also showed up a number of technological limitations that degraded their effectiveness. In particular, sensors better able to operate in environments of poor weather and other visibility-reducing conditions are clearly required. Also, there is a need for sensors better able to operate with precision at medium and high altitudes and in the context of operations conducted to maximize pilot and aircraft survivability.[61] The in-progress conversion of the guidance systems in cruise missiles from terrain-following computer maps to Global Positioning System receivers, allowing precise designation and determination of target location without the need for visual cues, is an example of the direction of procurement I have in mind.

Third, the Gulf War disclosed more sharply than ever before the interdependence of air power effectiveness and intelligence, both in target identification and in bomb damage assessment. Only insofar as theater commanders possess reliable target identification information can they successfully conduct air operations against truly essential military targets and diminish unnecessary disruption to civilian life and infrastructure. Further, only insofar as BDA is accurate and timely can unnecessary restriking of targets be avoided, further diminishing the risks to aircrews and the destruction of civilian life and property that is part of the friction of war.

## Conclusion

This paper has been a thought experiment regarding the continuing utility of JWT in the context of contemporary air war. I have shown that, at least for the United States and other technologically advanced military powers, it is now possible to use air power in ways which are vastly more discriminate and precise than has ever been possible hitherto. I have shown that the limitations of existing weapons systems and tactics at the time of the Persian Gulf War indicate directions for future acquisition of weapons systems and training of military officers. Developments in that direction can further extend the possibility of controlling considerably the damage inflicted on civilian populations by air war.

Obviously the cost of precision weapons systems and of the delivery platforms necessary for their effective use places limitations on the numbers and range of such weapons we can acquire. Further acquisition in these areas, very careful review of the effectiveness of attacks on various infrastructural elements, and improved BDA in future conflicts combine to make possible a nearly indefinite improvement toward the goal of restriction of death and destruction to targets which truly bear on military effectiveness of enemy forces.

I conclude by flagging issues this paper has not addressed. Obviously, I have only considered the *jus in bello* portion of JWT. I have not addressed one way or another the *jus ad bellum* questions of the Persian Gulf War, or of any future conflict. Nor have I addressed the global question whether modern war with modern weapons is inherently so destructive that nothing, or virtually nothing, can justify engaging in it. My issue has been focused rather narrowly on the specifics on weapons, tactics, and legal requirements of modern air war, and the degree to which modern air war can be conducted within the constraints of JWT.

My conclusion here is tentative, but still clear: current developments in weapons, doctrines and tactics promise the possibility of air war which comes closer than ever before imagined to meeting the moral strictures of JWT. As citizens and Christians, we have the opportunity and obligation to urge our military leaders and their civilian overseers to attend to our military affairs in such a way that our forces improve continually in their capabilities to perform along these lines.

## Notes

[1]A substantially different earlier version of this paper was commissioned by the Carnegie Council on Ethics and International Affairs and presented at the first meeting of the "Ethics and the Future of International Conflict" working group at the National War College in January, 1997.

[2]Perhaps most clearly in *When War is Unjust: Being Honest in Just-War Thinking* (Minneapolis: Augsburg, 1984).

[3]Each of these weapons systems had been employed to some degree in earlier conflicts, e.g., precision guided munitions in Vietnam and beyond, and F-117s saw some action in Panama. Still, "debut" seems an appropriate use here in that, for the first time, these systems were employed in large quantity and in pursuit of an integrated strategic vision.

[4]For a detailed discussion of whether the Gulf War is a "revolution in military affairs," see Eliot A. Cohen, dir., *Operations and Effects and Effectiveness*, vol. 2, *Gulf War Air Power Survey* (Washington, D.C.: U.S. Government Printing Office, 1993), 348-370.

[5]Michael S. Sherry, *The Rise of American Air Power: The Creation of Armageddon* (New Haven, CT.: Yale University Press. 1987), 2.

[6]Ibid., 5.

[7]Ibid., 19.

[8]Quoted in ibid., 25.

[9]Quoted in ibid., 25.

[10]Ibid., 53.

[11]See ibid., 99-100.

[12]Ibid., 256-300. Sherry uses this point as support of the thesis that the WWII Air Corp was in the total thrall of the ideal of terror bombing. Dr. Thomas Keaney helpfully points out that the B-29s were, in fact, designed for strategic bombing. The strategic theory of the time made it seem to the planners that diverting their efforts toward sea lanes would be a misuse of the weapons system and would prevent their efficient fulfillment of the goal of crippling Japan and ending the war without the need for an invasion. Whether such models were correct seems, in hindsight, unlikely.

[13]James L. Stokesbury, *A Short History of Air Power* (New York: William Morrow and Company, Inc., 1986), 190.

[14]*Air Force Manual* 1-1, v.2, 148.

[15]*Air Force Manual* 1-1, v.2, 148.

[16]*Air Force Manual* 1-1, v.2, 158, n. 3.

[17]In a much grimmer assessment of the future value of such weapons, Col. Charles J. Dunlap argues that enemies will quickly find was to exploit the very precision of such weapons to make it still more difficult for high-tech forces to fight effectively. For example, one would anticipate that the use of "human shields" of civilians or POWs would become routine. Charles J. Dunlap, Jr. "How We Lost the High-Tech War of 2007: A Warning from the Future," *The Weekly Standard* (January 29, 1996): 22-28.

[18]Geoffrey Best, *War and Law Since 1945* (Oxford: Oxford University Press, 1994), 200.

[19]Quoted in ibid., 200.

[20]Ibid., 204.

[21]Private communication, Lt. Col. William G. Schmidt, USAF, United States Air Force Academy, Department of Law.

[22]International Committee of the Red Cross, *Summary of the Geneva Conventions of August 12, 1949 and Their Additional Protocols* (Geneva: International Committee of the Red Cross, 1988), 17.

[23]Ibid.

[24]W. Hays Parks, W. Hays, "Air War and the Law of War," *The Air Force Law Review* 32 (1980): 113. Parks very extensively and helpfully analyzes the difficulties with the language of Protocol I in five areas: 1) the definition of "attack," 2) the definitions of "civilian" and "combatant," 3) the definition of military object, 4) the apparent equation in value of civilian life and civilian property, and 5) the weight of responsibility for civilian welfare assigned to attacker and to defender. For our purposes, however, this level of detail in not important. What is important is the clear and agreed upon prohibition of indiscriminate bombing.

[25]Michael Walzer, in *Just and Unjust Wars*, makes a complex and interesting argument in favor of area bombing in the very early phases of the war. He argues that military necessity made such attacks acceptable for a small window of time when it was the only practical means to attack Germany. Whatever one thinks of this argument, however, he agrees as well that the justification for area bombing ceased fairly quickly when other means became available Michael Walzer, *Just and Unjust Wars: A Moral Argument with Historical Illustrations* (New York: Basic Books, 1977), 255-263.

[26]Ibid., 5-3 a.1.a.

[27]However, for a much grimmer assessment of the future value of such weapons, see Col. Charles J. Dunlap, Jr.'s provocative piece, "How We Lost the High-Tech War of 2007."

[28]Rich Atkinson, *Crusade: The Untold Story of the Persian Gulf War* (Boston: Houghton Mifflin Co., 1993), 56.

[29]John A. Warden III, *The Air Campaign: Planning for Combat*, (Washington, DC: National Defense University Press), 4.

[30]Atkinson, 58.

[31]Quoted in Ibid., 59.

[32]Ibid., 63.

[33]E.g., *Air Force Manual* 1-1, Volume II: *Basic Aerospace Doctrine of the United States Air Force* (March, 1992).

[34]Ibid., 151.

[35]Ibid., 152.

[36]Warden, 8.

[37]*Air Force Manual* 1-1, vol. 2, 148.

[38]Ibid.

[39]Ibid., 158.

[40]Personal communication, Lt. Col. William G. Schmidt, Dept. of Law, USAF Academy. Lt. Col. Schmidt was the chief of the International Law Division in Riyadh, Saudi Arabia, during the Gulf War.

[41]For a nuanced discussion of this claim, see chapter 10 of Thomas A. Keaney and Eliot A. Cohen, *Gulf War Air Power Survey Summary Report* (henceforth *GWAPS*) (Washington, DC: US Government Printing Office, 1993).

[42]Middle East Watch, *Needless Deaths in the Gulf War: Civilian Casualties During the Air Campaign and Violations of the Laws of War* (New York: Human Rights Watch), 4.

[43]Ibid., 17-20.

[44]United States General Accounting Office, *Operation Desert Storm: Evaluation of the Air War* (PEMD-96-10) (Washington, DC: General Accounting Office, July 1996).

[45]It is important to note that there is always tension between the desire to protect one's own troops and the development of weaponry. For example, laser-guided munitions, which clearly make possible highly accurate bombing, also require pilots to fly straight and level in order to hold the laser designator on the target. This requires pilots to forego evasive maneuvers they would commence immediately after release of more traditional bombs.

[46]For a specific GAO analysis of these shortcomings, see United States General Accounting Office. June, 1997. *Operation Desert Storm: Evaluation of the Air Campaign* (GAO/NSIAD-97-134) (Washington, DC: General Accounting Office, June 1997), 40-41.

[47]GAO, PEMD-96-10, 4

[48]It is important to note that "Contrary to the general public's impression about the use of guided munitions in Desert Storm, . . . approximately 95 percent of the total bombs delivered against strategic targets were *unguided*; 5 percent were guided. Unguided bombs accounted for over 90 percent of both total bombs and bomb tonnage. Approximately 92 percent of the total tonnage was unguided, compared to 8 percent guided" (GAO/NSIAD-97-134, 69). Given these numbers, the lack of significant civilian collateral damage is extraordinary—perhaps an artifact of the location of many strategic targets in Iraq away from population centers? The accuracy of weapons delivery from the F-117 Stealth was also overplayed considerably in the popular media. See the detailed analysis of the accuracy of F-117 bombing at GAO/NSIAD-97-134, 127-143. In general, this study shows that there were considerable numbers of bomb misses—counting as "misses" anything from 3.2 meters to 178.1 meters from aimpoints. This moderates considerably the expectation of certain destruction of targets through the use of guided munitions in future conflicts. On the other hand, this is an improvement of orders of magnitude in the distance of misses from World War II or even Vietnam—a fact which is important when one focuses on civilian collateral damage. That is, even if targets were not destroyed by such weapons, at least they seem largely to have fallen in the immediate target area rather than far afield where the probability of damage to civilian life and property would be raised considerably.

[49]See GAO/NSIAD-97-134, 123 for a detailed analysis of the degree to which this "one bomb, one target" goal was not attained. The main conclusion was that "the average number of LGBs [laser guided bombs] dropped per target was four."

[50]Ramsey Clark, *The Fire This Time: U.S. War Crimes in the Gulf* (New York: Thunder's Mouth Press, 1992), 59-84. I am entirely sympathetic to Clark's concern and insistence that a great deal of care needs to be taken in future conflicts to make good faith judgments of the relative military value of such targets in comparison to the costs to civilian populations. I do not agree, however, that international law is, as yet, very clear on this point—and certainly not that

we can with any confidence refer to the infrastructure destruction in the Gulf War as "war crimes."

[51]Ibid., 62-63.

[52]*GWAPS, Summary Report*, 71.

[53]*GWAPS, Summary Report*, 73.

[54]*Harvard Study Team Report: Public Health in Iraq after the Gulf War*, May 1991, 12-13; quoted in *GWAPS*, Summary Report, 75.

[55]Beth Osborne Daponte, "Iraqi Casualties from the Persian Gulf War and Its Aftermath"; quoted in *GWAPS*, Summary Report, 75.

[56]*GWAPS, Summary Report*, 74.

[57]*GWAPS, Summary Report*, 75. See also p. 75, footnotes 44-45 for additional citations on point.

[58]Parks, 156.

[59]This lack of balanced assessment in the responsibilities of both attackers and defenders is one of the major flaws in the critique offered by Ramsey Clark and other extreme critics. While they are right to document the destruction of the war, they are often lacking in even-handed assessment of the moral and legal responsibilities of the parties.

[60]GAO, PEMD-96-10, 4.

[61]GAO, PEMD-96-10, 12.

# Two Rival Versions of Just War Theory and the Presumption Against Harm in Policing

*Tobias L. Winright*

## Abstract

In recent years, there has been a debate, centrally between James Turner Johnson and James F. Childress, on how to understand the just war tradition. The international arena has historically served as the context for demonstrating the normative and political utility of the just war tradition. Contemporary experience shows, however, that violence is not only a distant issue, but it is also a local, domestic problem. Investigation into contemporary police practice, a lacuna in Christian ethics, with regard to the justifiable use of force can help clarify which understanding of the just war tradition is preferable.

## Introduction

"It was right in front of me the whole time!" In embarrassment I have uttered these words on several shopping occasions during which, in exasperation at failing to find the object of my desire, I finally succumb to requesting assistance from a clerk, who simply points to where it sits practically under my nose. Instead of an illusion, or perceiving what is *not* there, I have experienced visual agnosia, or not perceiving what *is* there. A similar problem exists, I think, among Christian ethicists in a debate that is currently rekindling.

A few years ago, J. Bryan Hehir predicted that during the 1990s "another review of the ethical premise of the just war theory" would occur.[1] And recent articles by James F. Childress and James Turner Johnson, about whether or not the just war tradition rests upon a presumption against harm and violence, have proven

Hehir correct.[2] In his piece, Childress recounts his espousal, over the past two decades, of what I will call *the presumption-against-harm version* of just war theory, which holds that "war is at least *prima facie* wrong and thus requires justification." It is upon this "shared starting point" that pacifists and proponents of justified violence putatively converge. "This has been," Childress reflects, "one of the most important moves in my work and also one of the most controversial."[3] *Important*, I suppose, in that an affirmative response has been developed and advanced in parallel ways by other ethicists and, moreover, officially recognized in various denominational documents, including the U.S. Catholic bishops' pastoral letter *The Challenge of Peace* (1983) and the United Methodist bishops' *In Defense of Creation* (1986). *Controversial*, I gather, in that critics of this understanding of a mutual presumption against violence contend that it represents an abandonment of the classic just war heritage. Thus Johnson, in his own recent essay, counters that the tradition has been "broken" and that the real "font" and "core" of the just war tradition is based on the *jus ad bellum* criterion of "just cause as a response to injustice." In other words, Johnson advocates what I will call *the presumption-against-injustice version* of just war theory, in which the starting point (which is not shared with pacifism) is the duty "to prevent, punish, and remedy injustice," or, to "police injustice."[4]

It is not my aim in this essay to adjudicate the historical debate between Childress and Johnson. Rather, what I will attempt to do is draw upon a limited case (just alluded to above by Johnson's metaphor, viz., domestic policing) to begin to establish an empirical base for a normative argument about which way the just war tradition ought to go. Indeed, proponents of *both* the presumption-against-harm and the presumption-against-injustice versions of just war theory occasionally mention policing but, like the experience of visual agnosia, fail to perceive it as meriting a closer look. Perhaps this should not be surprising, however, given that policing, as a subject itself, is a lacuna in Christian ethics. Yet, I wish to focus on domestic policing precisely because it is a limited case with fewer variables. To be sure, my argument is not determinative or conclusive, but only a first step in the empirical part of a normative argument. For the argument to be more conclusive, the range of cases would need to be expanded. Nevertheless, it is my view that investigation of domestic policing in the United States can make a contribution to the empirical investigation.

The essay will develop in three sections. First, I will sketch the state of the question concerning the supposed presumption against harm in the just war tradition, while noting any references to policing on either side. Second, I will turn to the preliminary work of Edward Malloy, a Christian ethicist who *has* dealt with policing, in order to consider more closely the analogous logic of the use of force justifications in policing and in the just war tradition. And third, I will draw upon recent literature in the field of criminal justice ethics, especially the work of philosopher John Kleinig, in order to help clarify which understanding of the just war tradition is preferable.

## Two Rival Versions of Just War Theory

*Proponents of the Presumption*

The publication last decade of the Catholic and Methodist bishops' respective pastoral letters on war and peace initially kindled the debate concerning a supposed presumption against harm and violence shared by the just war tradition and pacifism.[5] In their document, for example, the Catholic bishops claim that both just war teaching and pacifism share a "complementary relationship" (24; par. 74). In a "new moment" in the Catholic church's evaluation of war and peace, the bishops view "just-war teaching and non-violence as distinct but interdependent methods of evaluating warfare" (37; par. 120). Admittedly, the two stances "diverge on some specific conclusions," but they at least "share a common presumption against the use of force" (37; par. 120) or a "presumption *in favor of peace* and *against* war" (27; par. 83). According to the bishops, all Christians alike are called to defend peace against aggression, but it is the question of "the *how* of defending peace which offers moral options" (23; par. 73). Hence, the just war tradition begins with the pacifist presumption against harm and violence, but it sometimes considers it necessary, in defense of the common good, to override that presumption while still restricting and reducing the horrors of war (27; par. 83). Especially when confronted with modern warfare, both pacifists and just war advocates "agree in their opposition" to unjust and total warfare (37; par. 121). Similarly, in their own statement on war and peace, the United Methodist bishops "invite pacifists and nonpacifists among our people . . . to recapture their common ground," their shared "moral presumption against all war and violence . . ." (13).

In actuality, however, the presumption-against-harm thesis did not originate with these church statements. Rather, it was initially articulated by ethicists James Childress and Ralph Potter. Moreover, this thesis has been assumed, accepted, defended or developed variously by Bryan Hehir (who is credited for incorporating it into the Catholic bishops' letter), David Hollenbach, Charles Curran, Richard Miller, and Lisa Sowle Cahill.[6] Because some of these scholars presuppose the work of Childress and Potter, the positions of only these two presumption-against-harm authors will be examined.[7]

Building upon philosopher W. D. Ross's ethical framework of *prima facie* duties, which is utilized "whenever we face conflicting obligations or duties, whenever it is impossible to fulfill all the claims upon us, to respect all the rights involved, or to avoid doing evil to everyone," Childress claims that occasionally "we confront two or more *prima facie* duties or obligations, one of which we cannot fulfill without sacrificing the other(s)."[8] Two *prima facie* duties that flow from the principle of love are the duty to do justice by protecting the innocent and the duty to do no harm. Because of this latter duty of nonmaleficence, pacifism and just war share the same starting point, namely, that "war is at least *prima facie* wrong and thus requires justification."[9] According to Childress, "The moral tension arises when these two *prima facie* obligations conflict."[10] For pacifism, nonmaleficence is an absolute stance admitting no exceptions; whereas, for the just war advocate the presumption against harm is *prima facie* and may be overridden for the sake of other *prima facie* duties, such as protecting the innocent. In this way, there exists no *prima facie* duty to go to war, "but because some other *prima facie* duties (for example, to protect the innocent) may override the *prima facie* duty not to injure or kill, there may be an *actual* duty to fight. . . ."[11] The proponent of just war, therefore, "bears a heavy burden of proof" for justifying the overriding of the *prima facie* presumption against harm. In addition, Childress points out that, throughout the remaining, assorted just war criteria, the *prima facie* presumption retains a "trace" or "residual" effect, in which the conduct that follows the overriding of the *prima facie* presumption of nonmaleficence continues to be affected by it.[12]

As an example, Childress tersely posits, "Even a policeman who has a duty to try to stop an escaped criminal who has taken hostages still must respect certain moral and legal limits."[13] The *duty* to use force, according to Childress, arises when the *prima facie* duty of nonmaleficence (*vis-à-vis* anyone) is overridden (in this case, *vis-à-vis* the criminal) by the *prima facie* duty to protect the innocent (viz., the hostages). For Childress, this duty follows from the overall framework of *prima facie* duties, but the presumption against harm and violence remains central, as is evident in the leaning toward restraint in the other criteria of the just war tradition. Thus, I suspect that Childress would rule out shooting the criminal as a first rather than as a last resort, rule out shooting the criminal with hollow point bullets when a standard bullet would suffice, and rule out blowing away the criminal with an inaccurate shotgun blast (which would probably harm the hostages).

Similar to Childress, Potter proposes the relevance of just war theory "to all situations in which the use of force must be contemplated," and he holds that it is especially appropriate as "a mode of thinking for assessing the use of domestic police power. . . ."[14] Beginning with a "debt of love that Christians owe to their neighbors," Potter identifies two moral claims that are at "opposite poles of the continuum of Christian attitudes toward war and violence."[15] At one end is the claim to "contend for justice" or "protect the innocent," and at the other end is the claim "that we should not harm any neighbor." Both claims, Potter insists, must be held in tandem through the "framework" of the just war tradition. Accordingly, the first claim establishes a burden of proof upon those, including pacifists, who reject resorting to force in certain instances. That is, if they refuse to take up arms to protect the innocent, they must nevertheless resort to other nonviolent methods of defense or promoting justice. Conversely, the second claim places a burden of proof upon those, including just warriors, who justify the use of force. That is, there exists a "strong presumption against the use of violence, a presumption established for the Christian by the non-resistant example of Jesus and for the rational non-Christian by prudent concern for order and mutual security."[16] And this presumption may be overridden only by the other strong claim, to do justice and protect the innocent against unjust aggressors.

As an example of the latter, Potter appeals to the role of the police, "as servant[s] of the community," who "promise to risk [their] own life in defense of . . . any who need protection from unjust attack."[17] Indeed, Potter is one of the few Christian ethicists who specifically addresses the role of the police, and he calls on other Christian ethicists to help police officers, who "deserve counsel and instruction," to carefully "reflect upon the mode of reasoning appropriate to their office that would guide them in determining when they should act, how they should act, and why."[18] (Vividly etched in my memory is a question posed by a panelist during my own oral board interview fourteen years ago within the application process for a position with a sheriff's department in Florida: "Would your Christian faith hinder or prevent you from a performance of duty, such as shooting to kill a criminal?" I was at a loss as to how to respond, for it seemed to me that scripture and church teaching may not directly apply to this question. Yet, even before I read Potter, I instinctively assumed that the basic thrust of the church's just war teaching was analogous enough to the department's policies when I responded "No" to the question. But the specific guidance for which Potter calls certainly would have helped.) Employing the just war "mode of reasoning" to the context of policing, therefore, Potter proposes that if a Memphis police officer had seen the rifle aimed at Martin Luther King, Jr., the claim to protect the innocent would have overridden the claim to do no harm, thereby obligating the officer to fire upon the assailant.

This basic lexical structure of presumption and exception proposed by Childress and Potter has become conventional wisdom among a number of ethicists and has been incorporated into the statements of various churches.[19] Proponents of this version of just war theory offer a generally accepted framework that purports to boil down the just war criteria into a single, coherent logic of presumptive duties, claims, and rules which, when they conflict with each other, are permitted to be overridden conditionally for the sake of the stronger duty or claim. In this way, the presumption-against-harm proponents maintain that their approach reinforces a posture of restraint, placing a strong burden of proof on those who find it necessary to resort to force. And the brief references made by Childress and Potter to policing seem to give support to the actual application of this version of just war theory in at least that domestic context.

### *Opponents of the Presumption-Against-Harm*

James Turner Johnson, however, takes issue with the "idea that the just-war tradition is rooted in a 'presumption against war,'" a version of just war theory that he critically characterizes as being "clearly an innovation."[20] In contrast to the presumption-against-harm version, Johnson retorts that a survey of the classic just war tradition (for example, Ambrose, Augustine, Aquinas, Vitoria, and Grotius) "suggests that, above all, the first requirement of *jus ad bellum*—that it have a just cause as a response to injustice—is the font of the entire tradition."[21] If anything, therefore, there is a presumption against injustice. Ambrose and Augustine, for example, began with "the duty of love to protect the innocent, not with a presumption against doing harm, even to an enemy." It is only subsequent to the duty to use force to protect the neighbor that restraint comes into consideration, and it, too, follows from the duty to love. In Johnson's view, then, the use of force *per se* never constitutes a moral problem in itself, although he, for some reason, uses the language of "permission" in his discussion, which seems curious if the use of force is a duty of love and justice.[22] The presumption-against-harm proponents, on the other hand, appear to perceive force, itself, to be problematic, and their strong presumption against it, Johnson warns, pushes "just-war theory close to outright rejection of any resort to force."[23] For Johnson, the right question is not "*whether* the political community should exercise power but what kind of power it should exercise, when, and for what reasons."[24]

Johnson believes that the mistaken emphasis on the presumption against harm is to blame for the narrowing down of just cause in this century—in, for example, international law and Catholic social teaching—to defense against wrongful aggression. He advocates, instead, a renewed emphasis on the presumption against injustice, which would reclaim two other instances of classic just cause in addition to defense: viz., "retaking something wrongly taken, or punishment of evil." In this way, the classic just war calls for the use of force to prevent, remedy, or punish injustice—in other words, to "police injustice." Johnson believes that his version helpfully applies to today's conflicts such as humanitarian interventions, which are also sometimes referred to as "police actions."[25]

Much of Johnson's critique of the presumption-against-harm position echoes and updates the work of Paul Ramsey on this issue. Ramsey's alternative account holds that just war is a positive service of love to the victim of wrongful aggression and the community as a whole. For him, there are no *prima facie* duties or goods that are commensurable, so that any one could override another. Rather than being an exception to a prior rule, the just war, for him, is a rule of its own, not a lesser evil but a positive duty of love. It is not surprising, then, that Ramsey inveighs against the Methodist bishops' document: "I am bewildered overall, puzzled in detail, as to what to make of the Bishops' statements about pacifism and just-war traditions," especially their claim about a "common ground" and a "moral presumption against all war and violence."[26] According to Ramsey, "justified-war Christians *do not believe that killing is intrinsically wrong*."[27] Only after a just cause has been identified is there, with the secondary principle of last resort, a presumption against harm similar to that of pacifism. With the duty to protect against injustice as the overarching principle and lexically prior to other considerations, including any presumption against violence associated with last resort, Ramsey also calls for a return to a broader, three-pronged understanding of just cause, rather than only defense against aggression.[28] Thus Ramsey, himself, allows for "aggressive just war."[29]

Undergirding his version of just war theory, Ramsey often asserts, is an "Augustinian insight" about "the *logic*, the heart and soul, of such protective love."[30] In other words, "the interior ethics of Christian love, or what John XXIII termed 'social charity'" produced the just war tradition. As an example of such charity or disinterested love of the neighbor, Ramsey mentions the Good Samaritan who assisted the man victimized by thieves on the Jericho road. Suppose, however, that one encounters an enemy-neighbor. Ramsey insists, with Augustine and Ambrose, that love requires nonresistance in one-to-one neighbor relations, but if there is more than one neighbor involved, love requires shifting to a tactic of resistance on behalf of the victim-neighbor against the enemy-neighbor. Augustine, according to Ramsey, shows how, "in a world of conflicting neighbor relations," it is "possible to move from the presumption of universal love for all to preference for some neighbors, and to the idea of a justifiable use of lethal force."[31]

So, returning to the story of the Good Samaritan, Ramsey suggests, "By another step it would have been a work of charity, and not of justice alone, to maintain and serve in a police patrol on the Jericho road to prevent such things from happening." After all, what would Jesus have made the Samaritan do "if he had come upon the scene while the robbers were still at their fell work?"[32] Answer: act like a police officer. Whenever a choice must be made between "the perpetrator of injustice and the many victims of it," the latter are to be preferred. Therefore, the just use of force is not an exception to but an expression of Christian love.[33] This duty of Christian love, moreover, requires that the application of force must also be limited, but Ramsey appears to restrict his concern here solely to safeguarding the innocent neighbor, that is, non-combatant immunity. In this way, Ramsey thinks that the two elements—"(1) a specific justification for sometimes killing another human being; and (2) severe and specific restrictions upon anyone who is under the hard necessity of doing so"—are both "exhibited in the use of force proper to the domestic police power."[34] Indeed, he warns that the police officer should never forget this distinction between the victim-neighbor, the enemy-neighbor, and bystander-neighbors. But Ramsey's version of just war theory applied to policing seems to ignore ethical considerations *vis-à-vis* the perpetrator.

By now it should be apparent that the disagreement runs deep between these two versions of just war theory concerning whether or not there is a presumption against harm at the tradition's core. However, a point of contact exists, though it is often not noticed—namely, references to policing. In the version of just war theory offered by Childress and Potter, the emphasis is on a presumption against harm, which is overridden if someone's life is threatened by an attacker. This is a tighter, more restrained version of just war theory that seems consonant with police practice. It advocates protection from harm for innocent persons, but through methods that attempt to do as little harm as possible to the attacker. In contrast, the version of just war theory proposed by Johnson and Ramsey seems to focus so much on just cause that it is in danger of underemphasizing other criteria. By stressing the criterion of just cause, and by expanding this criterion to include punishment, the presumption-against-injustice version certainly calls for police to protect the innocent, but concern for the perpetrator may drop out of the picture. Indeed, Childress fears that this position may lead to the "use of force without any reservation or any hesitation about that use of force, so long as it remains within the limits of justice that require the protection of noncombatants against direct attack."[35] The language of duty associated with this concentration on just cause, moreover, may lead to or support crusades and holy wars. Hence, the presumption-against-injustice version seems more consonant with the general public demands in the U.S. for a "war on crime" in which law enforcement gets tough, rather than consonant with the actual guidelines and practices currently being advocated in policing to avert or at least mitigate the use of force. Attention to ethical treatments of the use of force in contemporary U.S. policing, I think, will substantiate these reflections about the difference it makes to emphasize either a presumption against harm or a presumption against injustice.

### *Speak Up For Policing*

I have noted how an analogy with policing has frequently been postulated in the just war debate, but there has been a conspicuous absence of critical reflection by Christian ethicists on policing, itself. This state of affairs is especially surprising given the long and rich history of Christian theological reflection on violence. As Lisa Cahill observes, "The challenge to decide about violence, especially state-supported and institutionally perpetuated violence, has been with Christians from the beginning."[36] More incisively, Stanley Hauerwas claims that the "the question of violence is the central issue for any Christian social ethic."[37] To be sure, the question of police violence has commanded the attention of the U.S. public in recent years with incidents like the Rodney King beating in 1991 by Los Angeles police.[38] And yet, while much theological attention has been given to whether or how Christians should participate in war, Edward Malloy accurately perceives "a noticeable deficiency in applying such analysis to the domestic context of crime" and police use of force in response to it.[39]

Indeed, Malloy is the only Christian ethicist, to my knowledge, who offers a fairly substantial treatment of police use of force. The first chapter of his *The Ethics of Law Enforcement and Criminal Punishment* stands as one of the few theological treatments of the topic of police use of force that, although preliminary and brief, deals with this issue as a subject worthy of attention. He writes:

> At the theoretical level, most ethical reflection about the problem of violence has centered on difficulties in personal relations or on the horror of warfare. In between these two extremes stands the role of the police in a contemporary setting.[40]

In response to this lack of attention to policing, Malloy recommends the just war tradition as a "helpful ethical framework for analysis." With it he conducts "an exercise of analogical interpretation" that, he hopes, "has not stretched the just war tradition too far," in which each criterion of the just war tradition is analyzed *vis-à-vis* guidelines for the use of force in policing, yielding a coherent, restrained ethical grid for application in the latter context.[41] Malloy also intends that his "modest venture in a field which is ripe for interdisciplinary cooperation might encourage other Christian ethicists to grapple with this problem of the control of, and response to, domestic violence."[42]

It will be helpful to discern the ways in which the logic of the ethical framework is analogous between the use of force in policing and the use of force in the just war tradition by giving attention to Malloy's list of criteria particularly pertinent for this essay. The first criterion with which he deals is "legitimate authority," that is, war may be waged only by a recognized government. Adapting this to the police context, the police officer may only use coercive force when he or she truly represents the body politic.[43] Sworn to uphold the law, police possess an enormous amount of discretion and cannot always consult with a superior or make a decision in advance; in many cases, therefore, they are required to determine on the spot when and how to use force. Yet, such authority is derivative and is thereby withdrawn when other criteria for justifiable use of force are not satisfied. Criminologists Jerome Skolnick and James Fyfe corroborate this view: "[W]here police derive their authority from law and take an oath to support the Constitution they are obliged to acknowledge the law's moral force and to be constrained by it"; furthermore, if an officer uses excessive force, "he or she undermines the very source of police authority."[44]

The second criterion, according to Malloy's reckoning, is that war may be fought only for a "just cause."[45] Because the legitimate goals of war in the just war tradition, in Malloy's account, include both vindicating justice and restoring peace, traditional examples that he mentions are national defense and protecting allies. Importantly, Malloy does not include punishment in this category. So, adapting this criterion of just cause to the context of policing requires the existence of an operative legal code from which can be derived any situation where police use of force may be warranted. This, of course, presupposes the justice of the code as a whole. Therefore, when a just law is broken (that is, injustice or crime), intervention by police is justified. But Malloy immediately introduces consideration of the criteria of "proportionality" and "last resort," which together determine, in the first place, whether intervention is really necessary, and, in the second place, what level of intervention (that is, force) is appropriate.

Since the response must be proportionate to the offense, police officers possess the discretionary ability to perhaps issue a warning for many infractions, or to help persons in a conflict to talk and work things out, rather than make a forceful arrest. The pivotal role of proportionality and last resort especially comes into view by considering the use of lethal force. According to Malloy, a police officer may fire a weapon only to protect life (one's own or someone else's), for a "life may be taken only when a life is at stake."[46] Killing someone is equivalent to imposing "an irrevocable" sentence or punishment, which may be the reason that Malloy does not include punishment as an example of just cause. For him, the role of the police is not to punish but to apprehend or incapacitate the perpetrator. Thus, it should be a "reluctant decision to employ" force, especially lethal force, which is why it is a last resort.[47] The police should exhaust all other possible methods, in other words, for handling a situation before resorting to force. Again, Malloy's view finds corroboration in a process of tightening the restraints on use of force during the past two decades in the law and in departmental standard operating procedure guidelines. Most police agencies have limited the right to shoot a firearm to two categories: 1) the officer may shoot to defend herself or himself from grievous bodily injury, and 2) the officer may shoot to save another person from grievous bodily injury.[48] Departments no longer allow their officers to shoot fleeing felons in situations in which the perpetrator no longer poses an immediate threat to anyone's life.[49]

It should be readily apparent that, for Malloy, the criteria coalesce tightly as an interlocking framework. He does not make any claims about a primary starting point for his version of just war theory. It is based neither upon only a presumption against harm nor only a presumption against injustice. Both, though, seem to be implicit within it. Yet, Malloy's application of just war thinking to police use of force seems more consonant with the presumption-against-harm version in that it exhibits a strong leaning toward restraint. I attribute this to the fact that Malloy identifies himself as a "strict constructionist" just war theorist.[50] That is, he requires that each and every criterion be met before justifying war, or in this case, the use of force by police. If any of the criteria cannot be satisfied, a "no" to the use of force must be the result.[51] This differs from Ramsey, who says the "supravalent" presumption of just war is against injustice and that the presumption against harm is "infravalent."[52] Malloy's version might be understood as holding that all the criteria are *polyvalent*. In this way, it may stand closer to Childress's version which bonds each criterion closely together through the residual or trace effects of the presumption against harm. Like Childress's version, the result of Malloy's strict constructionist approach is that there is strong burden of proof to justify force, and this framework seems to find empirical support within the context of policing. Attention to more recent treatments of the topic of the police use of force, from the perspective of the nascent field of police ethics itself, will help to see if this is the case.

## *To Serve and Protect*

In the wake of the Rodney King incident, one criminal justice expert observed: "That beating was not unique in the history of policing. It probably has kin in every state in the Union, in every country, and indeed in every significant police force as far back as we can trace the police function."[53] With regard to the use of lethal force, researchers estimate that police officers kill nearly 600 suspects annually, shoot and wound an additional 1200, and fire at and miss another 1800.[54] All of this has provoked philosophers and criminal justice scholars in recent years to give attention to the ethics of police use of force. Philosopher John Kleinig provides the latest, most comprehensive book on the subject, *The Ethics of Policing*. In it he examines both the moral foundations of policing and the specific problem of the use of force, identifying models of policing currently advocated, along with their respective understandings of the use of force. The two main models in tension with each other are the "crimefighter" model and the "social peacekeeper" model, with the former striving to continue in the United States as the primary paradigm and the latter gradually gaining acceptance instead.[55] Consideration of his treatment of police use of force should help clarify which understanding of the just war tradition is preferable.

With regard to the moral foundations of policing, Kleinig begins with social contract theory, since it undergirds most liberal democratic thinking and seems to offer "good prospects for accountable policing."[56] Given that policing as we know it developed in Western liberal democracies, most philosophers and criminologists who address the subject—and in particular the use of force—turn to social contract theory. Jeffrey Reiman, for example, draws from classical social contract thinkers, who emphasize individual rights, personal freedom, and government through consent, in order to construct an ethical approach to police use of force.[57] According to this view, since the problem of some hypothetical "state of nature" is that "everyone's freedom to use force at his own discretion undermines everyone else's freedom to work and live as he wishes, it becomes rational for freedom-loving people to renounce their freedom to use force at their own discretion . . . if (and only to the extent that) the sacrifice of this freedom results in a gain in real and secure freedom to live as one wants."[58] Instead of the insecurity of some "state of nature," in which each person protects his or her own interests, and in which there is a danger of escalating, unlimited coercion, citizens in the social contract consent to an exchange of some of their freedoms to a civil government authorized to have the power to protect their fundamental rights. The institution of law enforcement is a manifestation of this government authority and power. At the same time, however, the right to use force that is deposited in the police, according to this social contract perspective, is not without limits.

Indeed, for liberalism there remains a normative cutting edge that hinges on "whether renouncing a private use of force and allowing a public agency to enforce this renunciation results in greater concrete freedom for everyone."[59] The liberal emphasis on freedom thus provides a general guide with which to distinguish between legitimate and illegitimate exercises of power. That is, coercive action by police that restricts or endangers citizen freedom, instead of securing and broadening it, undermines the authority of the police by reproducing the conditions of the state of nature that the police are supposed to remedy. Social contractarians, therefore, usually limit police use of force, first, to self-defense (private citizens actually retain this right in the absence of a police officer) and, second, to protect the lives of private citizens. Until recently, this approach justified police use of force, including lethal force, to protect property or to stop a fleeing felon who may or may not have posed a physical threat, but these have recently become unjustifiable causes for the use of lethal force.

To be sure, this philosophical perspective regards coercive power as the *raison d'être* of policing. As Vance McLaughlin puts it, "[Police] routinely use force to carry out their role as enforcers—the use of force is inherent in the profession. . . ."[60] Similarly, police are characterized by Robert Reiner as "specialists in coercion."[61] This is why Kleinig observes—I think rightly—that the predominant paradigm for policing associated with a liberal contractarian approach is the "crimefighter" or "war" model. As he puts it, "Classical social contract theory perceives such a role for police. Just as an army is needed to protect us from the barbarian without, a police force is required to protect us from the barbarian within."[62] Yet, although Kleinig acknowledges that "any model of policing that fails to take into account their authority to employ force will be inadequate," he correctly argues that there are "serious practical and moral problems" with the crimefighter model. Quite simply, it encourages an "us" versus "them" mentality, in which the police view their role as a punitive one, so that they are inclined to be cynical in their attitudes toward the public and treat suspects as though they are guilty criminals. More problematic, most police officers *like* to see themselves as crimefighters (some of my fellow officer friends and I often enjoyed *Dirty Harry*-type movies), even though their actual work is diversified, with such activities as helping injured accident victims, searching for lost children, calming quarreling spouses, or coaching youth basketball teams. Kleinig, therefore, believes that the crimefighter model "runs a risk of excess." And ethical perspectives on the use of force that are based on social contract theory, he suggests, are too minimalistic and attenuated to rein in this model.

As an alternative approach, Kleinig recommends the "social peacekeeper" model, which seems to be gaining adherence currently with the implementation of community-oriented policing. He believes that this model is historically rooted in the Anglo-Saxon tradition of the king's peace, in which the "role of the police is to ensure or restore peaceful order."[63] This model does not obviate the logic of restraint that social contractarians describe; rather, it reinforces restraint through couching it within a wider framework of community and social practices of service. This would counter the tendency toward excess. As Kleinig puts it, "So understood, the peacekeeper model is broad enough to encompass most of the work that police do, whether it is crimefighting, crime control, or interventions in crisis situations. But what is more important is the irenic cast that it gives to police work."[64] Accordingly, police use of force "becomes a last (albeit sometimes necessary) resort rather than their dominant *modus operandi*."

Such a perspective *does* perceive the use of force to be a problem. Indeed, Kleinig suggests that it is a "*prima facie* evil" or "the lesser of two evils" to use force in policing. He maintains that there is a *prima facie* "presumption against the use of force," which is why force requires justification, even in police use of force.[65] This is especially the case for lethal force, because its use is irrevocable, with "no room for mistake, for changes of mind, for remission or pardon, no room for compensating the person who is killed." Indeed, lethal use of force risks judging and punishing a person to death, which undercuts the principle "innocent until proven guilty." Upon this basis, Kleinig delineates some key principles of current moral and legal assessments of police use of force. With regard to the current moral assessments of intermediate and lethal force, Kleinig identifies the primary criteria currently employed, including right intention (which rules out punishment and instead calls for restraint and apprehension), reasonableness (that is, it should not "shock the conscience"), proportionality (that is, force used to achieve legitimate ends ought not to be disproportionate to the seriousness of the alleged offense), and minimization (that is, employing a use of force continuum with lethal force as last resort).

In line with this ethical perspective, Kleinig observes that, on the legal front in the past decade or so, there has been "a tightening up of state legislative permissions or, in many cases, departmental policies and practices."[66] For example, a monumental Supreme Court decision in 1985 ruled out the use of deadly force in instances of a non-life-threatening fleeing felon.[67] In other words, "we have arrived at a situation," says Kleinig, "in which the police use of deadly force has been significantly limited—one in which the fleeing felon privilege has been all but subsumed under the defense-of-life privilege."[68] The more a social peacekeeper model is implemented, with police officers trained to see themselves as serving the community in which they are integrally involved, the stronger the presumption against force is reinforced.

## Conclusion

At this point, it should be evident that the experience (in theory and, increasingly, in practice) of police in the U.S. indicates an empirical basis for favoring the presumption-against-harm version of the just war tradition. Indeed, Kleinig's social peacekeeper model, with its use of force guidelines based on a strong presumption against harm, seems quite consonant with the "mode of reasoning" offered by Potter and Childress. Moreover, Malloy's earlier attempt at providing a "strict constructionist" treatment of the use of force in policing seems to share more affinity with the presumption-against-harm proponents. Each of these perspectives aim at justifying force in a way that takes into consideration all of the agents involved in a possible conflict situation: the victim, the police officer, and the perpetrator. In this way, the presumption-against-harm version attempts to rein in excessive force by police. In contrast, the presumption-against-injustice version, by focusing primarily upon the criterion of just cause, and by including punishment as a just cause, may reinforce a crimefighter model that runs the risk of excess through calls for "crusades against crime" or the like. In this version, the rights of the perpetrator are in danger of dropping out of the equation. In my view, the trajectory over the past few decades—in police law and ethics, and in the just war teachings of the churches—has been strikingly parallel, with the restraints tightened in each through a strong presumption against harm.

Childress points out that his own position on this debate "can be assessed on several grounds, including its fidelity to tradition, broadly understood, its consistency and coherence, and its congruence with contemporary experience."[69] I have endeavored to investigate the "contemporary experience" of policing in the U.S. in order to begin to establish an empirical base for a normative argument about which way the just war tradition ought to proceed. The above attention to the justification of the use of force in policing, I think, is congruent with that version of the just war tradition calling for a coherent, restrained approach to the use of force, with a strong presumption against harm. Of course, a conclusive argument would require more case studies, especially those that cross national borders (e.g., international police actions and humanitarian interventions), but if the domestic U.S. case is analogous, then the initial evidence suggests that whatever the historical understanding of the just war tradition, normatively for now and in the foreseeable future the presumption-against-harm version of just war theory should be followed.[70]

## Notes

[1]J. Bryan Hehir, "Just War Theory in a Post-Cold War World," *Journal of Religious Ethics* 20/2 (1992): 248.

[2]James F. Childress, "Nonviolent Resistance: Trust and Risk-Taking Twenty-Five Years Later," *Journal of Religious Ethics* 25/2 (1997): 213-220; James Turner Johnson, "The Broken Tradition," *The National Interest* 45 (Fall 1996): 27-36. My teacher, the late John Howard Yoder, expressed a keen interest in this particular debate, writing, for example, unpublished letters to both Childress and Hehir in 1994 and 1996, respectively, inquiring about the history of the discussion and proposing to consider it at an upcoming conference or Society of Christian Ethics meeting. Yoder's enthusiasm was reflected, also, in his encouragement of another student, Joseph A. Capizzi, and me as we participated in a round table discussion on this debate at a conference. See my "The Complementarity of Just War Theory and Pacifism" and Capizzi's "Against: The Problems Associated with the Complementarity Thesis," in *Religion, War and Peace: Proceedings of the Conference at Ripon College* (Wisconsin: The Wisconsin Institute for Peace and Conflict Studies, 1996).

[3]Childress, "Nonviolent Resistance: Trust and Risk-Taking Twenty-Five Years Later," 216.

[4]Johnson, "The Broken Tradition," 27-28, 35. Moreover, Johnson describes this "recent metathesis" based on a "presumption against war," which has become generally accepted in the last three decades, as an "intellectual deterioration" of just war theory. In contrast, Hehir lauds

how the "last thirty years have been a time of substantial development in the just war tradition." See his "Just War Theory in a Post-Cold War World," 239.

[5]National Conference of Catholic Bishops, *The Challenge of Peace: God's Promise and Our Response* (Washington, DC: United States Catholic Conference, 1983); United Methodist Council of Bishops, *In Defense of Creation: The Nuclear Crisis and a Just Peace* (Nashville: Graded Press, 1986). Subsequent page and paragraph citations for these editions will be given in parentheses in the text. Hehir writes that the response to the Catholic bishops' position "ran from an indictment that it amounted to a confusion of tongues to an endorsement of the pastoral as a development in Catholic theology." See J. Bryan Hehir, "Catholic Teaching on War and Peace: The Decade 1979-1989," in *Moral Theology: Challenges for the Future*, ed. Charles E. Curran (New York: Paulist Press, 1990), 370. Commemorating the tenth anniversary of *The Challenge of Peace*, the U.S. Catholic bishops, reiterate that both traditions share "the strong presumption against the use of force." See *The Harvest of Peace is Sown in Justice* (Washington, DC: U.S. Catholic Conference, 1994), 4-5. It should be noted that these statements do not place just war teaching and pacifism on an equal par, in that just war is advocated for most Christians and nations, and pacifism is an option only for individuals. In addition to the shared presumption against harm, which is the subject of this essay, other areas of convergence include the following: 1) just war and pacifism both reject the "realist" and "crusade" approaches; 2) they both oppose total and nuclear warfare; and 3) they interlock concerning nonviolent resistance as a legitimate and effective option for fostering or defending peace and the common good. Interestingly, Yoder suggested to me that, just as over a decade ago the threat of nuclear war brought together serious just war and pacifist thinkers, so too might the development of low intensity conflict (that is, police actions). Policing, itself, has sometimes been an area of convergence between just war thinkers and pacifists; see my "From Police Officers to Peace Officers" in the *The Wisdom of the Cross: Essays in Honor of John Howard Yoder*, eds. Stanley Hauerwas, Mark Nation, and Harry Huebner (Grand Rapids: Eerdman's, forthcoming).

[6]See J. Bryan Hehir, "The Just-War Ethic and Catholic Theology," in *War or Peace? The Search for New Answers*, ed. Thomas A. Shannon (Maryknoll, NY: Orbis, 1980), 15-39; David Hollenbach, *Nuclear Ethics: A Christian Moral Argument* (NY: Paulist Press, 1983), 1-33; Charles E. Curran, "Roman Catholic Teaching on Peace and War in a Broader Theological Context," in his *Critical Concerns in Moral Theology* (Notre Dame: University of Notre Dame Press, 1984), 144-170; Richard B. Miller, *Interpretations of Conflict: Ethics, Pacifism, and the Just War Tradition* (Chicago: University of Chicago Press, 1991); and Lisa Sowle Cahill, *Love Your Enemies: Discipleship, Pacifism, and Just War Thinking* (Minneapolis: Fortress, 1994). To be sure, the views of each of these authors are not identical, but they all at least regard pacifism and just war as sharing significant points of contact.

[7]As far as I can determine, no one pinpoints when this way of understanding and articulating the logic of the just war tradition began. Potter was one of the first to present it this way, and Childress at a roughly contemporary point in time did the same. Hehir presumably inherited it from Potter, with whom he did his Ph.D. at Harvard. Hollenbach cites Childress's work; Miller and Cahill mention all of the above.

[8]James F. Childress, "Just-War Theories: The Bases, Interrelations, Priorities, and Functions of Their Criteria," *Theological Studies* 39 (1978): 429. See W. D. Ross, *Foundations of Ethics* (Oxford: Clarendon, 1939), and *The Right and the Good* (Oxford: Clarendon, 1930). Elsewhere, Childress draws upon another philosopher, William Frankena, in order to delineate four levels of beneficence, which is part of but not equivalent to "the very principle that supported pacifism: the principle of love": 1) one ought not to inflict evil or harm; 2) one ought to prevent evil or harm; 3) one ought to remove evil; and 4) one ought to do or promote good. Childress maintains that many Christians have held that '1 has priority over 2 through 4.' See James F. Childress, "Moral Discourse about War in the Early Church," in *Peace, Politics, and the People of God*, ed. Paul Peachey (Philadelphia: Fortress, 1986), 119.

[9]Childress, "Nonviolent Resistance: Trust and Risk-Taking Twenty-Five Years Later," 216. Elsewhere, Childress portrays how the early Christians opposed war and/or participation in war for a number of reasons, including an aversion to bloodshed, and that this "aversion to bloodshed was important and required attention even after the other reasons for opposing military service

became obsolete because of Christianity's dominant role." See his "Moral Discourse about War in the Early Church," 118.

[10]Childress, "Nonviolent Resistance: Trust and Risk-Taking Twenty-Five Years Later," 217; "Just-War Theories: The Bases, Interrelations, Priorities, and Functions of Their Criteria," 433, 435.

[11]Childress, "Just-War Theories: The Bases, Interrelations, Priorities, and Functions of Their Criteria," 444.

[12]Ibid., 431-433. Regarding "trace" or "residual" effect, Childress draws upon Robert Nozick, "Moral Complications and Moral Structures," *Natural Law Forum* XIII (1968): 1-50.

[13]Ibid., 444.

[14]Ralph B. Potter, *War and Moral Discourse* (Richmond: John Knox Press, 1973), 49-50. In addition to domestic police power, Potter mentions revolution and international peacekeeping.

[15]Ibid., 53-54.

[16]Ibid., 61; see also, 32.

[17]Ibid., 55-56.

[18]Ibid., 60. Anecdotal evidence of the need for a resource dealing with the intersection of policing and Christian faith is provided in a book targeted at a popular audience and edited by Judith A. Kowalski and Dean J. Collins, *To Serve and Protect: Law Enforcement Officers Reflect on Their Faith and Work* (Minneapolis and Chicago: Augsburg/ACTA, 1992).

[19]For example, Hehir accepts "the point that the moral tradition which legitimizes war as the *ultima ratio* must begin at the point where the nonviolent tradition stands, with a presumption against taking life." See Hehir, "Catholic Teaching on War and Peace: The Decade 1979-1989," 372. He adds, however, that the just war ethic "must be able to *legitimate* force as well as to limit it." Similarly, Cahill thinks that Hehir and Childress correctly note "that both pacifism and just war theory share a presumption against violence. . . ." See Lisa Sowle Cahill, "Theological Contexts of Just War Theory and Pacifism: A Response to J. Bryan Hehir," *Journal of Religious Ethics* 20/2 (1992): 260.

[20]Johnson, "The Broken Tradition," 33. Similarly, George Weigel believes that *The Challenge of Peace* represents the "abandonment of the classic Catholic heritage" on war and peace. See his *Tranquillitas Ordinis: The Present Failure and Future Promise of American Catholic Thought on War and Peace* (NY: Oxford, 1987), 280-284. Indeed, Weigel calls for "an abandonment of the 'dual tradition' concept promoted by" the Catholic bishops. See his "Back to Basics: Moral Reasoning and Foreign Policy 'After Containment,'" in *Peacemaking: Moral and Policy Challenges for a New World*, eds. Gerard F. Powers, Drew Christiansen, S.J., and Robert T. Hennemeyer (Washington, DC: U.S. Catholic Conference, 1994), 68.

[21]Ibid., 28.

[22]Ibid., 30. Similarly, James E. Dougherty thinks that the just war tradition with its "coercive power was a divinely appointed remedy for human sinfulness, but the coercive power itself was deemed good, not sinful." See his *The Bishops and Nuclear Weapons: The Catholic Pastoral Letter on War and Peace* (Hamden, CT: Archon Press/Institute for Foreign Policy Analysis, 1984), 33.

[23]Ibid., 33. See also Johnson, review of *Love Your Enemies*, by Lisa Sowle Cahill, *Horizons* 22 (Fall 1995): 284; "The Just War Tradition and the American Military," in *Just War and the Gulf War*, eds. James Turner Johnson and George Weigel (Washington, DC: Ethics and Public Policy Center, 1991), 6.

[24]Johnson, *The Just War Idea and the Ethics of Intervention*, The Joseph A. Reich, Sr., Distinguished Lecture on War, Morality and the Military Profession, no. 6 (Colorado: U.S. Air Force Academy, 1993), 5.

[25]Johnson, "The Broken Tradition," 35; also *The Just War Idea and the Ethics of Intervention*, 11, 15. Russell Sizemore similarly suggests that just cause "arguably has logical priority and is the most illuminating of tensions in the post-cold war world." See his "Just Cause and New World Order: Sovereignty, Rights, and International Community," *The Annual of the Society of Christian Ethics* (1992), 173. Interestingly, Hehir acknowledges that, with regard to interventionary wars, "we need to follow Johnson's lead in giving renewed attention to *jus ad bellum* issues." See his "Just War Theory in a Post-Cold War World," 247. Similarly, Hollenbach

recognizes the importance of this stress on just cause, in that it helps consideration of "the full range of human values that are at stake in international affairs: human rights, freedom, justice, security, and peace itself." He adds that just cause still "depends on whether the other criteria of the tradition are met." See his "War and Peace in American Catholic Thought: A Heritage Abandoned?" *Theological Studies* 48 (December 1987): 722-723.

[26]Paul Ramsey, *Speak Up for Just War or Pacifism: A Critique of the United Methodist Bishops' Letter "In Defense of Creation"*, with an epilogue by Stanley Hauerwas (University Park and London: The Pennsylvania State University Press, 1988), 51. With regard to this mistake, Ramsey also prolixically and polemically engages the Catholic bishops' letter, Hehir, Hollenbach, Potter and Childress, inquiring how all of them could have gotten just war wrong.

[27]Ibid., 104. This is because Ramsey incorporates the just war into a theory of statecraft which claims that the "use of power, and possibly the use of force, is the *esse* of politics." See Paul Ramsey, *The Just War: Force and Political Responsibility* (NY: Charles Scribner's Sons, 1968), 4-5, 7, 142. Thus, the criteria governing use of force apply to any use of power, armed or not. George Weigel attempts to preserve this "theory of statecraft implicit in the just war tradition" which seeks an ordered peace, with freedom, justice, security and order. See his "War, Peace, and the Christian Conscience," in *Just War and the Gulf War*, eds. James Turner Johnson and George Weigel (Washington, DC: Ethics and Public Policy Center, 1991), 71, 85.

[28]Ibid., 53-54, 81-86, 109. Warns Ramsey, "[A] reader must be careful to avoid recourse to the wrong presumption." Just cause is "the logically prior premise or assumption in just-war ethics."

[29]Ibid., 88.

[30]Ibid., 72.

[31]Ibid., 82. See his *The Just War: Force and Political Responsibility*, 142-143; *Basic Christian Ethics* (Louisville: Westminster/John Knox, 1950, 1993), 165, 169-171; *War and the Christian Conscience: How Shall Modern War Be Conducted Justly?* (Durham, NC: Duke, 1961), xvi-xvii.

[32]Ramsey, *The Just War: Force and Political Responsibility*, 142-143.

[33]Ibid., 151.

[34]Ibid., 144. The rules for the "laws of war are the same as the rules governing any use of force," including "the laws governing the use of force domestically." Ibid., 468, 475.

[35]Childress, "Nonviolent Resistance: Trust and Risk-Taking Twenty-Five Years Later," 217; and "Just-War Theories: The Bases, Interrelations, Priorities, and Functions of Their Criteria," 444. Also, see Cahill, *Love Your Enemies*, 94, 202; Miller, "Pacifism and Just War Tenets: How Do They Diverge?" *Theological Studies* 47 (1986): 469. And, as Yoder put it, "In sum: the 'just war tradition' is not a position but a broad stream of traditions. At one side of the stream it shades off into the crusade, in that a single criterion will suffice to justify a war; at the other bank it agrees with pacifism that war always has the burden of proof, and honorably faces this burden by respecting all the criteria. . . ." See Yoder, review of *Tranquillitas Ordinis*, by George Weigel, *The Journal of Law and Religion* 4 (1988): 505.

[36]Cahill, *Love Your Enemies*, ix.

[37]Stanley Hauerwas, *The Peaceable Kingdom: A Primer in Christian Ethics* (Notre Dame: University of Notre Dame Press, 1983), 114.

[38]Other examples include the 1985 bombing of the radical group MOVE's house by Philadelphia police, which destroyed 61 homes and killed six adults and five children, and the 1996 beating of two immigrants pulled out of their truck by Riverside County Sheriff's deputies in California. Examples at the level of federal law enforcement include the burning of the Branch Davidian compound in Waco and the shooting of Vicki Weaver at Ruby Ridge.

[39]Edward A. Malloy, *The Ethics of Law Enforcement and Criminal Punishment* (Lanham, MD: University Press of America, 1982), 2.

[40]Malloy, 10.

[41]Ibid., 24. Of course, analogies are neither univocal nor equivocal, rather they involve attributes which are neither precisely the same nor yet simply different. The similarities and dissimilarities between policing and war have been noted by various writers, including Roland H. Bainton, *Christian Attitudes Toward War and Peace: A Historical Survey and Critical Re-*

*evaluation* (NY: Abingdon, 1960), 240-241; Duane L. Cady, *From Warism to Pacifism: A Moral Continuum* (Philadelphia: Temple University Press, 1992), 36; Jenny Teichman, *Pacifism and the Just War: A Study in Applied Philosophy* (Oxford and NY: Basil Blackwell, 1986), 38-46; John Howard Yoder, *The Politics of Jesus: Vicit Agnus Noster*, rev. 2nd ed. (Grand Rapids: Eerdmans, 1994), 204. Most of the differences noted by these writers are that of degree rather than kind. Even if the analogy between war and policing has both strengths and weaknesses, the use of force in either context requires justification; hence, the ethical logic or framework used to evaluate the justifiability of the use of force in either case does seem to be analogous.

[42]Ibid., ix. Malloy initially considered the problem of police use of force in a paper, "Ethics and Police Intervention in Domestic Violence," that he presented at the 1979 annual meeting of the Society of Christian Ethics. See Edward LeRoy Long, Jr., *Academic Bonding and Social Concern: The Society of Christian Ethics 1959-1983* (Religious Ethics Incorporated, 1984), 117. For an updated expansion of Malloy's work, see Tobias L. Winright, "The Perpetrator as Person: Theological Reflections on the Just War Tradition and the Use of Force by Police," *Criminal Justice Ethics* 14/2 (Summer/Fall 1995): 37-56. A fuller analysis of the historical, jurisprudential, philosophical, and theological treatments of the use of force in policing may be found in my dissertation, directed by Todd David Whitmore and currently in progress, "The Challenge of Policing: An Analysis in Christian Social Ethics" (Ph.D. diss., University of Notre Dame).

[43]Ibid., 12.

[44]Jerome H. Skolnick and James J. Fyfe, *Above the Law: Police and the Excessive Use of Force* (NY: The Free Press, 1993), xvi.

[45]Malloy, 12-13.

[46]Ibid., 17-18.

[47]Ibid., 18, 22, 13.

[48]William A. Geller, "Police and Deadly Force: A Look at the Empirical Literature," in *Moral Issues in Police Work*, eds. Frederick A. Elliston and Michael Feldberg (Totowa, NJ: Rowman and Allanheld, 1985), 218. Geller calls this a "defense-of-life" shooting policy that has been adopted in recent years.

[49]Whereas in the 18th century the English jurist, William Blackstone, justified deadly force in stopping a felon who was fleeing, in recent years "the rationale for the rule is gone; that while all felonies were capital crimes in the 18th century, relatively few are in the 20th." See John C. Hall, "Deadly Force, the Common Law and the Constitution," *FBI Law Enforcement Bulletin* 53 (April 1984): 27.

[50]Malloy, 28, footnote 23.

[51]Ibid., 11.

[52]Ramsey, *Speak Up for Just War or Pacifism*, 92.

[53]Michael Davis, "Do Cops Really Need a Code of Ethics?" *Criminal Justice Ethics* 10 (Summer/Fall 1991): 14.

[54]Irene Prior Loftus, et al., "The 'Reasonable' Approach to Excessive Force Cases Under Section 1983," *Notre Dame Law Review* 64 (1989): 136.

[55]John Kleinig, *The Ethics of Policing* (NY: Cambridge University Press, 1996), 24-29. Two additional models identified—the "emergency operator" and the "social enforcer"—continue to focus "too directly on the coercive dimension of police authority" as their "distinguishing feature," although they each claim to downplay the "crimefighting" character of policing.

[56]Ibid., 11.

[57]Jeffrey H. Reiman, "The Social Contract and the Police Use of Deadly Force," in *Moral Issues in Police Work*, eds. Frederick A. Elliston and Michael Feldberg (Totowa, NJ: Rowman and Allanheld, 1985); Reiman relies on John Locke's *Second Treatise of Government*, Thomas Hobbes's *Leviathan*, Jean-Jacques Rousseau's *The Social Contract*, and John Rawls's *A Theory of Justice*.

[58]Ibid., 239.

[59]Ibid., 240.

[60]Vance McLaughlin, *Police and the Use of Force: The Savannah Study* (Westport: Praeger, 1992), 1.

[61]Robert Reiner, *The Politics of the Police*, 2d ed. (Toronto: University of Toronto, 1992), 2, 59-60.

[62]Kleinig, 24-25.

[63]Ibid., 27-28.

[64]Ibid., 29.

[65]Ibid., 96-98, 101. Kleinig does not indicate from where he gets this language, but it is strikingly similar to Childress's.

[66]Ibid., 112, 114-118.

[67]*Tennessee v. Garner*, 471 U.S. 1, 105 Supreme Court 1694, 85 L. Ed. 2d 1 (decided 27 March 1985).

[68]Kleinig, 116.

[69]Childress, "Nonviolent Resistance: Trust and Risk-Taking Twenty-Five Years Later," 217.

[70]For his helpful feedback, in the weeks prior to his death, on earlier drafts of this essay, I am grateful to Professor John Howard Yoder. I also wish to express my appreciation to Maria Malkiewicz, William Mattison, David Weiss, Professor Todd Whitmore, the editors of *The Annual of the Society of Christian Ethics*, and the three anonymous reviewers for their helpful suggestions concerning the revision of this essay.

# APPLIED ETHICS

# Business and "Family Values"

*George D. Randels, Jr.*

## Abstract

Feminist theologians and ethicists reject the normative nature of traditional gender roles as unjust, and as part of a sinful social order. In its place, they advocate mutuality and alternative anthropologies. Although I find much of this work compelling, I question its rejection of capitalism as endemic of the old sexual-political order. Capitalism is not monolithic, nor is it necessarily hostile to women. I advocate a stakeholder model of capitalism, which can more readily address the feminist critique. Such a model would reject both the rigid traditional family roles that denigrate women, and the radical individualism that undermines family.

*The perfect fund manager is the guy who can't pick his kids out in a police lineup.*[1]
- Michael Stolper, investment consultant

*I refuse to buy into the traditional role of motherhood.*[2]
- Marie Holman-Rao, divisional president, The Limited

For families that only need one income, the mother's working outside the home "becomes similar to an illicit pleasure, almost akin to having an affair."[3] So states a recent *New York Times* "Business Day" article. Normative notions of the traditional family apparently continue to reign, undaunted by the approaching millennium. Even women at the top of their profession feel that the pressure to balance home and career falls on primarily on their shoulders, as evidently was the case for Pepsi-Cola North America CEO Brenda Barnes, who resigned last September to spend more time with her three children.[4] Gender roles remain strong at home and in the workplace, in spite of Barnes' rising above the glass ceiling to the executive suite.

These conditions contribute to an on-going theme in the literature of religious ethics. Quite rightly, feminist (and other) theologians and ethicists reject the normative nature of traditional gender roles as unjust, and even part of a sinful social order. In its place, they advocate mutuality and alternative anthropologies. I find much of this work compelling. Yet, in the process of promoting a progressive social agenda, these scholars often go on to reject capitalism as endemic to the old sexual-political order. We can see this rejection in Christine Gudorf's relatively recent, *Body, Sex, and Pleasure*,[5] although it admittedly plays only a minor role. It is much more prominent, however, in the work of Mary Hobgood and Beverly Harrison, whose analyses Gudorf accepts in this regard, as well as others, such as Rosemary Radford Ruether. Although I have much sympathy with these scholars and others regarding their concern for social justice and desire to reconstruct social ethics, historical analysis and many contemporary cases illustrate the need for a more fine-grained analysis regarding business and its possibilities. Gudorf and Hobgood apparently have an overly narrow understanding of business, and base their critique upon that image. Harrison's account is more sophisticated, but is also too narrow inasmuch as it focuses primarily on neoclassical economic theory as providing "the ideological boundaries of capitalism."[6] While these critiques contain much validity, these scholars make the same mistake as their right-wing opponents by assuming that they discern the essential nature of business. I contend that no such essential nature exists, and so their critiques pertain only to a particular manifestation of business in a larger, patriarchal social structure. Capitalism may bring its own set of problems, but any economic system would be skewed under such conditions.

For the sake of clarity, I should note here at the outset my understanding of the traditional family and its acceptable alternatives, as well as capitalism and business. At base, the traditional family is the ideal of modern nuclear family, consisting of husband, wife, and children, with the husband as the bread-winner through work done outside of the house and the wife as the domestic worker. This ideal is most often not met but is still controlling when the wife's role is expanded beyond that of homemaker. She may also work outside of the home in support of her husband's income, or perhaps just for something to do. What she brings in may be more than "pin money"—indeed, it may be crucial for the family's well-being—but it remains supplemental income, and does not free her from her domestic responsibilities. The husband's role remains as the primary bread-winner, and the wife's as primary domestic worker, even when they deviate from these roles to various degrees.

Rejection of the traditional family model as a normative concept that assigns women and men rigid roles does not mean that all other possible arrangements are therefore morally acceptable. A more liberal conception of family rejects both rigid traditional roles and radical individualism. Instead, it invokes mutuality as the standard for career and domestic responsibilities. Gudorf and other feminist theologians have been instrumental in making the case for mutuality as opposed to self-sacrifice as the ideal for familial and other relations,[7] and I support this shift. Mutuality is not an exact science, however, and particular democratized families could determine that traditional roles or their reversal are best. Mutuality will not necessarily lead to perfectly equal roles. As Don S. Browning, et al, contend, mutuality should not devolve into individualistic reciprocity.[8] A family's structure should be oriented to the family's common good, not strictly to any individual's separate good. Moreover, nothing in this formulation excludes same sex couples and parents.

Besides family, two other crucial concepts for this paper are capitalism and business. While any dictionary will provide several definitions for business, in its collective sense it is almost interchangeable with capitalism, as well as with free market. These all can refer to a particular type of economic system. What is capitalism? Typically, it is understood as an exploitative economic system focused on self-interested—often understood as selfish—pursuit of wealth. Profit is king and acquisition is the chief good. Many neo-classical economists extend this point in an attempt to explain not only capitalism, but also much of human behavior.

But just as the traditional family model does not articulate the essential nature of men, women, or family, this typical understanding of capitalism fails to articulate the essential nature of business. I submit that there is no one way to conduct business, no one form of capitalism. One can reject particular forms of capitalism and economic theory without rejecting free enterprise. Likewise, one can reject the normative rigidity of the traditional family structure and roles without rejecting free enterprise. In fact, one can accept much of the Marxist-feminist critique, albeit with some question regarding capitalism's historic support of the traditional family. I see vulgar capitalism, or what R. Edward Freeman calls "cowboy capitalism,"[9] and neoclassical economic theory as rejecting the traditional family in favor of radical individualism.

In contrast, I would advocate the type of capitalism that can converse with theological ethics, and that would support families—not *the* family—more broadly conceived. This type of capitalism would reject both the rigid traditional family roles that denigrate women, and the radical individualism that undermines family. It would more clearly serve the common good, not a narrowly conceived individual good at the expense of the larger community.

Harrison contends that "to provide justice for women under advanced capitalist economies would require fundamental political and economic change."[10] Perhaps we are in the process of such change, although not fundamental in the revolutionary sense that she envisions. Instead of rejecting capitalism per se, we can reject business as usual in favor of progressive forms of capitalism. This revisioning would not merely provide female access to a "male-defined" activity, but would also address the concerns of women and diminish the hyper-individualism that negatively impacts families.

## Patriarchy and Capitalism

When examining western culture and its economics, secular and theological feminists generally argue that home and work are divided into separate spheres, the former being the domain of the woman, and the latter being domain of the man, with the man dominant in both. This radical separation and its associated patriarchy are unjust. At the same time, many of these same scholars make a "bleeding spheres" argument, contending that these spheres reinforce one another.[11] Hobgood's thesis is that in the dominant U.S. culture, "sexual and capitalist ideologies work in tandem to impoverish human relationships within and outside marriage."[12] So far, so good for Hobgood's argument, because there is much evidence that the traditional ideologies have had that effect. Hobgood gets into trouble, however, when she claims that "traditional marriage is essential to capitalism"[13] and so reinforced by it. She distinguishes five particular ways in which she contends this is so. All of them are problematic, but I will focus on only one of them here: the necessity for gender inequality in the labor market. Hobgood contends that the gender system of the traditional family relegates women to "a secondary labor sector of lower-paying, low-benefit, dead-end jobs." Domestic roles serve "capitalism by making people assume that segmented public labor is natural. Wage differentials . . . between men and women make a tremendous amount of profit for individual capitalists and are essential to their survival in the economic system."[14] In a statement that supports several of these items, Harrison contends that "advanced industrial technological systems of production, developed under the aegis of private capital, weaken women's social role while supporting and strengthening ideologies of women's 'special nature' and 'special place' because those ideologies serve the smooth workings of these economic systems."[15] Both scholars' positions coincide with that of Marxist-feminist Iris Young, who claims that the "*marginalization of women and thereby our functioning as a secondary labor force is an essential and fundamental characteristic of capitalism.*"[16]

Clearly these scholars raise issues that have been and continue to be problems for capitalist societies. Two recent studies of pay for male executives find that men with stay-at-home wives earn significantly more than men whose spouses work,[17] and women, on average, continue to receive lower pay and status, although there has been some improvement in recent years.[18] Men continue to work long hours and neglect their families, reinforcing the husband's role strictly as a provider. While fewer office parties include strippers, sexual harassment in the workplace remains alive and well. Although most members of U.S. society no longer expect that women should aspire to be only homemakers and mothers, social pressure nevertheless remains on working women to hold primary responsibility for the domestic life. When nominated for U.S. Attorney General, Zoe Baird was condemned not only for her nanny problems, but at least implicitly for having one at all, indicating that she neglected her children. Her high-salaried position was not a matter of economic necessity for her family, and so its time demands made her suspect as a mother.

Nevertheless, the more-or-less essentialist argument regarding capitalism's necessary subordination of women in both domestic life and the workplace is problematic on both historical and theoretical grounds. It is a historically contingent subordination, not an essential one. As Harriet Bradley notes, "it is misleading to detach an analysis of sex relations at work from an understanding of sex relations in the society as a whole and their historical evolution."[19] Patriarchy clearly predates capitalism. Long before Adam Smith sketched his "system of natural liberty," men dominated the political, legal, and economic systems, including the sexual division of labor. Early capitalism was highly dependent on these antecedent practices and traditions for its own gender arrangements. Law, medicine, and academia all share this same historical, patriarchal background with capitalism. Each one has perpetuated this background in its own way, developing particular role structures for men and women that only relatively recently have begun to erode.[20] Arguments regarding them, however, generally call for only reforming the institutions, rather than eliminating them in favor of something else.

Like the rest of these practices, capitalism does not require a gender hierarchy for its internal structure nor the traditional family standard as an external support, in spite of inheriting those things at its inception. To avoid repetition, I will leave discussion of capitalism's internal structure for the next section of this paper, and now will address the notion of traditional family as a necessary external support. Historically, this role is quite problematic, because during the vulgar capitalism of the industrial revolution, the use of female and child labor prompted the complaint that capitalism was undermining the traditional family. (Religious and moral conservatives raise similar complaints today about working mothers without condemning capitalism in the process.) This complaint came not just from social conservatives, but also from Marx and Engels. In the *Communist Manifesto*, they contended that the bourgeoisie "has put an end to all feudal, patriarchal, idyllic relations. . . . [It] has torn away from the family its sentimental veil, and has reduced the family relation to a mere money relation."[21] They viewed the condition as even worse for the proletarians "in the practical absence of the family." For them, "all family ties . . . are torn asunder, and their children transformed into simple articles of commerce and instruments of labor."[22] In *Das Kapital*, Marx wrote that the workman previously sold only "his own labour power, which he disposed of nominally as a free agent. Now he sells wife and child. He has become a slave dealer."[23]

In a somewhat different vein, Engels contended in his later writing that capitalism's impact on women would be at least somewhat salutary because it would begin the process of abolishing the patriarchal family as the economic unit of society.[24] According to Heidi Hartmann, Engels held that "women's participation in the labor force was the key to their emancipation. Capitalism would abolish sex differences and treat all workers equally. Women would become economically independent of men and would participate on an equal footing with men in bringing about the proletarian revolution." Capitalism would erode patriarchal relations.[25] Large-scale industry thus provides a means for the wife to escape her domestic servitude, but also creates the modern work-family dilemma. "[W]hen she fulfills her duties in the private service of her family, she remains excluded from public production and cannot earn anything; and when she wishes to take part in public industry and earn her living independently, she is not in a position to fulfill her family duties."[26]

Of course, traditional families fared somewhat better than Marx and Engels predicted, and Jane Humphries argues that they may have taken on a role radically different than the one that Hobgood describes. Humphries' Marxist perspective leads her to claim that proletarian families can survive and even thrive under capitalism, but not as a support of the system. Humphries contends that the working class family is not "an essential component of the conditions of existence of the capitalist mode of production." Working class families have resisted alternatives to the traditional family structure, viewing its erosion as "a threat to its standard of living and ability to engage in class struggle."[27] Furthermore, "the family does not merely respond to capitalism, or worse still, reflect capitalism; it also shelters working people from capitalist oppression and—most neglected function of all—plays a crucial role in their struggle against capitalism and toward a better life."[28] Maintenance of the traditional family, then, may be a revolutionary act, rather than a supporting one. Although I would not argue that all or even most families fit the role that Humphries articulates, her argument along with others suggests that a much more complicated landscape exists regarding the relation between traditional families and capitalism than one of simple support.

Furthermore, if bleeding indeed occurs between the domestic and economic spheres, then changes in the traditional gender structure of families should influence changes in corporate structures. Likewise, improvements for women in the economic sphere should influence changes in the domestic sphere.[29] Changes in both spheres would indicate that an essentialist understanding of gender roles in a capitalist system is just as flawed as an essentialist view of the traditional family.

I now turn to the internal structure of capitalism, which is often associated with neoclassical economic theory. While not the essence of capitalism—indeed, there is no such thing—neoclassical economics clearly has been strongly influential and has provided a forcefully articulated framework that claims to articulate that essence.

## Neoclassical Economic Theory

Neoclassical Economic Theory posits atomistic individuals with narrowly self-interested outlooks. As economist Julie Nelson notes, "The subject of the economist's model world is an individual who is self-interested, autonomous, rational, and whose active choices are the focus of interest, as opposed to one who would be social, other-interested, dependent, emotional, and directed by an intrinsic nature."[30] Nelson calls it a gendered "male" perspective that pays no heed to family or affective relationships, ignores much productive human activity, and too often neglects the common good. Neo-classical theorists would reject the gender-specific charge, claiming that all humans seek to maximize their individual utility, whatever that might be. The rational individual weighs the cost of obtaining these desired goods against their perceived benefits.

Harrison rightly rejects neoclassical economic theory as inadequate for the task of theological ethics. She is too hasty, however, in acquiescing to the commonly held belief among economists and others that ethics falls outside of the realm of economic theory and business activity.[31] Milton Friedman, whom Harrison and many others cite as the primary spokesperson for this school of thought, himself provides a normative framework for capitalism. When Friedman assails the notion of corporate social responsibility, he expounds his conception of business ethics in the process. Friedman holds that managers have a fiduciary duty to the stockholders to maximize profits within variously articulated limits, such as avoiding deception and fraud.[32] Not attending to stockholder interests is unethical, and so is engaging in deception and fraud, even in the pursuit of profit. Friedman thus presents a normative argument, attempting to persuade the reader how individuals and corporations should operate in a free and democratic society. Friedman's vision is, of course, too narrow for the marketplace, let alone for other spheres of life. It provides a minimalist ethic for a libertarian worldview, with no guidance for what to do with one's freedom. Even its version of commutative justice is impoverished. Within Friedman's narrow "rules of the game," the sole yardstick for measuring one's actions is that of profitability. Yet, while far from satisfactory, this yardstick nevertheless provides a small starting point for addressing and rejecting traditional, segmented, subordinate roles for women.

Because of the mandate to maximize profit, neoclassical economic theory is forced to reject the glass ceiling for women and the pigeon-holing of them into traditional roles. Refusal to develop and utilize their talent runs contrary to the theory—if good employees are not developed and allowed to succeed, then financial performance will be less than optimal. At least one study shows that among the Standard and Poor 500 companies, those with better records regarding various equity issues outperform the ones with the worst records by a better than 2-to-1 margin.[33] There is every indication that female-friendly and family-friendly businesses outperform their rivals. Contrary to standard business ideology, doing right by the employees in this way can, and often does, improve the bottom line.[34] Organizations and businessmen that fail on these fronts fail to maximize profits, and put themselves at a competitive disadvantage with their rivals. Family-friendly corporations provide additional motivation, improving productivity, and find it easier to recruit and keep good employees. Research by the Families and Work Institute and the University of Chicago provides evidence that employees who have access to, and take advantage of, family-oriented programs such as day care and flex hours are more productive. They do not feel compelled to choose between work and family, because they can have both. Similarly, *Working Mother* magazine says of AT&T, its top firm for women: "When the company goes out of its way to accommodate employees' family needs, they feel obliged to go out of their way for AT&T."[35]

A conversation with neoclassical economics regarding the rejection of traditional family roles and in support for children is thus possible, but the results are only partially satisfactory because of the approach's strict focus on profit maximization as its sole good, validating nearly anything that serves this goal. The limited conversation provides sufficient evidence, however, against Hobgood's bald claim that the traditional family is essential to capitalism, or the claim that capitalism cannot address women's and family issues. The problem, then, is not capitalism per se, but that the larger culture and particular—even most—capitalist practices; corporate cultures and business people are prisoners of a problematic ideology.[36]

## Alternative Theories for Capitalism

With the rejection of cowboy capitalism and the inadequacy of neoclassical economic theory comes the need for new theory. As a replacement, Harrison proposes a neo-Marxian "radical political economic" theory that she claims correlates far better with theological ethics, and so provides a richer conversation. The four points of overlap between this radical political economic theory and theological ethics are: 1) the attention to concrete conflict and suffering; 2) the understanding of political economy as a transformable sociohistorical reality; 3) the acceptance of "responsibility for concretely illuminating the experiences of everyday life"; and 4) the recognition that "all economic activity is intrinsically and directly related to the overall cultural and institutional matrix of human social life." Contrary to the capitalist framework, says Harrison, human life does not exist in isolated, unrelated spheres (e.g., economics, politics, morality, and religion), nor are all spheres subsumed under the neo-classical rubric. Harrison's proposed theory would address these issues.[37]

I agree that all four features of Harrison's radical theory are crucial to an ethically superior economic theory; clearly Harrison rightly rejects the notion of isolated spheres in favor of an integrated view. I would argue, however, that a "kinder, gentler" capitalism can also converse with theological ethics on these same four points. Interestingly, unlike Hobgood, Harrison leaves the door slightly ajar for retaining capitalism. Following Marx, she holds that capitalism's successes create the conditions for economic democracy. She also claims that "radical political economists do not treat capitalism as irrevocably evil, but they do insist that its pattern of exploitation must be transcended historically."[38] Nevertheless, the tenor of her writings indicate a rejection of this prospect, except as a logical possibility.

One reason that Harrison may find capitalism's prospects dubious at best is her reading of the business ethics literature. She criticizes it as "boring" and, along with corporate responsibility ethics, inadequate as an economic ethics, because it remains tied to the assumptions of neoclassical economic theory and preoccupied with questions regarding its relevance because of those assumptions.[39] While that critique may have been true enough twelve years ago when she published *Making the Connections*, much has happened since then that makes business ethics look more like the radical theory and feminist theory that she espouses, blurring the distinction between reform and revolution. Most business ethics scholars are not Chamber of Commerce cheerleaders or lacking in conceptual resources, but engage in critical reflection on the traditional assumptions of capitalism and problems with its practice. They develop alternative visions that can connect with theological ethics, providing a basis for much richer conversation.

This is not to say, however, that nothing interesting and important was going on in the management literature to challenge the assumptions of neoclassical economics. For example, in a 1960 issue of *California Management Review*, Keith Davis argued that "it is hardly possible to separate economic aspects of life from its other values. Business deals with a *whole* man in a *whole* social structure, and all aspects of this situation are interrelated."[40] And in 1954, management guru Peter Drucker maintained that the business enterprise has an economic responsibility to strengthen society, but doing so "in accordance with society's political and ethical beliefs," which he recognized would change over time.[41]

Nevertheless, it was probably R. Edward Freeman's 1984 publication of the revolutionary *Strategic Management: A Stakeholder Approach* that began a marked shift not only in the business ethics literature, but also in management textbooks. In this work, Freeman builds on this earlier thread in the management literature, rejecting the stockholder theory of the firm—the notion that managers' purpose is to maximize stockholder value (an offshoot of neoclassical economics). In its place, Freeman expounds the first systematic account of "stakeholder theory," contending that managers are responsible to a larger and diverse constituency who can affect, or are affected by, a firm's actions. Managers must create value not only for stockholders, but also for employees, consumers, suppliers, local communities, and so forth. When stakeholder interests conflict, managers must balance the competing claims.[42]

Stakeholder theory has proved to be a popular model, and it has been developed in several directions. Freeman and various co-authors have also refined the theory several times. In one article, he and co-author William Evan characterize it as "Kantian Capitalism." They claim that no stakeholder group may serve as mere means to the ends of others; all deserve respect, and each has a legitimate claim on the firm. "The very purpose of the firm is . . . to serve as a vehicle for coordinating stakeholder interests." Moreover, each stakeholder group must participate in the decisions that substantially affect its welfare.[43] More recently, Freeman and co-authors Andrew C. Wicks and Daniel R. Gilbert, Jr.

provide a feminist reinterpretation of the stakeholder concept that attempts to integrate individual and community. This view holds that "the corporation is constituted by the network of relationships, which it is involved in with the employees, customers, suppliers, communities, businesses and other groups who interact with and give meaning and definition to the corporation."[44] Other authors have gone further, arguing that notions of justice and rights provide insufficient grounding for stakeholder theory, but feminist theory and its ethic of care supply the necessary elements.[45] Rather than merely providing access for women, these versions provide a complete revisioning of the firm and its relationship to the larger society. Instead of a single theory, it might be better to say that Freeman, his co-authors, and many other scholars have developed several theories that utilize the stakeholder concept.

Besides the work in stakeholder theory, much other recent work in the field "makes the connections," employing virtue theory, narrative theory, and moral imagination, among other things, in their discussions of business and ethics.[46] More importantly, however, we can see these connections in business practice. Tom Chappell, founder and CEO of Tom's of Maine, explicitly adopts stakeholder principles in the management of his company. He explicitly connects them to lessons from Buber, Jonathan Edwards, and Kant learned from his days at Harvard Divinity School. From Buber, Chappell learned the value of developing I-Thou rather than I-It relationships with his customers and employees. From Edwards's notion of being-as-relation, he learned that one's identity comes from a sense of connection with others and accountability to them. Being an individual does not mean being isolated from others. Chappell applied this lesson not only to himself, but also to his company. Tom's of Maine's statement of beliefs, mission statement, and, crucially, its day-to-day operations show that the firm is not driven exclusively by the profit-motive as per neoclassical economics, but rather integrates profit-making with other values, such as environmental concern, respect for others, and sharing wealth with the local community through donations and on-the-payroll volunteer work.[47] It also has a Leadership and Career Development Program for women, who make up 45% of the employees, 50% of the managers, and 33% of the board of directors.[48]

Although we might expect such attitudes to reside exclusively at small firms, we can find larger examples of what Tom Peters calls "excellent corporations." Robert Haas, CEO of Levi Strauss, is an outspoken advocate of stakeholder theory. Haas has changed Levi's ethical focus from mere legal compliance to a values-oriented approach. Six ethical principles serve as its basis: honesty, promise-keeping, fairness, respect for others, compassion, and integrity. Like Chappell, Haas seeks to link good ethics with good business by empowering employees through participatory management, and aspiring to a range of values. Deserving special mention are Levi's Global Sourcing Guidelines, which ban the use of child labor, and how its reaction to discovering that a few of their contractors were violating those guidelines. Rather than fire the children, whose loss of income would harm their families, or violate its principles, Levi decided to pay wages and send the children to school full time.[49]

Stakeholder theory clearly overlaps with theological ethics. Chappell's use of Buber and Edwards nicely dovetails with the feminist emphasis on mutuality in human relationships. It also connects with Pope John Paul II's vision of the firm's purpose as

> not simply to make a profit, but . . . as a community of persons who in various ways are endeavoring to satisfy their basic needs, and who form a particular group at the service of the whole society. Profit is a regulator of the life of a business, but it is not the only one; other human and moral factors must also be considered which, in the long term, are at least equally important for the life of a business.[50]

It would seem, then, that stakeholder theory can manifest itself in concrete ways that can dialogue with theological ethics on the same four points as Harrison's radical economic theory. Freeman's various versions of stakeholder theory and Chappell's and Haas's practical applications concur with Harrison's insights that we should not attempt to separate business from other spheres of life, and that the connections should be based on mutuality and the common good, rather than patriarchy and hyper-individualism.

## Business, Family, and Values

The autonomy-supporting element of the Kantian capitalism version of stakeholder theory rejects the rigid traditional family structure as normative for business practice. It allows for a range of possible family and career structures and rejects discrimination based on such things as gender and sexual orientation. The feminist reinterpretations highlight community and mutuality, more clearly rejecting the atomistic individualism of neoclassical economics in favor of recognizing that we exist in a larger social framework, with responsibilities to others. Business is not an isolated sphere of activity but is intimately connected with everything else that we do. Further, corporations themselves ought to be communities, their members holding common values and working together to achieve goals that fit with the larger community. To hold both liberty and community as important values means that corporations themselves need to be liberal communities.

A modified "family values" version of stakeholder theory would recognize that not only are individual employees stakeholders, but so also are their families. Many employees join organizations not strictly as individuals, but as members of families, or they may form families during their tenure. Families reap various benefits from business enterprises but also bear certain risks and burdens (e.g., time and work pressures that negatively impact domestic life), both clearly giving them a stake in the business. Catholic social thought has long viewed families as stakeholders, although not using the term itself, in its call for organizations to pay a "living wage" to male heads of households sufficient to support their families. My modified family values version of stakeholder theory would reject the traditional family model associated with the living wage idea, but uphold its recognition that employer obligations reach beyond individual employees.

In rejecting the traditional family model as normative, corporations must reject the automatic association of men with career and women with family, and all of the trappings that go along with this association, such as rewarding men with stay-at-home wives. The traditional family is, of course, one possibility, but with increasing opportunities for women and a decline in "family wage" manufacturing jobs for men, it is a choice that is decreasing in incidence with less than 30% of all families meeting its ideal standard. The alternative is not the creation of two tracks—a career track for women who want to join the traditional male model and a second-tier "mommy track" for women who also want families, as proposed by Felice Schwartz[51]—but various tracks. Or better yet, no tracks. Instead, corporations can and should provide room for all employees to attend to family and other projects, providing them with necessary institutional support. The principle of subsidiarity thus should be applied to the firm. Possible ways to implement that principle include allowing flex-time (77% of Fortune 1000 companies have some form of it already), day care (13% of the same companies), job-sharing, tele-commuting, and parental leave. It is difficult to specify in the abstract the upper and lower limits of institutional support that must be provided, or the particular forms they should take. The principle of subsidiarity would reject undue interference in family life, and the standard of mutuality would indicate that conversation must take place to determine what is appropriate in a particular context.

Control Data Corporation CEO Lawrence Perlman testified before Congress in support of the Family and Medical Leave Act, because of Control Data's success with a similar policy of its own. Although Perlman rejects a federal solution for every workplace problem, he sees this act as one that "can make a real difference in the quality of employees' lives and in the quality and efficiency of businesses. Family and medical leave . . . responds to fundamental changes in the composition of the American workforce and recognizes that each employee is a whole person with a life that extends beyond the workplace."[52]

Perlman, then, advocates the type of capitalism that can converse with theological ethics. Rather than dictating a particular family structure, capitalism can support various potential family structures. That is precisely what Apple Computer did, in spite of opposition from a Texas community where it sought to locate a facility. According to Apple spokeswoman Lisa Byrne, "We don't feel that we're in the business of defining what a family is. But we want to treat all our employees with respect and fairness" regarding their families.[53] Other imperfect but important exemplars like Hewlett-Packard provide female-friendly programs like leadership development and mentoring, family-friendly programs like job flexibility and dependent care, and benefits for domestic partners. This is a type of capitalism theological ethics can and should support.

## Notes

[1]Quoted in *The Chicago Tribune* (21 March 1993): 4-3; cited by Todd David Whitmore, "Children and the Problem of Formation in American Families," *Annual of the Society of Christian Ethics* (1995): 272.

[2]Quoted in Reed Abelson, "When Waaa Turns to Why: Mom and Dad Both Work? Sure. But What to Tell the Children?" *New York Times* (11 November 1997): C6.

[3]Ibid.

[4]Ibid.

[5]Christine Gudorf, *Body, Sex, and Pleasure: Reconstructing Christian Social Ethics* (Cleveland: Pilgrim Press, 1994).

[6]Beverly Harrison, *Making the Connections: Essays in Feminist Social Ethics* (Boston: Beacon Press, 1985), 68.

[7]See, e.g., Christine E. Gudorf, "Parenting, Mutual Love, and Sacrifice," *Women's Consciousness, Women's Conscience*, ed. Barbara Hilkert Andolsen, Christine E. Gudorf, and Mary D. Pellauer (Minneapolis: Seabury, 1985).

[8]Don S. Browning, et al, *From Culture Wars to Common Ground: Religion and the American Family Debate* (Louisville, KY: Westminster John Knox Press, 1997), 47.

[9]R. Edward Freeman, *Ethics Digest* 1 (1989), quoted in Robert C. Solomon, *Ethics and Excellence: Cooperation and Integrity in Business* (New York: Oxford University Press, 1992): 65.

[10]Harrison, 52-53.

[11]Thanks to Ann Mongoven for supplying the term "bleeding spheres" during the discussion at the annual meeting to characterize this argument.

[12]Mary E. Hobgood, "Marriage, Market Values, and Social Justice: Toward an Examination of Compulsory Monogamy," *Redefining Sexual Ethics: A Sourcebook of Essays, Stories, and Poems*, ed. Susan E. Davies and Eleanor H. Haney, (Cleveland: Pilgrim Press, 1991), 116.

[13]Ibid., 119.

[14]Ibid.

[15]Harrison, 42.

[16]Iris Young, "Beyond the Unhappy Marriage: A Critique of the Dual Systems Theory," *Women and Revolution: A Discussion of the Unhappy Marriage of Marxism and Feminism*, ed. Lydia Sargent (Boston: South End Press, 1981), 58 (emphasis in the original).

[17]Associated Press, "Men Earn Less When Wives Work;" available from C-ap@clarinet.com; accessed 27 October 1994. Having a wife to take primary responsibility for domestic matters enables men to devote more time and energy to their careers.

[18]Federal Glass Ceiling Commission, *Good for Business: Making Full Use of the Nation's Human Capital* (Washington, DC, 1995).

[19]Harriet Bradley, *Men's Work, Women's Work: A Sociological History of the Sexual Division of Labour in Employment* (Minneapolis: University of Minnesota Press, 1989), 171.

[20]To take a relatively recent example from academia, Vassar College was harshly criticized by a federal judge for consistent prejudice against married women in the hard sciences. U.S. District Court Judge Constance Baker Motley wrote that Vassar's Biology Department operated under the stereotype "that a married woman with an active and ongoing family life cannot be a productive scientist and therefore, is not one despite much evidence to the contrary." Gail

Appleson, "Judge Rules Against Vassar in Discrimination Case," Reuters, available at clarinews@clarinet.com; accessed 23 May 1994.

[21]Karl Marx, *The Communist Manifesto*, *The Marx-Engels Reader* (2nd ed.), ed. Robert C. Tucker (New York: W.W. Norton Co., 1978, 1972), 475-476.

[22]Ibid., 487-488.

[23]Karl Marx, *Capital* (vol. I), Karl Marx and Frederick Engels, *Collected Works* (vol. 35) (New York: International Publishers, 1996), 399.

[24]Friedrich Engels, *The Origin of the Family, Private Property, and the State*, *The Marx-Engels Reader* (2nd ed.), ed. Robert C. Tucker (New York: W.W. Norton Co., 1978, 1972), 744.

[25]Heidi Hartmann, "The Unhappy Marriage of Marxism and Feminism: Towards a More Progressive Union," *Women and Revolution: A Discussion of the Unhappy Marriage of Marxism and Feminism*, ed. Lydia Sargent (Boston: South End Press, 1981), 4.

[26]Engels, 744.

[27]Jane Humphries, "The Working Class Family: A Marxist Perspective," *The Family in Political Thought*, ed. Jean Bethke Elshtain (Amherst, MA: University of Massachusetts Press, 1982), 199-200.

[28]Ibid., 222, (emphasis in the original).

[29]On this latter point, see Scott Coltrane, *Family Man: Fatherhood, Housework, and Gender Equity* (New York: Oxford University Press, 1996).

[30]Julie A. Nelson, *Feminism, Objectivity, & Economics* (New York: Routledge, 1996), 22.

[31]Harrison, 69.

[32]Milton Friedman, *Capitalism and Freedom* (University of Chicago Press, 1962, 1982); and "The Social Responsibility of Business is to Increase Its Profits," *New York Times Magazine* (Sept. 13, 1970).

[33]Federal Glass Ceiling Commission, 14.

[34]Jay Mathews, "Easing an Employee's Family Strains Reaps Benefits for Employers Too," *Washington Post* (May 2, 1993): H2.

[35]Reuters, "ATT, Xerox among top firms for mothers," available from C-reuters@clarinet.com; accessed 13 Sept 1994.

[36]I say "business people" and not "businessmen" here because some businesswomen can be part of the problem. In her summer internship, my former research assistant, Jennifer Dellapina, witnessed ostracism of a lesbian manager by other female managers, as well as by male managers.

[37]Harrison, 76-77.

[38]Ibid., 77.

[39]Ibid., 69.

[40]Keith Davis, "Can Business Afford to Ignore Social Responsibilities?" *California Management Review* 2/3 (1960): 74 (emphasis in the original).

[41]Peter Drucker, *The Practice of Management* (New York: Harper & Bros, 1954), 35.

[42]R. Edward Freeman, *Strategic Management: A Stakeholder Approach* (Boston: Pitman, 1984).

[43]William M. Evan and R. Edward Freeman. "A Stakeholder Theory of the Modern Corporation: Kantian Capitalism," *Ethical Theory and Business* (4th edition), ed. Tom Beauchamp and Norman Bowie (Englewood Cliffs, NJ: Prentice-Hall, 1993), 82.

[44]Andrew C. Wicks, Daniel R. Gilbert Jr., and R. Edward Freeman. "A Feminist Reinterpretation of the Stakeholder Concept," *Business Ethics Quarterly* 4/4 (1994): 483.

[45]Brian K. Burton and Craig P. Dutton, "Feminist Ethics as Moral Grounding for Stakeholder Theory," *Business Ethics Quarterly* 6/2 (1996). See also Jeanne M. Liedtka, "Feminist Morality and Competitive Reality: A Role for an Ethic of Care," *Business Ethics Quarterly* 6/2 (1996); John Dobson and Judith White, "Toward the Feminine Firm," *Business Ethics Quarterly* 5/3 (1995); and Robbin Derry, "Toward a Feminist Firm: Comments on John Dobson and Judith White," *Business Ethics Quarterly* 6/1 (1996).

[46]See, e.g., Robert C. Solomon, *Ethics and Excellence: Cooperation and Integrity in Business*, (New York: Oxford University Press, 1992); Daniel R. Gilbert Jr., "A Critique and A Retrieval of Management and the Humanities," *Journal of Business Ethics* 16 (1997); and

Patricia Werhane, "Moral Imagination and the Search for Ethical Decision-making in Management," *The Ruffin Lectures in Business Ethics* (Charlottesville, VA: The Darden School, University of Virginia, 1994).

[47]Tom Chappell, *The Soul of a Business: Managing for Profit and the Common Good* (New York: Bantam, 1993).

[48]Federal Glass Ceiling Commission, 179.

[49]Robert D. Haas, "Ethics—A Global Business Challenge," *Vital Speeches of the Day* 60 (1 June 1994): 507-508.

[50]Pope John Paul II, *Centesimus Annus* (Washington, DC: United States Catholic Conference, 1991) 69.

[51]Felice N. Schwartz, "Management Women and the New Facts of Life," *Harvard Business Review* 67 (Jan-Feb 1989).

[52]Christopher Dodd, et al., "Should the Congress Approve the Family and Medical Leave Act," *Congressional Digest* (April 1991): 18.

[53]Associated Press, "Apple Gets Offer After Rejection," *St. Petersburg Times* (5 December 1993): 91.

# A Cabbit in Sheep's Clothing: Exploring the Sources of Our Moral Disquiet About Cloning

*Timothy M. Renick*

## Abstract

Emerging from the first successful cloning of a mammal, a sheep named "Dolly," is a critical but under-asked question: "Why do so many of us find this feat (and its potential application to human subjects) to be deeply disturbing?" This paper suggests that the answer rests not primarily in the theological and philosophical arguments most often heard against cloning but in the threat the act poses to our foundational "cosmological categories." Building upon theories introduced by Mary Douglas and Jeffrey Stout, the essay argues that Dolly becomes a "cabbit" in sheep's clothing—an outwardly innocuous entity which, like Stout's cat/rabbit, offends at a deep and visceral level. Like the cabbit, the cloned sheep and especially the cloned human are disturbing not because of the way they are produced nor by the physical threat they pose but because they challenge the very way we understand and organize our world.

## Introduction

On February 23, 1997, the world awoke to an announcement that managed to rattle the foundations of both biology and philosophy. Researchers at the Roslin Institute near Edinburgh, Scotland had accomplished what many biologists had thought, and many moralists had hoped, was a scientific impossibility. That day, the world was introduced to a six-month-old sheep named Dolly, an animal almost jarringly innocuous by all appearances, and told that she had been genetically constituted from a single cell taken from an adult donor.

Removing a cell from the mammary gland of a six-year-old sheep, embryologist Ian Wilmut and his colleagues at Roslin extracted the cell's nucleus and planted it into a hollowed-out, unfertilized egg from another sheep; they then placed the altered egg in the womb of a third adult. What resulted from this "nuclear transfer" was the birth of an animal that was the genetic clone of the first sheep, an identical twin six years the junior of her sister. The technique was astoundingly simple—so simple in fact that, as Princeton University molecular biologist Lee Silver writes, ". . . there is every reason to expect that the technology can be transferred [to humans]. It requires only equipment and facilities that are already standard or easy to obtain by biomedical laboratories and free-standing *in vitro* fertilization clinics across the country. . . ."[1] If Silver is correct, then for the first time in history human life does not have to have its origins in an embryo formed through the merger of gametes from a mother and a father. A single parent can produce new human life.

Almost as striking as the revelations from Roslin were the public reactions to these events. While scientists reveled in the technical accomplishment, politicians and public alike more often voiced grave concern, even disgust, in the face of Dolly and her prospective human counterparts. On February 24, the day after the news broke from Scotland, President Bill Clinton appointed a National Bioethics Advisory Commission, asking it to report within ninety days "with recommendations on possible federal actions" to prevent the "abuse" of cloning of human beings. A week later, unable to wait for the findings of his commission, Clinton announced, "I believe we must . . . resist the temptation to replicate ourselves." On June 7, the Commission, chaired by Harold Shapiro, concurred, recommending a ban on human cloning for at least five years.[2] In the interim, Senator Christopher Bond declared, "This type of research on humans is morally reprehensible;"[3] National Institutes of Health director Harold Varmus testified that cloning a person is "repugnant;" and *Time*, in a two-page color spread, graphically depicted a *really* frightening implication of the new technology: a Bulls starting lineup consisting of nothing but five cloned Dennis Rodmans. Perhaps predictably, a subsequent national poll found that over ninety percent of Americans "strongly oppose" human cloning and two out of three consider even the cloning of animals to be immoral.[4]

The swift and harsh reactions to this new bio-technology were not limited to politicians and the public. The ethics community has viewed these developments with comparable alarm. Leon Kass writes, "Science is close to crossing some horrendous boundaries;" his most recent article on the topic is peppered with the words "offensive," "grotesque," "revolting," "repulsive," and "repugnant."[5] Richard McCormick finds defenses of cloning on humans to be "appalling" and "frightening;" he asserts, "I can't think of a morally acceptable reason to clone a human being." Jeremy Rifkind calls human cloning "an horrendous crime."[6] George Annas writes of a "nightmare scenario come true," while Germain Grisez advises with disgust, "the people doing this ought to contemplate splitting themselves in half and see how they like it."[7]

With such an overwhelming outcry against the cloning of humans, it would seem that the ethical reasons for this widespread moral disquiet, indeed disgust, ought to be very clear. It would seem that cloning must violate moral values of such universal recognition and fundamental importance that the need to preserve these values is commonly manifest to the public, politician and academician alike.

But this simply is not the case. While moralists have been writing on the topic since at least 1970, when Paul Ramsey devoted a chapter to the subject in *Fabricated Man,*[8] there is little consensus about what makes human cloning immoral. Just as significantly for my project, the arguments that *are* offered against cloning seem incapable of generating the strength of the moral opposition so often voiced against the practice. A few examples will suffice to illustrate my point.

Steven G. Post is a strong opponent of cloning in part because it is, he argues, destructive to the family. "Marriage is a union of female and male that alone allows for procreation in which children can benefit developmentally from both mother and father," Post asserts. In creating single parent genetic, if not necessarily social, offspring, cloning disrupts the "core nucleus [of] wife, husband and children" and threatens to "unravel what is both naturally and eternally good."[9] But precisely what good is unraveled by cloning? It is not clear. If Post's concern is that the cloned child is not the product of the genetic union of both social parents, it is difficult to see how the clone is, in this sense, different from the child resulting from *in vitro* fertilization by sperm donor or, for that matter, from the adopted child. All are lacking a genetic link to at least one social parent. Is his concern, then, that we make single parenthood more likely through cloning? Maybe so, but if this is the case, the uniqueness of the threat posed by cloning is undermined. Cloning should, by this logic, engender no more disgust than does the woman who elects to conceive of a child by natural means and raise it on her own. Why is cloning, then, seen as "reprehensible" and the single mother's act (most commonly) is not?

Perhaps it is the case that cloning poses a unique threat to the genetic diversity of the species. Post and Ronald Bailey, among others, have expressed this concern. "Surely no scientist would doubt that genetic diversity produced by procreation between man and woman will always be preferable to cloning, because procreation reduces the possibility for species annihilation through particular diseases and pathogens," Post writes.[10] Yet cloning is by most accounts more expensive and, presumably, considerably less fun than traditional means of reproduction. It is not likely to become a widespread practice any time soon. Moreover, even if every man, woman and child on earth *were* to wake up tomorrow with the desire and resources to reproduce exclusively by cloning for the rest of his or her life, the resulting next generation of the human population would be *exactly* as genetically diverse as today's (for it would be a genetic carbon-copy of the present species population). When was the last time you heard someone voice moral "revulsion" over the lack of genetic diversity in the present-day population?

Leon Kass, Richard McCormick, Jean Bethke Elshtain and Allen Verhey all express various concerns about the psychological pressure we might place on children brought into the world as clones.[11] Consider, for example, the burden placed on the child who is cloned in order to "replace" a child killed tragically by disease, or the child who is cloned to serve the ego or fulfill the lost dreams of a narcissistic individual. Even Peter Singer, who finds most arguments against cloning to be less than compelling, has grave concerns here. He writes (with Deane Wells): "Would [such parents] be able to love their children with the uncritical love of parents who accept their children for what they are—a love that does not depend on the extent to which children measure up to some preconceived standard of excellence? And will the children not suffer from the knowledge that they are not living up to the parents' expectations?"[12] While these are deeply important moral considerations, the sad fact is that many of the same psychological burdens are placed on non-cloned children by grieving, narcissistic, or demanding parents. If we recoil in disgust in the face of the above scenarios, is it not in response to the "obscene" abuses of parental responsibility evidenced rather than to the cloning *per se*?

My point here is not to offer a comprehensive refutation of existing moral arguments against human cloning. Quite the contrary, I believe some of the arguments are valid ones. I strongly agree with Shapiro's Commission, for example, that a five-year moratorium on human experimentation is warranted out of concern for the genetic health and general well-being of the clone. Other commentators already have explored the conventional moral arguments in considerable detail, and I commend these materials to the interested reader.[13] No, my point is not to under*mine* the arguments but to under*line* a curious disjunction: the arguments voiced—even when valid—are simply inadequate to generate the intensity of the moral outrage expressed. For Post, Kass, McCormick, Elshtain and others, the "disgust" and "revulsion" that they admit to in the face of the practice seem incommensurate with the moral arguments they put forth. Just as significantly, the same seems true of many of us: we feel deeply uneasy in the face of human cloning but are unable to articulate why.

Interestingly, Kass, one of the strongest opponents of cloning, seems to acknowledge the very disjunct I am positing. He asks, "Can anyone really give an argument fully adequate to explain the horror of father-daughter incest (even with consent), or having sex with animals, or mutilating a corpse, or eating human flesh. . . ? Would anybody's failure to give full rational justification of his or her revulsion make that revulsion ethically suspect?" Kass concludes: "Human cloning belongs to this category. We are repelled by the prospect of cloning human beings not because of the strangeness or novelty of the undertaking, but because we intuit and feel, immediately and without argument, the violation of things that we rightfully hold dear."[14] Lisa Geller's experiences are simpler but similar. While conceding that intellectually she can find little moral difference between *in vitro* technologies and cloning, Geller admits, cloning "makes my stomach feel nervous."[15]

What is it that makes so many stomachs nervous about human cloning? What are the sources of the widespread and deep, if not universal, moral disquiet felt in the face of the practice? And what are those things that we "rightfully hold dear" that are at stake in this debate? It is upon these questions that I would like to focus in this essay. Making use of theories originally advanced by Jeffrey Stout and Mary Douglas (but for very different heuristic purposes than my own), I will offer an account of the sources of the common moral discomfort in the face of cloning—an account very different from the ones suggested by traditional moral theories. As will become evident, it is not my point to argue here that human cloning is or is not an immoral practice. Rather, I will suggest that our judgments about cloning are secondary to and contingent upon far more foundational issues concerning who we are as individuals and as a society. It is my belief that our failure to acknowledge the actual sources of the widespread disquiet experienced in the face of human cloning—a disquiet which, by the way, I share—has been a hindrance to constructive ethical debate and has fueled the emotional nature of much of our existing discourse on the subject. An alternate account of the roots of our reactions is needed. It is to that task of suggesting one that I now turn.

## Of Cabbits and Strange Bedfellows

Jeffrey Stout tells of his encounter with a cabbit. A cabbit is allegedly the product of crossbreeding. (I say allegedly because some have claimed the cabbit is, in fact, a physically altered Manx cat.[16]) Take a rabbit ovum, fertilize it *in vitro* with feline sperm, and implant the fertilized egg in a fecund female rabbit and, with a little patience and far too much federal grant money, one is able to produce a cabbit. "I do not know why you would want one," writes Stout, for the cabbit is a rather disturbing creature. Featuring the hindquarters of a rabbit, replete with hopping legs and bushy tail, and the head of a cat, the cabbit is what can only be called an "abomination." This is precisely the reaction it received when it made an appearance on the "Tonight Show" several years ago; squeals of disgust and nervous laughter filled the crowd on hand. As Stout points out, this was a visceral phenomenon: it was not so much the intellectual concept of the cabbit but the actual sight of this creature simultaneously hopping and meowing that he found, at the gut level, "revolting." He goes on to contrast his strong reaction here to that of his two-year old daughter who, he is confident, found the cabbit to be, far from offensive, just another cute, furry creature like puppies and raccoons.[17]

What accounts for the dramatic difference between the two's reactions? Stout explains that his daughter "had not yet learned to treat [cats and rabbits] as distinct kinds of things, having only begun to master the requisite vocabulary. A person who lacks the concepts of cat and rabbit would not be fascinated by the anomalous combination: no distinction, no anomaly. . . . The offense one takes depends upon the concepts one brings to the scene." Still, even Stout's reaction to the blending of cat and rabbit was, by his own admission, comparatively mild. Take categories more significant to one's cosmology, categories fraught with social and legal consequence like the distinction between human and animal, for example, and blend them—say in the form of the "elephant" man—and the revulsion will be even stronger. Or think of the fascination and disgust generated by the "bearded woman" to the customers of side-shows in early twentieth-century America—a time and place in which the categories of male and female had profound societal implications.[18]

Stout uses these examples as the basis for his concept of "moral abomination." Moral abominations occur when we are faced with entities or acts which are anomalous or ambiguous with respect to some system of categories. Increase the vividness of a person's experience of the abomination or the social significance of the categories it challenges, and one will increase the disquiet experienced by that person.

Stout is here applying theories developed by anthropologist Mary Douglas in her attempt to explain a variety of perplexing religious phenomena, ranging from Hindu brahministic purity laws to the Levitical eating codes. In the latter instance, for example, Douglas theorizes that the Levitical ban on eating animals such as shellfish and bats has less to do with "medical materialism"—the idea that these foods pose some kind of medical risk to the ancient Israelites—than it does with the "threat" these animals pose to Hebrew cosmology. Amid a context in which God has established "the fish in the sea, the birds of heaven, and the cattle and wild animals on dry earth" (Genesis 1:26) as the basic animal phyla, the animals proscribed in Leviticus confound. The lobster walks on legs like a land animal but is in the sea; the bat flies in the heavens but is not a bird. "The initial recognition of anomaly leads to anxiety and from there to suppression and avoidance," she writes.[19]

Why would we have such strong reactions to that which contradicts cosmological categories? Douglas explains that the organization of the world into categories is one of the most basic and universal stages in human learning. In fact, early childhood development is, at times, nothing *more* than this. Through trial, error, and parental guidance, a child learns to distinguish colors, shapes, and sounds. She learns to identify "mommy" and "daddy" and, eventually, acquires the more complex distinction between male and female. She learns to categorize cat and rabbit. Errors are made. The two-year-old, for example, may at first refer to all adult males as "daddy." If so, the child is taught to refine her categorizations so as to conform to the established system.

According to Douglas, without this process, we would be unable to navigate our incredibly complex world—a world in which each moment is filled with a myriad of potential stimuli. To offer a mundane example, while out for a stroll in the park, we subconsciously place particular objects we are seeing for the first time into familiar general categories and adjust our behavior and expectations accordingly: that object is a tree and hence will remain stationary; this object is a dog—expect motion and potential biting—and so forth. Douglas writes: "In a chaos of shifting impressions, each of us constructs a stable world in which objects have recognisable shapes, are located in depth, and have permanence. . . . As time goes on and experiences pile up, we make a greater and greater investment in our system of labels. It gives us confidence."[20] We develop what Douglas calls a "conservative bias" in favor of the system of organization we have adopted; we have a stake in preserving our way of classifying and systematizing the world, for such is equivalent to the way we *understand* the world.

And what of those things that simply do not fit into our established schema? What of the anomalous? As Douglas puts it, "Even to gaze steadily at distorting apparatus makes some people feel physically sick, as if their own balance was attacked. . . . There is a whole gradient on which laughter, revulsion, and shock belong at different points and intensities."[21] Hence we titter nervously in the presence of a cabbit, recoil in disgust at the sight of the elephant man, and the ancient Israelites looked with revulsion on the prospect of consuming a lobster.

Stout's important insight here is that this same process of categorization (and the "conservative bias" it engenders) may rest at the root of our seemingly unaccountable and disproportionate reactions to certain phenomena. Take bestiality. While bestiality certainly is considered to be among the most repugnant of human acts, it is difficult to explain *why* by prevailing moral standards. One may attempt to attack bestiality on the grounds that it violates rights (the animal's) or creates negative utility (most identifiably to the perpetrator himself), but the fact remains that the arguments generated by these efforts pale next to the rights violated and negative utility created for persons by a host of acts which many people would judge far less harshly than bestiality (e.g., cheating on taxes, adultery). Your uncle, the tax fraud, likely would have a welcome place at your dinner table despite his moral flaw; your uncle, the lover of barnyard animals, likely would be treated as a social and moral pariah.

Stout's theories provide a possible explanation. We recoil in disgust at bestiality not because of our deep concern for the animal or for the well-being of the perpetrator, but out of concern for *ourselves*. Bestiality is a threat to our cosmology and our conception of the world. In the act of bestiality, we see challenged one of the categorical distinctions most central to our society: the line between human and animal. Here is a line fraught with social and legal significance if ever there was one. We accord to human persons a host of rights and expectations that we do not accord to animals. To dismantle these lines would be, in effect, to dismantle society as we know it. In confronting the act of bestiality, we experience, viscerally, our established cosmology being threatened. The perpetrator, by treating the animal as we normally treat only a fellow human and by behaving as we expect only an animal to behave, simultaneously undercuts both the animal's status and his own. "His abominable act has made him an abomination," writes Stout.[22] But just as importantly, he undercuts *our* status. Are we humans not qualitatively different than the beasts?

Similarly, the necrophiliac is made abominable by an unnerving challenge to another critical social category: the line between the living and the dead. In our society so dedicated to the freedom and self-determination of the individual, how else can we account for our nearly unspeakable moral disgust in the face of necrophilia? Would we be any less outraged if the deceased party signed a contract consenting to the act before her death? No, the necrophiliac is *dangerous*, not most markedly to himself or the corpse, but to us and our society. As Douglas explains, "pollution beliefs indicate the areas of greatest systematization . . . . [They] protect the most vulnerable domains, where ambiguity would most weaken the fragile [societal] structure."[23] We often speak of "enculturating" moral values in our children; here the literal meaning of the word is in evidence. The person who commits necrophilia, like the person engaged in bestiality, quite literally "lacks culture"—stands as an outsider to the rules and categories that define society. I thus disagree with Kass who, as we have seen, assumes that no rational light can be shed on our deep repugnance in the face of abominable acts like incest, bestiality, and necrophilia—that these feelings simply *are*. If my theory is correct, these feelings have a great deal to do with "the things we rightfully hold dear," as Kass puts it: our society, its rules, its organization, and its preservation.

Of course, this is not to say that any given established order necessarily *should* be preserved. My ninety-eight-year old relative who, born and raised in the South, still recoils at the sight of an inter-racial couple is, through her reaction, subconsciously attempting to hold on to cultural categories of significance to her. But these are categories best surrendered. For someone who is the product of a time and place in which one's racial category determined where one could work, go to school, buy a sandwich, and take a sip of water, the interracial couple emerges as the equivalent of the perpetrators of bestiality or necrophilia: people who, through their actions, threaten the way one organizes and understands the world.[24] If blacks are the social equivalent of whites, then one's worldview is turned on its head—but here is a worldview that is best overturned, despite the feelings of disgust it may engender in some people.

Thus, societal rules serve to reinforce and preserve the cosmological categories, and vice-versa. In contrast, anomalous practices, over time, undermine the categories. A society cannot survive for long with too pronounced a disjunct between its accepted practices and its cosmological categories. One or the other must change. With these theoretical parameters now established, we are equipped to return to our discussion of cloning.

## Cloning As A Moral Abomination

If my portrayal in the introductory section of this essay is correct, the reaction that has greeted cloning is very similar to those that have traditionally greeted bestiality and necrophilia. In all three cases, there is an exceptionally strong repugnance voiced about the practices but a comparatively weak, indeed incommensurate, set of conventional moral arguments to ground the disquiet we feel. What if the *roots* of our reactions to all three phenomena are similarly related? What if the reason Dolly is gazed upon as "offensive," "grotesque," "repulsive," and "revolting" is not because she threatens to violate anyone's rights or to inflict negative utility but because she threatens our cosmology? What if she is less a sheep than a cabbit?

These suggestions become plausible, I believe, when we begin to explore the implications of cloning—not from the perspective of traditional moral standards like rights and utility but with an eye to our newly developed theory of cosmological categories. When we do so, we see that several socially significant categories are indeed threatened by Dolly and her prospective human counterparts.

First, there are crucial classifications of familial relations that are not merely called into question but are all but dismantled by cloning. Indeed, from the theoretical perspective that I have suggested, we (at last) can locate ways in which the threats posed by cloning are, in fact, novel ones. The lines between mother and sister or father and son, for example, necessarily are blurred by somatic cell nuclear transfer cloning in a way they are not by *in vitro* fertilization, artificial insemination, or even cloning by embryo splitting.[25] The unsettling fact is that the woman who seeks reproduction by nuclear transfer cloning is simultaneously the biological *mother* and the genetic *sister* of her cloned offspring. A man who clones himself in order to become a parent becomes both genetic *brother* and social *father* to the cloned. Listen for a moment to the efforts of Silver, a defender of human cloning, to explain the resulting familial connections:

> If Jennifer gives birth to a clone of herself named Rachel, then Jennifer is clearly Rachel's birth mother. And if Jennifer raises Rachel herself, then she is clearly Rachel's social mother as well. In genetic terms, however, Jennifer is not Rachel's mother, she's Rachel's identical twin. This means that Rachel's genetic parents are the same as Jennifer's genetic parents. In other words, Rachel's social grandparents are also her genetic parents. And this means that Rachel and all other cloned children always have two genetic parents, not one.[26]

Note that the confusion is not limited to a single generation but effects our notions of the entire extended family. The mother of the woman who is cloned, for example, becomes both grandmother and mother to the offspring: grandmother in a social sense but mother in a genetic sense (since the new mother now has, in effect, a twin sister, both sharing the same genetic mother). The clone's aunt is simultaneously her sister, since genetically the clone and the aunt share the same mother and father.

If you have difficulty following the machinations here, that is precisely my point: one *cannot* follow the machinations since our society lacks the categories and vocabulary to adequately describe the situation. Our language—and our existing classifications—simply collapse under the weight and novelty of the phenomenon. With the clone, we have created a true anomaly.

As we have seen Stout suggest, a moral abomination is nothing more than what we now see before us: an entity that defies categorization in the established societal cosmology. The more important the categories confounded are to us and our culture, he tells us, the stronger the reaction to the anomaly will be. In this case, the categories in question are some of those most crucial to understanding ourselves and our world: mother, father, sister, brother, grandmother, grandfather, aunt, uncle. In our society, as in most, there are acute differences between the social, legal, financial, and emotional obligations which accrue, depending upon how we are classified with regard to these categories. As Kass writes, "Would 'grandpa,' who thought his paternal duties concluded, be pleased to discover that the clonant looked to him for paternal attention and support?"[27] Would the cloned man behave as father or brother to "his" newly produced son/twin, or as both? And what of the woman who decides to clone herself after she has already had children by natural conception, producing a child who is in fact the genetic mother of her older brothers and sisters? Any entity which poses such deep questions about identity is, I would suggest, bound to conjure fears and disquiet of the deepest sort.

Significantly, the explanatory power of the "cosmological category" theory extends beyond its ability to account for why we are disgusted by cloning. It allows us to see why some people are more disturbed than others. Given the thesis that one's revulsion toward an anomaly will increase with one's commitment to the categories being challenged, it is understandable why commentators like Kass and McCormick experience the greatest repugnance for cloning. Those people who are committed most strongly to the "traditional" family will be more disturbed by the clone than will those who already have come to reject many of its structures. I would *expect* Kass and McCormick to experience more repugnance toward cloning than do, say, TV's Murphy Brown and Ellen, for the former's world view is more fundamentally threatened. Similarly, I would expect almost all of us to experience greater disquiet in the face of human cloning than animal cloning, for the categories we possess to distinguish different humans and their roles are far more complex and socially significant to us than those we maintain concerning, for example, sheep. And as for Kass's claim that the disgust he feels toward cloning is comparable to the disgust he feels toward incest, from my theoretical perspective this connection becomes far more than coincidental. Cloning in essence is substantially like incest, for both undermine traditional familial lines and boundaries, blurring the status of the participants involved.

Even if its threat to familial lines were the only cosmological challenge posed by human cloning, I would argue that we have taken a significant step toward explaining the common visceral disgust at the practice. In fact, though, the challenge to traditional family classifications is not only not the sole, it may well not even be the most significant, cosmological threat that human cloning entails.

The human clone poses a profound challenge to the line drawn between self and other. It is hard to imagine a line more basic to our ability to navigate the world. Who am "I" and who is "other"? On the answer hinges our ability to formulate and pursue life projects, conceive of and own personal property, make sense of basic human concepts ranging from "independence" to "theft," indeed comprehend the whole notion of "identity." And yet with human cloning, the answer to this most basic of identity questions becomes disturbingly unclear. Standing face to face with my genetic replica, I see a mirror reflection of an entity that simultaneously both is and is not me.

This argument may seem implausible at first, but the connections here to the notion of a moral abomination are strong. Stout contends, for example, that precisely because they strike such guttural and seemingly inexplicable fear in us, moral abominations provide the perfect recipe for monsters in horror films. Take social categories infused with meaning, create an entity anomalous to these classifications, and emerge with a "monster" that will scare and titillate. The wolfman horrifies by blending the categories of human and animal; Dracula by challenging the division between living and dead. To this mix in recent years has been added the stock horror/science-fiction figure of the clone. Imagine this scene from a recent televison show: an F.B.I. agent, on the trail of a serial killer, traces the perpetrator to a seedy apartment, knocks on the door and finds standing on the other side . . . his clone, the exact replica of the agent himself. The simultaneous jolt of surprise and disorienting confusion is exactly what the producers are after—and what attracts (and scares) an audience. The show in question is *The X-Files*, a series which has turned human replication into an art form, using clones and their equivalents no less than five times in its first three years on the air.[28] As series co-producer Frank Spotnitz explains, "It's much scarier if the monster looks just like you and me—if the man sitting next to you on the bus isn't what he seems."[29]

And that is precisely my point about the cosmological threat posed by the clone: the clone is not what it seems. It seems to be self and is in fact other (or seems to be other and is in fact self). Who "I" am is brought into question. Once again it is the visceral experience more than the intellectual concept which frightens; brought face to face with one's clone, one is left literally shaken by the experience of temporarily losing hold on who one is.[30] While for obvious reasons we must turn to science fiction for depictions of this phenomenon, many of us have had a similar, momentary jolt of anxiety-provoking confusion when we have walked into an unfamiliar room and caught a glimpse of an eerily familiar person standing nearby, only to find it to be our own reflection in a mirror. The mind races to process the incoming data, and we find comfort in the conclusion that "it is only me." But what if it were more than that? What if it were not merely a reflection? The clone makes this a question we must face with every corner we turn. Of course, if human cloning were to become reality, the clone *in fact* would be a distinct rights-bearing individual, shaped uniquely by "nurture" despite the identicalness wrought by "nature." She in fact would be other than self. But it is the visceral experience that concerns me here, and it is this imagined experience that, I believe, conjures fear and disquiet in many individuals.

In fact, a second approximation of the experience I have in mind is one that has faced the human species since its inception: the phenomenon of the identical twin. In some senses this example may seem to undermine my argument, since twinning shows that the loss of identity due to genetic identicalness is neither wholly new nor novel. I grant this point. But it also reveals that historically even the occasional and *natural* loss of genetic uniqueness has been the source of great human anxiety.

Even a brief survey of the anthropological literature reveals a human fascination with, and fear of, twins. Of the Chaya of East Africa, O. F. Raum writes, "A disaster is the birth of identical twins, of whom, in the past, one was killed and still nowadays many die of neglect . . . . In the case of twins, we have a particular instance of primitive bewilderment."[31] Other anthropologists contend, "killing one or both twins seemed an ideal solution for several Brazilian and American Indian tribes" and report that yet other tribes regarded identical twins to be oracles "able to regulate the weather or foretell misfortune or death."[32] (Can it be a coincidence, then, that behind their journalistic pseudonyms the two most influential American oracles, Ann Landers and Abigal Van Buren, are identical twins?[33])

The fear of the replicated child is not foreign to Christian history. Indeed, Christians have long conjured connections between the birth of supertwins and divine wrath. In 1276, a Dutch woman, Margaret of Henneberg, was said to have been "punished by Providence" for a moral crime "by being delivered of three-hundred-and-sixty-five children [at one time], in bigness all like newbred mice."[34] Of the "litter," 182 were allegedly sons, 182 daughters, and the last one an hermaphrodite. According to the historical record, the Bishop of Utrecht baptized them (all the boys under the name "John" and all the girls under the name "Elisabeth," time being of some importance), and immediately after children and mother alike promptly died. The Reverend Samuel Clarke reports that Anne Hutchinson, banished from the Massachusetts Bay Colony in 1638, brought forth "thirty monstrous births at once, in punishment for her monstrous heresies."[35] With the theory of "cosmological categories," we have a tool for understanding why so many cultures would vilify, even exterminate, the seemingly innocuous twin. It is not that the identical twin poses a particular threat to rights or utility,[36] but that she poses a threat to foundational notions of identity. As Hillel Schwartz writes: "Identical twins are creatures of terrible ambiguity, for they compromise values we place upon the individual even as they promise that which we so desperately want: faithful companionship and mutual understanding."[37] Psychologist Richard Ainslie, who clinically studies the psychological challenges faced by identical twins, concurs. He discovers in twins: "overt feelings that one's sense of self can be lost, at least temporarily, that one's sense of self is seriously threatened in certain situations, or that the stability for one's sense of self is contingent upon another."[38] This is a phenomenon that someone attuned to the significance of cosmological categories can well appreciate.

Interestingly, my theory additionally serves to question the often heard assertion that cloning is an inevitable, if regrettable, outgrowth of a "culture which views human persons as isolated and autonomous agents."[39] For Kass and McCormick, our individualistic culture is seen as the culprit in the move toward cloning, breeding the idea that whatever the individual wants to do, he or she should be able to do. While on one level this may be true, on another level I believe that this very individualism is a critical ingredient in preserving our *aversion* to cloning. By threatening to blur the lines between self and other, the prospect of human cloning attacks our very notion of individuality. Indeed, it would only be amid a cultural context in which the individual is unimportant—a Hitlerian vision of society constituted by a sea of identical blue-eyed, blond-headed children, for example—that cloning could be embraced as non-threatening. It is, in part, *because* of our individualism that the clone (like Ainslie's twin) causes "overt feelings that the sense of self can be lost." Cloning threatens to make anomalies of us all.

This realization is vital, I believe, to our attempts to understand the sources of the widespread disquiet about human cloning. In its undermining of familial roles and, now, personal identity, cloning suddenly sets into flux long-established notions of who we and who others *are*: brother or father? sister or aunt? self or other?

But as I close this essay, do not think that I have gone further than I have. While the insight that the clone threatens to make anomalies of us all is indeed crucial, I believe, to understanding our reactions to human cloning, it is important to recognize that the realization is not, in and of itself, sufficient moral reason to *condemn* human cloning. The cosmological categories embraced by societies and individuals are not necessarily right, and they certainly are not static.

Most human communities, for example, have come to accept identical twins. Oftentimes by a complex and protracted process, cosmologies have been adapted to account for the possibility of the "natural" multiple birth. The twin does not confound amid a cosmology of which somehow she is a part. Perhaps our society will do the same for (or to?) the "clone." Other cultures, oftentimes those with high mortality rates, have tended to de-emphasize the uniqueness of the parental relationship to the child by regarding all blood relatives as equals of sorts; all relations alike become socially and financially responsible for all offspring. If my theory is correct, such a move by our society would diminish our discomfort in the face of cloning's tendency to blur traditional familial categories like mother, sister, and aunt. Hence, I can imagine *in theory* a society in which the clone might not prove markedly anomalous.

The obvious question—a moral question I can only pose here—is: *should* we seek such a re-envisioned society? In other words, we must ask whether cloning is more like necrophilia or inter-racial dating. Are the categories confounded by the practice, and hence the sources of our aversion, classifications that we *should* preserve? In the case of necrophilia, the lines blurred are those between the living and the dead. To envision our society moving toward a cosmology in which this distinction is unimportant stretches the bounds of the imagination and, more importantly for my discussion, the bounds of ethical desirability. We morally should not aspire to a society in which the dead are accorded the same rights, responsibilities, and support as the living—and there is no movement to do so. As long as this is true, our aversion to necrophilia surely will remain widespread and deep. In the case of the alleged abomination of interracial dating, on the other hand, my theory suggests a causal connection to cosmological categories that are morally bankrupt. We should expect interracial dating to become increasingly *un*problematic in a society which opposes legal and social distinctions between the races. In fact, the racist is facing a losing battle, I would argue, when he or she tries to hold on to a social separation of the races amid a culture which increasingly sees the categories of "black" and "white" as lacking social significance.[40]

The question, then, is which of these two scenarios is appropriate in the case of human cloning? Are the cosmological categories at stake—those of mother and sister, father and brother, self and other—ones that we morally should wish to preserve or ones better re-envisioned or even rejected? If my theory is correct, to permit cloning would be to undermine these categories, if not fatally then at least significantly. Is this something that is desirable? Is it *acceptable*?

While the answers to these last questions go well beyond the scope of an essay dedicated to exploring the *sources* of our disquiet about cloning, they are answers we best not delay in seeking. Within two weeks of the cloning of Dolly, a Bahamas-based company was formed under the direction of French scientist Brigitte Boisselier and with international financial backing. Named "Clonaid," its announced end is to offer cloning services to individuals for a fee of $200,000. According to the company's web site, Clonaid provides "a fantastic opportunity to parents with infertility problems or homosexual couples to have a child cloned from one of them."[41] Meanwhile, in Chicago, physicist G. Richard Seed, one of the researchers involved in early embryo transfer efforts in the 1970s, has vowed to open a Chicago-based cloning clinic and to "produce at least a two-month pregnancy in a female within a year and a half's time."[42]

The rattling of our ethical foundations and of our cosmologies, it would appear, has only begun.[43]

## Notes

[1]Lee M. Silver, *Remaking Eden: Cloning and Beyond in a Brave New World* (New York: Avon, 1997), 93.

[2]"To Clone or Not to Clone," *Christian Century* (March 19-26, 1997): 287; "All the Same," *National Review* (June 30, 1997): 17; Harold T. Shapiro, "Ethical and Policy Issues of Human Cloning," *Science* 277 (July 11, 1997): 195-196. I find Shapiro's (and the commission's) stance on the topic to be prudent and well thought out.

[3]Ronald Bailey, "The Twin Paradox: What Exactly is Wrong with the Cloning of People," *Reason* (May 1997): 52.

[4]Jeffrey Kluger, "Will We Follow the Sheep," *Time* (March 10, 1997): 70; Silver, 92 and 275.

[5]Leon Kass, "The Wisdom of Repugnance," *The New Republic* (June 2, 1997): 17-26; see also *Time* (March 10, 1997): 70.

[6]Richard McCormick, "Should We Clone Humans?: Wholeness, Individuality, Reverence," *Christian Century* (November 17-24): 1993, 1148; Kluger, 70.

[7]Ruth Macklin, "Splitting Embryos on the Slippery Slope: Ethics and Public Policy," *Kennedy Institute of Ethics Journal* 4, 3 (1994): 215.

[8]Paul Ramsey, *Fabricated Man: The Ethics of Genetic Control* (New Haven: Yale University Press, 1970), see especially chapter two.

[9]Stephen G. Post, "The Judeo-Christian Case Against Human Cloning," *America* (June 21, 1997): 22.

[10]Post, 20. See also Bailey, 21.

[11]Kass, esp. 23-25; McCormick, 1993; Jean Bethke Elshtain, "The Hard Questions: Our Bodies, Our Clones," *The New Republic* (August 4, 1997): 25; and Allen Verhey, "Theology After Dolly: Cloning and the Human Family," *Christian Century* (March 19-26, 1997): 285-286. See also Ramsey, 60-103.

[12]Peter Singer and Deane Wells, *Making Babies: The New Science and Ethics of Conception* (New York: Charles Scribner's Sons, 1985), 145.

[13]In addition to essays already cited, see Ruth Macklin, "Splitting Embryos on the Slippery Slope: Ethics in Public Policy," *Kennedy Institute of Ethics Journal* 4, 3 (1994): 209-255; Ruth Chadwick, "Cloning," *Philosophy* 57 (1982): 201-209; John A. Robertson, "The Question of Human Cloning," *Hastings Center Report* (March-April 1994): 6-14; and Melinda A. Roberts, "Human Cloning: A Case of No Harm Done," *Journal of Medicine and Philosophy* 21 (1996): 537-554.

[14]Kass, 20.

[15]Kluger, 70.

[16]As will become evident, whether the cabbit is an actual hybrid or altered Manx cat is not critical to the argument that follows. Nonetheless, burning academic inquisitiveness led me to pursue the matter to its highest possible source. I located a column of "Dear Abby" which claims the cabbit is legitimate. Case closed?

[17]Jeffrey Stout, "Moral Abominations," *Soundings*, LXVI, 1 (Spring 1983): 7; and Stout, *Ethics After Babel: The Languages of Morals and Their Discontents* (Boston: Beacon Press, 1988), ch. 7.

[18]Stout, "Moral Abominations," 8.

[19]Mary Douglas, *Purity and Danger* (Boston: Routledge & Kegan Paul, 1966), 5. See especially chapter 3.

[20]Ibid., 36.

[21]Ibid., 37.

[22]Stout, "Moral Abominations," 13.

[23]Mary Douglas, *Implicit Meanings: Essays in Anthroplogy* (Boston; Routledge & Kegan Paul, 1975), 57-8.

[24]For another vivid example, think of the harsh proscription against inter-racial marriage before the dismantling of Apartheid in South Africa—the ultimate late-twentieth-century example of a society organized around racial classifications.

[25]In this last case, a practice available years before the events in Roslin, the "clone" is created by splitting a genetically unique embryo formed by natural means (at least in the sense of having genetic mother and father) to produce, in effect, "artificial" twins.

[26]Silver, 169.

[27]Kass, 23.

[28]Rick Schindler and Stephanie Williams, "An X-Files Encyclopedia from A to Z," *TV Guide* (May 17, 1997): 22. For those scoring at home, the authors elaborate: "There were the two Eves (evil spawn of a genetic experiment); multiple copies of Mulder's missing sister, Samantha; and hordes or red-headed boys and men all named Kurt Crawford. And who could forget the morphers? Both an alien bounty hunter and Eddie Van Blundht have transformed themselves into spitting images of Mulder."

[29]Ibid., 22.

[30]Of course, the first generation of human clones would not be the same age as their human sources (and hence would be distinguishable in that respect), but if cloning were practiced for several generations into the future, one might well encounter an heretofore unknown identical clone—an identical twin one had no knowledge existed.

[31]O. F. Raum, Chaya, *Childhood: A Description of Indigenous Education in An East African Tribe* (New York: Oxford University Press, 1967), 88-89.

[32]Judy W. Hagedorn and Janet W. Kezziar, *Gemini: The Psychology and Phenomena of Twins* (Anderson, S.C.: Droke House/Hallux, 1974), 11-12.

[33]Hillel Schwartz, *The Culture of the Copy: Striking Likenesses, Unreasonable Facsimiles* (New York: Zone Books, 1996), 44.

[34]Amran Scheinfeld, *Twins and Supertwins* (New York: J.B. Lippincott Company, 1967), 252.

[35]Ibid.

[36]Not that utility is totally inapplicable here; one reason to fear or eliminate twins may be out of a concern for the resource drain they might place on family and village. But such "logical" considerations seem incapable of generating the near-hysterical fear of twinning evidenced in the cited examples.

[37]Schwartz, 7.

[38]Richard C. Ainslie, *The Psychology of Twinship* (Lincoln: University of Nebraska Press, 1985), 80.

[39]McCormick, "Blastomere Separation," 16.

[40]Of course, even categories diminished in significance carry some weight, hence many American continue to feel some discomfort with inter-racial dating. I hope, however, that we can expect fewer episodes like that in Alabama in 1996, in which a high school principal attempted to cancel the prom rather than have an interracial couple attend.

[41]The web site is found at http://www.clonaid.com. Clonaid advertises that it also "will provide the sampling and safe storage of cells from a living child or from a beloved person in order to create a clone if the child dies of incurable disease or through an accident." The anticipated cost of such peace of mind: $50,000. ( See also Silver, 123.)

[42]*USA Today* (January 7, 1998).

[43]The author would like to thank Kenneth Smith, Thomas Atwood, and Jeffrey Wilson for their valuable assistance in the preparation of this essay; and Louis Ruprecht, Jr., Jeffrey Stout, Scott Davis, and participants at the 1998 Annual Meeting of the Society of Christian Ethics, most particularly the reviewers for The Annual, for their helpful comments. Any errors or deficiencies in the essay, of course, remain the author's own.

# PROFESSIONAL RESOURCES

# Introduction: Doing Health Care Ethics Today

*Dennis Brodeur and John Kilner*

Ethical reflection on health related issues is not new, although many people still describe the current field of *health care ethics*[1] as "emerging." Ample evidence of ethical concerns about health, illness, and the roles of health care professionals resides in histories of health care ethics, an overview of which can be found in the *Encyclopedia of Bioethics.*[2] This encyclopedia, plus the *Bibliography of Bioethics*[3] provide overviews and resources on virtually every issue in bioethics. The theological content of both, however, is very limited and must be supplemented from other sources, such as bibliographies provided by the Christian centers identified below and indexes such as *Religion Index One and Two*.[4]

In light of the geographical center of gravity of the SCE, this professional resources section will focus on Western thinking and the attempts to approach health care ethics in a systematic fashion over the last forty years. Particularly in the 1950s and 1960s, much of this ethical reflection was done in the context of theological or other religious discourse. In the Roman Catholic tradition, scholars such as Gerald Kelly and later Richard McCormick[5] reflected on particular ethical problems within Catholic theological tradition. Issues of respect for life, dying and death, transplantation, and the moral obligation to accept treatment or the moral freedom to reject treatment were addressed. In the Protestant traditions, scholars such as Paul Ramsey and later James Gustafson[6] examined similar issues in the context of their theological convictions, the sacredness of life, and the particular moral obligations incumbent upon the physician caring for a vulnerable population. Still other religious authors addressed concerns from a Jewish perspective as did Immanuel Jakobovits in his commentary on the halakhic tradition.[7] At the same time, communities such as Christian Scientists, Jehovah's Witnesses, and Orthodox Christianity contributed particular religious perspectives and raised special questions.[8]

While sustained religious discourse has given way in most settings to more philosophical approaches as people have sought common language for a pluralistic society (see next essay), the voice of Christian ethics in health care ethics now appears to be strengthening. At the end of the twentieth century there are many places in which the theological dimension of ethical reflection on health care matters is taking place. Centers of higher education continue to play a key role. Health care ethics is addressed there in various locations, including theological circles, seminaries, philosophy departments, medical schools, schools of public health, hospital administration programs, nursing schools, and schools for allied health professionals. Each of these places in the world of academia has claimed for itself a chair of health care ethics, professor in health care ethics, shared professional resources across campuses, or some form of ethics throughout the health professional curriculum. Some places have developed entire graduate degree programs in health care ethics, though only a few of these degree programs—including Trinity International University (Deerfield, IL),[9] Loma Linda University (Loma Linda University, CA),[10] and St. Louis University (St. Louis, MO)[11] —are explicitly Christian in focus. To obtain sample syllabi for courses in health care ethics, contact these schools directly; or, for a broader range of samples, contact the National Reference Center for Bioethics Literature.[12] For a broader list of graduate and post-doctoral programs in bioethics, contact the University of Pennsylvania Center for Bioethics.[13]

Various other organizations and communities are actively involved in health care ethics as well. As the three issue-oriented essays in this section document, some major church denominations such as the Methodists, Episcopalians, Southern Baptists, and Roman Catholics have convened groups to study particular problems in health care in general or certain clinical problems such as those related to death and dying. Many large heath care systems, as they have developed over the last fifteen years, have institutionalized ethics concerns and ethics exploration. Many major systems of all religious denominations, and large systems not sponsored by religious bodies, have hired health care ethics persons as staff members to support their ethics education, their ethics committees, their ethics consultation, or to guide boards and senior administrative groups in ethical matters as they relate to clinical and organizational concerns. As discussed in the next essay, the voice of Christian ethics in such settings is not usually very audible, but sorely needed nevertheless.

Probably the best sources for Christian and other religious audio, video, printed, electronic, and live resources for health care ethics today are a variety of centers specializing in health care ethics. Some are explicitly Christian in focus—for example, The Center for Bioethics and Human Dignity[14] and the Center for Christian Bioethics.[15] Others are attached to larger Christian institutions but are not as explicitly Christian in their publications--for example, the Center for Health Care Ethics of Saint Louis University,[16] the Kennedy Institute for Ethics,[17] and the Center for Healthcare Ethics of St. Joseph Health System.[18] Still others, such as the Park Ridge Center[19] and the Institute of Religion, [20] are broadly religious (as opposed to particularly Christian) in focus. Among the many non-religious centers--which only occasionally address religious perspectives—the oldest and most widely known is the Hastings Center.[21] There are two journals devoted to exploring issues in bioethics from a Christian perspective, *Ethics and Medicine: An International Christian Perspective on Bioethics*,[22] and *Christian Bioethics: Non-Ecumenical Studies in Medical Morality*.[23]

There is certainly no shortage of ethical topics for consideration today. Multiple issues arise at the beginning of life, including abortion, contraception, reproductive technologies, the treatment of neonates, and many other maternal/fetal questions. Other issues may also have special application at the beginning of life, but touch a wider range of people. These include genetics, informed consent, proxy consent, general medical decision making, and experimentation both with adults and children. End of life issues, such as assisted suicide and forgoing treatment, abound as well. Some groups have focused their attention more on public policy and organizational matters, addressing critical issues of access, resource allocation, health care organization, physician responsibility, managed care, and other institutional financial responsibilities.

There are multiple ethical topics, competing methodologies and various places where ethical debate takes place. While this professional resources section cannot address all of them, it endeavors to orient the reader to the arena of health care ethics generally and to three of its most prominent issues. The first essay focuses on matters of methodology and the settings in which health care ethics is done. The next three essays address the issues of genetics, access, and end-of-life care, respectively. Throughout, this section attempts not only to spotlight the insights and resources of Christian ethics, but also to locate them in the larger contemporary debate.

## Notes

[1]This professional resources section will primarily employ the term "health care ethics" to describe this field. That term is broader than "medical ethics," which refers only to health-related activities within the practice of medicine and, in the minds of many, relates more to physicians than to other health care professionals. "Bioethics," on the other hand, may address all issues in the biosphere, including environmental ethics, and so may cover more than issues in health care. Nevertheless, people writing here and elsewhere sometimes use the three terms interchangeably.

[2]Warren Reich, ed. *Encyclopedia of Bioethics,* rev. ed. (New York: Macmillan, 1995).

[3]Leroy Walters and Tamar Joy Kahn, eds. *Bibliography of Bioethics* (Washington, DC: Kennedy Institute of Ethics, annual volumes).

[4]Chicago and Evanston, IL: American Theological Library Association, annual volumes.

[5]See next essay in this section, notes 1 and 20.

[6]See next essay in this section, note 1.

[7]Ibid.

[8]See the overview of volumes and series in note 27 of the next essay in this section.

[9]2065 Half Day Road, Deerfield, IL 60015. Telephone: 800-533-0975. World Wide Web site: http://www.tiu.edu.

[10]Loma Linda, CA 92350-0001. Telephone 800-422-4558. World Wide Web site: http://www.llu.edu.

[11]3663 Lindell Blvd, Suite 100, St. Louis, MO 63108. Telephone 314-977-2240. World Wide Web site: http://www.slu.edu.

[12]Located on the campus of Georgetown University, Washington, D.C. 20057. Telephone: 800-633-3849.

[13]3401 Market St., Suite 320, Philadelphia, PA. Telephone: 215-898-7136.

[14]2065 Half Day Road, Bannockburn, IL 60015. Telepone: 847-317-8180. World Wide Web site: http://www.bioethix.org.

[15]Loma Linda University, Loma Linda, CA 92350. Telephone: 909-824-4956. World Wide Web site: http://www.llu.edu/llu/bioethics/.

[16]1402 S. Grand, St. Louis, MO 63104. Telephone: 314-577-8195. World Wide Web site being constructed.

[17]Box 571212, Georgetown University, Washington, DC 20057. Telephone:202-687-8099. World Wide Web site: http://guweb.georgetown.edu.kennedy/.

[18]P.O. Box 14132, Orange, CA 92613. Telephone: 714-997-7690. World Wide Web site: http://www.chce.org.

[19]211 E. Ontario #800, Chicago, IL 60611. Telephone: 312-266-2222. World Wide Web site being constructed.

[20]Texas Medical Center, 1129 Wilkins St., Houston, TX 77030. Telephone: 713-797-0600. World Wide Web site not available.

[21]P.O. Box 5555, Garrison, NY 10524. Telephone: 914-424-4040. World Wide Web site being constructed.

[22]*Ethics and Medicine* is jointly published by The Center for Bioethics and Human Dignity (2065 Half Day Road, Bannockburn, Illinois, 60015 USA), The Centre for Bioethics and Public Policy (London, England), and The Lindeboom Institute (Ede, The Netherlands). Its main editor is C. Ben Mitchell.

[23]*Christian Bioethics* is published by Swets & Zeitlinger (P.O. Box 825, 2160 SZ Lisse, The Netherlands). Its main editors are H. Tristram Engelhardt, Jr., B. Andrew Lustig, and Joseph Boyle.

# Methodology and Theology in Health Care Ethics

*Ron Hamel*

Theology played a significant role in the earliest days of modern health care ethics. Not only were theologians among the major contributors to the field,[1] but their work shaped discussions on a wide variety of issues being addressed at the time. In the late 1970s, however, a secular philosophical methodology emerged that has virtually dominated the field ever since, in effect reducing the frequency and significance of theological approaches and contributions.[2] Known today as the "principles-approach," or principlism, this methodology first appeared in *The Belmont Report*[3] and subsequently defined the approach of Beauchamp and Childress in their *Principles of Biomedical Ethics,*[4] the premiere text in health care ethics. While they are not alone in employing such a methodology,[5] it is their use of four principles—respect for autonomy, beneficence, non-maleficence, and justice—in conjunction with several rules, that constitutes the framework so influential and formative of the way health care ethics is done in the United States and, increasingly, abroad.

Principlism is so commonly accepted as the way to do health care ethics that even many of those in the field who are theologically trained have replaced their theological approaches with principlism's language, concepts, and methodology.[6] There is evidence of this in the literature, in public discourse and debate, in university and seminary classrooms, in the ethical framework employed and taught by many ethics committees in faith-based health care institutions, and even within communities of faith. Not surprisingly, the tendency to use a secular approach to health care ethics is stronger in more pluralistic contexts. It is said to afford a "common language" in the face of religious pluralism, to avoid offending the religious sensibilities (or lack thereof) of any particular individual or group, and to diminish the chances of conflict that might result from introducing religious perspectives. Recently, however, theology has not only begun to regain its voice in health care ethics, but is increasingly being recognized as a legitimate contributor to the field.[7]

## Alternatives to Principlism

This development comes amidst other challenges to the "standard" approach. In the early 1990s, critics from a variety of disciplines, both within and outside of the field of health care ethics, began to challenge the adequacy of a principles-based approach as well as its privileged status.[8] Alternative or complementary approaches began to be introduced—casuistry, virtue, feminist/care, and narrative among the most common. While principlism has largely survived the challenge, there is greater diversity today in approaches to the issues in health care ethics than there was some twenty years ago. While these other approaches have not supplanted principlism, they have in their own ways complemented it. None is explicitly theological, but some have affinities to existing theological approaches.

Casuistry, which has its roots in the classical rhetoricians and sixteenth and seventeenth-century Roman Catholic moral theologians, has been retrieved as a contemporary form of practical moral reasoning by Albert Jonsen and Stephen Toulmin in particular.[9] It begins with the concrete case and seeks to resolve cases not by the application of abstract principles but by comparing new cases needing a decision with paradigm cases that are morally unambiguous. The paradigmatic cases guide the decision at hand by analogy. The "revived casuistry" of Jonsen and Toulmin has not received much attention in theological circles. However, comparing situations with paradigm cases can and does occur in a natural law approach. Doing so is also compatible with a more biblical approach, whether the analogy be made with certain biblical narratives or with exemplary historical expressions of faithfulness to the God revealed in the Hebrew and Christian scriptures. Considerable work remains to be done in this area.

While principlism and casuistry both exemplify a preoccupation with cases and the resolution of conflicts, virtue ethics shifts the focus to the moral agent. More precisely, it is concerned with the agent's moral character—the intentions, motives, and dispositions that do and should characterize the agent. Virtue ethics thereby broadens the concerns of the moral life, and of health care ethics, from matters of doing to matters of being. Edmund Pellegrino and David Thomasma are two of the strongest proponents of the place of virtue in philosophically-based health care ethics,[10] while theologians James Gustafson and Stanley Hauerwas have made significant contributions to restoring the place of virtue in theological ethics and, to a lesser degree, in health care ethics.[11] The former look to the nature of the healing relationship for those virtues which should "characterize" the good or virtuous health professional.[12] The latter look to God's story as told first by the people of Israel, then in Jesus, and now within the Christian community, for those virtues that are normative for shaping the identity of the Christian and the Christian community. With the exception of Gustafson and Hauerwas, virtue ethics does not appear to be a prominent methodological factor among those who are doing health care ethics theologically. Rather, it seems to be woven into other approaches, especially those that are more biblically-based.

Closely related to virtue ethics, though considerably broader in scope, is narrative ethics.[13] Here the focus is on the story that is unfolding in the situation as well as on the multiple stories that have shaped its protagonists and of which they are a part, including the teller and hearer of the story. Narrative ethics is sensitive to the complexity and layered quality of human relationships, experiences and situations. It seeks to uncover, understand, and interpret them through a careful "reading of the story." When the concern is with the right course of action, narrative ethics looks for that alternative which most coheres with the story and its meaning. Because of their inherently narrative character, the Hebrew and Christian scriptures readily lend themselves to narrative ethics. Stanley Hauerwas and Allen Verhey are examples of theologians in whose work story or narrative plays a prominent role.[14]

Finally, feminist ethics also offers an alternative to the standard approach. While it takes a variety of expressions, it characteristically brings the experience and perspective of women to bear on the issues (e.g., reproductive technologies), concepts (e.g., autonomy), methodologies (e.g. principlism), and structures of health care (e.g., the role of women and medical research on women). The goal of feminist ethics is to uncover how male-centeredness and assumptions about gender permeate and distort people's perceptions, thinking, and behavior, and to identify how these biases harm all people, especially women.[15] Feminist ethics seeks to transform those theories, practices, structures and systems that contribute to and sustain the oppression of women and other groups.[16] Other concerns of feminist ethics include the individual, his or her relationships in the concrete situation, and responding to the needs of others out of empathy and care.[17] Typically feminist ethics looks to the primacy of women's experience as a source for theology and ethics. This starting point variously impacts the significance of scripture and doctrine. Some feminists reject them altogether, others relativize portions, while yet others transform their meaning from a feminist perspective.[18]

These various approaches to health care ethics, each in its own way, supplements or complements rather than replaces principlism. Each contributes to a fuller, richer understanding of the moral life in the context of health care. Each is also capable of being integrated into a theological approach, some more so than others—though for the most part this work remains to be done. If neither principlism nor its alternatives serve as adequate or prominent theological approaches to health care ethics, how *is* theology primarily being employed in this discipline?

## Theological Approaches

Theological methodologies in health care ethics do not lend themselves to the discrete categories that describe recent developments in philosophical ethics. Not only is there a broad diversity of methodologies among religious traditions, there is also considerable diversity within those traditions. Categorization and generalizations are hazardous. Any thorough discussion of theological methodology in health care ethics would at least need to consider the fundamental biblical/theological/philosophical convictions that ground and give shape to a particular approach to the moral life, as well as the role of scripture, human nature and experience, law, conscience, church teaching, and the community of faith.[19] How any given approach deals with these elements will give it its distinctiveness and profoundly influence its understanding of the moral life and its approach to ethical analysis.

One of the methodological elements that most distinguishes Roman Catholic from Protestant approaches to health care ethics has traditionally been the former's emphasis on natural law and the latter's on Scripture. These basic commitments, which themselves are methodological options, have significant implications for the further unfolding of methodology in each one's approach to health care ethics.

Along with the role of the authoritative teaching of the church on moral matters, natural law is probably the most distinctive feature of Catholic contributions to ethics generally and to health care ethics in particular. While recognizing both faith and reason, Scripture and the natural law, as sources of moral insight, Catholicism has traditionally given greater emphasis to the natural law. Generally speaking, this approach contends that human beings, through the use of reason, are able to participate in God's plan of creation, that is, they are able to discover the "patterns of creation" or the ends for which God created various entities, including human beings and their faculties. The end for which something is created is normative; it is a source of moral obligation. In order to act morally, one must act in a way consistent with God's plan as written in nature and discoverable by reason. Hence, it is possible to know right and wrong without appealing to revelation, and the dictates of the natural law should apply to all. Accordingly, Catholic moral teaching based on natural reasoning is said to apply beyond Catholics to "all people of good will."

There have been two strands of natural law within Catholicism—one focusing on the "order of nature" and the other on the "order of reason." The former tends to focus on physical and biological structures of nature as the source of moral obligation, while the latter focuses on the human capacity to discover in experience what befits human well-being. This difference is extremely significant methodologically. The more "physicalist" approach is employed in most ecclesiastical teaching and pronouncements on issues in sexual and medical ethics, as well as in the "textbooks" of medical ethics common in the 1950s.[20] It has been described as a universalist, absolutist, deductive ethic. While this approach continues in some sectors, a more "personalist" approach typifies many if not most Catholic moral theologians today who employ a natural law methodology. It tends to focus on the whole person in all his/her relationships, is sensitive to historical contexts and experience, and proceeds more inductively. Such an approach also influences both the interpretation accorded to official church teaching on moral issues as well as the weight given to it. Church teaching is viewed as an extremely significant word, but not as the first or final word.

What is the role of theology in a natural law approach? The concept of natural law is itself grounded in certain theological beliefs. Beyond that, however, it has been possible for Catholic moral theologians to engage in moral reflection and argument without ever taking account of Scripture. More often than not, religious beliefs have made very little difference for moral claims argued on purely philosophical grounds. Appeals to Scripture, when made at all, have been done in a "proof-texting" manner. Many Catholic moral theologians today, however, are following the lead of Bernard Haring[21] and the urging of the Second Vatican Council for a more biblically-based theology and are far more biblical and theological in doing moral theology and health care ethics. Hence, there is no longer a monolithic approach to health care ethics within Catholicism. There are a variety of interpretations and uses of natural law, and an increasing number of Catholic moral theologians are employing a variety of theological arguments.

This theological diversity, among other factors, has led to various approaches to Scripture in Christian health care ethics.[22] For some, Scripture's primary role is in shaping the identity of the individual Christian as well as the community of Christians. In other words, a variety of biblical materials can and ought to shape the perspectives, dispositions, intentions and motives of those who profess to live their lives in accordance with the narrative one finds in the Scriptures. Some will appeal to the full range of biblical materials, while others will take a much more limited approach. Generally, some biblical theme or themes provide a framework for theological and ethical reflection—covenant for Paul Ramsey; God as Creator, Provider, and Redeemer along with covenant for Allen Verhey; a perspective that is God-centered, reality-bounded, and love-impelled for John Kilner.[23] Identity in turn shapes what is seen, how it is interpreted, what is valued, what is chosen, and what is done.

In addition to the formation of character, Scripture can also influence decision-making, though some scholars would argue that its influence here is more complex and, perhaps, less significant. For some, Scripture provides a source of revealed norms—prescriptions and prohibitions—to be applied to specific challenges in health care. A less stringent approach might look to biblical norms to provide guidance on an issue, or to establish the burden of proof, or to mark the boundaries of what is morally permissible conduct, or to provide an alternative content to commonly accepted non-biblical norms. Some maintain that Scripture is a decisive source of moral judgments (whether one appeals to norms, ideals, patterns of behavior, or events in making those judgments), whereas others believe that Scripture informs moral judgments, but is not in itself sufficient. Ultimately, the use of Scripture in health care ethics, as in ethics and theology generally, depends on how one views the nature of biblical revelation, one's principles of interpretation and choice of biblical materials, and how one relates Scripture to other sources of moral insight.

## The Relevance of Context

To some degree, the role of Scripture and theology in health care ethics depends on the *context* in which health care ethics is done.[24] If it is being done in a community of faith, whether for the community as a whole or for individual believers, one would expect a very deliberate and explicit application of the biblical and theological resources of the tradition to the issues at hand. As Allen Verhey observes: "Faithful members of Christian community want to live and die and give birth and suffer and care for the suffering with Christian integrity, not just with impartial rationality. The longing of faith and faithfulness for Christian integrity is not served by ignoring the resources of the tradition or by silencing the peculiar voices of scripture. It is served by talking together and thinking together and praying together about the ways in which the story Christians love to tell and long to live can form and inform a response" to the events of our lives and the uses of new medical powers.[25]

In faith communities, the theological and biblical resources of the tradition can serve to form the character of community members (narrative discourse), inform the moral reflection and deliberation of the community (ethical discourse), and call the community to greater faithfulness to its traditions while challenging the prevailing assumptions of the culture (prophetic discourse).[26] All the more would a theologically and biblically informed health care ethics be appropriate in programs (whether seminary-based or otherwise) preparing individuals for ordained and non-ordained ministries in the church. Since they will be speaking out of, to, and for their communities, the language of impartial rationality embodied in principlism makes little sense as a primary language.

A somewhat more challenging context is that of faith-based health care institutions. There the language of principlism often supplants theologically informed approaches to health care ethics in response to a diversity of religious views amongst staff and patients. The challenge in this setting is to preserve and nourish the religious traditions of the particular institution and bring them to bear on the full range of health-related ethical issues while respecting religious pluralism. Abandoning the culture and language of a particular tradition for the generic language of principlism constitutes a betrayal of one's tradition in a most critical area.

Academic institutions and their departments of religion or theology are another context—one in which a good deal of health care ethics is developed, taught, and learned. Here, too, the language of principlism often marginalizes theological approaches, due to a multiplicity of factors. Among them are religious pluralism among students, the role (or lack) of religion in their lives, the training and personal methodologies of faculty, the belief of some faculty that they will not get a hearing unless they use some generic language and approach, and the relative paucity of teaching materials (at least in comparison to the bulk of the literature in health care ethics).[27] These factors, however, do not excuse avoiding religion in religion courses and theology in theology courses.

The way Christian content is introduced will likely depend on how closely a given institution is affiliated with a particular religious tradition, the religious backgrounds of students, whether the course in health care ethics is taught in a department of religion or a department of theology, and whether the courses in question are undergraduate or graduate. In most instances, the approach will likely be less "confessional" and more ecumenical than in communities of faith. In the undergraduate setting, courses may focus on acquainting students with a wide range of issues in health care ethics in conjunction with the relationships and contributions of theology past and present in one or a variety of religious traditions. In graduate programs, the concern might be less on the issues and more on various theological methodologies that have been and are employed in doing health care ethics, in order to provide students with the tools to do theological ethical reflection. Both settings—graduate and undergraduate—afford faculty opportunities for breaking new ground (e.g., by creatively integrating secular methodologies into theological approaches).

One of the most difficult and complex settings for giving theology a voice in health care ethics is the public arena. Some would maintain that theology should not lose its distinctive voice just because it is involved in public discourse.[28] Other would argue that if the contributions are to be heard, explicitly theological language must give way to language that is more conducive to a pluralistic society,[29] or even that theology must resort to the language of liberalism.[30]

It may well be the case that theological methodologies in health care ethics are influenced not only by the fundamental presuppositions of one's religious tradition, but also by the contexts in which religious ethical reflection is done, the audiences to whom it is addressed, and the methodological currents in secular health care ethics. However, the validity of this observation will be hard to assess as long as the theological voice in health care ethics remains muted. It is not only legitimate but also necessary that theology regains its voice in bioethics: speaking the language of principlism ultimately impoverishes both health care ethics and theology.

## Notes

[1]A few of the more prominent of these early contributors are James M. Gustafson, *Christian Ethics and the Community* (Philadelphia: Pilgrim Press, 1971); *Theology and Christian Ethics* (Philadelphia: Pilgrim Press, 1974); *The Contributions of Theology to Medical Ethics* (Milwaukee: Marquette University Press, 1975); *Can Ethics Be Christian?* (Chicago: University of Chicago Press, 1975); "Theology Confronts Technology and the Life Sciences," *Commonweal* 105 (June 16, 1978): 386-92; Immanuel Jakobovits, *Jewish Medical Ethics: A Comparative and Historical Study of the Jewish Religious Attitudes to Medicine and Its Practice,* 4th ed. (New York: Bloch Publishing, 1975); *Hospital Compendium: A Guide to Jewish Moral and Religious Principles in Hospital Practice* (New York: Commission on Synogogue Relations of the Federation of Jewish Philanthropies, 1963); Richard A. McCormick, *How Brave a New World?* (Garden City: Doubleday, 1981); "To Save or Let Die: The Dilemma of Modern Medicine," *Journal of the American Medical Association* 229 (July 8, 1974): 172-76; "Does Religious Faith Add to Ethical Perception?" in *Personal Values in Public Policy: Conversations on Government Decision-making,* ed. John C. Haughey (New York: Paulist Press, 1979); Paul Ramsey, *The Patient as Person* (New Haven: Yale University Press, 1970); *Fabricated Man* (New Haven: Yale University Press, 1970); *Ethics at the Edges of Life* (New Haven: Yale University Press, 1978).

[2]For a discussion of this development, see Daniel Callahan, "Religion and the Secularization of Bioethics," *Hastings Center Report* 20 (July-August 1990): 1-4; Courtney S. Campbell, "Religion and Moral Meaning in Bioethics," *Hastings Center Report* 20 (July-August 1990): 4-10; Albert R. Jonsen, "American Moralism and the Origin of Bioethics in the United States," *The Journal of Medicine and Philosophy* 16 (1991): 113-30; Stephen Lammers, "The Marginalization of Religious Voices in Bioethics," in *Religion and Medical Ethics: Looking Back, Looking Forward*, ed. Allen Verhey (Grand Rapids: Eerdmans, 1996), 19-43; David H. Smith, "Religion and the Roots of the Bioethics Revival," in *Religion and Medical Ethics*, pp. 9-18.

While the four principles are typically grounded philosophically, it is possible to offer theological justification for them. For an example of a theological reinterpretation of the principles, see Courtney Campbell, *op. cit.*

[3]National Commission for the Protection of Human Subjects of Biomedical and Behavioral Research, *The Belmont Report: Ethical Principles and Guidelines for the Protection of Human Subjects of Research*, DHEW Publication No. (OS) 78-0012 (Washington, D.C.: U.S. Government Printing Office, 1978).

[4]Tom L. Beauchamp and James Childress, *Principles of Biomedical Ethics* (New York: Oxford University Press, 1979). This book is now in its fourth edition.

[5]Tristram H. Engelhardt, Jr., *The Foundations of Bioethics* (New York: Oxford University Press, 1986); Robert Veatch, *A Theory of Medical Ethics* (New York: Basic Books, 1981).

[6]For a strong critique of this development, see James M. Gustafson, "Theology Confronts Technology and the Life Sciences," *op. cit.*, note 1.

[7]For example, Daniel Callahan and Courtney S. Campbell, eds., "Theology, Religious Traditions, and Bioethics," *Hastings Center Report, Special Supplement* 20 (July/August 1990); Lisa Sowle Cahill, issue editor, "Theology and Bioethics," *The Journal of Medicine and Philosophy* 17, no. 3 (June 1992). The entire issue is devoted to the topic with articles by Cahill, Martin Marty, Karen Lebacqz, Louis E. Newman, Edward C. Vacek, and J. Bryan Hehir. See also Lisa Sowle Cahill, issue editor, "'Playing God': Religious Symbols in Public Places," *The Journal of Medicine and Philosophy* 20, no.4 (August 1995).

[8]For examples of these critiques, see John Arras, "Getting Down to Cases: The Revival of Casuistry in Bioethics," *Journal of Medicine and Philosophy* 16 (February 1991): 29-51; Daniel Callahan, "Religion and the Secularization of Bioethics," *The Hastings Center Report* 20, a Special Supplement (July/August 1990): 2-4; Courtney Campbell, "Religion and Moral Meaning in Bioethics," *The Hastings Center Report* 20, a Special Supplement (July/August 1990): 4-10;

Alisa Carse, "The 'Voice of Care': Implications for Bioethical Education," *Journal of Medicine and Philosophy* 16 (1991): 5-28; Danner K. Clouser and Bernard Gert, "A Critique of Principlism," *Journal of Medicine and Philosophy* 15 (April 1990): 219-36; Renee Fox, "The Entry of U.S. Bioethics into the 1990s: A Sociological Analysis," in *A Matter of Principles? Ferment in U.S. Bioethics,* ed. Edwin R. DuBose, et al. (Valley Forge: Trinity Press International, 1994), 21-71; Leon Kass, "Practicing Ethics: Where's the Action?," *Hastings Center Report* 20 (January/February 1990): 5-12; Susan Sherwin, "Feminist and Medical Ethics: Two Different Approaches to Contextual Ethics." *Hypatia* 4 (Summer 1989): 57-72; Allen Verhey, "Talking of God—But with Whom?" *Hastings Center Report* 20 (July/August 1990): 21-24.

[9]Albert Jonsen and Stephen Toulmin, *The Abuse of Casuistry: A History of Moral Reasoning* (Berkeley: University of California Press, 1988). See also Albert Jonsen, "Casuistry and Clinical Ethics," *Theoretical Medicine* 7, no.1 (1986): 67-71; "Case Analysis in Clinical Ethics," *Journal of Clinical Ethics* 1, no.1 (1990): 63-65; "Casuistry as Methodology in Clinical Ethics," *Theoretical Medicine* 12 (December 1991): 295-307; "Casuistry: An Alternative or Complement to Principles?" *Kennedy Institute of Ethics Journal* 5 (September 1995): 237-52. For critiques of this approach, see John Arras, *op. cit.*, note 8; Loretta Koppelman, "Case Method and Casuistry: The Problem of Bias," *Theoretical Medicine* 15 (March 1994): 21-37; Benjamin Levi, "Four Approaches to Doing Ethics," *The Journal of Medicine and Philosophy* 21 (1996): 7-39; Tom Tomlinson, "Casuistry in Medical Ethics: Rehabilitated, Or Repeat Offender?" *Theoretical Medicine* 15 (March 1994): 5-20.

[10]Edmund Pellegrino, "The Virtuous Physician and the Ethics of Medicine," in *Virtue and Medicine: Explorations in the Character of Medicine*, ed. Earl Shelp (Dordrecht: D. Reidel, 1985): 237-56; "Toward a Virtue-Based Normative Ethics for the Health Professions," *Kennedy Institute of Ethics Journal* 5 (September 1995): 253-77. Also, Edmund Pellegrino and David Thomasma, *The Virtues in Medical Practice* (New York: Oxford University Press, 1993) and *The Christian Virtues in Medical Practice* (New York: Oxford University Press, 1996). For one critique of virtue theory, see Robert Veatch, "Against Virtue: A Deontological Critique of Virtue Theory and Medical Ethics," in *Virtue and Medicine*, ed. Earl Shelp (Dordrecht: D. Reidel, 1985): 329-46.

[11]See the essays in James Gustafson, 1971, 1974, 1975, *op. cit.*, note 1. Also, see Stanley Hauerwas, *Vision and Virtue* (Notre Dame: Fides Publishers, 1974), *Truthfulness and Tragedy* (Notre Dame: University of Notre Dame Press, 1977), *A Community of Character* (Notre Dame: University of Notre Dame Press, 1981), *Suffering Presence* (Notre Dame: University of Notre Dame Press, 1986), and "On Medicine and Virtue: A Response," in *Virtue and Medicine, op. cit.*, note 10, pp. 374-55. Theologian James Drane has also written on virtue and medicine. See his *Becoming a Good Doctor: The Place of Virtue and Character in Medical Ethics* (Kansas City: Sheed & Ward, 1988) and "Character and the Moral Life: A Virtue Approach to Biomedical Ethics," in *A Matter of Principles?, op. cit.*, note 8, pp. 284-309. The volume edited by Shelp, *Virtue and Medicine*, is an important discussion of the role of virtue in medicine. The volume provides historical analyses, discussions of various virtue theories, and considerations of the role of virtue in medicine.

[12]Edmund Pellegrino, 1995, *op. cit.*, note 10, pp. 269-70. See also Drane, *op. cit.*, note 11 for an identification of physician virtues.

[13]See Howard Brody, "The Four Principles and Narrative Ethics," in *Principles of Health Care Ethics,* ed. G. Raanan (New York: John Wiley, 1994), pp. 207-15; Tod Chambers, "The Bioethicist as Author: The Medical Ethics Case as Rhetorical Device," *Literature and Medicine* 13 (1994): 60-78; Rita Charon, "Narrative Contributions to Medical Ethics," in *A Matter of Principles?, op. cit.*, note 8, pp. 260-83; Kathryn Hunter, "The Whole Story," *Second Opinion* 19 (1993): 97-103; Steve Miles and Kathryn Hunter, "Case Stories," *Second Opinion* 15 (1990): 60-69.

[14]In addition to Hauerwas' works cited earlier, see Stanley Hauerwas and L. Gregory Jones, *Why Narrative? Readings in Narrative Theology* (Grand Rapids: Eerdmans, 1989). For an example of Verhey's use of a narrative approach, see Allen Verhey, "Assisted Suicide and Euthanasia: A Biblical and Reformed Perspective," in *Must We Suffer our Way to Death?*

*Cultural and Theological Perspectives on Death by Choice,* ed. Ronald P. Hamel and Edwin R. DuBose (Dallas: SMU Press, 1996), 226-65.

[15]See Barbara Hilkert Andolsen, "Elements of a Feminist Approach to Bioethics," in *Religious Methods and Resources in Bioethics*, ed. Paul Camenisch (Dordrecht: Kluwer Academic Publishers, 1994), 227-57; Margaret Farley, "Feminist Theology and Bioethics," in *Women's Consciousness, Women's Conscience: A Reader in Feminist Ethics*, ed. Barbara Andolsen et al. (Minneapolis: Winston Press, 1985); Christine Gudorf, "A Feminist Critique of Biomedical Principlism," in *A Matter of Principles?, op. cit.*, note 8, pp. 164-81; Margaret Olivia Little, "Why a Feminist Approach to Bioethics?" *Kennedy Institute of Ethics Journal* 6 (March 1996): 1-18.

[16]Barbara Andolsen, "Elements of a Feminist Approach to Bioethics," *op. cit.*, note 15; Christine Gudorf, "A Feminist Critique of Biomedical Principlism," *op. cit.*, note 15. For feminist discussions of justice, see again Christine Gudorf; Carter Heyward, *Our Passion for Justice: Images of Power, Sexuality and Liberation* (New York: Pilgrim Press, 1984); Virginia Held, "Non-Contractarian Society," in *Science, Morality and Feminist Theory*, ed. Marcia Hanen and Kai Nelson, *Canadian Journal of Philosophy* supp. 13 (1987): 11-138; Karen Lebacqz, "Feminism and Bioethics: An Overview," *Second Opinion* 17 (October 1991): 11-25; Diana Meyers, "The Socialized Individual and Individual Autonomy: An Intersection Between Philosophy and Psychology," in *Women and Moral Theory* ed. Eva Feder Kittay and Diana Meyers (Totowa, N.J.: Rowman & Littlefield); Charlotte Muller, *Health Care and Gender* (New York: Russell Sage Foundation, 1990).

[17]Alisa Carse and Hilde Lindemann Nelson, "Rehabilitating Care," *Kennedy Institute of Ethics Journal* 6 (March 1996): 19-36; Sarah T. Fry, "The Role of Caring in a Theory of Nursing Ethics," *Hypatia* 4 (Summer 1989): 88-103; Sarah T. Fry, Aileen Kellen, and Ellen Robinson, "Care-Based Reasoning, Caring, and the Ethic of Care: A Need for Clarity," *The Journal of Clinical Ethics* 7 (Spring 1996): 41-7; Christine Gudorf, "A Feminist Critique of Biomedical Principlism;" Nel Noddings, *Caring: A Feminist Approach to Ethics and Moral Education* (Berkeley: University of California Press, 1984).

[18]For two helpful overviews of feminist theology and bioethics, see Margaret Farley, "Feminist Theology and Bioethics," in *Theology and Bioethics: Exploring the Foundations and Frontiers,* ed. Earl Shelp (Dordrecht: D. Reidel, 1985), and Barbara Hilkert Andolsen *op. cit.*, note 15. Another useful resource is Charles E. Curran, Margaret Farley and Richard A. McCormick, eds., *Feminist Ethics and the Catholic Moral Tradition* (Mahwah, N.J.: Paulist, 1996).

[19]For a very helpful discussion of methodological differences between Catholic and Protestant ethics, see James M. Gustafson, *Protestant and Roman Catholic Ethics* (Chicago: University of Chicago Press, 1978).

[20]For example, Gerald A. Kelly, *Medico-Moral Problems* (St. Louis: Catholic Health Association, 1958); John Kenny, *Principles of Medical Ethics* (Westminster, MD.: Newman Press, 1952); Thomas O'Donnell, *Morals in Medicine* (Westminster, MD.: Newman Press, 1956).

[21]See Bernard Haring, *Free and Faithful in Christ,* 3 vols. (New York: Crossroad, 1978, 1979, 1981); *Medical Ethics* (Notre Dame, IN: Fides, 1971); *Ethics of Manipulation* (New York: Seabury, 1975).

[22]Allen Verhey is one of the few theologians who have written explicitly on the relation of Scripture to health care ethics. See Allen Verhey, "Scripture and Medical Ethics: Psalm 51:10a, the Jarvik VII, and Psalm 50:9," in *Religious Methods and Resources in Bioethics, op. cit.*, note 15, pp. 261-88. For the relation of Scripture and ethics, see Allen Verhey, "The Use of Scripture in Ethics," *Religious Studies Review* 4 (1978): 28-39; William C. Spohn, *What Are They Saying About Scripture and Ethics?* (New York: Paulist Press, 1984); Bruce C. Birch and Larry Rasmussen, *Bible and Ethics in the Christian Life*, revised edition (Minneapolis: Augsburg, 1989).

[23]Paul Ramsey, *The Patient as Person* (New Haven: Yale University Press, 1970); Allen Verhey et al., *Christian Faith, Health, and Medical Practice* (Grand Rapids: Eerdmans, 1989); John Kilner, *Life on the Line* (Grand Rapids: Eerdmans, 1992).

[24]For other discussions related to the contexts of health care ethics, see James M. Gustafson, "Moral Discourse about Medicine: A Variety of Forms," *The Journal of Medicine and Philosophy* 15 (1990): 125-42; Stephen Lammers, "The Marginalization of Religious Voices in Bioethics," in *Religion and Medical Ethics, op. cit.*, note 2, pp. 19-43

[25]Allen Verhey, "Scripture and Medical Ethics," *op. cit.*, note 22, p. 265.

[26]See James M. Gustafson, "Moral Discourse about Medicine: A Variety of Forms," *The Journal of Medicine and Philosophy* 15 (1990): 125-42.

[27]The resources for teaching health care ethics theologically are expanding. In addition to the works of individual theologians working in health care ethics, the following may be helpful either as personal resources or texts: Laura Jane Bishop and Mary Carrington Coutts, "Religious Perspectives in Bioethics, Part I," *Kennedy Institute of Ethics Journal* 4, no.2 (1994): 155-183; Laura Jane Bishop and Mary Carrington Coutts, "Religious Perspectives on Bioethics, Part II," *Kennedy Institute of Ethics Journal* 4, no. 4 (1994): 357-86; Paul Camenisch, ed., *Religious Methods and Resources in Bioethics* (Dordrecht: Kluwer, 1994); Richard A. McCormick, "Bioethics and Method: Where Do We Start?" *Theology Digest* 29 (Winter 1981): 303-18; Richard A. McCormick, "Theology and Bioethics," *Hastings Center Report* 19 (1989): 5-10; Ronald Numbers and Darrel W. Amundsen, eds., *Caring and Curing: Health and Medicine in the Western Religious Traditions* (New York: Macmillan Publishing Company, 1986); Earl Shelp, ed., *Theology and Bioethics* (Dordrecht: D. Reidel, 1985); Lawrence E. Sullivan, ed., *Healing and Restoring: Health and Medicine in the World's Religious Traditions* (New York: Macmillan, 1989); James B. Tubbs, Jr., *Christian Theology and Medical Ethics: Four Contemporary Approaches* (Dordrecht: Kluwer, 1996); Allen Verhey, ed., *Religion and Medical Ethics: Looking Back, Looking Forward* (Grand Rapids: Eerdmans, 1996; Allen Verhey and Stephen Lammers, eds., *On Moral Medicine: Theological Perspectives in Medical Ethics* (Grand Rapids: Eerdmans, 1987); Allen Verhey and Stephen Lammers, eds., *Theological Voices in Medical Ethics* (Grand Rapids: Eerdmans, 1993); John Williams, *Christian Perspectives on Bioethics* (Ottawa: Novalis, 1997). In addition, The Park Ridge Center for the Study of Health, Faith and Ethics has published a multi-volume series called *Health and Medicine in the Religious Traditions*. Each volume is devoted to a different religious tradition and is written by a different author. Moreover, The Center for Bioethics and Human Dignity publishes two explicitly Christian book series with annual releases: the *Horizons in Bioethics* Series and the *Critical Issues in Bioethics* Series. (See Introduction to this section of the *Annual* for information on these centers.)

[28]See Stephen Carter, *The Culture of Disbelief* (New York: Basic Books, 1993); Michael J. Perry, *Love and Power: The Role of Religion in American Politics* (New York: Oxford University Press, 1991); Allen Verhey, "Talking of God—But with Whom?" *Hastings Center Report*, Special Supplement 20 (July/August 1990): 21-24, especially 23-24. Stanley Hauerwas is also a strong proponent of this position, though he is far more concerned that the church focus on its own religious and moral formation and its faithfulness to its religious convictions, rather than on shaping public policy.

[29]See for example Lisa Sowle Cahill, "Can Theology Have a Role in 'Public' Bioethical Discourse?" *Hastings Center Report,* Special Supplement 20 (July August 1990): 10-14. She maintains that religious ethicists should speak *out of* their traditions, but also *beyond* them using language that can communicate to a plurality of traditions. Holding a similar position are David Novak, "Bioethics and the Contemporary Jewish Community," *Hastings Center Report*, Special Supplement 20 (July/August 1990): 14-17; and Louis Newman, "Jewish Theology and Bioethics," *The Journal of Medicine and Philosophy* 17, no. 3 (June 1992): 309-27. For a discussion of the dangers of using non-theological language see, Courtney Campbell, "Religion and Moral Meaning in Bioethics," *Hastings Center Report,* Special Supplement 20 (July/August 1990): 4-10, especially 5-6; and Stanley Hauerwas, "The Testament of Friends," *The Christian Century* 107 (February 28, 1990): 213.

[30]Kent Greenwalt seems to move in this direction. See his *Religious Convictions and Political Choices* (New York: Oxford University Press, 1988).

# Ethics and Human Genetics

*Audrey R. Chapman*

Genetic discoveries during the past half-century and their potential applications to engineer or bring about deliberate genetic changes in plants, animals, and human beings have raised a series of ethical and theological issues. The explosion of knowledge about the biological basis of life has been further accelerated by the inception of the Human Genome Project (HGP), a $3 billion initiative begun in 1998 to map and sequence the human genetic code and to identify the 4,000 genes whose defects are assumed to be the cause of genetically based diseases. To respond to public concerns about the project, Congress allocated three percent and then five percent of the HGP's budget for research on the ethical, legal, and social implications of the human genetics revolution. A working group overseeing this funding identified nine topics deemed to be of particular importance, among them: fairness in the use of genetic information with respect to insurance; the impact of knowledge of genetic variation on the individual, including issues of stigmatization and impact on self-image; privacy and confidentiality of genetic information and related consent issues; impact on genetic counseling and reproductive decisions influenced by genetic information; questions raised by the commercialization of the products from the project; and conceptual and philosophical implications on the concept of human responsibility and the issue of free will versus determinism.[1]

That the genetics revolution raises major questions for the religious community was quickly recognized. Some early reflections by moral theologians, such as Karl Rahner[2] and Paul Ramsey,[3] reflect a diffuse sense of unease or anxiety about genetic engineering and the implications of altering the genetic basis of life. Like many of the religious writings that followed, these ethicists raised, but did not resolve, questions about the appropriate limits of human intervention into the Creation and the basis of making such a determination. Other writers have acknowledged that "[D]evelopments in genetic science and technology compel our reevaluation of accepted theological/ethical issues, including determinism versus free will, the nature of sin, just distribution of resources, the status of human beings in relation to other forms of life, and the meaning of personhood.'"[4]

This essay will review the religious literature on human genetics during the past thirty years. Given space limitations it will not cover related developments in reproductive technologies, cloning, or genetic patenting.

## Public Theology: Protestant Ecumenical and Denominational Initiatives

Many ecumenical and denominational bodies have commissioned committees or individual experts to study aspects of genetic engineering, develop resources, and/or draft position statements, some of which have become the basis of official policy. Consistent with its interest in the significance of science and technology, the World Council of Churches has published several booklets on genetics, including *Genetics and the Quality of Life* (1975),[5] *Manipulating Life: Ethical Issues in Genetic Engineering* (1982),[6] and *Biotechnology: Its Challenges to the Churches and the World* (1989).[7] Likewise the National Council of Churches of Christ issued two study documents, *Human Life and the New Genetics* (1980)[8] and *Genetic Engineering: Social and Ethical Consequences* (1984),[9] and the Governing Board adopted a 1986 statement entitled "Genetic Science for Human Benefit."[10]

Nine North American Protestant denominations have addressed genetics issues. These denominational documents differ in focus, purpose, and emphasis, as well as the process by which they were drafted. Six denominations—the United Methodist Church,[11] the United Church of Christ,[12] the Episcopal Church,[13] the Presbyterian Church (U.S.A.),[14] the Reformed Church in America,[15] and the Southern Baptist Convention[16]—have drafted reports, policy statements, or study resources on genetic science, genetic engineering or procreational ethics, and a seventh, the United Church of Canada, has prepared a brief.[17]

Despite having been drafted by and for a religious audience, these documents do not generally have a theological character. Roger Shinn, the chair of one National Council of Churches' initiative, described the ensuing task force report as drawing "from theology not a set of prescriptions but 'a context of awareness.'"[18] The same could be said of much of the denominational and ecumenical literature. In several cases the theological framework amounts to little more than a recitation of confessional teachings without direct application to the issues posed by the developments in genetics. Instead, the fundamental purpose appears to be to educate members about the significance of the discoveries in genetics, to promote a better understanding of the science, and to establish a policy framework regarding appropriate and inappropriate applications of genetic technologies.

Most of these documents have a hopeful and respectful attitude toward genetic science, taking care that the concerns expressed will not appear unqualifiedly critical and thus position the religious community as Luddites. This makes it difficult to engage in the prophetic inquiry to which some of these writings explicitly aspire.[19] That is not to say that the documents fail to raise valid ethical concerns. However, they frequently read like laundry lists of issues and related policy affirmations with little theological or ethical analysis.

Ethical issues outlined in a 1992 United Methodist statement[20] reflect the concerns of many of the denominations and ecumenical agencies. Like several other statements, the text has a strong justice commitment and to that end urges that the benefits of genetic research and application accrue to the broadest possible public. It supports adequate public funding of genetic research so that there will be greater accountability to the public. Relatedly, the text advocates that there be a public role in setting research priorities and formulating guidelines for various types of applications. In addition, the statement emphasizes the need for measures to assure the privacy and confidentiality of genetic information and opposes discriminatory or manipulative use of these data as, for example, in the limitation, termination, or denial of insurance or employment. The United Methodist statement also goes beyond other denominational positions in two ways. It urges that genes and genetically modified organisms be held as common resources and to that end not be exclusively controlled or patented. In addition, the document affirms both the right of all persons to health care and health care resources regardless of preexisting genetic or medical conditions, and supports equal access to medical resources, including genetic testing and genetic counseling.

Several of the documents refer to claims that genetic engineering amounts to "playing God." While the statements acknowledge that the ability to alter the building blocks of life represents a new threshold, they disappointingly do not attempt to define the appropriate limits of human knowledge and power. Unable to provide answers as to where Christian theology or the church should draw lines, they opt for the "need for further study." Some assign society the primary responsibility for decision-making in this area, seemingly abdicating any role for the churches in providing society with ethical guidance.

On the topic of human gene therapy, these documents generally support somatic gene therapies that seek to alter or replace "defective" genes with those that are well functioning, equating these interventions with other curative medical innovations. However, the documents are more cautious about germ-line alterations that will be passed on to future generations. Those that deal with the topic also oppose the use of recombinant DNA for eugenic purposes or genetic enhancements designed for cosmetic purposes or perceived economic, social, or sexual advantage.[21] Positions on the appropriateness of human germ-line therapy range from the studied and apparently intentional silence on the matter in the National Council of Churches statement to recommendations in several others that experiments involving genetic engineering on the human germ-line be banned for the present. Other than acknowledging that such genetic therapy would have potential long-term effects on the human species, especially loss of genetic diversity, none of the documents specifically address the theological issues involved in permanently altering the genetic makeup of human beings. Instead, the reasoning in these documents tends to be on grounds of the risks the technology entails.

The role proposed for the religious community in these documents tends to be surprisingly modest. Although many of the statements eloquently justify the churches addressing the genetic revolution, they do not seem to envisage a major continuing role for the religious community. One shared priority is expanding education, resources, and dialogue around ethical issues associated with the development of genetics. Another is training clergy in order that they be able to provide pastoral counseling for persons with genetic disorders and their families and those facing difficult choices as a result of genetic testing. A third is supporting persons who, because of the possibilities of severe genetic disorders, have to make difficult decisions regarding reproduction. They also mention the need for the churches to monitor and participate in governmental, legislative, and public policy debates.

## Official Catholic Teaching on Human Genetics

In contrast with the Protestant context, official Roman Catholic teaching on human genetics proceeds from an explicit framework of church doctrine on human sexuality, the beginning of human life from the moment of conception, and the prohibition on abortion.[22] In a 1983 statement Pope John Paul II differentiated between the acceptability of genetic manipulation that is strictly therapeutic action enhancing personal well-being, and the unacceptability of any intervention that affects the origin of human life and the biological nature of the human being.[23] The Catholic Health Association of the United States' 1990 resource, *Human Genetics: Ethical Issues in Genetic Testing, Counseling, and Therapy,* recommends that Catholic health care institutions be encouraged to establish programs in medical genetics and that the freedom of persons to participate in genetic testing and counseling be protected.[24] Acknowledging that germ-line intervention is potentially the only means of treating genetic diseases that do their damage early in embryonic development, this document proposes an approach consistent with Catholic teaching: to develop techniques for making genetic corrections in the gonadal cell tissues of prospective parents before their children are conceived.[25]

## Works by Moral Theologians on Human Genetics

To provide a brief overview of the literature, Ronald Cole-Turner's book *The New Genesis: Theology and the Genetic Revolution* was published in 1993.[26] Cole-Turner also co-authored a second book with Brent Waters on *Pastoral Genetics: Theology and Care at the Beginning of Life* that fills the important need of providing clergy with a scientifically informed and theologically sensitive resource.[27] In 1994, J. Robert Nelson published a work entitled *On the New Frontiers of Genetics and Religion* which recounts and sometimes reproduces the presentations of participants at two conferences organized by the Institute of Religion at the University of Texas in 1990 and 1992.[28] Roger Shinn, who might be described as the doyen of religious ethicists working on genetics issues, contributed a 1996 book entitled *The New Genetics: Challenges for Science, Faith, and Politics*[29] which nonetheless is not written from an explicitly religious perspective. Ted Peter's 1997 book, *Playing God? Genetic Determinism and Human Freedom*,[30] represents the first truly comprehensive and in-depth theological analysis of human genetics focussing, as the title implies, on the role of genes in determining human nature and behavior. He has also written a second book, *For the Love of Children: Genetic Technology and the Future of the Family*[31] that addresses the implications of genetic screening and selective abortion for conceptions of personhood and dignity, eugenics, and an acceleration of discrimination in the employment insurance health care loop. Jan Heller's work, *Human Genome Research and the Challenge of Contingent Future Persons: Toward an Impersonal Theocentric Approach to Value*,[32] attempts to develop a framework for evaluating the implications of contemporary genetic interventions on persons who will live in the future. In terms of multi-authored works with multi-media options, a 1997 volume *Genetic Ethics: Do the Ends Justify the Genes?*, edited by John Kilner, Rebecca Pentz, and Frank Young, has a wide range of short articles and a very useful glossary of genetic terms.[33] Another collection of articles by religious ethicists entitled *Genetics: Genes, Religion, and Society*, edited by Ted Peters, focuses on justice and social issues.[34] Additionally, there are many chapters of books and articles on genetics written by moral theologians. These works begin the task of developing a constructive theological ethics on genetics.

In 1969, James Gustafson, anticipating the implications of the new genetics, called for the reconceptualization of the traditional non-evolutionary, fixed, unchanging, and essentially dualistic concept of humans.[35] It has taken some twenty-five years for religious ethicists to respond to the challenge that genetics research poses to traditional theological anthropologies. While many ethicists may assume an evolutionary perspective, few have been as explicit as Thomas Shannon who notes that genetic research shows that "[W]hat our nature is now is not what it was nor is it necessarily what it will be."[36] On the important question as to whether human nature is the sum of its parts or whether there is a transcendent dimension, a long-time query, Christian theology has, of course, claimed the latter. Genetics, like neuroscience research, makes it difficult to maintain the traditional dualistic conception of the self divided into a body and soul. However, in doing so it may motivate us to look for other sources of integration and transcendence. And there are some preliminary efforts to speak of the soul in a way that does not contradict an understanding of human nature as a psychosomatic unity.[37]

A related issue that ethicists and theologians have long debated and that genetic research both illuminates and complicates is the relationship between biological inheritance and cultural or learned patterns of behavior. Philip Hefner describes humans as genuinely biocultural creatures, but understands this dual heritage as bequeathing fundamental tensions. According to Hefner, as creatures of evolution we carry within our genes the history of the planet's experiments with living forms. Because the human neocortex has evolved on a reptilian and ancient paleo-mammalian brain, we have the task of humanizing these aspects of ourselves. Another set of tensions is rooted in the conflict between our individual and social nature, between the selfishness bequeathed by our genes and our complex social existence as well as the limits and innate fallibility of both.[38]

Of the topics considered in the literature, one of the most important is the assessment of the extent to which genes shape human nature and determine human behavior. Peters' *Playing God?* offers insightful criticism of "genetic essentialism," also sometimes referred to as the "gene myth," the notion that human nature and behavior is solely or predominantly determined by our genes. His book argues forcefully that science does not support the view that humans are the sum total of their DNA, and provides an eloquent defense of human creativity, moral responsibility, and freedom. According to Peters, molecular biology has provided little or no evidence supporting a philosophy of human determinism that undermines traditional philosophical and theological conceptions of human freedom. Peters concludes that because freedom is exercised at the level of the person in the form of deliberation, decision, and responsible action, determinism at the genetic level does not obviate having free moral will.[39]

Despite assumptions to the contrary,[40] most religious thinkers, like the drafters of the ecumenical and denominational statements, have a positive attitude toward the developing science of genetics and do not consider genetic engineering as intrinsically problematic theologically. Cole-Turner, for example, metaphorically describes God as engaging in genetic engineering and views human genetic engineering as an extension of God's activity.[41] Adopting Hefner's terminology,[42] Peters conceptualizes the human being as God's "created cocreator," a creature created by God and vested with creativity to share in the transforming work of God's ongoing creation, with genetic engineering understood as an expression of human creativity.[43] Peters disputes what many critics claim, that genetic engineering and other reproductive technologies go beyond the limits of a reasonable dominion over nature or at least provide temptations in that direction.[44] Much like the 1982 report *Splicing Life: The Social and Ethical Issues of Genetic Engineering with Human Beings*[45] issued by the President's Commission for the Study of Ethical Problems in Medicine and Biomedical and Behavioral Research, these thinkers tend to dismiss the concern that genetic engineering is "playing God" or that this notion even has a specific religious meaning.[46] Allen Verhey goes so far as to suggest that Christians should "play God," by emulating God's example in exercising responsible stewardship, providing healing, promoting life and its flourishing, and taking the side of the poor.[47]

Venturing beyond the caution in the ecumenical and denominational documents, some moral theologians move a few steps closer to a qualified endorsement of germ-line intervention and by implication enhancement applications as well. Shinn, for example, advocates caution, but wants to stop short of an ethical prohibition for an unforeseeable future.[48] Peters argues that realism about current technological limits and risks is insufficient warrant for prematurely ruling out possibilities for an improved human future through germ-line intervention.[49] The very important question, now much debated by secular ethicists, of the moral acceptability of gene therapy for enhancement purposes or nonmedical uses,[50] receives relatively little attention in this literature. There is nothing, for example, comparable to the careful analysis of the issues involved and the difficulty of drawing a line between prevention and enhancement applications contributed by secular ethicists.[51]

The ethical literature is disappointingly underdeveloped in formulating norms for evaluating potential applications of genetic science. This is particularly curious because several of the ethicists are well aware of the possibilities of questionable uses. Philip Hefner, for example, assumes that human sinfulness ensures that genetic interventions will be manipulated by social class interests, that alterations will be made in individuals and in the germ-line that are unwise, and that the Human Genome Project will threaten to define human life in ways that violate basic human dignity,[52] all of which are serious issues. There is something of a consensus that genetic research and therapies should seek to promote the relief of human suffering and the benefit of the human population, particularly the poor and vulnerable, but these broad principles are not easily applied to determine the appropriateness of specific applications. Two ethicists, Roger Shinn[53] and James Peterson,[54] put forward general standards to define an ethically responsible program of genetic research and practice. As valuable as they are, these efforts represent starting points. Shinn himself characterizes his effort as referring "less to precise decisions than to the personal and cultural climate in which decisions are made."[55]

One subject on which there is a clear religious divide is the use of genetic testing as the basis for therapeutic abortions. Abortion is already one of the most divisive moral issues in this country. Advances in genetic knowledge pose increasing dilemmas as to how to respond to the opportunity for prenatal genetic screening and then use the information gained from these diagnoses. These painful choices, usually made by the parents with the assistance of clergy or a genetic counselor, are all the more wrenching because genetic testing is still a relatively imprecise science that cannot determine the potential seriousness of a mutation or usually correct it *in utero*. Positions on whether and how to use prenatal screening often, but not always, reflect views on abortion.

C. Ben Mitchell, an ethicist who serves as a consultant for the Southern Baptist Convention, points out that "the expansive use of prenatal genetic screening casts a shadow of suspicion over every unborn baby. Every pregnancy becomes a 'tentative pregnancy,' pending the results of prenatal screening."[56] He argues that it is morally offensive to treat human babies as chattel to be disposed of when they do not meet our criteria of normalcy. He warns that the effort to prevent children from being born with fatal and debilitating diseases is likely to increase discriminatory prejudice and reduce life prospects for persons with disabilities. Mitchell's conclusion is that the church must provide support and encouragement for couples who choose either not to undergo prenatal screening or decide to maintain their pregnancy despite the diagnosis of genetic anomaly.[57]

Mainline Protestant ethicists have dealt less with these issues, possibly because of the turmoil over abortion in many of these denominations. While most of these ethicists undoubtedly support genetic screening of pregnancies at risk, they are reluctant to be directive on the central moral issue of whether or when to terminate a pregnancy if a defect is identified. The Cole-Turner and Waters book, *Pastoral Genetics,*[58] makes an important contribution by better enabling parents and genetic counselors to consider the religious and moral issues that confront those coping with difficult pregnancies. This relatively brief book should be required reading for all pastoral theology courses in Christian seminaries. Nevertheless, it is analytical and theological rather than prescriptive. Peters also examines the implications of genetic technologies in his book *For the Love of Children*. Although Peters is quite critical of the use of selective abortion to achieve "designer children," he recommends restricting rather than eliminating therapeutic abortions. His "minimalist middle axioms" offer perceptive and balanced guidelines for prospective parents and Christian ethicists alike.[59]

In light of the historical commitment of the Christian community to justice and the concerns identified in the ecumenical and denominational statements and study documents, it is surprising that there is relatively little emphasis on justice issues in this literature. Just as gene therapy offers possibilities for ameliorating human suffering, it could also be the basis for practicing eugenics.[60] Demonstrable advances in biomedicine have created an openness, perhaps even a receptivity, to some of the more regressive formulations of the genetic reductionism characteristic of social Darwinism. Troy Duster points to the danger signs in the growing popularity of genetic explanations of violence and deviance.[61] For some groups who were marginalized in the past, the discovery of an increased disposition to genetically-based disease--for example, sickle cell among African Americans and Tay-Sachs in the Jewish community--raise potential new issues of stigmatization.[62] Karen Lebacqz's article on genetic privacy issues and their disproportionate burden on the poor offers one of the few Christian analyses of this critical societal problem.[63]

## Further Work Needed

The religious literature on genetics surveyed in this article attests to the concern of the religious community with human genetics but also underscores the need for additional work. As yet there has been more attention to defining and analyzing the issues than in developing a constructive and prescriptive moral theology. While it is difficult to identify just a few topics deserving of attention from moral theologians, three stand out: (1) development of a better ethical foundation, particularly in the form of norms, to determine whether potential applications of genetic science are morally appropriate; (2) evaluation of the implications of using genetics for enhancement purposes and the social consequences of doing so; and (3) further exploration of justice issues relative to access to genetic therapy and its potential for new forms of inequality.

## Notes

---

[1]National Institutes of Health and US Department of Energy, *Understanding our Genetic Inheritance: The U.S. Human Genome Project: The First Five Years,* FY 1991-1995, appendix 7, 67-69.

[2]Karl Rahner, "The Experiment with Man: Theological Observations on Man's Self-Manipulation," *Theological Investigations: IX*: 225-52, trans. G. Harrison (New York: Seabury).

[3]Paul Ramsey, *Fabricated Man: The Ethics of Genetic Control* (New Haven: Yale University Press, 1972).

[4]United Methodist Church, "New Developments in Genetic Science," *The Book of Resolutions of the United Methodist Church* (Nashville: The United Methodist Publishing House, 1992), 329.

[5]Charles Birch and Paul Albrecht, *Genetics and the Quality of Life* (Elmsford, New York and Potts Point, New South Wales, Australia: Pergamon Press, 1975).

[6]Church and Society, *Manipulating Life: Ethical Issues in Genetic Engineering* (Geneva: World Council of Churches, 1982).

[7]Church and Society, *Biotechnology: Its Challenges to the Church and the World* (Geneva: World Council of Churches, 1989).

[8]*Human Life and the New Genetics: A Report of a Task Force Commissioned by the National Council of Churches of Christ in the U.S.A.* (New York: NCC, 1980).

[9]Panel of Bioethical Concerns, *Genetic Engineering: Social and Ethical Consequences*, ed. Frank M. Harron (New York: Pilgrim Press, 1984).

[10]"Genetic Science for Human Benefit: A Policy Statement of the National Council of the Churches of Christ in the U.S.A." Adopted by Governing Board, 1998.

[11]"New Developments in Genetic Science," *The Book of Resolutions of the United Methodist Church* (Nashville: The United Methodist Publishing House, 1992), 325-338.

[12]"Pronouncement, Church and Genetic Engineering," and "Resolution, The Church and Reproductive Technologies," *Minutes, Seventeenth General Synod, United Church of Christ* (St. Louis: United Church Resources, 1991), 45-47.

[13]"Resolution on Guidelines in the Area of Genetic Engineering," 70th General Convention of the Episcopal Church, 1991.

[14]"The Covenant of Life and the Caring Community and Covenant and Creation: Theological Reflections on Contraception and Abortion," Policy Statements and Recommendations adopted by the 195th General Assembly (Louisville: The Office of the General Assembly, 1983); and "The Covenant of Life and the Caring Community adopted by the 195th (1983) General Assembly," *Social Policy Compilation* (Louisville: Advisory Committee on Social Witness Policy, 1992), 97 and 846 (the resolution of the 202nd (1990) General Assembly, which is untitled in the compilation, is on p.776.)

[15]"Genetic Engineering," Reports on Christian Action, *Minutes of the General Synod 1988*, New York: Reformed Church of America.

[16]C. Ben Mitchell, "Genetic Engineering: Bane or Blessing," (Nashville: The Christian Life Commission, n.d.) and C. Ben Mitchell, "Was Jesus an Embryo? The Ethics of Human Embryo Research and the Brave New World," (Nashville: The Christian Life Commission, n.d.).

[17]The Division of Mission in Canada, "A Brief to the Royal Commission on New Reproductive Technologies on Behalf of the United Church of Canada," approved by the Executive of the Division of Mission, January 17, 1991.

[18]Roger Shinn, "Genetics, Ethics, and Theology," in Ted Peters, ed., *Genetics: Issues of Social Justice* (Cleveland: The Pilgrim Press, 1998), 132.

[19]Presbyterian Church (U.S.A.), "On Implications of Genetic Research and the Church's Response," 776-777.

[20]United Methodist Church, "New Developments in Genetic Science."

[21]See, for example, United Methodist Church, "New Developments in Genetic Science," 333.

[22]Sacred Congregation for the Doctrine of the Faith, *Instruction on Respect for Human Life in its Origin and on the Dignity of Procreation* (Rome, 1987).

[23]Address of Pope John Paul II to participants in the World Medical Association convention, *Origins*, November 17, 1983, 385, 387.

[24]Catholic Health Association of the United States, *Human Genetics: Ethical Issues in Genetic Testing, Counseling, and Therapy* (St. Louis: The Catholic Health Association of the United States, 1990), 37.

[25]Ibid., 21.

[26]Ronald Cole-Turner, *The New Genesis: Theology and the Genetic Revolution* (Louisville: Westminster/John Knox, 1993).

[27]Ronald Cole-Turner and Brent Waters, *Pastoral Genetics: Theology and Care at the Beginning of Life* (Cleveland: The Pilgrim Press, 1996).

[28]Barry Freundel, "Personal Religious Positions Individually Expressed: Judaism," in J. Robert Nelson, *On the New Frontiers of Genetics and Religion* (Grand Rapids: Wm. B. Eerdmans, 1994), 120-135.

[29]Roger Shinn, *The New Genetics: Challenges for Science, Faith, and Politics* (Wakefield, Rhode Island and London: Moyer Bell, 1996).

[30]Ted Peters, *Playing God? Genetic Determinism and Human Freedom* (New York: Routledge, 1997).

[31]Ted Peters, *For the Love of Children: Genetic Technology and the Future of the Family* (Louisville: Westminster/John Knox Press, 1996).

[32]Jan Christian Heller, *Human Genome Research: The Challenge of Contingent Future Persons* (Omaha: Association of Jesuit University Presses, 1996).

[33]John F. Kilner, Rebecca D. Pentz, Frank E. Young, eds., *Genetic Ethics: Do the Ends Justify the Genes?* (Grand Rapids: William B. Eerdmans Publishing Company, 1997). Related series of videos on "The [Ethical] Challenges of Genetics" and audio tapes on "Genetics and Ethics" are available from The Center for Bioethics and Human Dignity (see Introduction to this section of the *Annual*).

[34]Ted Peters, ed., *Genetics: Genes, Religion, and Society* (Cleveland: The Pilgrim Press, 1998).

[35]Cited in Nelson, *On the New Frontiers of Genetics and Religion*, 18.

[36]Thomas A. Shannon, "Genetics, Ethics, and Theology: The Roman Catholic Discussion," in Peters, ed., *Genetics*, 170.

---

[37]James Bachman discussed this subject in a paper prepared for the 1992 Houston conference. See the citation in Nelson, *On the New Frontiers of Genetics and Religion*, 106-107.

[38]Philip Hefner, "Determinism, Freedom, and Moral Failure," in Peters, ed., *Genetics*, 112-117.

[39]Peters, *Playing God*?, 176.

[40]Secular commentators sometimes erroneously equate the interest and concerns of the religious community with a negative mind set. See for example the comments of Francis S. Collins, Director of the U.S. Human Genome Project, "The Human Genome Project," in Kilner, Pentz, and Young, *Genetic Ethics*, 101-102.

[41]Cole-Turner, *The New Genesis*, 109.

[42]Philip Hefner, *The Human Factor* (Minneapolis: Fortress Press, 1993).

[43]Peters, *Playing God?,* 15.

[44]This is one of the fundamental themes of Peter's book *Playing God?*, particularly the first chapter.

[45]President's Commission for the Study of Ethical Problems in Medicine and Biomedical and Behavioral Research, *Splicing Life: The Social and Ethical Issues of Genetic Engineering with Human Beings* (Washington, D.C.: Government Printer, 1982), 53-60.

[46]Peters, *Playing God*, 2; Shinn, *The New Genetics*, 143-145; Allan Verhey, "Playing God," in Kilner, Pentz, and Young, eds., *Genetic Ethics*, 60-74.

[47]Verhey, "Playing God," 69-71.

[48]Shinn, *The New Genetics*, 144-145.

[49]Peters, *Playing God?*, 156.

[50]The National Institutes of Health, for example, sponsored a two-day meeting on this topic in September 1997.

[51]See, for example, Eric T. Juengst, "Can Enhancement Be Distinguished from Prevention in Genetic Medicine?" *The Journal of Medicine and Philosophy* 22 (1997): 125-142.

[52]Hefner, "Determinism, Freedom, and Moral Failure," 120.

[53]Shinn, *The New Genetics*, 108-121.

[54]James C. Peterson, "Ethical Standards for Genetic Intervention," in Kilner, Pentz, and Young, *Genetic Ethics*, 197-200.

[55]Shinn, *The New Genetics*, 120-1.

[56]C. Ben Mitchell, "The Church and the New Genetics," in Kilner, Pentz, and Young, *Genetic Ethics*, 238.

[57]Mitchell, "The Church and the New Genetics," 240.

[58]Cole-Turner and Waters, *Pastoral Genetics*.

[59]Peters, *For the Love of Children*, 116-118.

[60]Arthur J. Dyck, "Eugenics in Historical and Ethical Perspective," in Kilner, Pentz, and Young, *Genetic Ethics*, 25-39.

[61]Troy Duster, "Persistence and Continuity in Human Genetics and Social Stratification," in Peters, ed., *Genetics*, chapter 10.

[62]Laurie Zoloth-Dorman, "Mapping the Normal Self: The Jew and the Mark of Otherness," in Peters, ed., *Genetics*, chapter 8.

[63]Karen Lebacqz, "Genetic Privacy: No Deal for the Poor," in Peters, ed., *Genetics*, chapter 11.

# The Ethics of Access to Health Care

*Charlene A. Galarneau*

Confounding the predilection of bioethics for individual and crisis-oriented dilemmas, the issue of access to health care raises fundamental concerns about the complex institutional structuring of health care organization and finance, as well as the political processes of resource allocation and rationing. The temptation to turn away from this daunting subject has been great, as intimated by Paul Ramsey's oft-recited claim: "The larger questions of medical and social priorities are almost, if not altogether, incorrigible to moral reasoning." Indeed, medical and social priorities are deeply rooted in health care, and their expressions in organizational and financing arrangements shape virtually all other health care concerns. Yet, medical and social priorities are also dynamic, continually reshaped with or without the benefit of self-conscious ethical reflection. As Ramsey also states: "there is no avoiding this question of choosing societal priorities. We must choose how we shall go about choosing and ordering our medical and societal goals."[1] If medical and social priorities appear incorrigible to moral reasoning, perhaps it is because we have not yet developed suitable moral tools to understand them descriptively and normatively.

Recent ethical attention to health care access in the United States has been motivated by the prospect of health care reform at the national and state levels, the increasingly visible restructuring of the health care "non-system" in the name of managed care, the claims of injustice by the "have-nots," as well as the fears of the "haves" whose access is becoming increasingly tenuous. That the current situation of access to health care in the United States is a moral problem is commonly asserted by ethicists. Less extensive, but growing, is the ethical reflection devoted to the etiology, definition, and resolution of this moral problem.

## The Literature: Basic Assumptions, Conceptual Contours, and Questions

Attention to access to health care is often nested within broader ethical discussions of health care reform, resource allocation, and rationing. The present essay highlights access as a discrete issue warranting specific ethical discernment.[2] Critical ethical examination of the moral and empirical meanings of *access to health care* is uncommon. People generally presume *health care* to mean the personal health care services provided by trained personnel employed by formal health care institutions (in contrast to family care-giving and population-based public health activities). In ethical terms, health care is commonly understood as a fundamental social good that promotes human dignity and well-being and thus has moral standing as an individual right and/or as a communal obligation. *Access to health care* typically refers to the means, usually financial, of obtaining health care services, as is reflected in the common assumption that persons with health insurance have access to health care. Analogously, people commonly accept the routine litany of statistics regarding the number of uninsured persons in the United States as evidence and measure of an access problem. However, personal possession of health insurance is a weak proxy for access. It neglects both the systemic and the non-financial dimensions of access such as the availability of particular services and personnel in a given health care plan or institution, facility location and transportation needs, and the cultural competency of care.

Three statements made by Presidential commissions and task forces in the last half-century reflect the most widely employed ethical frameworks applicable to access. In 1953, the President's Commission on the Health Needs of the Nation declared that "access to the means for attainment and preservation of health [including health care] is a basic human right." In 1983, another Presidential Commission self-consciously dismissed the earlier rights claim, declaring instead that "society has an ethical obligation to ensure equitable access to health care for all." In 1993, President Clinton's proposal for health care reform, the Health Security Act, affirmed the principle of universal access. Grounded in "fundamental national beliefs about community, equality, justice, and liberty," this principle claimed that "every American citizen and legal resident should have access to health care without financial and other barriers."[3]

Justice, rights, and obligations constitute the central ethical concepts invoked to address access to health care. These notions connect and intertwine in myriad ways, and as such, each stands as a useful entree to the ethical landscape of access to health care.[4] Common ethical questions regarding access reflect these diverse elements: Is there a right to health care? What does justice require regarding access to health care? What standard or level of access is appropriate? What is a just health care community and who belongs? Is there a societal obligation to provide access to health care?

## Bibliographic Resources

One approach to the ethics of access examines the implications of general theories of justice for health care.[5] This approach typically understands justice as distributive and asks the question: according to which criterion—need, ability to pay, or merit—should the benefits and burdens of health care be distributed? Given the multiplicity of general theories of justice, it is not surprising to find multiple visions of access and justice for health care. In his classic 1976 essay, "Social Justice and Equal Access to Health Care," Gene Outka evaluates various conceptions of justice for health care and argues for a form of equal access compatible with a Christian notion of *agape*. H. Tristram Engelhardt's libertarian account understands just health care as the procedural outcome of an unconstrained market; access inevitably will be unequal, though not necessarily unfair. Robert Veatch offers a strong egalitarian interpretation and identifies equal health or well-being, not simply equal access to care, as the justice standard. John Rawls's work on justice has inspired several contractarian interpretations for health care: among these, Norman Daniels's fair equality of opportunity account advances equitable access as access to a basic package of health care services which insures fair equality of opportunity through the promotion of "normal species-typical functioning." Ronald Green, offering a different Rawlsian interpretation, asserts health care to be an important primary social good, akin to civil liberties, and thus argues for a "substantial (and equal) right to equal access to health care."[6]

A different approach to the ethics of access takes the notion of a right to health care as its starting point.[7] Even for those who affirm the validity of this right, important questions arise about a right to health care, including its grounding, content, and scope. Is a right to health care an individual and/or social right? a negative and/or positive right? a moral, legal, political, and/or human right? What are its moral justifications, substantive requirements, correlative responsibilities, and policy implications? These questions are well-addressed in Audrey R. Chapman's edited volume, *Health Care Reform: A Human Rights Approach*.[8] These 16 critical essays offer numerous insights from a range of ethicists long concerned with access-related ethics including Dan Brock, Robert M. Veatch, Larry R. Churchill, James Lindemann Nelson, and Michael J. Garland. The 1963 papal encyclical *Pacem in Terris* affirmed a right to medical care, and more recently, a wide range of Catholic representatives have elaborated this right.[9] Arguing on behalf of a political-legal right to health care grounded in the principles of fairness and beneficence, James F. Childress concisely presents the definitional terrain of rights as well as broader issues including rationing and managed care.[10]

Most discussions of access to care address a normative and substantive standard of access commonly known as *equitable* or *equal access*.[11] The many interpretations of this standard include equal access as similar treatment for similar medical need; equal access as a "basic," "adequate," or "decent minimum" level of care for all; and equitable access as access to equitable health or well-being, not simply to equitable health care.[12]

Rising costs as well as the recent institutional restructuring of health care delivery and finance have prompted state and federal policy changes that impact access. Oregon's Medicaid reforms and the federally-created diagnosis-related groups (DRGs) for Medicare have prompted ethical comment.[13] Managed care, with its access-restricting features such as the gatekeeper function of the primary care physician, is the subject of growing ethical analysis.[14]

National health care reform efforts of the early 1990s prompted the development of many sets of ethical criteria for current and future reform proposals.[15] The principle of *universal access*, as promoted in President Clinton's Health Security Act, was closely scrutinized.[16] The Interreligious Health Care Access Campaign developed a set of working principles, including a call for universal access, which was endorsed by nearly 75 state and national faith-based organizations.[17] Many of these religious institutions have passed their own resolutions and policy statements in support of universal or adequate access to health care.[18]

Three recent essays in the *Bioethics Yearbook*[19] attend to denominational statements regarding equitable access: Judith A. Granbois and David H. Smith describe the theological underpinnings of the call for equitable access by the Standing Commission on Health - Episcopal Church of the United States of America.[20] Allen Verhey traces the theological statements and resolutions of the Presbyterian Church (USA) which undergird the Church's 1993 support of a universal health care plan.[21] And Robert L. Shelton describes the variety of explicit and implied positions on access in resolutions and statements created and approved by Methodist churches including the United Methodist Church, the Wesleyan Church, the Christian Methodist Episcopal Church, the African Methodist Episcopal Church, and the Church of the Nazarene.[22]

Attention to the theo-ethical grounding of concern about access to health care is growing. The Fellows of the Calvin Center for Christian Scholarship offer a covenental perspective on justice and access.[23] Sondra Ely Wheeler, Arthur J. Dyck, and John F. Kilner, among others, present biblically-informed perspectives on health care reform, rationing, resource allocation, and managed care in multi-media formats.[24] Philip S. Keane and B. Andrew Lustig develop Catholic perspectives on access, and on health care reform and rationing more generally.[25] Jewish understandings of access and justice based on notions of community, needs, and the relational self are offered by Laurie Zoloth-Dorfman and Aaron L. Mackler.[26] Hindu and Islamic perspectives on justice and access are also being developed.[27]

To date, serious attention to the barriers to health care access has concentrated on financial barriers, and, in particular, on the individual's lack of employment-based health insurance. This narrow view is due, in part, to a lack of critical attention to the concrete social realities that contribute to the inaccessibility of care.[28] New ethical lenses are needed to identify and analyze social and non-financial barriers to care including gender and racial discrimination, the lack of inclusion and participation in health care priority-setting, and the restructuring of health care institutions in the context of managed care.

That women comprise the majority of patients and health care workers, and that they have a disproportionately high representation among the poor, the elderly, and those without employment-based health insurance, make gender and sexism critical dimensions of the ethics of access.[29] Vernellia R. Randell documents well how racism impedes access to care and argues for the strengthening of Title VI Civil Rights legislation as the primary means to improved access.[30] Cheryl Sanders reminds us that the particular moral contexts of African-Americans are shaped by "the broader moral context of Euro-American racism," thus pointing to racism, not race, as the ethical problem.[31]

Annette Dula and Sara Goering, in *"It Just Ain't Fair": The Ethics of Health Care for African Americans*, point to a unifying tendency in conventional discussions of the ethics of access and recommend a different approach:

> Certainly, medical ethics has acknowledged the inequities in access and the fact that, in general, some groups are not well served by the health care system. However, the view taken in traditional medical ethics homogenizes the different groups into just one large category of underserved people. The large and growing group of the underserved has no face, no features, color, sex, age, ethnic or cultural differences, or political history. To understand the morality and the real-life effects of unfair access, medical ethicists need to look at the health experiences of real people . . . and at real populations, like African Americans.[32]

The reasons for a lack of access to health care vary considerably among different groups, and may include poverty, discrimination, the decline in availability of employment-based health insurance, closed and distant facilities, and the unavailability of particular services such as obstetrics and other reproductive health services. These distinct factors warrant distinct assessments and normative recommendations, both ethical and programmatic.

## Future Directions

In line with Ramsey's counsel that "we must choose how we shall go about choosing and ordering our medical and societal goals," greater public discussion of access to health care is imperative. Access to health care must be engaged as a moral, and not simply an economic, issue. Concepts familiar to Christian theo-ethical reflection such as need, the common good, love, solidarity, social justice (in addition to distributive justice), and the preferential option for the marginalized await more insightful exploration in relation to access. Important arenas for future reflection include the experiences of persons directly affected by a lack of access, actual institutional practices and health policies, and the empirical work on access done by health policy analysts. Understanding access as context-specific means that access involves the relationship between individual health care needs and the social-economic-political and institutional situations within which those needs exist. This understanding of access expands the relevant ethical domain to include issues of poverty (not simply the lack of health insurance), the private-public interstructuring of health care, the cultural competency (and thus the quality) of care, and access to access-relevant decision-making. Ultimately, participation in the shaping of health care delivery and financing systems is essential to meaningful access.

## Notes

[1]Paul Ramsey, *The Patient as Person: Explorations in Medical Ethics* (New Haven: Yale University Press, 1970), 240. Two early anthologies dedicated to social bioethical questions are: Robert M. Veatch and Roy Branson, ed. *Ethics and Health Policy* (Cambridge: Ballinger, 1976) and Earl E. Shelp, ed. *Justice and Health Care* (Dordrecht: D. Reidel, 1981).

[2]The literature reviewed here concerns the ethics of access to health care in the United States, nearly all of which has been published within the last 25 years in article and/or chapter form. Dominated by contributions from moral and political philosophy, this literature also includes works rooted in Christian and Jewish ethics, law, and health policy. This essay emphasizes Christian contributions, as well as a broader survey of the most recent literature. As will become apparent, there is a relative lack of explicitly Christian analyses of access issues. Much of the recent literature, while useful for clarifying the implications of a Christian outlook, contains little explicitly Christian content.

[3]President's Commission on the Health Needs of the Nation, *Building America's Health* (Washington, D.C.: U. S. Government Printing Office, 1953), 3. President's Commission for the Study of Ethical Problems in Medicine and Biomedical and Behavioral Research, *Securing Access to Health Care: The Ethical Implications of Differences in the Availability of Health Services* (Washington, D.C.: U.S. Government Printing Office, 1983), 4. The White House Domestic Policy Council, *The President's Health Security Plan* (New York: Times Books, 1993), 11. This principle of universal access eschews the languages of both rights and obligations.

[4]Equality is yet another central concept. Multiple Christian perspectives on equality and health care are featured in the November 1996 issue of *Christian Bioethics* 2, no. 3. See especially Kevin Wm. Wildes, "Health Care, Equality, and Inequality: Christian Perspectives and Moral Disagreements," *Christian Bioethics* 2, no. 3 (1996): 271-279.

[5]Tom L. Beauchamp and James F. Childress present a concise overview of general theories of justice and their implications for health care in *Principles of Biomedical Ethics,* 4th ed. (New York: Oxford University Press, 1994), 334-341.

[6]Gene Outka, "Social Justice and Equal Access to Health Care," *Journal of Religious Ethics* 2 (Spring 1974): 11-32; H. Tristram Engelhardt, "Health Care Allocations: Responses to the Unjust, the Unfortunate, and the Undesirable," in Shelp, *supra* note 1, and *The Foundations of Bioethics*, 2d.ed (New York: Oxford University Press, 1996), 375-410; Robert M. Veatch, *The Foundations of Justice: Why the Retarded and the Rest of Us Have Claims to Equality* (New York: Oxford University Press, 1986); "What is "Just" Health Care Delivery? in Veatch and Branson, *supra* note 1; John Rawls, *A Theory of Justice* (Cambridge, MA: Harvard University Press, 1971); Norman Daniels, *Just Health Care* (Cambridge: Oxford University Press, 1985);

Ronald M. Green, "Health Care and Justice in Contract Theory Perspective," in Veatch and Branson, *supra* note 1; and "The Priority of Health Care," *Journal of Medicine and Philosophy* 8 (1983): 373-380.

[7]Arguments against a positive right to health care are offered predominantly from libertarian perspectives which give priority to the freedom of health care professionals to chose whom they serve. See H. Tristram Englehardt, *supra* note 6; Robert M. Sade, "Medical Care as a Right: A Refutation," *The New England Journal of Medicine* 285 (Dec. 2, 1971): 1288-1292; and Garvan F. Kuskey, "Health Care, Human Rights and Government Intervention: A Critical Appraisal," in *Ethical Issues in Modern Medicine,* ed. Robert Hunt and John Arras (Palo Alto, CA: Mayfield, 1977), 465-471.

[8]Audrey R. Chapman, ed., *Health Care Reform: A Human Rights Approach* (Washington, D.C.: Georgetown University Press, 1994). Chapman's introductory essay offers a good overview of both health care as a right in general, and health care as a human right in particular, 1-32.

[9]Pope John XXIII, *Pacem in Terris*, Part 1: 11. U. S. Catholic Bishops, "Resolution on Health Care Reform," *Origins* 23, no. 7 (July 1, 1993): 99; National Conference of Catholic Bishops, "Pastoral Letter on Health and Health Care," in *Pastoral Letters of the United States Catholic Bishops* Vol. IV, 1975-1983, ed. Hugh J. Nolan (Washington, D.C.: National Conference of Catholic Bishops, 1983), 472; Charles E. Curran, "The Right to Health Care and Distributive Justice," Chapter 6 in his *Transition and Tradition in Moral Theology* (Notre Dame: University of Notre Dame Press, 1979), 139-170. According to Joseph Boyle, "there does not exist a detailed account of the nature and extent of this right [to health care] either in papal or episcopal teaching or in the theological literature . . . . Whatever the right to health care means exactly, it requires access for all to some decent level of health care; and rationing schemes that target the poor cannot be just if such a right is assumed to exist." Joseph Boyle, "The Roman Catholic Tradition and Bioethics," in *Bioethics Yearbook*, Volume 3, ed. B. Andrew Lustig, Baruch A. Brody, H. Tristram Engelhardt, and Laurence B. McCullough (Dordrecht: Kluwer, 1993), 23.

[10]James F. Childress, *Practical Reasoning in Bioethics* (Bloomington: Indiana University Press, 1997), see Chapter 13, "Rights to Health Care in a Democratic Society."

[11]For two analyses of the multiple meanings of equal access, see Childress, *supra* 10, 249-254, and Arthur L. Caplan, *If I Were a Rich Man Could I Buy a Pancreas? And Other Essays on the Ethics of Health Care* (Bloomington: Indiana University Press, 1992), 329-332.

[12]Interestingly, the standard of equitable health has been rejected by many ethicists as idealistic (for an exception, see Veatch *supra* note 6, 1986), while health policy analysts—rarely labeled idealists—have developed a set of indicators for access based, in part, on improved health measures. For example, the Institute of Medicine has defined access as "the timely use of personal health services to achieve the best possible health outcomes," and has developed corresponding measurements. See Michael Millman ed., *Access to Health Care in America* (Washington, D.C.: National Academy Press, 1993), 4. See also Center for Health Economics Research, *Access to Health Care: Key Indicators for Policy* (Princeton, N.J.: The Robert Wood Johnson Foundation, 1993). Ethical analysis has rarely incorporated this empirical work. One exception is Thomas B. Jabine, "Indicators for Monitoring Access to Basic Health Care as a Human Right," in Chapman, *supra* note 8, 233-259. Some health policy analysts began attending to the ethics of access in the mid-1970s, that is, about the same time that bioethicists took up the issue. See, for example, David Mechanic, "Rationing health care: public policy and the medical marketplace," *Hastings Center Report* 6, no. 1 (February 1976): 34-37. For a more recent example, see Karen Davis, "Inequality and Access to Health Care," *The Milbank Quarterly* 69, no. 2 (1991): 253-273.

[13]On Oregon, see Martin A. Strosberg, Joshua M. Wiener, Robert Baker with I. Alan Fein, ed. *Rationing America's Medical Care: The Oregon Plan and Beyond* (Washington, D.C.: The Brookings Institute, 1992); and Robert Castagna, "State Health-Care Rationing Plan Opposed," *Origins* 21, no. 17 (October 3, 1991): 265-268. The August 1994 issue of *The Journal of Medicine and Philosophy* 19, no. 4, entitled "The Oregon Plan," features five substantial articles which address the moral elements of policy formation in Oregon. On the ethical dimensions of DRGs, see Robert M. Veatch, "DRGs and the Ethical Reallocation of Resources," in *The Crisis*

*in Health Care: Ethical Issues*, ed. Nancy F. McKenzie (New York: Meridian, 1990), 187-207; also Ruth Macklin, *Mortal Choices: Ethical Dilemmas in Modern Medicine* (Boston: Houghton Mifflin, 1987), 161-162.

[14]Cardinal Joseph Bernardin, "Managing Managed Care," *Origins* 26, no. 2 (May 30, 1996): 21-26; Edmund D. Pellegrino, "Ethics," *Journal of the American Medical Association* 271, no. 21 (June 1, 1994): 1668-1670; Marc A. Rodwin, "Conflicts in Managed Care," *Journal of the American Medical Association* 332 no. 9 (March 2, 1995): 604-606; Leonard M. Fleck, "Justice, HMOs, and the Invisible Rationing of Health Care Resources," *Bioethics* 4 no. 2 (1990): 97-119.

[15]William F. May, "The Ethics of Health Care Reform" in *The Annual of the Society of Christian Ethics 1994* (Boston: Society of Christian Ethics, 1994), 173-178; The Catholic Health Association, *Charting the Future: Principles for Systemic Healthcare Reform* (St. Louis: Catholic Health Association, 1990); Dan Brock and Norman Daniels "Ethical Foundations of the Clinton Administration's Proposed Health Care System" *Journal of the American Medical Association* 271, no. 15 (April 20, 1994): 1189-1196; and Charles J. Dougherty "An Axiology for National Health Insurance," *Law, Medicine & Health Care* 20 nos.1-2 (Spring-Summer 1992): 82-91.

[16]Rebecca Voelker, "Is Reform Coverage Really Universal?" *Journal of the American Medical Association* 270, no. 22 (December 8, 1993): 2663-2665. Charlene A. Galarneau, "Missing Persons: Undocumented Immigrants," *Dissent* (Spring 1994): 203-205; Robert Pear, "What Is 'Universal' is Center Of Fight Over a Health Plan," *New York Times*, Feb. 16, 1994, A1.

[17]Interreligious Health Care Access Campaign, "Working Principles," (Washington, D.C.: National Council of Churches, 1991). As part of this effort, the National Council of Churches collected the policy statements and resolutions of many religious organizations into a packet still available upon written request (110 Maryland Ave. N.E., Washington, D.C. 20002). With the demise of federal health care reform, the Interreligious Health Care Access Campaign was effectively dissolved though some members continue to work together on access issues.

[18]These resolutions and policy statements are available directly from the denominations and groups themselves. See, for example, the American Baptist Churches USA's 1991 "Resolution on Health Care For All;" the 1989 "Church of the Brethren Statement on Health Care in the United States;" and Church Women United's 1991 "Position on Health Care Reform." Access to health care is a relatively low priority for some Christians. Paul D. Simmons suggest why some Baptists and Evangelicals have not fully engaged issues of health care reform, including access, in "Baptist-Evangelical Medical Ethics," in *Bioethics Yearbook*, Volume 5, ed. B. Andrew Lustig (Dordrecht: Kluwer, 1997): 247-251. Courtney S. Campbell describes a different set of reasons for the "silence" of Latter-Day Saints regarding social and clinical ethics in "Sounds of Silence: The Latter-Day Saints and Medical Ethics," *Bioethics Yearbook*, Volume 1, ed. Baruch A. Brody, B. Andrew Lustig, H. Tristram Engelhardt, Laurence B. McCullough, and Thomas J. Bole (Dordrecht: Kluwer, 1991), 38-40.

[19]Volumes 1, 3, and 5 of the *Bioethics Yearbook* (Dordrecht: Kluwer) offer a rich collection of theological resources on a dozen bioethical issues from a dozen religious traditions.

[20]Judith A. Granbois and David H. Smith, "The Anglican Communion and Bioethics" in *Bioethics Yearbook*, Volume 3, ed. B. Andrew Lustig, Baruch A. Brody, H. Tristram Engelhardt, and Laurence B. McCullough (Dordrecht: Kluwer, 1993): 100-102.

[21]Allen Verhey, "Bioethics in the Reformed Tradition" in *Bioethics Yearbook*, Volume 5, ed. B. Andrew Lustig (Dordrecht: Kluwer, 1997): 276.

[22]Robert L. Shelton, "Biomedical Ethics in Methodist Traditions" *Bioethics Yearbook*, Volume 5, ed. B. Andrew Lustig (Dordrecht: Kluwer, 1997): 199-201.

[23]Hessel Bouma III, Douglas Diekema, Edward Langerak, Theodore Rottman, and Allan Verhey, *Christian Faith, Health, and Medical Practice* (Grand Rapids: William B. Eerdmans, 1989), 162-170.

[24]Sondra Ely Wheeler, "Broadening Our View of Justice in Health Care," and Arthur J. Dyck, "Rationing Health Care: A Case of Justice Denied," in *The Changing Face of Health Care: A Christian Appraisal of Managed Care, Resource Allocation, and Patient-Caregiver*

*Relationships,* ed. John F. Kilner, Robert D. Orr, and Judith Allen Shelly (Grand Rapids, Mich: William B. Eerdmans, 1998). Also John F. Kilner, "Rationing and Health Care Reform," in *Bioethics and the Future of Medicine: A Christian Appraisal,* ed. John F. Kilner, Nigel M. de S. Cameron, and David L. Schiedermayer (Grand Rapids: William B Eerdmans, 1995), 290-301; and his "Health-Care Resources, Allocation of" in *Encyclopedia of Bioethics*, revised ed. A series of videos ("Bioethics and Contemporary Health Care" Series) and audio tapes ("Changing Health Care" Series) on these issues is available from The Center for Bioethics and Human Dignity (see Introduction to this section of the *Annual*).

[25]Philip S. Keane, *Health Care Reform: A Catholic View* (New York: Paulist Press, 1993). B. Andrew Lustig, "Needy Persons and Rationed Resources," in *Duties to Others*, ed. Courtney S. Campbell and B. Andrew Lustig (Dordrecht: Kluwer, 1994), 217-233. Also B. Andrew Lustig, "Reform and Rationing: Reflections on Health Care in Light of Catholic Social Teaching," in *Secular Bioethics in Theological Perspective* ed. Earl E. Shelp (Dordrecht: Kluwer, 1996), 31-50.

[26]Laurie Zoloth-Dorfman, "First, Make Meaning: An Ethics of Encounter for Health Care Reform," *Tikkun* 8, no. 4 (July-August 1993): 23-26, 89. Aaron L. Mackler, "Judaism, Justice, and Access to Health Care," *Kennedy Institute of Ethics Journal* 1, no. 2 (June 1991): 143-161.

[27]Issues of justice, access, and resource allocation are addressed in Cromwell Crawford's "Hindu Developments in Bioethics," 65-68, and in Gamal I. Serour's "Islamic Developments in Bioethics," 181-182, both in *Bioethics Yearbook*, Volume 5, *supra* note 18.

[28]For an analytical description of the wide range of barriers to access, see Institute of Medicine, *Assessing Health Care Reform* (Washington, D.C.: National Academy Press, 1993), 6-17. Some churches have attempted to address the problem of limited access to health care by establishing parish nurse programs and neighborhood clinics, by offering counseling and referral services, and by giving direct financial assistance for health care services. For example, see Granger E. Westberg, "What a Congregation Looks Like that takes Wholistic Health Seriously," in *Health Care and Its Costs: A Challenge for the Church, Essays Commissioned by the Task Force on Health Costs and Policies of the Presbyterian Church* (USA), ed. Walter E. Wiest (Lanham: University Press of America, 1988): 320-328.

[29]Theological and methodological explorations of gender and bioethics are offered by Christine E. Gudorf, "A Feminist Critique of Biomedical Principlism," in *A Matter of Principles? Ferment in U.S. Bioethics*, ed. Edwin R. DuBose, Ronald P. Hamel, and Laurence J. O'Connell (Valley Forge, PA: Trinity Press International, 1994), 164-181; Barbara Hilkert Andolsen, "Elements of a Feminist Approach to Bioethics," in *Religious Methods and Resources in Bioethics*, ed. Paul F. Camenisch (Dordrecht: Kluwer, 1994), 227-257; Margaret A. Farley, "Feminist Theology and Bioethics," in *Feminist Theological Ethics: A Reader*, ed. Lois K. Daly (Louisville, Kentucky: Westminster John Knox Press, 1994), 192-212. On feminism and bioethics from philosophical perspectives, see Susan M. Wolf, ed., *Feminism & Bioethics: Beyond Reproduction* (New York: Oxford University Press, 1996), especially "Justice in the Allocation of Health Care Resources: A Feminist Account" by Hilde Lindemann Nelson and James Lindemann Nelson, 351-370. Also Susan Sherwin, *No Longer Patient: Feminist Ethics and Health Care* (Philadelphia: Temple University Press, 1992), see especially Chapter 11, "Gender, Race, and Class in the Delivery of Health Care."

[30]Vernellia R. Randall, "Racist Health Care: Reforming an Unjust Health Care System to Meet the Needs of African-Americans" in *Justice and Health Care: Comparative Perspectives*, ed. Andrew Grubb and Maxwell J. Mehlman (Chichester: John Wiley & Sons, 1995), 147-224. For a perspective on organized medicine's response to the changing landscape of health care, see Frank E. Staggers and Barbara C. Staggers, "The Impact of Changes in Health Care Delivery On Minority Communities," in Kilner, Orr and Shelly, *supra* note 24.

[31]Cheryl J. Sanders, "Problems and Limitations of an African-American Perspective in Biomedical Ethics: A Theological View," in *African-American Perspectives on Biomedical Ethics*, ed. Harley E. Flack and Edmund D. Pellegrino (Washington, D.C.: Georgetown University Press, 1992), 170.

[32]Annette Dula and Sara Goering, eds. *"It Just Ain't Fair": The Ethics of Health Care for African Americans* (Westport, Conn.: Praeger, 1994), 4. For a narrative account of the barriers to access encountered by one African-American family in Chicago, see Laurie Kaye Abraham,

*Mama Might Be Better Off Dead: The Failure of Health Care in Urban America* (Chicago: University of Chicago Press, 1993).

# Ethical Issues at the End of Life

*Sondra Ely Wheeler*

Although ease of reference dictates that we separate end-of-life issues into subtopics, the connections among these matters are pervasive and vital. For example, we deceive ourselves if we foist off patients' decisions to seek death onto the realm of inviolable autonomy but do not address the economic burdens that may make such choices anything but free, or the isolation that can make life unendurably bleak and empty for the old and the sick. Divisions are convenient, but potentially misleading. Any serious answer to the question of how we care for human beings when death looms will engage how we live as well as how we die.

## Formulating the Questions

Perhaps the most promising development of recent years in the area of end-of-life issues has been increased attention to the moral and practical questions of how we care for people who are dying. Even ten years ago one could find the statement that "Health care professionals have an obligation to control distressing symptoms in dying patients . . . not only from physical causes, but from emotional, social and spiritual ones as well. Their total care requires professionals to pay attention to all these potential origins of distress."[1] But now as then, such clear statements of the ethical obligations regarding palliative care have to be accompanied by acknowledgment that such comprehensive attention is the exception rather than the rule.[2] Practice is often behind theory in this area, and the moral necessity and the practical difficulty of providing high quality care for the dying is the subject of ongoing research.

From the battle over Karen Ann Quinlan more than 20 years ago to the present, a series of highly-publicized court cases has focused national attention and debate on questions of when and for what reasons life-sustaining care may be refused, withheld, or withdrawn. A voluminous literature traces the facts, legal decisions, ethical rationales, and broader implications of Quinlan (1976), Saikewicz (1977), Spring (1979), Bouvia (1983), Brophy (1985), and Cruzan (1990), among others.[3] The result has been an extensive body of case law affirming that, without consent by competent patients or genuine benefits for incompetent patients, medical treatment is an unwarranted intrusion.[4] More interesting from a theological standpoint is the attention this debate has prompted to the deeper set of questions underlying medical practice. What are the legitimate ends and limits of medicine? What is the nature of the goods and harms received in and through the body? Questions like these continue to animate intense theological and philosophical debate. Although a wide moral consensus supports the general trend of court rulings permitting treatment termination by competent patients or surrogates acting in their interests, there are ongoing and stubborn disagreements. These have been fueled by unresolved issues about basic duties to one another, and about the nature of personal and social goods and harms. These disagreements are manifested in the continuing discomfort of many practitioners with terminating artificial feeding, and in the fierce debate about medical futility. Both issues raise profound questions about the nature of the relation between self and body, and self and community, with implications for the entire range of bioethical questions.

The most publicly controverted bioethical issue concerning the end of life is the moral permissibility of active measures to bring about death. In the American context, the current prominence of this debate is related to three factors: generalized public fear of the modern conditions of dying; overwhelming emphasis on autonomy as the linchpin of moral claims; and high levels of uncertainty and anxiety about the rising costs of health care added to the perception that great resources are being wasted on lives that are of no value to anyone. All of these find their way into the enormous and expanding literature on physician-assisted suicide and euthanasia.

## Ethical Issues in Palliative Care

After 50 years of preoccupation with developing and refining tools to cure disease and thwart death, health care providers confronting AIDS and an aging population have been forcibly returned to the oldest of their roles: attending the sick and dying when the course of illness cannot be reversed. Based on clinicians' reported experience, the skill and success with which this role is filled varies widely. Such a mixed report is found in a collection of essays compiled from a 1994 conference co-sponsored by Yale's Program for the Humanities in Medicine and Boston's Goethe-Institut: *Facing Death: Where Culture, Religion and Medicine Meet.*[5] This volume, containing fairly short and non-technical essays by both clinicians and ethicists, could be used in an advanced college or graduate level course, or in a clinical or CPE setting. In it, writers from clinical fields celebrate the advances in pain management and the wider range of pharmacological responses available to those suffering with such conditions as end-stage cancer, AIDS, and heart disease. At the same time they decry the lack of adequate education and clinical training received by most physicians in pain management and other aspects of palliative care.

Critics also lament a more subtle barrier to attentive treatment of the dying: the attitude that, in keeping with recent history, defines medicine as effective intervention to cure disease and prolong life. Since the Quinlan case, there has developed among health care professionals a much greater willingness to withhold or withdraw treatment that is not beneficial. However, termination of aggressive curative therapies has sometimes been equated with withdrawal of all care, resulting in an unconscionable abandonment of dying patients in acute care facilities.[6] Such failures of care may be attributed to various factors, including inadequate training in comfort care and facilities whose staffing patterns, procedures and even physical facilities are designed more for quick action to thwart death than for careful attention to the process of dying itself. The results of the 1995 "Study to Understand Prognosis and Preferences for Outcomes and Risks of Treatment," in particular, paint a sobering picture of how far we have to go in improving and directing treatment of the dying in our current institutional framework.[7] Additional volumes of particular interest to advanced students in clinical settings are *Palliative Care Ethics*[8] and *Approaching Death: Improving Care at the End of Life*.[9]

More deeply, the inadequacy of palliative care may manifest our lack of an adequate framework to provide meaning and support for those facing death either as patients or as caregivers. Essays in the second half of the just-cited volume *Facing Death* seek to address this problem by offering religious and cultural-historical perspectives on death. But the difficulty in recognizing what are called the "spiritual" dimensions of the work of caring for the dying is that we have no shared religious or philosophical basis for such work. It is questionable whether any generic "spirituality" exists which can be offered to those who confront death, regardless of the particular beliefs of patient and caregiver. The promotion of such general goals as "harmony," "balance," or "acceptance" may obscure or directly offend the commitments of particular religious adherents.[10] Additional research and reflection upon the challenge of offering genuine spiritual care to patients of differing (or no) religious convictions is sorely needed.

Also needed are more explicit and more seriously developed resources for laity and for seminary students which restore the care and companioning of the dying to their historic place in the service and witness of the church. The community of faith has paid a high price for the specialization and professionalization of health care, namely the isolation of its members from one another at the very point when the comfort and affirmation of the faith are most needed. The development of materials for clinical pastoral education with a more confessional center and theological character might enhance many CPE programs that focus on the tools of secular psychotherapy rather than the nurture and discernment of the church.[11] Similarly, materials for lay education could help to reclaim the ministry of the baptized, and restore a sense of shared responsibility for incarnating the body of Christ in the mundane ministry of presence with the sick and dying. Existing resources in this area include ecclesial statements[12] and some fairly accessible treatments of care for the dying in the various volumes on health and medicine in the denominational traditions.[13]

The rapid rise of the hospice movement has been one of the most significant developments in the improvement of care for those near death.[14] Many experts in the care of the dying assert that hospice services are the only contemporary medical context in which reliable attention and expertise are devoted to relieving symptoms and providing comfort and support. But hospice advocates face new challenges presented by AIDS and the controversy concerning physician-assisted suicide and euthanasia.[15] Apart from the struggle to define the aims and appropriate means of hospice care there is the ongoing and acute problem, both moral and practical, of providing access to this specialized and intensive palliative care for those who need it. Critics of the form hospice development has taken in the U.S. also assert that acceptance of current federal funding guidelines, together with the effort to remain in close relation with mainstream technological medicine, have diluted or compromised the ideals and goals of hospice care. In their view, the result has been a re-emphasis on a physical, technical and pharmacological approach to pain rather than the integrated and comprehensive emotional, psycho-social, and spiritual approach advocated by Cicely Saunders and other pioneers.[16] Without comprehensive health care reform, both the quality and accessibility of hospice will remain inconsistent and inadequate, and some patients will suffer cruelly as a result. Additional research is needed on the institutional structures best suited to provide terminal care, and on funding requirements and strategies for their support.[17]

## Withholding and Withdrawing Treatment

The watershed court decisions of the last twenty years have affirmed and clarified the rights of both competent and incompetent patients to have unwanted treatment withheld or withdrawn at their request or that of a surrogate.[18] But this movement has been much broader than the legal recognition of autonomy-based claims against treatment. Medical technology now has the problematic power to sustain vital functions almost indefinitely, and thus to prolong considerably the process of dying. Confrontation with this reality and the suffering it can cause has helped to shape the moral consensus that treatment is justified jointly by the benefits it provides and by the consent of the patient. This is a matter not just of respect for autonomy, but also of responsible and faithful exercise of the power for good and for harm conferred by medical knowledge and technique. Philosophical and theological arguments from a wide range of traditions and perspectives have been adduced to support the legal consensus (in multi-media formats).[19]

Two areas of continued debate remain within this general agreement. These are disagreements about the termination of artificial nutrition and hydration, especially for incompetent patients, and the intense, ongoing argument about the definition and moral implications of futility in medicine. The former controversy arises partly from the powerful emotional and symbolic significance in human culture of the giving and receiving of food and water. Feeding is a nearly universal metaphor for care and nurture. Conversely, starvation represents not only severe suffering and death, but abandonment by the human community. It is easy to see an omission as culpable if it *guarantees* that the patient will die, and die *of* a lack of the food and water needed by all living things. This problem is particularly acute when the patient is not competent to refuse artificial feeding and has not executed a living will or empowered a surrogate to make treatment decisions on her or his behalf.

In such cases, the majority view of the permissibility of ending artificial nutrition and hydration is based upon one of two applications of the proportionality argument. Treatment may be terminated because of the disproportionate burdens it imposes upon the patient, which can be physical or emotional. Alternatively, treatment may be ended because it offers no benefit to the patient, as when artificial nutrition sustains the metabolism of a patient who has irreversibly lost the capacity for consciousness. This second argument, however, hinges upon premises concerning what makes sustained life a benefit to its possessor—premises that may not be universally granted.[20] The underlying disagreement about what constitutes a beneficial treatment relates directly to the debate about the meaning and consequences of futility in medicine.

The controversy over futility has both substantive and procedural dimensions. The procedural questions concern whether physicians have the right and/or obligation unilaterally to refuse to provide forms of treatment they deem useless for a particular patient. A related issue is whether doctors have a right not to disclose treatment possibilities they regard as futile and contraindicated to patients or their families. Defenders of such rights or duties on the part of physicians argue that the whole medical enterprise entails making educated, considered judgments about what serves the patient's welfare. They assert that such judgments and the professional conduct pursuant to them are intrinsic to medical practice as a responsible moral activity. To force physicians to abrogate such professional discretion is to deny their moral agency and thus violate the basic obligation of caregivers to benefit those entrusted to their care.

Opponents of this view regard it as simply a cloak for reasserting physicians' power to make and impose their own judgments about the modes and goals of treatment. They claim that it illegitimately extends doctors' medical expertise and authority to non-medical judgments about what kind of life should be valued and preserved. On this view, the procedural debate about decision-making authority is inseparable from the substantive debate about goods and harms. A sampling of the current arguments and a useful current bibliography can be found in *Medical Futility and the Evaluation of Life-Sustaining Intervention*, edited by Marjorie

Zucker and Howard Zucker.[21] Howard Brody's introductory essay "Medical Futility: A Useful Concept?" is particularly helpful. While most of the literature on medical futility is not explicitly Christian, some such analysis is beginning to emerge.[22]

## Physician-Assisted Suicide and Active Euthanasia

After decades of denial, Americans are beginning to talk—and read—about death. Sherwin Nuland's *How We Die*, a clinically detailed account of the course of the most common fatal illnesses, was a major seller,[23] and Derek Humphrey's 1991 how-to manual on suicide[24] remained on the New York Times' bestseller list for 18 weeks. Prompted by ballot initiatives on physician-assisted suicide in Oregon, Washington and California, major newspapers and newsmagazines have done numerous stories on euthanasia and the "right to die." In fact, the volume of popular literature alone is daunting.[25] Meanwhile, discussions of euthanasia and physician-assisted death have proliferated in academic and clinical journals. They include broad discussions of the state of the argument;[26] panel-style presentations and public debates on the issues, featuring a variety of viewpoints;[27] and numerous essays detailing arguments for particular positions of all kinds. As will be documented later in this essay, several book-length treatments have recently appeared, as well as a number of anthologies gathering essays from all the fields and professions with a stake in this argument. The discussion is taking place at many levels and on several fronts, and it is helpful to identify the context and interests of various contributions to the conversation.

Particularly since an anonymous 1988 article recounting a case of euthanasia[28] prompted a public furor, major medical journals have published a number of editorials, commentaries and proposals regarding physician involvement in aiding death. These have addressed both professional ethics and public policy, and have taken positions ranging from strong advocacy for physician aid in dying under specified circumstances,[29] to firm opposition to active measures to bring about death under any circumstances.[30] Other practitioners have taken a different tack, arguing that euthanasia or suicide would not be requested if we employed what we know about palliative care,[31] or that justified cases of euthanasia are rare and should be treated as special exceptions to normal medical practice rather than made part of public policy. These articles generally have both the strengths and weaknesses of brevity, in that they are constrained to articulate a position without a full acknowledgment or defense of their assumptions or their use of ambiguous terms. They reveal how far the legal and professional discussion has gotten ahead of the more fundamental moral conversation about the aims and limits of human care for the dying. However, their concreteness and attachment to the actual practice of care make them invaluable, not only in clinical education but in classroom and ecclesial settings as well.

Academic journals of ethics, philosophy, and theology contain articles on this topic suitable for use in advanced undergraduate settings or for graduate students in ethics, philosophy or medicine. The better of these pay attention to larger questions that underlie the controversy. These include the moral character of medicine[32] and the nature and limits of human control over life,[33] as well as recurrent debates about the import of distinctions between acts and omissions, and the significance of intention in the moral judgment of actions.[34] There are also multiple discussions of the Dutch policy of not prosecuting physicians who aid patients in suicide, provided certain criteria are met. These consider the policy's rationale, its actual operation, and its effects on medicine and society.[35] Analyses of the legal reasoning and jurisprudence underlying recent court decisions regarding assistance in death debate the validity of due process and equal protection claims against the prohibition of assisted suicide on philosophical and theological grounds.[36]

Even these more extended discussions often fail to engage one another because of incommensurable claims and fundamental shifts in vision. Some of this disconnection can be attributed to disparate basic understandings of the meaning of human embodiment and mortality, and of the moral implications of social connection. There is a growing body of literature which reckons directly with these matters of fundamental conviction, either by placing their arguments about bioethical problems within a framework of explicit theological or philosophical commitments, or by arguing for a realm of generally negotiable public morality within which patients and professionals must place their private convictions and practices. Examples of the former strategy include extended essays such as John Kilner's discussion in *Life on the Line,*[37] William May's *Testing the Medical Covenant: Active Euthanasia and Health Care Reform,*[38] Kenneth Vaux's *Death Ethics,*[39] and Orthodox theologian Vigen Guroian's *Life's Living Toward Dying.*[40] Also in this general category is the somewhat older, but still very useful study of Robert Wennberg, *Terminal Choices: Euthanasia, Suicide, and the Right to Die.*[41] Examples of the latter approach include most notably H. Tristram Engelhardt's *Bioethics and Secular Humanism: The Search for a Common Morality,*[42] which takes up the issues of bioethics, including euthanasia, as a demonstration and a test for the necessity and the limits of a generally negotiable ethics.

A number of anthologies offer developed theological or philosophical treatments of suicide and euthanasia, either from a broad selection of perspectives or from a single theological standpoint. They include: *Must We Suffer Our Way to Death?*;[43] *Dignity and Dying: A Christian Appraisal*;[44] *Choosing Death: Active Euthanasia and the Public Debate*;[45] *Intending Death: The Ethics of Physician Assisted Suicide and Euthanasia*;[46] and the euthanasia issue of *Studies in Christian Ethics.*[47] These offer a broad range of positions on the moral, legal and public policy questions surrounding active measures to cause death, and open up for consideration the basic, intractable issues at stake for society and communities of faith in resolving these dilemmas. Most of these resources are best suited for graduate educational contexts. Badly needed are clear, accessible treatments of the issue from a wide range of theological positions, suitable for use in undergraduate, ecclesial, and professional continuing education settings.

## Notes

[1]The Hastings Center, *Guidelines on the Termination of Life-Sustaining Treatment and the Care of the Dying* (Indianapolis: Indiana University Press, 1987), 71.

[2]Ibid, p. 72. See also Marcia Angell, "The Quality of Mercy," *New England Journal of Medicine* 306/1 (1982): 98-99; Eric J. Cassell, "The Relief of Suffering," *Archives of Internal Medicine* 143 (1983): 522-523.

[3]For outlines and decision texts of these and other cases, see Furrow, Johnson, Jost and Schwartz, *Health Law: Cases, Materials and Problems* (St. Paul: West Publishing Co., 1987); for Cruzan, see *Cruzan v. Director Missouri Department of Health*, 497 U.S. 261 (1990). Analyses and commentaries, especially regarding Quinlan, Saikewicz, Brophy, and Cruzan, are too numerous to list; see indices to *Hastings Center Report*, *Journal of the American Medical Association*, *Lancet*, and *New England Journal of Medicine* for the relevant years.

[4]For a detailed study of the question of defining and determining competence, see Becky Cox White, *Competence to Consent* (Washington D.C.: Georgetown University Press, 1994).

[5]Howard Spiro, Mary McCrea Curnen, and Lee Palmer Wandel, eds., *Facing Death: Where Culture, Religion and Medicine Meet* (New Haven: Yale University Press, 1996).

[6]Physician-philosopher Eric Krakauer tells a harrowing story of such a case from his own experience in "Attending to Dying," in *Facing Death*, p. 27.

[7]This extensive, multi-institutional study, aimed at assessing and improving care of the dying and facilitating patient control over their own care, failed to demonstrate any significant degree of improvement despite intensive effort. The results and various interpretations of them are the subject of a special supplement to *Hastings Center Report* 25 (Nov.-Dec. 1995): S1-34.

[8]Fiona Randall and R. S. Dowie, *Palliative Care Ethics* (Oxford and New York: Oxford University Press, 1996.)

[9]Derek Doyle, Geoffrey Hanks and Neil MacDonald, *Approaching Death: Improving Care at the End of Life* (Oxford: Oxford University Press, 1993.)

[10]For an example, see Susan Salladay and Judith Shelly, "Spirituality in Nursing Theory and Practice," *Christian Bioethics* 3/1 (1993): 20-38.

[11]A very modest effort in this direction is my own introductory *Stewards of Life: Bioethics and Pastoral Care* (Nashville: Abingdon Press, 1996). There are also a few valuable anthologies of theological treatments of a variety of issues, most notably Stephen Lammers and Allen Verhey's *On Moral Medicine: Theological Perspectives in Medical Ethics*, 2nd ed. (Grand Rapids, MI: Eerdmans, 1998).

[12]See, for example, the 1992 resolution regarding "Living and Dying as Faithful Christians" in the *Book of Resolutions of the United Methodist Church* (Nashville: Methodist Publishing House, 1996), 139.

[13]See, for example, Stanley Harakas, *Health and Medicine in the Eastern Orthodox Tradition* (New York: Crossroad, 1990); Martin Marty, *Health and Medicine in the Lutheran Tradition* (New York: Crossroad, 1983); and Kenneth Vaux, *Health and Medicine in the Reformed Tradition* (New York: Crossroad, 1984).

[14]A popular introduction to hospice care can be found in the works of its founder Cicely Saunders, such as *Care for the Dying* (London: Macmillan Journals, 1976). A brief introduction intended for use in clinical settings is Joanne Lynn's "Supportive Care for Dying Patients: An Introduction for Health Care Professionals," Appendix B of *Deciding to Forego Life-Sustaining*

*Treatment* (Washington D.C.: Government Printing Office, 1983). Extensive discussions of the practices and issues of hospice care can be found in such journals as *Hospice* and *The American Journal of Hospice and Palliative Care*.

[15]For accounts of the struggle over assistance in suicide among hospice providers, see Courtney Campbell's "Dying Well: Hospice Confronts Physician-Assisted Suicide," *Biolaw* 11/4 (April 1993): 29-36, and C. Campbell, J. Hare and P. Matthews, "Conflicts of Conscience: Hospice and Assisted Suicide," *Hastings Center Report* 25 (May-June 1995): 36.

[16]Cathy Siebold, *The Hospice Movement*, op. cit., 96-97; 134-136; 185-187.

[17]For a good statement of the problem, see Joanne Lynn, "Caring for Those Who Die in Old Age," in *Facing Death*, op. cit.

[18]Summaries of the development of jurisprudence surrounding treatment refusal can be found in Robert Veatch, *Death, Dying, and the Biological Revolution*, rev. ed. (New Haven and London: Yale University Press, 1989), chs. 4-5, and more recently in Alan Meisel, "The Legal Consensus on Forgoing Life-Sustaining Treatment," *Kennedy Institute of Ethics Journal* 2 (1992): 309.

[19]Ethical and theological reflection on these cases has found rationales in the traditional rejection of extraordinary measures to prolong life, and in the concept of proportionality that excludes treatment modalities in which burdens outweigh benefits. See, for example, Sacred Congregation for the Doctrine of the Faith, *Declaration on Euthanasia* (May 5, 1980) and David F. Kelly, *Critical Care Ethics: Treatment Decisions in American Hospitals* (Kansas City: Sheed & Ward, 1991). Both are suitable for use in advanced undergraduate or Masters level classes.

Additional theological rationales for forgoing treatment have been found in the idea of a faithful acceptance of death that includes the freedom to judge the usefulness and reasonableness of life-sustaining measures. A careful and nuanced account of such Christian discernment is woven through the volume *Christian Faith, Health, and Medicine* (Grand Rapids: Eerdmans Publishing, 1989), jointly authored by Bouma, Diekema, Langerak, Rottman, and Verhey, with a discussion of rationales for withholding treatment on p. 290ff. For a brief and readable discussion suitable for use in congregational contexts, consult Gilbert Meilaender, *Bioethics: A Primer for Christians* (Grand Rapids: Eerdmans, 1996). End-of-life series of videos ("Dying with Dignity" series) and audiotapes ("Ethics at the End of Life" series) are available from The Center for Bioethics and Human Dignity (see the article by Dennis Brodeur and John Kilner in this volume of the *Annual*). See also the related book, John Kilner, Arlene Miller, and Edmund Pellegrino, eds., *Dignity and Dying: A Christian Approach* (Grand Rapids, MI: Eerdmans, 1996).

[20]For a brief, non-technical presentation of the dominant view, see David Kelly, *Critical Care Ethics*, op. cit., ch. 2. A more recent theological argument for the permissibility of ceasing artificial feeding under certain circumstances, drawing mostly on Roman Catholic sources, is Patricia Talone's *Feeding the Dying* (New York: Peter Lang Publishers, 1996). For influential arguments against the prevailing position, see Callahan, "On Feeding the Dying," *Hastings Center Report* 13 (1989); Meilaender, "On Removing Food and Water: Against the Stream," *Hastings Center Report* 14 (1990); and more recently Meilaender's *Body, Soul, and Bioethics* (Notre Dame, IN.: Notre Dame University Press, 1995), 37-56. These are best suited to graduate level educational settings.

[21]Marjorie Zucker and Howard Zucker, eds., *Medical Futility and the Evaluation of Life-Sustaining Intervention* (Cambridge: Cambridge University Press, 1997).

[22]For discussions of the 1991 Wanglie case that brought this debate to the fore, see Michael Rie, "The Limits of a Wish," *Hastings Center Report* 21 (1991): 24; Felicia Ackerman, "The Significance of a Wish," *Hastings Center Report* 21 (1991): 27; Daniel Callahan, "Medical Futility, Medical Necessity: The Problem-Without-a-Name," *Hastings Center Report* 21 (1991): 32; and Alexander Capron, "In Re Helen Wanglie," *Hastings Center Report* 22 (1992): 26. A recent and commonly-cited attempt to define futility and its moral implications for medical practice is Schneiderman and Jecker, *Wrong Medicine: Doctors, Patients, and Futile Treatment* (Baltimore: Johns Hopkins University Press, 1995). For an assessment of the debate from an explicitly Christian standpoint, see C. Christopher Hook, "Medical Futility," in *Dignity and Dying*, op. cit., note 19.

[23] Sherwin Nuland, *How We Die: Reflections on Life's Final Chapter* (New York: Alfred P. Knopf, 1993).

[24]Derek Humphry, *Final Exit: The Practicalities of Self Deliverance and Assisted Suicide for the Dying* (New York: St. Martin's, 1991).

[25]Recent books include: Lonny Shavelson, *A Chosen Death* (New York: Simon and Schuster, 1995); Lofty L. Basta, *A Graceful Exit* (New York: Plenum Press, 1996). There are also thoughtful articles by specialists written for general readership magazines, e.g., Ezekiel Emanuel, "Whose Right to Die?" *Atlantic Monthly* 279 (March 1997).

[26]For example., Thomasma, Kushner, and Heilig, "Physician-Aided Death: The Escalating Debate," *Cambridge Quarterly of Health Care Ethics* 5 (1996): 1-31. For a longer-term view of the controversy, see Ezekiel Emanuel, "History of the Euthanasia Debate," *Annals of Internal Medicine* 121 (1994): 121.

[27]For example, *Hastings Center Report* has twice devoted all or most of an issue to this topic. See "Assisted Suicide," *Hastings Center Report* 25 (May-June 1995) and "A Colloquy on Euthanasia and Assisted Suicide," *Hastings Center Report* 22 (March-April 1992). A lively debate between Kevorkian's attorney Geoffrey Fieger and Christian physician and scholar Edmund Pellegrino is available from The Center for Bioethics and Human Dignity in audio or video recordings (see Brodeur and Kilner's article in this *Annual*).

[28]"It's Over, Debbie," *Journal of the American Medical Association* 259 (1988): 272.

[29]E.g., Timothy Quill, "Doctor, I Want to Die. Will You Help Me?" *Journal of the American Medical Association* 270 (1993): 870; Timothy Quill, Christine Cassel, and Diane Meier, "Care of the Hopelessly Ill: Proposed Clinical Criteria for Physician-Assisted Suicide," *New England Journal of Medicine* 327 (Nov. 5 1992): 1380; and Marcia Angell, "The Supreme Court and Physician Assisted Suicide," *New England Journal of Medicine* 336 (1997): 1348.

[30]For example, W. Gaylin, et al., "Doctors Must Not Kill," *Journal of the American Medical Association* 259/14 (1988): 2139; E. Pellegrino, "Doctors Must Not Kill," *Journal of Clinical Ethics* 3 (1992): 95.

[31]For example, K. Foley, "Competent Care for the Dying Instead of Physician Assisted Suicide," *New England Journal of Medicine* 336/1 (1997); see also the discussion of the deficiencies of palliative care in the report of the New York State Task Force on Life and the Law, *When Death is Sought: Assisted Suicide and Euthanasia in the Medical Context* (New York, State Task Force, 1994), 35-48.

[32]See F. Miller and H. Brody, "Professional Integrity and Physician-Assisted Death," *Hastings Center Report* 25 (May June 1995): 8; cf. Stephen Miles, "Physician-Assisted Suicide and the Profession's Gyrocompass," *Hastings Center Report* 25/3 (1995): 17.

[33]See the often-cited article by Daniel Callahan, "When Self-Determination Runs Amok," *Hastings Center Report* 22/2 (1992); also Leon Kass, "Is There a Right to Die?" *Hastings Center Report* 23/1 (1993): 34.

[34]Most recently, see Patrick Hopkins, "Why Does Removing Machines Count as 'Passive' Euthanasia?" *Hastings Center Report* 27/3 (1997): 29, which challenges the relevance not only of acts versus omissions but of artificial versus natural means of bodily support. For an analysis that also rejects a morally relevant distinction between rejecting life-sustaining treatment and requesting aid in dying, see Dan Brock, "Voluntary Active Euthanasia," *Hastings Center Report* 22/2 (1992): 10.

[35]For a range of responses to the tolerance of euthanasia in the Netherlands, see articles by Capron, de Wachter, and ten Have & Welie in *Hastings Center Report* 22/2 (1992). Severe critiques are offered in Herbert Hendin, "Seduced by Death: Doctors, Patients, and the Dutch Cure," *Issues in Law and Medicine* 10/2 (1994): 123, and in Carlos Gomez, "Reaping the Whirlwind: the Dutch Experiment with Euthanasia," *Bioethics Forum* 10 (1994): 20. Both Gomez and Hendin have also published book-length studies and critiques of the Dutch policy in practice. See Gomez, *Regulating Death: Euthanasia and the Case of the Netherlands* (New York: The Free Press, 1991) and Hendin, *Seduced by Death: Doctors, Patients and the Dutch Cure* (New York: W.W. Norton, 1997). For an explicitly Christian and theological critique, see Henk Jochemsen, "The Netherlands Experiment," in *Dignity and Dying*, *op. cit.*, note 19.

[36]For contrasting views of the legitimacy of constitutional challenges to laws against assisted suicide, see Yale Kamisar, "Are Laws Against Assisted Suicide Constitutional?" *Hastings Center Report* 23/3 (1993): 32; Robert Sedler, "The Constitution and Hastening Inevitable Death," *Hastings Center Report* 23/5 (1993): 20; and Arthur Dyck, "North American Law and Public Policy," in *Dignity and Dying, op. cit.*, note 19.

[37]John Kilner, *Life on the Line* (Grand Rapids, MI, Eerdmans Publishing, 1992).

[38]William May, *Testing the Medical Covenant: Active Euthanasia and Health Care Reform* (Grand Rapids, MI: Eerdmans Publishing, 1996).

[39]Kenneth Vaux, *Death Ethics* (Philadelphia: Trinity International Press, 1992).

[40]Vigen Guroian, *Life's Living Toward Dying* (Grand Rapids, MI: Eerdmans Publishing, 1996).

[41]Robert Wennberg, *Terminal Choice: Euthanasia, Suicide, and the Right to Die* (Grand Rapids, MI: Eerdmans Publishing, 1989).

[42]H. Tristram Engelhardt, *Bioethics and Secular Humanism: The Search for a Common Morality* (Philadelphia: Trinity Press International, 1991). See especially pp. 103-140.

[43]Ron Hamel and Edwin DuBose, eds. *Must We Suffer Our Way to Death?* (Dallas: SMU Press, 1996).

[44]Kilner, Pellegrino, and Miller, op. cit., note 19.

[45]Ron Hamel, ed., *Choosing Death: Active Euthanasia and the Public Debate* (Philadelphia: Trinity International Press, 1991).

[46]Thomas Beauchamp, ed. *Intending Death: The Ethics of Physician Assisted Suicide and Euthanasia* (Englewood Cliffs, NJ: Prentice-Hall, 1995).

[47]*Studies in Christian Ethics* 11:1 (Edinburgh, Scotland: T&T Clark, 1998).

# Contributors

**Maria Antonaccio** is an Assistant Professor of Religion at Bucknell University. She is the co-editor, with William Schweiker, of *Iris Murdoch and the Search for Human Goodness* (University of Chicago Press, 1996). Her essay "Imagining the Good: Iris Murdoch's Godless Theology" appeared in *The Annual* in 1996.

**Dennis Brodeur** is Senior Vice President for Stewardship at SSM Health Care. He formerly served as Associate Director for the Center for Health Care Ethics of St. Louis University School of Medicine. He has published numerous articles and co-authored, with Fr. Kevin O'Rourke, *Medical Ethics: Common Ground for Understanding*, volumes I and II (Catholic Health Association of the United States, 1986).

**Peter D. Browning** is Associate Professor of Philosophy and Religion and Chaplain at Drury College. He is currently working on a project exploring ethical decision-making in mainline Protestant denominations.

**Lisa Sowle Cahill** is J. Donald Monan, S. J., Professor in the Theology Department at Boston College, where she has taught since 1976. Her areas of research include sex and gender, war and peace, and New Testament and ethics. Her most recent book is *Sex, Gender, and Christian Ethics* (Cambridge University Press, 1996).

**Audrey Chapman** directs the Program of Dialogue Between Science and Religion at the American Association for the Advancement of Science. She is the author, coauthor, or editor of ten books. Her current work in progress is *Religious Ethics at the Frontiers of Science*.

**Martin Cook** has taught at Gustavus Adolphus College, The College of William and Mary, St. John's College, Santa Clara University, and the United States Air Force Academy. Beginning in the Fall, 1998, he will assume new duties as

Professor of Ethics at the United States Army War College in Carlisle, Pennsylvania.

**John P. Crossley** is Associate Professor of Religion and Director of the School of Religion at the University of Southern California in Los Angeles. He has published articles on Schleiermacher's ethics in the 1991 *Annual*, the *Journal of Religious Ethics*, *New Athenaeum*, and in a forthcoming *Festschrift* in honor of Terrence N. Tice to be published by Edwin Mellen Press.

**Charlene A. Galarneau** is Lecturer in the Community Health Program at Tufts University in Medford, MA. She is a Ph.D. candidate in The Study of Religion at Harvard University and is completing her dissertation on community, justice, and U.S. health care policy.

**Vigen Guroian** is Professor of Theology and Ethics at Loyola College in Maryland. His works include *Life's Living Toward Dying: A Theological and Medical-Ethical Study* and *Ethics After Christendom*, both from Wm. B. Eerdmans. His most recently published book is *Tending the Heart of Virtue: How Classic Stories Awaken a Child's Moral Imagination* (Oxford University Press, 1998).

**James Gustafson** has taught at Yale University, the University of Chicago, and Emory University. He is now retired.

**Ron Hamel** is Senior Associate for Ethics with the Catholic Health Association in St. Louis. He has authored several articles and books, including *Introduction to Christian Ethics: A Reader* (Paulist, 1989), *A Matter of Principles?* (Trinity, 1994), *Must We Suffer our Way to Death?* (SMU, 1995), and *Three Levels of Managed Care* (Sheed & Ward, 1997).

**Stanley Samuel Harakas** is the author of *Health and Medicine in the Eastern Orthodox Tradition* (Crossroad, 1990, 1996). He retired in 1995 after 29 years of teaching Orthodox Christian Ethics on the faculty of Holy Cross Greek Orthodox School of Theology, Brookline, MA and now lives and writes in Spring Hill, FL.

**John Kilner** is Director of The Center for Bioethics and Human Dignity in Bannockburn, Illinois. He has authored and co-edited books in Christian bioethics including *The Changing Face of Health Care* (1998), *Genetic Ethics* (1997), *Dignity and Dying* (1996), *Bioethics and the Future of Medicine* (1995), and *Life on the Line* (1992).

**Cheryl A. Kirk-Duggan** is the Director of the Center for Women and Religion, and Assistant Professor of Theology and Womanist Studies in the Graduate Theological Union, Berkeley, CA. An ordained minister in the Christian Methodist Episcopal Church, she has written *African-American Special Days* (Abingdon Press, 1996); *It's In the Blood: A Trilogy of Poems Harvested from a Family Tree* (River Vision, 1996); and *Exorcising Evil: A Womanist Perspective on the Spirituals* (Orbis Press, 1997).

**M. Therese Lysaught** is an Assistant Professor in the Department of Religious Studies at the University of Dayton and is a member of the Recombinant DNA Advisory Committee at the National Institutes of Health. Her work focuses on theological bioethics and on the relationship between liturgy and ethics.

**William O'Neill, S.J.** is an Associate Professor of Christian Social Ethics at the Jesuit School of Theology at Berkeley and the Graduate Theological Union. He has served as a visiting professor at Hekima College in Nairobi, Kenya. Publications include *The Ethics of Our Climate: Hermeneutics and Ethical Theory* from Georgetown University Press, and journal articles on the privilege of the poor in Christian social ethics and the ethics of immigration and refugee policy.

**George D. Randels, Jr.** is Assistant Professor of Social Ethics in the Religious Studies Department of the University of the Pacific (Stockton, CA). He has published articles about business ethics, medical ethics, and computer ethics. Current projects include virtue theory and business, stakeholder theory in health care management, and ethics and the internet.

**Timothy M. Renick** is Associate Professor of Religious Studies in the Department of Philosophy and the Director of the Religious Studies Program at Georgia State University.

**William Schweiker** is Associate Professor of Theological Ethics at the Divinity School of Chicago. He is the author of *Responsibility and Christian Ethics* (Cambridge, 1995) and *Power, Value, and Conviction in a Post-Modern Age* (Pilgrim, 1998). Professor Schweiker is also a member of the Board of Directors in the Society of Christian Ethics.

**Timothy F. Sedgwick** is Professor of Christian Ethics at Virginia Theological Seminary, Alexandria, VA. His forthcoming book on the Christian moral life will be published by Eerdmans.

**Cristina L. H. Traina** is an Assistant Professor in the Department of Religion at Northwestern University. She is the author of *Undoing Anathemas* (working title; forthcoming, Georgetown University Press) and essays on sexual and environmental ethics. She is currently working on a book on the ethics of maternal eroticism.

**Sondra Ely Wheeler** spent one year on the faculty of Duquesne University before moving to Wesley Theological Seminary in Washington, D. C., where she teaches theological and social ethics, including bioethics. She is the author of two books, most recently *Stewards of Life: Bioethics and Pastoral Care* (Abingdon, 1996) as well as a number of reviews, articles, and essays.

**Tobias L. Winright** is completing his doctorate in moral theology at the University of Notre Dame, and he currently teaches social ethics in the Department of Religion at Simpson College. Other publications include "Children: An Undeveloped Theme in Catholic Teaching" (with Todd David Whitmore), in *The Challenge of Global Stewardship: Roman Catholic Responses*, eds. Maura A. Ryan and Todd David Whitmore (University of Notre Dame Press, 1997), and "Virgil Michel on Worship and War," *Worship* 71 (September 1997): 451-462.

**Werner Wolbert** is Professor for Moral Theology at the Catholic Theological Faculty of the University of Salzburg, Austria.